Adam Smith's *Wealth of Nations*

Adam Smith's *Wealth of Nations* is regarded by many as the most important text in the history of economics. Jerry Evensky's analysis of this landmark book walks the reader through the five "Books" of *The Wealth of Nations*, analyzing Smith's terms and assumptions and how they are developed into statements about economic processes in Book I, his representation of the dynamics of economics systems in Book II, and his empirical case for his model in Book III. With that framework in place, Evensky examines Smith's critique of two alternative models, Mercantilism and Physiocracy, in Book IV, and Smith's presentation of the policy implications of his analysis in Book V. This guide highlights the nexus of Smith's economics and his work on ethics and jurisprudence. In doing so Evensky sets his examination of *The Wealth of Nations* into a larger, holistic analysis of Smith's moral philosophy.

Jerry Evensky is a professor of economics and a Meredith Professor for Teaching Excellence at Syracuse University. He has published widely on Adam Smith's work including in *History of Political Economy*, *Journal of the History of Economic Thought*, *Scottish Journal of Political Economy*, *Journal of Economic Perspectives*, *Southern Economic Journal*, *American Journal of Economics and Sociology*, and the *Review of Social Economy*. He coedited, with Robin Malloy, *Adam Smith and the Philosophy of Law and Economics* (1994). In 2005 his book *Adam Smith's Moral Philosophy: A Historical and Contemporary Perspective on Markets, Law, Ethics, and Culture* was published by Cambridge University Press. Professor Evensky is past president of the History of Economics Society.

This work is dedicated to the memory of those
I loved and lost too young
Judi Kops
Herbert Behrend
Mazen Elhassan
Tom Franey
Paul O'Connor
"'Tis better to have loved and lost
Than never to have loved at all."
Alfred, Lord Tennyson, In Memoriam

Adam Smith's
Wealth of Nations

A Reader's Guide

JERRY EVENSKY
Syracuse University, Syracuse, NY

CAMBRIDGE
UNIVERSITY PRESS

CAMBRIDGE
UNIVERSITY PRESS

University Printing House, Cambridge CB2 8BS, United Kingdom

One Liberty Plaza, 20th Floor, New York, NY 10006, USA

477 Williamstown Road, Port Melbourne, VIC 3207, Australia

4843/24, 2nd Floor, Ansari Road, Daryaganj, Delhi - 110002, India

79 Anson Road, #06-04/06, Singapore 079906

Cambridge University Press is part of the University of Cambridge.

It furthers the University's mission by disseminating knowledge in the pursuit of
education, learning and research at the highest international levels of excellence.

www.cambridge.org
Information on this title: www.cambridge.org/9781107043374

First published 2015

A catalogue record for this publication is available from the British Library

Library of Congress Cataloging in Publication data
Evensky, Jerry, 1948–
Adam Smith's wealth of nations : a reader's guide / Jerry Evensky,
Syracuse University, NY.
pages cm
Includes bibliographical references and index.
ISBN 978-1-107-04337-4 (hardback) – ISBN 978-1-107-65376-4 (pbk.)
1. Smith, Adam, 1723–1790. 2. Economics – History. 3. Smith, Adam,
1723–1790. Inquiry into the nature and causes of the wealth of nations. I. Title.
HB103.S6E94 2015
330.15′3–dc23 2015003113

ISBN 978-1-107-04337-4 Hardback
ISBN 978-1-107-65376-4 Paperback

Contents

Acknowledgments   *page* vii

    Prologue: The Purpose of This Work   1

1   Adam Smith's Moral Philosophical Vision:
    The Context of His Economic Analysis   7

2   *The Wealth of Nations*: Book I   17

3   *The Wealth of Nations*: Books II and III   64

4   *The Wealth of Nations*: Book IV   106

5   *The Wealth of Nations*: Book V   170

    Epilogue: Adam Smith and Laissez-Faire   253

References   267
Index   273

Acknowledgments

I have been richly blessed to have very dear friends who go back a very long way: Martin Gilman – since two months old. Rupert Barkoff, Charlie Carrera, John Kops, and Richard Zander – since fourth grade. (We refer to ourselves as the "Allgood's Five" in honor of a diner we used to frequent when we were in high school.) Bill Fricke – since sophomore year of college. Jean LeLoup and Agnes Gregg – from the first days of my teaching career, which began with six years as a junior high social studies teacher in Webster Groves, Missouri. Tod Porter, Teri Riley, and Hussein Mirghani – since graduate school. Jay Meacham, Kisha Montgomery, and John Collins – for many years. There is nothing sweeter, more to be cherished, than old friends.

I begin my acknowledgments here because this work would not exist but for the persistent insistence, since my earlier publication at Cambridge (*Adam Smith's Moral Philosophy*, 2005), of one of those old and dear friends. When I talked with John, he never failed to ask me, "How's Adam Smith II coming along?" Well, John, here it is. Thank you very much for the push.

This work started as an aborted mission in *Research in the History of Economic Thought and Methodology* to explore the entire *Wealth of Nations*. That project only got through "Book I: Its relationship to Adam Smith's full moral philosophical vision: An inquiry into the nature and causes of the wealth of nations" (Warren J. Samuels, Jeff E. Biddle (ed.), Volume 21 Part 1, Emerald Group Publishing Limited, pp. 1–47 v. 21 Part 1, 2003), wherein I presented a much less developed version of what is Chapter 2 in this work. (My sincere thanks to Emerald Publishing for permission to build on that earlier work.) As with much of my work it was Warren Samuel's support that planted the seed of this project.

When I considered returning to this project, the encouragement of my good friend Scott Parris, then at Cambridge University Press, gave me the confidence to pursue it. Since Scott left Cambridge I have had the good fortune to work with Karen Maloney as the project has come to fruition.

As was the case with my first Smith book, I could not have realized the finished product without the support of Syracuse University, the Maxwell School, and the SU Department of Economics.

SU provided me with a sabbatical and a library carrel. That gave me the time and space to concentrate on this project.

On those mornings that I head to my carrel to work I generally stop for a coffee and a coffee roll at the Schine Student Center to gather my thoughts for the day. For many years I've been greeted there not only with hot coffee, but also with the warm smiles and greetings of the three delightful women who work at Dunkin' Donuts: Mary Beth Stiles, Kathleen Stenner, and Deborah LeClair. Mary Beth retired after she saw me through my first Smith book, Deb retired once she had seen me through this work, and Kathy is still there (missing her buddies) with her lovely smile and that good cup of coffee.

On those days when I can't trundle off to the library because I'm teaching, my day usually starts with coffee in the Economics Department office with my Department "family" – the staff that has included Dee Ficcaro, Laura Sauta, Sue Lewis, Patty Stach, Maureen Eastham, and Faye Shephard. I can't say enough about how wonderful they are. It's good to have a haven for sharing ... they are my haven.

I also benefit from the good company, good sharing, and good advice of three other dear SU community friends: Don Dutkowsky, Robert Rubinstein, and Jerry Edmonds. Don is "Mr. A to B" ... If it needs to be done, let's do it. And he does it, whatever "it" is, with a wonderful smile, a laser-like focus, and total integrity. Robert is my teaching savior. My Parkinson's has impeded me a bit and he's shown me a number of technological workarounds that have made the challenge much more manageable. He's also a very sweet heart and a joy to share time with. Jerry is my poster person for excellence in administration. He moves a team along to great achievements with care and caring, and with a very sharp wit that's a joy. Each is a very special person who brings great insight, great laughs, and great support to my world.

For many years I've had the pleasure of being the faculty liaison to the first-year program at SU. I've worked with a number of program directors but two are extra special: Mariana Lebron and Carrie Abbott. Mariana was the first director I worked with, and she set an amazingly high standard. I was really in awe of her ability to choreograph such a huge operation with a tiny staff. Carrie is the director with whom I work now. She is an extraordinarily accomplished professional. That and her infectious sparkle make it a joy to work with her.

My one colleague and very dear friend who actually does work on Adam Smith and with whom I can therefore share thoughts on my research is Robin Malloy. Indeed, it was in the process of developing a coedited work with Robin, *Adam Smith and the Philosophy of Law and Economics* (Kluwer Academic Publishers, 1994), that I came to appreciate the importance of institutional evolution in Smith's moral philosophy, a central theme that informs this book. Robin has not only given me insights into Smith, he has given me something much more precious – an extended family, for his family and mine are now tightly woven into one another's lives – and it is a blessing.

To help me cope with my Parkinson's I've turned to my former very good student and now very good friend, Master Trainer Karl Sterling. Karl is a tough, sweet human being who has really helped me maintain my balance – literally and figuratively. I also look to my longtime primary care physician, David Small, for support on this front. My office conversations with David cover the necessary and sufficient issues related to my health, and then turn to engaging talk about the state of the world, or our worlds.

When I need an evening of grounding and sharing I turn to Barry Berg. Barry is a mensch. It's a joy to laugh and kvetch with him, to talk with him of life – its joys and challenges – over dinner and his choice of wines. And speaking of mensch, I must also cite Bill Bogatz – my poster person for what it means to be a dedicated teacher – and Bob Waters – who represents the essence of the term "good neighbor." Barry, Bill, and Bob all fully deserve the appellation "mensch."

During the past year, as I worked on this book, I lost two women who were very dear to me.

My mom, Sylvia Kapelow Evensky, died at ninety-five. My momma was at one and the same time a classic Jewish mother and a brilliant, frustrated entrepreneur. She always had an agenda. If it was an agenda for you … it was always a good-hearted agenda, even if it wasn't always a welcomed agenda. If it was her own agenda, she was on it … always moving, always imagining the possibilities. She started several businesses when I was growing up, each one more successful than the last. I'm quite certain that in a different time and place she would have been a real business mover and shaker (or with her wonderfully imaginative eye, a great architect, as she dreamed of being). But in her time (1950s and 1960s) and her place (New Orleans) just getting a loan from the bank to start a small business involved having her brother cosign as the "responsible party," after all … what woman could be responsible with money for a business? My momma could, if they'd given her a chance.

My aunt Elsie Friedlander Evensky also passed away this past year at ninety-five. Aunt Elsie was the quintessential steel magnolia. Born and bred in Alabama, she was sugar and spice on the outside and rock solid on the inside. She faced heart-stopping pain, the loss of her daughter, Emily – her only child – in a car accident when Emmy was twenty-one. Yet she refused to let that pain diminish her life even as she carried it with her every hour of every day. She was a beautiful person and a truly unique character.

These two strong women along with my "Mom" (Ennis) Kops (who endured the same unthinkable pain as Aunt Elsie when she lost her daughter Judi when Judi was twenty-one … a pain she endured with the same amazing strength), my aunt Rosalind Gilman, Martha Barkoff, Helen Cohen, my "Pop" (Murray) Kops, my uncle Seymour Gilman, my uncle Nathan Evensky, Abe Cohen, and my dad – Herbert Evensky, who was the sweetest person I have ever known – these folks shaped my world as I grew up. I was a very, very fortunate kid to have such wonderful people to put up with me and to nurture me.

This parade of special people in my life may seem irrelevant to my subject here – Adam Smith – but it isn't. In the many pages of Smith's work that I've poured over so many times for so many years, I have long since identified one quotation that I think is a clear insight into who Smith was, and that I find a wonderful expression of the beauty we each have to offer one another as human beings:

"Kindness is the parent of kindness." (*Theory of Moral Sentiments*)

All the folks I've mentioned in this acknowledgment are exemplars of Smith's words. They have each enriched the world with their kindnesses and in so doing have given birth to so much more.

Prologue

The Purpose of This Work

My subject is Adam Smith's economics as he presents it in his *Inquiry into the Nature and Causes of the Wealth of Nations* (sometimes abbreviated *WN* in what follows).[1]

Smith's rhetorical strategy in *The Wealth of Nations* is to lay out his narrative in a stepwise process of analytical presentation, empirical persuasion, and policy implications.

There are five "Books" in *WN*. Smith begins his analytical presentation in Book I, defining his terms and arranging them into statements about economic processes. In Book II he turns to the dynamics of economics systems, analyzing how and why the wealth of a nation grows, stagnates, or declines. In Book III he offers an empirical case for his model by demonstrating the power of his analysis to explain both the twists and turns and the long view of humankind's history.

Having presented his model and made his empirical case for it, in Book IV Smith examines two alternative models, Mercantilism and Physiocracy, highlighting their weaknesses and the perverse consequences of their application as policy. Finally, in Book V Smith turns to the policy implications of his own analysis, offering his perspective on the role of government in a liberal society with a special emphasis on the importance of establishing security and justice, providing public goods, optimal revenue generation, and properly aligning incentives.

The Wealth of Nations (first edition published in 1776) is one piece of Smith's planned body of work that was to offer a moral philosophical (a

---

[1] Smith writes that inquiries into what is "properly called Political Economy ... [are inquiries into] the nature and causes of the wealth of nations" (*WN*, 678–9).

holistic) analysis of the human condition. He makes this agenda clear in the original "Advertisement" to the first published piece in this analysis, the first edition (1759) of his *Theory of Moral Sentiments*. Therein he tells us that there are more dimensions of his analysis yet to be written concerning law and government (never written, but his *Lectures on Jurisprudence* reflect his thinking on this dimension[2]) and economics (realized in *WN*).[3]

What I offer here is an analysis of the economics of Adam Smith as presented in *The Wealth of Nations* that weaves those other dimensions of his moral philosophy into his economics so that the integrated character of his moral philosophy becomes clear. To that end, I highlight the central role of the ethical standards and legal institutions in Smith's understanding of how and why the wealth of a nation grows, stagnates, or declines. This integrated analysis of *WN* has not been done before.[4]

---

[2] "The first of the two reports relates to Smith's Jurisprudence lectures in the 1762–3 [Glasgow University] session [*LJ*(A)], and the second, in all probability, to the lectures given in the 1763–4 session [*LJ*(B)].... [Clearly] what really matters ... is the *reliability* of the document [(referring to *LJ*(B))], does it or does it not give a reasonably accurate report of what was actually said in the lectures at which the original notes were taken? Now that we have another set of notes [*LJ*(A)] to compare it with, we can answer this question with a fairly unqualified affirmative" (Meek, Raphael, and Stein, 1978, 5, 7 emphasis in original).

[3] Even at the end of his life as he publishes the last revision of *TMS* in the year he dies (1790) Smith harkens back to this agenda in the "Advertisement":

"In the last paragraph of the first Edition of the present work, I said, that I should in another discourse endeavour to give an account of the general principles of law and government, and of the different revolutions which they had undergone in the different ages and periods of society; not only in what concerns justice, but in what concerns police, revenue, and arms, and whatever else is the object of law. In the Enquiry concerning the Nature and Causes of the Wealth of Nations, I have partly executed this promise; at least so far as concerns police, revenue, and arms. What remains, the theory of jurisprudence, which I have long projected, I have hitherto been hindered from executing, by the same occupations which had till now prevented me from revising the present work. Though my very advanced age leaves me, I acknowledge, very little expectation of ever being able to execute this great work to my own satisfaction; yet, as I have not altogether abandoned the design, and as I wish still to continue under the obligation of doing what I can, I have allowed the paragraph to remain as it was published more than thirty years ago, when I entertained no doubt of being able to execute every thing which it announced." (*TMS*, 3)

[4] In the course of my analysis I also examine several elements of Smith's *WN* that I do not believe have been developed in the literature. These include:

- In Book I, Smith's take-off theory of growth.
- In Book II, Smith's analysis of circuits of growth as self-expanding cycles driven by capital deepening and spilling over into ever widening circuits of trade.

Ethics and law, as the keys to a "well-governed society" (*WN*, 22), are a constant theme in what follows because the progressive maturation of "government" is the *sine qua non* of Smith's moral philosophical vision of humankind's material progress. For Smith it is the content of and balance between individual ethics and institutional laws that "governs" a nation. And, it is the character of this *enlarged conception of "government"* that determines the prospect for a nation's progress. In my "Epilogue: Adam Smith and Laissez-Faire," I explore Smith's complex view on the relationship between the citizen and the state. Smith's is a nuanced view informed by what he clearly believes to be the messy business of the human condition.

It is not my purpose to offer a meticulous tome that addresses every issue that has ever been raised about Smith's *WN*. *WN* has been dissected page by page by very thoughtful scholars for well over 200 years. A work written to address all the issues that have been examined with regard to every element of Smith's *WN* would require multiple volumes.

My goal is at once less ambitious, and at the same time more so. It is to offer a persuasive analysis[5] of Smith's *Inquiry into the Nature and Causes of the Wealth of Nations* as a unified theory of the evolution of humankind's growing capacity for material production. And, to demonstrate how Smith's economics is integrated into his larger moral philosophical vision of humankind's progress from past to present to prospect.[6]

- In Book III, Smith's analysis of the twists and turns of history in the short and mid-term to complement his understanding of the longer-term trajectory of the human condition.
- In Book IV, an analysis of the evolution of Smith's views on the Mercantile system.
- In Book V, Smith's focus on the role of government as an instrument for aligning incentives.

[5] If this is to be a persuasive representation of Adam Smith's economics, I must at least meet the standards Smith would set for me:

- My interpretations of the individual elements of his analysis must efficiently and effectively represent a persuasive reading of his text, and
- I must weave a thread through these individual elements that "makes the sense of the author flow naturally upon our mind" (*LRBL*, 6) so that his *Inquiry into the Nature and Causes of the Wealth of Nations* makes sense as a narrative.

[6] Smith was a professor of Moral Philosophy at Glasgow. "Adam Smith did not think of himself as an economist, and so limited to familiar subject matter disciplinary boundaries. He was, instead, a moral philosopher, whose intellectual curiosity extended to the origins of the explanatory structure being applied" (Buchanan, 2008, 23).

To date, the most significant book-length analysis of the entire *Wealth of Nations* is Samuel Hollander's *The Economics of Adam Smith* (1973). Hollander's is a very valuable contribution to Smith scholarship, but it approaches Smith from a perspective that differs from the one I offer here. As Hollander himself notes, his purpose is to analyze Smith through a modern lens, applying modern techniques[7] to assess Smith's contributions.[8] The chapter headings in Hollander's work make clear that he is deconstructing Smith's analysis and exploring its elements one by one (Ch. 1 Automatic Equilibrating Processes, Ch. 2 Economic Development, Ch. 3 Industry Structure, Ch. 4 Theory of Value, and so on).

My purpose is different. It is to represent what Adam Smith *as moral philosopher* is doing in his *Inquiry into the Nature and Causes of the Wealth of Nations* as a part of his "grand vision" (Buchanan, 2008, 27).[9]

How do I *know* what Smith is "doing"? I don't. But, while it is impossible to know Smith's intentions with certainty, it is possible, by presenting an analysis that efficiently and effectively weaves together the threads of his *Inquiry* into a unified, coherent narrative, to offer a persuasive account of what he seems to be trying to communicate.[10]

[7] This is certainly a legitimate approach if, as Paul Samuelson writes: "Inside every classical economist is a modem economist trying to get out" (Samuelson, 1977, 42). But as the next footnote makes clear, Hollander has a more restrained view of the retrofitting of modern concepts on our predecessors.

[8] "[W]e adopt the position that the use of modern analytical tools, concepts, and procedures may be of considerable aid in an analysis of the work of an earlier writer, *provided that he was operating within the general frame of reference for which these devices are appropriate.* In particular, we believe that there is justification for the utilization of the current state of knowledge regarding the general equilibrium process in a study of the economics of Adam Smith insofar as he adopted the position that the price mechanism can be relied upon to clear product and factor markets.... The historian must, however, be alive to the danger that, in following this procedure, he will end up with an account of 'Smithian' ... economics rather than the economics of Adam Smith ..., it cannot be too strongly emphasized that it is with the latter that we are concerned" (Hollander, 13–14, emphasis in original).

[9] "How absurd to think of the author of the *Wealth of Nations* as interested only in the wealth of nations! Adam Smith's great work is more than a treatise on economics; it is a philosophical work, in that sense of the word 'philosophy' which has almost passed out of usage in the last hundred years" (Morrow, 322).

[10] "At the heart of Smith's thinking, his doctrine, and his method of presentation (the three are always related) is the notion of the chain (see ii. 133 and cf. Astronomy II. 8–9) – articulated continuity, sequence of relations leading to illumination. Leave no chasm or gap in the *thread*: 'the very notion of a gap makes us uneasy' (ii. 36)" (Bryce, 13, emphasis added). I follow Griswold's standard: that the "plausibility of my reconstruction of his basic framework rests primarily on its fit with his work" (Griswold, 170).

Smith asserts in his *Lectures on Rhetoric and Belles Lettres* that the point of good writing is to communicate with one's reader: "[T]he perfection of stile consists in Express<ing> in the most concise, proper and precise manner the thought of the author … which he designs to communicate to his reader" (*LRBL*, 55).[11]

Adam Smith had something to say that he believed could contribute to humankind's progress.[12] My focus has been on listening carefully in order to understand as clearly and to relate as effectively as possible what Smith is trying to communicate. James Buchanan writes: "Perhaps, only perhaps, by concentrating carefully on Adam Smith's grand vision, paying heed both to what he actually wrote and to what he must have had in mind, we can, finally, come to a consensus understanding of his inclusive message as well as its current implications" (Buchanan, 2008, 27). I agree.

This work is offered as a scholarly contribution to the Smith literature, the domain of Smith specialists. That said, I have endeavored to write a piece that an interested nonspecialist will find a worthy read. There are, after all, very few Smith specialists, but there are many folks who reference Smith.

For well over 200 years Smith's work has been a constant reference, cited for authority in the thoughtful, and sometimes not so thoughtful,[13] public discourse about the nature of markets and the role of government in a market system.[14] If Smith is going to be called upon to "participate"

---

[11] "Smith's range of interests includes rhetoric and belles-lettres, in the pursuit of which he developed theories as to the best literary form for getting your message over to your audience" (Campbell, 574).

[12] "The Historians again made it their aim not only to amuse but by narrating the more important facts and those which were most concerned in the bringing about great revolutions, and unfolding their causes, to instruct their readers in what manner such events might be brought about or avoided" (*LRBL*, 111).

[13] See Amartya Sen's "Uses and Abuses of Adam Smith" (Sen, 2011). Smith is often treated like the Soviet Central Committee of the Communist Party treated Marx, as a deep well of expressions (taken out of context) that one can dip into in order to justify the next Five Year Plan. Another classic example of this selective citation process is that enlisted by Mrs. B. J. Gaillot to "prove," using the Bible as the textual resource (the "well"), that segregation is the will of God. See "God Gave the Law of Segregation (as well as the 10 Commandments) to Moses on Mount Sinai" (Gaillot, 1960). Mrs. Gaillot was doing her thing in New Orleans when I was growing up there. She was "effective" enough to get herself excommunicated from the Catholic Church.

[14] "One of the consequences of becoming a celebrated authority and father of a discipline like Adam Smith is that one inevitably becomes subject to recruitment drives on the part of a variety of one's successors. Appealing to the authority of a great thinker or seeking

in this discourse, those who cite him should at least do him the courtesy of trying to understand his ideas in his own terms.

Herein I offer my understanding of Smith's ideas in his own terms.

inspiration in their work are regular occurrences in political and academic life, so fighting over Smith's legacy is no new sport" (Smith, Craig, 539). "[A]n economist must have peculiar theories indeed who cannot quote from *The Wealth of Nations* to support his special purposes" (Coats, 219).

Adam Smith's Moral Philosophical Vision

The Context of His Economic Analysis

ADAM SMITH AS MORAL PHILOSOPHER

Philosophy, by representing the invisible chains which bind together all these disjointed objects, endeavours to introduce order into this chaos of jarring and discordant appearances, to allay the tumult of the imagination, and to restore it, when it surveys the great revolutions of the universe, to that tone of tranquility and composure, which is both most agreeable in itself, and most suitable to its nature. Philosophy, therefore, may be regarded as one of those arts which addresses themselves to the imagination. Adam Smith's *History of Astronomy* (hereafter *HA*) (45–6)

Adam Smith was a philosopher,[1] one who believed that there is an order underlying what we observe in our universe and that to imagine and represent those "concealed connections[2] that unite the various appearances of nature" (*HA*, 51) is an intellectual joy,[3] an emotional balm,[4] and a social benefit.[5]

---

[1] See *Adam Smith's Moral Philosophy* (Evensky, 2005) chapters 1–4 for a more detailed presentation of what is covered here.

[2] Smith alludes to this concept of a natural system to be revealed in various ways. See Raphael and Skinner (p. 6) for examples.

[3] "[P]hilosophical effort involved not only an escape from the contemplation of 'jarring and discordant appearances' but also a source of pleasure in its own right" (Raphael and Skinner, 6). "It gives us a pleasure to see the phaenomena which we reckoned the most unaccountable all deduced from some principle (commonly a wellknown one) and all united in one chain, far superior to what we feel from the unconnected method where everything is accounted for by itself without any reference to the others" (*LRBL*, 146).

[4] "Philosophy, by representing the invisible chains which bind together all these disjointed objects, endeavours to introduce order into this chaos of jarring and discordant appearances, to allay the tumult of the imagination, and to restore it, when it surveys the great revolutions of the universe, to that tone of tranquility and composure, which is both most agreeable in itself, and most suitable to its nature" (*HA*, 45–6).

[5] "Science is the great antidote to the poison of enthusiasm and superstition, and where the superior ranks of the people were secure from it, the inferior ranks could not be much exposed to it" (*WN*, 796).

In his day philosophy was divided into two domains: Natural and Moral Philosophy.

Natural Philosophy focused on the physical universe. Natural philosophers carefully observed the universe and imagined what invisible connecting principles would be consistent with the "jarring and discordant appearances" we observe. Why, for example, do a few stars appear to wander through the heavens among the multitude of fixed stars?[6]

For centuries successively more complex epicycles of explanation seemed to offer ever more accurate explanations of these wandering stars. Each "success" encouraged even more careful observation. But keen observation brought not more understanding – just more epicycles. Then the earth was moved by Copernicus from the center of the "universe" and, with the benefit of Kepler's elliptical orbits, a much simpler and more coherent explanation of the motion of these "wandering stars," the planets,[7] was achieved.

But if the earth is indeed spinning on its axis and orbiting around the sun, why don't we feel a brutal wind?[8] If we speed along in a carriage the wind is in our face, and yet as we hurtle around the sun – no wind. This and other questions remained unanswered. Enter Newton.

Newton's analysis seemed to explain all that we could see, and to correctly predict things that were as yet unseen when he wrote (e.g., the return of Halley's comet[9]). His laws of physics seemed *as if* they were the actual laws that ruled the physical universe.

This "as if" is not my phrase; it is Adam Smith's. In his *History of Astronomy* Smith concludes his analysis of this history with glowing praise for Newton's work, qualified by "as if":

And even we, while we have been endeavouring to represent all philosophical systems as mere inventions of the imagination, to connect together the otherwise disjointed and discordant phaenomena of nature, have insensibly been drawn in, to

---

[6] My never to be forgotten high school teacher Mr. Herbert Behrend introduced me to this question.

[7] "The Stars, when more attentively surveyed, were some of them observed to be less constant and uniform in their motions than the rest, and to change their situations with regard to the other heavenly bodies; moving generally eastwards, yet appearing sometimes to stand still, and sometimes even to move westwards. These, to the number of five, were distinguished by the name of Planets, or wandering Stars" (*HA*, 55).

[8] "How, therefore, could the imagination ever conceive so ponderous a body to be naturally endowed with so dreadful a movement?" (*HA*, 78). "If the Earth, it was said, revolved so rapidly from west to east, a perpetual wind would set in from east to west, more violent than what blows in the greatest hurricanes" (*HA*, 79).

[9] See Smith's *HA* (p. 103).

make use of language expressing the connecting principles of this one [Newton's], *as if* they were the real chains which Nature makes use of to bind together her several operations. (*HA*, 105, emphasis added)

"As if" reflects Smith's philosophical humility.[10] The chains of causation that connect the natural events we observe are invisible. All we can know is what we observe, the events as they appear on the face of nature.[11] We can only imagine the invisible links based on what we can observe. We can never "know" nature, but with keen observation and building on the analysis of our predecessors, we can imagine and represent ever more persuasively what may lie behind the face of nature.[12] Smith "fully realized that science was a succession of approximations" (Bittermann, 733).

Newton was a Natural philosopher. Smith was a Moral philosopher.

Natural philosophers sought to represent the invisible connecting principles that underlie the order around us. Moral philosophers did the same for the order among us – the order of humankind.

Following Newton, observation and imagination are the keys to Smith's moral philosophical method. As a Moral philosopher, Smith observed all things human. His data included histories of past societies, stories of contemporary societies, and observations of his own society. His goal, based on these data, was to present a persuasive analysis[13] of the nature and causes of humankind's past and present course with an

---

[10] For a lovely example of Smith's admiration for philosophical humility, see his letter written as a eulogy for David Hume and in particular his description of Hume's imagined conversation with Charon as he tries to negotiate a delay in crossing the River Styx (*Correspondence*, 217).

[11] "Who wonders at the machinery of the opera-house who has once been admitted behind the scenes? In the Wonders of nature, however, it rarely happens that we can discover so clearly this connecting chain. With regard to a few even of them, indeed, we seem to have been really admitted behind the scenes, and our Wonder accordingly is entirely at an end" (*HA*, 42–3).

[12] So too, I can't know Smith's mind. I can only imagine and offer what I hope will be a persuasive analysis based on what is observable ... his works.

[13] "The desire of being believed, the desire of persuading, of leading and directing other people, seems to be one of the strongest of all our natural desires. It is, perhaps, the instinct upon which is founded the faculty of speech, the characteristical faculty of human nature. No other animal possesses this faculty, and we cannot discover in any other animal any desire to lead and direct the judgment and conduct of its fellows. Great ambition, the desire of real superiority, of leading and directing, seems to be altogether peculiar to man, and speech is the great instrument of ambition, of real superiority, of leading and directing the judgments and conduct of other people" (*TMS*, 336).

eye toward contributing to the realization of its prospect,[14] which, he believed based on the patterns he observed from the past to the present, is progress.[15]

Smith's *Inquiry into the Nature and Causes of the Wealth of Nations* is one dimension of his larger moral philosophical inquiry into humankind's past, present, and prospect.

SMITH'S MORAL PHILOSOPHY AND
THE WEALTH OF NATIONS

Adam Smith comes to his *Inquiry into the Nature and Causes of the Wealth of Nations* with some principles of his analysis of humankind already well developed.

In his first book, *The Theory of Moral Sentiments* (1759), he lays the foundation for his analysis of humankind by examining human nature, the attributes we share as the individuals who collectively make up humankind.

Our nature is, according to Smith, like a "coarse clay" (*TMS*, 162),[16] very malleable but with some universal characteristics:

- We all act on the same set of basic sentiments (self-love, justice, and beneficence) – individuals' different actions in similar circumstances are explained by the differing balance of these sentiments among us.
- We all desire to enjoy the approbation (praise) and avoid the disapprobation (blame) of those with whom we share our social world.
- We each have the capacity to transcend the societal pressures that derive from our desire for praise or abhorrence of blame, and in pursuit of

---

[14] For Smith "the historian's aim as an author consisted, not in seeking to entertain the reader ... but rather in offering him instruction, so that mankind, by coming to know the more interesting and important events of human life and by coming to understand what caused them, could learn the means by which good effects might be produced and evil effects avoided in human affairs" (Howell, 27–8).

[15] "Smith along with his contemporaries expected the world to become more intelligent, more tolerant, and more humane with the decline of superstition and the advance of knowledge.... Smith was undeniably a 'progressivist' ... Yet progress was not automatic. He did not look to Providence for direct aid in the economic and moral improvement of mankind. Man had to act on his own behalf ... Smith's own work as economist and philosopher were [*sic*] intended, most probably, as contributions toward this progress (Bittermann, 733–4).

[16] "Man [as individual] is perpetually changing ... [b]ut humanity, or human nature, is always existent, is always the same.... This, therefore, is the object of science, reason, and understanding" (*EPS*, 121). See Meek for more on this malleable conception of being as pervading "Enlightenment thought" (Meek, 1976, 20).

praiseworthiness (*TMS*, 113) to follow the dictates of a higher authority, our conscience.[17]

Born as this coarse clay and with a desire for approval, our society impresses upon us our first shape – inculcating in each of us a common sense of "duty" (*TMS*, 161) to the existing societal standards of behavior.[18] But we each have a unique biography, so socialization is never perfectly complete nor uniform. Given our varying life experiences we become unique beings, and as such we develop an autonomous perspective on our society.

From that autonomous perspective we can make independent judgments about the societal norms we have inherited and we can set our own standards. Based on those personal standards we can, if we choose, try to influence extant societal norms in order to reshape our society. Thus, individuals and societies coevolve, each shaping the other – in some times and places at a glacial pace, at other times and places in rapid and even radical ways.

This concept, evolve, is an essential principle in Smith's analysis of humankind's past, present, and prospect. Based on his data, Smith believed that the natural course of humankind has been a progression

---

[17] "Man naturally desires, not only to be loved, but to be lovely; or to be that thing which is the natural and proper object of love. He naturally dreads, not only to be hated, but to be hateful; or to be that thing which is the natural and proper object of hatred. He desires, not only praise, but praiseworthiness; or to be that thing which, though it should be praised by nobody, is, however, the natural and proper object of praise. He dreads, not only blame, but blame-worthiness; or to be that thing which, though it should be blamed by nobody, is, however, the natural and proper object of blame" (*TMS*, 113–14). Smith's initial version of the impartial spectator didn't reflect this autonomy, but in response to criticism from Sir Gilbert Elliot, Smith refined his analysis (see Raphael, 90–2).

[18] In contrasting standards of assessment of human beings Smith writes: "The first is the idea of complete propriety and perfection, which, in those difficult situations, no human conduct ever did, or ever can come up to; and in comparison with which the actions of all men must for ever appear blameable and imperfect. The second is the idea of that degree of proximity or distance from this complete perfection, which the actions of the greater part of men commonly arrive at" (*TMS*, 26). He continues later in *TMS*:

> Nature ... has not left this weakness [our human frailty], which is of so much importance, altogether without a remedy; nor has she abandoned us entirely to the delusions of self-love. Our continual observations upon the conduct of others, insensibly lead us to form to ourselves certain general rules concerning what is fit and proper either to be done or to be avoided....

> The regard to those general rules of conduct, is what is properly called a sense of duty, a principle of the greatest consequence in human life, and the only principle by which the bulk of mankind are capable of directing their actions....

> [U]pon the tolerable observance of these duties, depends the very existence of human society, which would crumble into nothing if mankind were not generally impressed with a reverence for those important rules of conduct. (*TMS*, 159, 161–2, 163)

through four stages – from hunting and gathering to pasturage to agriculture to commerce, and that this progress has been an evolutionary process.[19]

Note the term "progress."[20] It is Smith's term and he uses it in a normative sense. In his analysis this four-stage evolution is not only *natural*, it represents progress ... as in improvement.[21]

It is here, with the term "natural," that the analyses of Smith and Newton part ways. The natural path of a planet or a comet is the path it *will* take, the path we *will* observe. Neither the planet nor the comet has the free will to affect or effect its path. Each simply obeys the laws of nature.

According to Smith, humans have been endowed by nature with a unique capacity. Given our self-awareness and free will, we have in our nature the capacity to violate nature's laws. This makes Smith's task more challenging than Newton's. Newton's planets always act *in harmony with nature*. People don't. We can and do sometimes exercise our free will in unnatural ways. To understand what makes behavior unnatural, we need to understand the norm: natural.

The natural path of humankind, as Smith envisions it, is a path of progress toward the limiting case,[22] an ideal state of liberty and justice for all, and the greatest wealth for the nations. This potential for progress is a gift of nature. To facilitate this progress is to act *in harmony with nature*. To act in harmony with nature is to be a moral being. Thus moral human behavior is "natural" human behavior.

But we are not born as moral or immoral beings. We are born as coarse clay, and that coarse clay from which we are shaped has the capacity to take on an immoral form, to act unnaturally[23] ... and thus to distort natural progress.[24]

---

[19] In *LJA* Smith states: "There are four distinct states which mankind pass thro: – 1st, the Age of Hunters; 2dly, the Age of Shepherds; 3dly, the Age of Agriculture; and 4thly, the Age of Commerce" (*LJA*, 14). See Meek (1976).

[20] Smith uses the term "progress" well over 100 times in *WN*.

[21] "The belief in the natural progress of opulence, almost in its inevitability, is so strong throughout *WN* that, when dealing with a contemporary problem, Smith's main objective is to isolate those barriers which lay in the path of natural progress as he saw it" (Campbell and Skinner, 59).

[22] I use the concept of a "limit" because Smith believed we can approach but never realize the ideal.

[23] Why nature would embody in humans this capacity to act unnaturally is as much of a mystery to Smith as it is to us. What could possibly have possessed Adam Lanza to murder innocent little children at Sandy Hook Elementary School? From whence the "banality of evil" that made possible the Holocaust?

[24] As Dugald Stewart wrote regarding Smith's view in his "Account of the Life and Writings of Adam Smith": "[A]s paradoxical as the proposition may appear, it is certainly true,

As a society the key to nurturing progress is to nurture individuals to behave morally. In one sense, morality is to a social system as gravity is to a solar system. It is the invisible force that holds the system together and keeps it functioning smoothly and, in the case of humankind, productively.[25] In another sense, however, there is a significant difference. The nature of gravity is not debatable; the "nature" of morality is.

There is an absolute ideal of morality in Smith's Moral Philosophical analysis,[26] but the ideal standards of morality are among those connecting principles that are invisible. We cannot know the ideal, we can only imagine it.

In practice, in the real as opposed to the ideal world, moral standards are contingent, based on the norms as they have evolved in a given society, and they are subject to change.[27] And, because socialization is never perfect, even these contingent standards are not fully inculcated into each and every member of society.

It was clear to Smith from historical, contemporary, and personal cases that given free will, their balancer of sentiments, and their alignment of incentives, some individuals will try to better their condition in ways that are immoral by extant social standards. People cheat, lie, steal, murder, and so on, to get ahead. So, how does society protect itself from such behavior?

In the rude state it does so by tribal council that assesses behavior according to extant standards and enforces consequences for deviance from the norm. But as society becomes more complex this council system becomes unworkable. More complex institutions are required to define and enforce the socially sanctioned principles of moral behavior (one's "duty"). With each successive stage the complexity of society and thus the complexity of the institutions necessary for society to cohere increases. In

that the real progress is not always the most natural. It may have been determined by particular accidents, which are not likely again to occur, and which cannot be considered as forming any part of that general provision which nature has made for the improvement of the race" (Stewart, 296).

[25] Or as Smith puts it using a different image: "[V]irtue, which is, as it were, the fine polish to the wheels of society, necessarily pleases; while vice, like the vile rust, which makes them jar and grate upon one another, is as necessarily offensive" (*TMS*, 316).

[26] An individual is perfectly moral if his motives enjoy the complete sympathy of an ideal, well-informed, impartial spectator. Such a person will be acting based on perfectly balanced moral sentiments: "The man who acts according to the rules of perfect prudence, of strict justice, and of proper benevolence, may be said to be perfectly virtuous" (*TMS*, 237).

[27] See Smith's commentary on the sanction of infanticide "in almost all the states of Greece, even among the polite and civilized Athenians" (*TMS*, 210).

his *Lectures on Jurisprudence* (carefully recorded lecture notes from his students in a course that covered this subject) Smith explores the evolution of the jurisprudential institutions of human society, civil government.

He recognizes that just as individual humans are corruptible, so too these institutions are corruptible – they are, after all, a human construct.

This presents Smith with a conundrum: progress through the four stages requires an evolving, progressive development of morals and laws in a world in which individuals and institutions are corruptible, and such corruption takes society down unnatural paths that are destructive for society. The world is a messy place. So how is humankind's progress possible?

Smith believes that evolutionary progress emerges as a consequence of natural selection.

Those societies that are more successful at approximating the moral and legal conditions necessary for progress are more capable of realizing the increased material productivity that comes with progress. *Ceteris paribus*, greater productivity increases the capacity of a society to defend itself.[28]

Immoral individuals and/or distorted, unjust institutions put the fruits of individuals' labors at risk and/or monopolize market opportunities. These conditions reduce incentives for effort, innovation, and inventiveness; constrain the extent of the market; and discourage capital accumulation. Therefore moral and/or institutional distortions ultimately lead to stagnation or decline.

Individual morals and institutional standards are never perfectly aligned with the ideal in any society. Nevertheless, Smith believed that the story of humankind's history is a story of progress because, through natural selection, ever closer societal approximations of the ideal slowly prevail over those that are more distorted.

But distortions are the nature of the human beast, so the progress of any particular society is not inexorable. All societies are a work in progress. Individual societies emerge, grow, and decline, but ultimately the path of humankind has led to progress. As we will see, this relationship between the development of the division of labor, the extension of markets, the material well-being of individuals, and the evolution of "laws and institutions" (*WN*, 89) is a key theme Smith returns to again and again in

---

[28] Greater productivity means increased capacity for a larger population with the resources to support a division of labor that includes professional soldiers, and those who enlist, outfit, and support that military force for defense.

his *Inquiry into the Nature and Causes of the Wealth of Nations*. Indeed, it is on the twenty-second page of his 947-page tome[29] that Smith sets the frame for the whole of what is to follow by laying out the importance of laws and institutions that establish a "well-governed society":

It is the great multiplication of the productions of all the different arts, in consequence of the division of labour, which occasions, in a *well-governed society*, that universal opulence which extends itself to the lowest ranks of the people. (*WN*, 22, emphasis added)

"Well-governed" here refers to Smith's enlarged conception of government including both institutional government ... laws and police – and personal government ... civic ethics and self-command. In Smith's moral philosophy these two dimensions of "government" complement and inform one another. Both are improvable, but given "human frailty" (*Correspondence*, 221) neither is perfectible. For Smith the ideal is a limit – not achievable, but approachable.[30]

The raison d'être of Smith's body of work is to contribute to the approximation of that ideal[31] by representing the factors that lead to maturation of the economic/political/social nexus.[32] This nexus and its maturation is a thread woven through his *Inquiry into the Nature and Causes of the Wealth of Nations*. In Books I and II, as he models how markets work and the dynamic of growth, the degree to which the society is well-governed is the litmus test for the success and sustainability of its market system. In Book III he turns to history to make his case empirically, demonstrating that the emergence of more mature government was the key to successful growth in Europe after the Middle Ages. In Book IV he criticizes the Mercantile faction for undermining the tremendous progress that his own Great Britain has achieved thanks, as he demonstrates in his *Lectures on Jurisprudence*, to the maturation of its

---

[29] Pagination based on *The Glasgow Edition*.

[30] It is our human frailty, our inability to be perfectly moral beings by the ideal standards of the impartial spectator, that makes perfection a limit – approachable but not attainable (see Raphael, 94). In a "Note" in *TMS* Smith writes of "the present depraved state of mankind ... [and of] so weak and imperfect a creature as man" (*TMS*, 77 note).

[31] A. W. Coats writes that "[a]lthough the prevailing theories and practices of government fell far short of his [Smith's] ideal – which he realized was unattainable in practice ... – he certainly hoped that his *magnum opus* would contribute to ... reform" (Coats, 223–4).

[32] "The progress of opulence can be seen ... as a virtuous circle, in which legal and political improvement leads to economic improvement, and economic improvement in turns leads to further improvement in political and legal institutions" (Rothschild and Sen, 336). "[E]thics, jurisprudence, and economics were ... seen by Smith as the parts, separate but interconnected, of an even wider system of social science" (Skinner, 1979, 12).

laws and institutions.[33] And finally in Book V he examines the characteristics of effective institutional government.

This concept of a "well-governed society" is the thread that stitches Smith's *Wealth of Nations*, his *Theory of Moral Sentiments*, and his *Lectures on Jurisprudence* together into a holistic moral philosophical vision of humankind's past, present, and prospect.[34] I will follow this thread as I analyze Smith's narrative in his *Inquiry into the Nature and Causes of the Wealth of Nations*. The implications of this analysis for the role of institutional government in a free market system will be examined in my "Epilogue: Adam Smith and Laissez-Faire."

Smith believed that the engine that drives growth in the wealth of a nation is increasing productivity. Thus, Smith's analysis of *The Wealth of Nations* begins in Book I with "[t]he causes of this improvement, in the productive powers of labour" (*WN*, 11). The first principle of this "improvement" is the division of labor, so it is with this concept that Smith begins his *Inquiry*.

---

[33] See Evensky (2005, chapter 3) for more on this.

[34] In the "Preface" to his *Principles of Political Economy* first published in 1848, John Stuart Mill cites as his intellectual mentor not David Ricardo with whom he came of age as an economist, but Adam Smith, whose *Wealth of Nations* appeared thirty years before Mill was born and seventy-two years before Mill wrote his "Preface."

In that "Preface" Mill writes of *The Wealth of Nations*:

> The most characteristic quality of that work, and one in which it most differs from some others which have equalled or even surpassed it as mere expositions of the general principles of the subject, is that it invariably associates the principles with their applications. This of itself implies a much wider range of ideas and of topics, than are included in political economy, considered as a branch of abstract speculation. For practical purposes, political economy is inseparably intertwined with many other branches of social [(Smith's "moral")] philosophy. Except on matters of mere detail, there are perhaps no practical questions, even among those which approach nearest to the character or purely economical questions, which admit of being decided on economical premises alone. And it is because Adam Smith never loses sight of this truth; because in his applications of Political Economy, he perpetually appeals to other and often far larger considerations than pure Political Economy affords – that he gives that well-grounded feeling of command over the principles of the subject for the purposes of practice. (Mill, 4–5)

Mill's words capture Smith beautifully. Smith's *Inquiry into the Nature and Causes of the Wealth of Nations* represents but one dimension of his full moral philosophical vision. As such, Smith's story of the connecting principles that determine from whence we derive our daily bread – Adam Smith's economics – cannot be fully understood or appreciated unless those principles are set into the context of his vison of how society approximates the ideal combination of civic ethics and institutional government – of how a well-governed society is achieved.

The Wealth of Nations: Book I

Of the Causes of Improvement in the productive Powers of Labour, and of the Order according to which its Produce is Naturally distributed among the different Ranks of the People

CHAPTER 1: "OF THE DIVISION OF LABOUR"

Smith believes that a key to material progress is increasing productivity. So, what better place to start his *Inquiry into the Nature and Causes of the Wealth of Nations* than with these words:

The greatest improvement in the productive powers of labour, and the greater part of the skill, dexterity, and judgment with which it is any where directed, or applied, seem to have been the effects of the division of labor. (*WN*, 13)[1]

The basic principles of the division of labor are straightforward: by focusing on one task, individuals enhance their "dexterity," save time "commonly lost in passing from one species of work to another," and become more inventive (*WN*, 17). Each of these advantages increases individuals' productivity.

The role of the division of labor in making possible our material well-being is obvious if we simply reflect on our own experience. Consider "[t]he woollen coat" of "the most common artificer or day-labourer in a civilized and thriving country" ...

---

[1] Sympathy and imagination are the central concepts in *TMS* that establish the foundation for the analysis of all that follows. On the first page of *TMS* Smith lays out the mechanism through which the approbation or disapprobation (the morality) of another human being, and ultimately of ourselves, is assessed: the degree to which through imagination we sympathize with sentiments of that other or oneself. So too in *WN*, Smith begins with the central concept of his analysis, the division of labor.

and you will perceive that the number of people of whose industry a part, though but a small part, has been employed in procuring him this accommodation, exceeds all computation. The woollen coat, for example, which covers the day-labourer, as coarse and rough as it may appear, is the produce of the joint labour of a great multitude of workmen. (*WN*, 22)

He proceeds to imagine the "great multitude of" invisible hands that played a part in producing this very common item including, among the many cited:

ship-builders, sailors, sail-makers, rope-makers, [who] must have been employed in order to bring together the different drugs made us of by the dyer, which come from the remotest corners of the world! What a variety of labour too is necessary in order to produce the tools of the meanest of those workmen! To say nothing of such complicated machines as the ship of the sailor, the mill of the fuller, or even the loom of the weaver, let us consider only what a variety of labour is requisite in order to form that very simple machine, the shears with which the shepherd clips the wool. (*WN*, 23)

Thanks to all these hands, each doing its part, in this divided labor of production "it may be true, perhaps, that the accommodation of an European prince does not always so much exceed that of an industrious and frugal peasant, as the accommodation of the latter exceeds that of many an African king, the absolute master of the lives and liberties of ten thousand naked savages" (*WN*, 24).

Smith summarizes his point about the division of labor as follows:

It is the great multiplication of the productions of all the different arts, in consequence of the division of labour, which occasions, in a *well-governed society*, that universal opulence which extends itself to the lowest ranks of the people. Every workman has a greater quantity of his own work to dispose of beyond what he himself has occasion for; and every other workman being exactly in the same situation, he is enabled to *exchange* a great quantity of his own goods for a great quantity, or, what comes to the same thing, for the price of a great quantity of theirs. (*WN*, 22, emphasis added)

In this summary Smith anticipates where his narrative will go: to an analysis of the process of exchange.

Also imbedded in this summary is a thread that enters the fabric of his narrative here and weaves its way through the entire narrative, a thread represented here by the phrase "well-governed society."

The division of labor creates interdependence. For interdependence to be constructive there must be rules governing ownership and transactions (e.g., standards of property rights and exchange). Such governance provides individuals the security they need if they are to expose their resources to the transactional process. Absent such rules, society can degenerate into chaos.

The more constructive and inclusive these rules, the more secure more individuals feel about participating in exchange. More participants means a more extensive market and, as we will see shortly, the greater the extent of the market the more finely tuned the division of labor can be – and in turn the greater the productivity.

This enhanced productivity makes possible in "a well-governed society, that universal opulence which extends itself to the lowest ranks of the people." This line highlights another theme in Smith's *Wealth of Nations*: his metric of a good society is the condition of the "lowest ranks of the people." And note the connection between themes: a "well-governed society" serves the well-being of the "lowest ranks of the people."

In chapter 1 Smith sets the scene for the narrative that follows: he identifies and examines the ultimate source of increasing productivity – the division of labor.[2] He frames the narrative in the context of his larger moral philosophy by introducing the importance of a "well-governed society." He anticipates the analysis to come by introducing the crucial role of exchange.

CHAPTER 2: "OF THE PRINCIPLE WHICH GIVES OCCASION TO THE DIVISION OF LABOUR"

The division of labor, from which so many advantages are derived, is not originally the effect of any human wisdom, which foresees and intends that general opulence to which it gives occasion. It is the necessary, though very slow and gradual consequence of a certain propensity in human nature which has in view no such extensive utility; the propensity to truck, barter, and exchange one thing for another. (*WN*, 25)

The progress of opulence in humankind moves at a "slow and gradual" pace because it is evolutionary. This evolution is not the calculated consequence of "human wisdom, which foresees or intends"; it is largely the unintended consequence of human "propensities" like "to truck, barter, and exchange … [which are] found in no other race of animals" (*WN*, 25).

---

[2] For interesting commentaries and issues related to Smith's presentation of the division of labor see Meek and Skinner (1973) on the development of Smith's views on the division of labor, Stigler (1951) and Buchanan (2008) on the question of scale economies, and Rosenberg (1965) on the internal consistency of Smith's logic regarding the division of labor.

Is this "propensity" "to truck, barter, and exchange" "one of those original principles in human nature" or is it "the necessary consequence of the faculties of reason and speech"? Smith considers the former "more probable," but goes on to say that the answer to this question "belongs not to our present subject to enquire" (*WN*, 25). Smith's agnosticism on this point is indicative of his agenda.

His purpose is to offer a compelling analysis of principles that underlie humankind's progress with an eye toward informing policy. He briefly reflects on the origin of the "propensity" "to truck, barter, and exchange" but quickly moves on, noting only that whatever the origin "[i]t is common to all men" (*WN*, 25). The assumed propensity in place, the metaphysics of its origins are left behind as he moves on to the question: Why do we, as individuals, choose to participate in this interdependent exchange system? With interdependence we lose autonomy. Why give that up? His answer: self-love.

When an individual becomes sufficiently productive to generate a surplus of a commodity he will naturally try to vent that surplus by selling it to others: "He will be more likely to prevail if he can interest their self-love in his favour, and shew them that it is for their own advantage to do for him what he requires of them" (*WN*, 26). In his classic statement of self-love as a spring for human action Smith writes:

> It is not from the benevolence of the butcher, the brewer, or the baker, that we expect our dinner, but from their regard to their own interest. We address ourselves, not to their humanity but to their self-love, and never talk to them of our own necessities but of their advantages. (*WN*, 26–7)

This may be the most famous passage in all of Smith's work.[3] It is surely the most dangerous if it is read out of context.

Smith's immediate point here is straightforward. Self-love is the spring for human action, and it can serve us. What is not on this page is the context. In Smith's moral philosophical analysis the benefits of self-love are premised on the presence of a "well-governed society."

In Smith's day liberal society, a society in which individuals are free to exchange through markets, was in its nascent state. He was trying to understand the invisible connecting principles that make individual freedom a constructive environment. He shared with those predecessors and contemporaries who sought to understand this liberal experiment a deep fear of unbridled self-interest. There was a keen sense that absent some form of governance of self-love, the potentially fruitful free market

---

[3] The "invisible hand" being the most famous phrase.

exchange process would degenerate into a Hobbesian war of all against all, or in modern terms a "rent-seeking" society.[4] Smith's contemporaries the Physiocrats suggested that the solution lay in a civil government managing human affairs to ensure constructive participation.[5]

Smith rejected this. He believed that the most desirable source of government in a liberal society, the locus of government that would not undermine the very freedom such a society is supposed to represent, is the self-government of individuals based on a personal commitment to a commonly held set of civic ethics.

In *The Wealth of Nations* Smith does not reiterate the analysis of civic ethics and civil institutions that he laid out in the *Theory of Moral Sentiments* and in his *Lectures on Jurisprudence*.[6] Nevertheless, this larger context of evolving civic ethics and civil institutions underlies the possibility that the butcher, brewer, and baker can indeed realize the benefits of serving one another's interests.

As Smith completes chapter 2's presentation on the human foundation of the division of labor he is careful to note that

[t]he difference of natural talents in different men is, in reality, much less than we are aware of; and the very different genius which appears to distinguish men of different professions, when grown up to maturity, is not upon many occasions so much the cause, as the effect of the division of labour. The difference between the most dissimilar characters, between a philosopher and a common street porter, for example, seems to arise not so much from nature, as from habit, custom, and education. (*WN*, 28–9)

This reflects another constant in his moral philosophy. We may turn out very differently, but we are all molded from the same "coarse clay" (*TMS*, 162).

CHAPTER 3: "THAT THE DIVISION OF LABOUR IS LIMITED BY THE EXTENT OF THE MARKET"

Suppliers to markets respond to effective demand.[7] There is no reward for great productivity from specialized production if there is not sufficient

---

[4] See *Toward a Theory of a Rent-Seeking Society* (Buchanan, Tollison, and Tullock, 1980).
[5] "[F]or all the passages either esoteric or mundane extolling the glories of the abstinence of civil government, of the pervasive existence of *liberté*, there are equally strong exclamations in support of what the Physiocrats called *autorite tutelairé*" (Samuels, 1962, 160). There is some controversy on this point. See Peter Gay (1954).
[6] See *Adam Smith's Moral Philosophy* (Evensky, 2005) for this larger context.
[7] "[T]he certainty of being able to exchange all that surplus part of the produce of his own labour … encourages every man to apply himself to a particular occupation" (*WN*, 28).

effective demand to vent one's surplus. Thus the pursuit of greater productivity, the ever finer division of labor, is limited by the extent of the market.

The extent of the market is a function of transaction costs[8] including transportation costs. "As by water-carriage a more extensive market is opened to every sort of industry than what land-carriage alone can afford it" (*WN*, 32), nations first emerged and grew where there was unfettered access to navigable routes through coastal ports and/or navigable rivers, for this afforded them access to an extensive market. Always the empiricist, to make his case Smith turns to history.

The nations that, according to the best authenticated history, appear to have been first civilized, were those that dwelt round the coast of the Mediterranean sea. That sea, by far the greatest inlet that is known in the world, having no tides, nor consequently any waves except such as are caused by the wind only, was, by the smoothness of its surface, as well as by the multitude of its islands, and the proximity of its neighbouring shores, extremely favourable to the infant navigation of the world; when, from their ignorance of the compass, men were afraid to quit the view of the coast, and from the imperfection of the art of ship-building, to abandon themselves to the boisterous waves of the ocean....

Of all the countries on the coast of the Mediterranean sea, Egypt seems to have been the first in which either agriculture or manufactures were cultivated and improved to any considerable degree.... The extent and easiness of ... inland navigation was probably one of the principal causes of the early improvement of Egypt. (*WN*, 34–5)

Smith has now transformed his narrative from one about human nature to one about human societies and their possibilities. As his analysis unfolds the extent of the market becomes a tipping point that determines which societies evolve from stage to stage. His Egypt example makes clear that fortuitous geography is an advantage in this respect. Similarly, the current (1776) advanced condition of Britain rests at least in part on the good fortune that it is an island, this giving it many opportunities for coastal trade, and that it has a large, navigable river running through it.

Here, as he does throughout this narrative, Smith presents his analysis and then offers the best available empirical evidence to make his case for the validity of that analysis. In the Egyptian case just cited he begins: "according to the best authenticated history." When he moves from the Egyptian example and suggests that "[t]he improvements in agriculture and manufactures seem likewise to be of very great antiquity in the provinces of Bengal in the East Indies, and in some of the eastern

---

[8] See Williamson (1979).

provinces of China; [(he adds the caveat:)] though the great extent of this antiquity is not authenticated by any histories of whose authority we, in this part of the world, are well assured" (*WN*, 35). History is Smith's data base, but he does not treat all histories as equally credible.

There are times when the line between history and "conjectural history," as Smith's biographer Dugald Stewart refers to it (Stewart, 293), gets blurred in Smith's narrative. Conjectural history is Stewart's term for Smith's representation of what happened in times and places of which Smith has no credible knowledge. Smith's "histories" are in those cases constructed conjectures based on his extrapolation of what the natural course of events would have been if his principles are valid. Thus, he can write that "[t]he improvements in agriculture and manufactures seem likewise to have been of very great antiquity in the provinces of Bengal in the East Indies, and in some of the eastern provinces of China" because, given the great rivers there that allow for an extensive market, that story seems plausible.[9]

As he closes his presentation on the extent of the market and the particular virtues of water-carriage, Smith observes that "[t]he commerce ... which any nation can carry on by means of a river ... which runs into another territory before it reaches the sea, can never be very considerable; because it is *always in the power of the nation* who possess that other territory to obstruct the communication between the upper country and the sea" (*WN*, 36, emphasis added). He cites the Danube as an example.

This point is made in passing but it lays essential groundwork for a theme that is going to be central to his narrative as it unfolds: a nation with sufficient power can limit other nations' access to markets. If trade is conceived of as a zero-sum game, there is a strong incentive to do so. This view of trade is a keen concern of Smith's and the central topic of Book IV.

CHAPTER 4: "OF THE ORIGIN AND USE OF MONEY"

As growing markets lead to the refinement of the division of labor, trade becomes more complex. In a complex trading environment barter clogs the system (*WN*, 37), so general equivalents, commodities acceptable in exchange for all others, emerge. Items Smith cites as having played this role historically include cattle, shells, and salt. "In all countries, however,

---

[9] He extends his description of this China case in Book IV, chapter 9 (*WN*, 680–1).

men seem at last to have determined ... to give the preference, for this employment, to metals above every other commodity" (*WN*, 38) because they are the least perishable and most finely divisible option (*WN*, 39).

But raw forms of metals posed problems of weighing and assaying, so marks were stamped on the metal to warrant quantity and quality. "Hence the origin of coined money" (*WN*, 40). There was, however, still the issue of getting "clipped" (see *WN*, 213), so full stamps "covering entirely both sides ... and sometimes the edges" (*WN*, 41) were introduced.

Money certainly facilitates trade but it is also problematic because of private or public manipulation (e.g., debasement, a revenue trick that Smith equates with fraud) that undermines its credibility – an issue to which he will return.

Chapter 4 closes with an introduction to the topic he will address in the next chapter: value. Money is by definition a nominal measure of value. Wherein lies the "real measure"?

He tells us that his purpose in chapter 5 is to determine the "real measure of ... exchangeable value; or, wherein consists the real price of all commodities," to identify "what are the different parts of which this real price is composed or made up," and to understand the forces that cause "the market, that is the actual price of commodities," to vary at any given time from their "natural or ordinary" price (*WN*, 46). He prepares us for this analysis by clarifying the distinction between value in use and value in exchange.

Ironically, "[t]he things which have the greatest value in use have frequently little or no value in exchange; and, on the contrary, those which have the greatest value in exchange have frequently little or no value in use" (*WN*, 44). For example, "[n]othing is more useful than water," and yet it normally has very little value in exchange, while "[a] diamond ... has scarce any value in use," but has immense value in exchange (*WN*, 44–5). This diamond-water paradox is not so strange if one considers that exchange value depends, as he will explain in chapter 7, on the relationship between the quantity supplied and effective demand.

Diamonds represent a case in which the quantity supplied cannot be sufficiently expanded by additional labor to meet the effective demand. (Wine from uniquely excellent vineyards is an example he cites in chapter 7.) This constraint on supply causes the price to be higher than the cost of production. In contrast, the quantity of water supplied can, under normal circumstances, be expanded easily by additional applications of labor so the exchange value is determined by the cost of production.

As he prepares to take the reader into this realm of value Smith offers the following caveat, for he recognizes that this is a difficult, "abstract notion" (*WN*, 49).

I must very earnestly entreat both the patience and attention of the reader: his patience in order to examine a detail which may perhaps in some places appear unnecessarily tedious; and his attention in order to understand what may, perhaps, after the fullest explication which I am capable of giving of it, appear still in some degree obscure. I am always willing to run some hazard of being tedious in order to be sure that I am perspicuous; and after taking the utmost pains that I can to be perspicuous, some obscurity may still appear to remain upon a subject in its own nature extremely abstracted.[10] (*WN*, 46)

CHAPTER 5: "OF THE REAL AND NOMINAL PRICE OF COMMODITIES, OR OF THEIR PRICE IN LABOUR, AND THEIR PRICE IN MONEY"

"Labour … is the real measure of the exchangeable value of all commodities." It represents the "toil and trouble of acquiring" a commodity and thus it reflects its real worth (*WN*, 47). But labor is rarely embodied in a pure, unaided form in the production process. Workers use training and/or tools (human and/or physical capital) that are themselves the product of labor, so the total amount of "labor embodied" in a product becomes a muddled concept.

Smith turns therefore to the concept of labor commanded: How much labor will a commodity exchange for?

He recognizes that it is "an abstract notion" (*WN*, 49), but he believes that it represents a pure image of the amount of labor value a commodity has. Subsequently when he discusses the value of a commodity in the abstract he consistently uses the labor command notion as his reference.[11]

But this is an abstract measure not an observable metric. "In such a work as this … it may sometimes be of use to compare the different real values of a particular commodity at different times and places" (*WN*, 55). To support this analysis Smith needs a measure of value that he can actually observe,[12]

---

[10] Hueckel (2000) does a very nice job of exploring and clarifying Smith's analysis of value. For more on Smith and value theory see Dobb (1973).

[11] See *WN* (162, 176, 185, 191–2, 194, 205, 207, 210, 224, 229, 236, 237, 255, 262, 264, 355, 356, 535) for some of the occasions on which he cites labor command as his metric.

[12] As he puts it: "[T]he distinction between the real and the nominal price of commodities and labour, is not a matter of pure speculation, but may sometimes be of considerable use in practice" (*WN*, 51).

a metric that allows him to make intertemporal comparisons of value as he presents his evolutionary narrative on the causes of changes in the material well-being of individuals and nations:

Gold and silver are not suitable because these metals are themselves subject to changes in value.[13] Labor is the "real price [of commodities]; money is their nominal price only." (WN, 51). But again, neither labor embodied nor labor commanded is directly observable and measurable.

The proxy for abstract labor that Smith settles on as the best available, observable, consistent metric of value over the long term is corn.

> Upon all ... accounts ... we may rest assured, that equal quantities of corn will, in every state of society, in every stage of improvement, most nearly represent, or be equivalent to, equal quantities of labour, than equal quantities of any other part of the rude produce of land. Corn accordingly ... is, in all the different stages of wealth and improvement, a more accurate measure of value than any other commodity or sett of commodities.[14] (WN, 206)[15]

Here Smith is not only explaining his choice of corn as a consistent measure of value, but he is making clear why he needs such a measure. He is going to be presenting a narrative of humankind's evolution "in every state of society, in every stage of improvement." If he is to demonstrate that there has in fact been material improvement across the four stages of humankind's history, he needs a value index for direct intertemporal comparisons.[16] Throughout the narrative he reminds us that corn is his index, his metric of value[17] (e.g., WN, 206, 217, 248).

---

[13] He compares them to other artificial metrics such as a "natural foot, fathom, or handful, which ... [are themselves] continually varying in ... [their] own value, [and thus] can never be an accurate measure of the value of other commodities" (WN, 50).

[14] "Through the world in general that value [(the value of corn)] is equal to the quantity of labour which it can maintain, and in every particular place it is equal to the quantity of labour which it can maintain in the way, whether liberal, moderate, or scanty, in which labour is commonly maintained in that place. Woolen or linen cloth are not the regulating commodities by which the real value of all other commodities must be finally measured and determined. Corn is" (WN, 516).

[15] "When he utilized corn as *numeraire* ... it was because it served better than any alternative but not because it was satisfactory in its own right" (Hollander, 312, emphasis in original).

[16] "In such a work as this ... it may sometimes be of use to compare the different real values of a particular commodity at different times and places" (WN, 55).

[17] Hueckel refers to "Smith's choice of corn as numeraire" (Hueckel, 336) as the "Corn-Command Proxy" (Hueckel, 321). More than halfway through the work he is still reminding us that "[w]oollen or linen cloth are not the regulating commodities by which the real value of all other commodities must be finally measured and determined. Corn is.... [It plays this role as intertemporal metric well because t]he real value of corn does not vary with those variations in its average money price, which sometimes occur from one century to another" (WN, 516).

Smith's caveat at the end of the last chapter regarding a "measure of value" as a difficult, "abstract notion" was correct then and it remains so to this day. After two centuries of examination, dissection, and debate the concept of value is still "obscure."[18]

So, if Smith did not feel he had done the subject of value justice why did he leave it in this form? In 1784 he made very significant additions and corrections to *The Wealth of Nations*, but the obscurity of value is not addressed.[19]

Smith did not return to the issue because he had accomplished what he wanted in this chapter. His objective was not to definitively determine the essence or source of value. His purpose was practical. He needed a metric or index of value in order to make price comparisons as he presents his evolutionary narrative of the changes in humankind's material condition.

He does offer his metaphysical perspective on value: he believes it is based on labor. But as in the earlier "propensity to truck, barter and exchange" case, here too if the metaphysics is muddled so be it.[20] It has no bearing on the narrative that follows.[21]

CHAPTER 6: "OF THE COMPONENT PARTS OF THE PRICE OF COMMODITIES"

Chapter 6 begins:

In the early and rude state of society which precedes both the accumulation of stock and the appropriation of land. (*WN*, 65)

These words encompass several of the central elements of Smith's analysis. The reference to "the early and rude state" reflects his four

---

[18] "Most readers would put this remark down as the greatest understatement in the history of economic thought: Book I, chapter 5, is particularly difficult to follow and has attracted a bewildering variety of interpretations" (Blaug, 39).

[19] Indeed, as Naldi points out, "in the second edition of WN, Smith deleted the phrase *sources of value* and replaced it with *component parts of price*" (Naldi, 301, emphasis in original).

[20] The subsequent obsession with this chapter reflects, I believe, a retrofitting of a Ricardian mentality on Smith. Ricardo begins his *Principles* with a chapter "On Value" and frames the focus of the discourse on that metaphysical question. Treating Smith as if he shares Ricardo's concern with value is, I believe, a mistake. It is hard to fault Smith for not resolving the question of value. No one has yet succeeded. Ricardo's effort suffered from its "93%" solution. See Stigler (1958). Marx faced the "transformation problem." See Meek (1977) and Samuelson (1971). And modern NeoClassical theory has not resolved the "reswitching" issue. See Robinson (1953) and Cohen and Harcourt (2003).

[21] Indicative of this, in two instances Smith altered his language in later editions to distance himself from metaphysical connotations. In chapter 6 in two places he replaces the phrase "source of value" with the term "component part." See editors' note (*WN*, 67).

stages theory, the first of these being this rude state. His definition of the rude state as preceding "the accumulation of stock and the appropriation of land" reflects two of the most significant forces in his narrative of humankind's evolution through the four stages:

Accumulated stock is the fuel for material improvement because, as he will make clear in Book II, it is accumulation that provides the resources for the ever finer division of labor.

Appropriation of land is a seminal development in humankind's evolution because it makes possible the agricultural stage of production, the stage in which the capacity to support large societies emerges.

Prior to accumulation and appropriation the entire output of production goes to the laborer who produced it because it is the product of his unaided labor. But such unaided labor is not very productive. Enter accumulation: Accumulation is both liberating and complicating. It is liberating because it empowers the productivity of the division of labor. It is complicating because it introduces capital into the analysis of production and distribution.

Prior to accumulation the worker enjoyed all the fruits of his labor. With accumulation, the worker must receive a share but so too "something must be given for the profits of the undertaker of the work who hazards his [accumulated] stock in this adventure" (*WN*, 66).

He could have no interest to employ them [workmen], unless he expected from the sale of their work something more than what was sufficient to replace his stock to him; and he could have no interest to employ a great stock rather than a small one, unless his profits were to bear some proportion to the extent of his stock. (*WN*, 66)

Similarly, with appropriation of land the landlord must be compensated as well. "As soon as the land of any country has all become private property, the landlords, like all other men, love to reap where they never sowed, and demand a rent even for its natural produce" (*WN*, 67). Rent is not a return to productive activity; it is simply a fee for the "licence" (*WN*, 67) to use the land. For that privilege the gatherer or tiller must "give up to the landlord a portion of what his labour either collects or produces" (*WN*, 67).

Thus with the "the accumulation of stock and the appropriation of land" the component parts of price must include a return to the worker (wage), to the undertaker (profit), and to the landlord (rent). "[I]n every improved society [one in which there is accumulation of stock and appropriation of land], all the three enter more or less, as component parts, into the price of the far greater part of commodities" (*WN*, 68).

To this Smith adds a fourth share that is included as a part of gross profit, but that is distinct from that share of the profit that rewards the undertaker for it represents no real contribution to production. This fourth share is interest. Smith carefully distinguishes profit and interest because the distinction becomes pivotal in his comparative analysis of societies' advancement.

That revenue derived from stock, by the person who manages or employs it, is called profit. That [return] derived from it [(stock)] by the person who does not employ it himself, but lends it to another, is called the interest or the use of money. It is the compensation which the borrower pays to the lender, for the profit which he has an opportunity of making by the use of the money [((Just as rent is a fee for the license to use land.)]. Part of that [gross] profit naturally belongs to the borrower, who runs the risk and takes the trouble of employing it; and part to the lender, who affords him the opportunity of making this profit. (WN, 69–70)

Later, in Book V, chapter 2, he clarifies his use of profit and interest further. The "interest on money … is a neat produce which remains after completely compensating the whole risk and trouble of employing the stock" (WN, 847–8). Thus for Smith pure profit, as compensation for the "whole risk and trouble of employing the stock," is a return to productive activity, but interest "[l]ike rent on land" is not (WN, 847). Interest is simply an unearned benefit derived from ownership of capital just as rent is an unearned benefit derived from ownership of land.

As he will explain in chapter 9, in a "well-governed society" competition among capitals drives down the rate of interest. So that:

In a country which had acquired its full complement of riches, where in every particular branch of business there was the greatest quantity of stock that could be employed in it,[22] as the ordinary rate of clear [gross] profit would be very small, so that usual market rate of interest which could be afforded out of it, would be so low as to render it impossible for any but the very wealthiest people to live upon the interest of their money.[23] (WN, 113)

"Holland [which 'in proportion to the extent of its territory and number of people, is a richer country than England' (WN, 108)] seems to be approaching near to this state" (WN, 113). In contrast, in "China [which] seems to have been long stationary … [t]welve per cent … is said to be the common interest of money … and the ordinary profits of stock must be

---

[22] In other words, when the stock of capital has grown so large as to have exhausted all domestic opportunities for further investment – more on the dynamic of capital accumulation in Book II.

[23] In the language of Keynes, the well-governed society would not support a "rentier" class (Keynes, 376).

sufficient to afford this large interest" (*WN*, 111–12). This high interest rate in China is a function of "laws and institutions ... [that] establish the monopoly of the rich" over capital (*WN*, 112).

With his distinction between profit and interest, Smith is setting out a language of distribution that will be an essential tool for his analysis of growth, stagnation, or decline of the *Wealth of Nations*. In this case the high interest rate in the "long stationary" economy of China is a signal of distortions in the extant "laws and institutions" that advantage the rich.

Smith concludes chapter 6 asserting that

As in a civilized country there are but few commodities of which the exchangeable value arises from labour only, rent and profit contributing largely to that of the far greater part of them, so the annual produce of its labour will always be sufficient to purchase or command a much greater quantity of labour than what was employed in raising, preparing, and bringing that produce to market. (*WN*, 71)

Thus with each circuit of production, thanks to the division of labor, the stock generated is capable of supporting a larger number of workers than were employed in the previous circuit. It follows that:

If the society was annually to employ all the labour which it can annually purchase [i.e., if it commits all the stock generated from the last circuit of production to the next circuit], as the quantity of labour would increase greatly each year, so the produce of every succeeding year would be of vastly greater value than that of the foregoing. (*WN*, 71)

This is the key to the *Causes of the Wealth of Nations*: the accumulation and allocation of the growing stock to successive circuits of production is, as he will explain in detail in Book II, the dynamic that causes the wealth of a nation to grow.

But this growth only occurs to the degree that the accumulation from a given circuit is committed to productive activities, that is, to the next circuit of production:

[T]here is no country in which the whole annual produce is employed in maintaining the industrious. The idle every where consume a great part of it; and according to the different proportions in which it is annually divided between those two different orders of people, its ordinary or average value must either annually increase, or diminish, or continue the same from one year to another. (*WN*, 71)

Again, Smith is framing our mind for what is to come. Increasing accumulation fuels growth because it is this growing accumulation that can finance an ever larger productive labor force and an ever finer division of labor in subsequent periods. But whether the production in a given year leads to accumulation and growth depends on the proportions of the current accumulation that are applied to "productive and unproductive labour" (*WN*, 330). His analysis of productive versus unproductive labor is still a long way off (Book II, chapter 3), but Smith alludes to the issue here for he is building the foundation for the analysis that is to come.

CHAPTER 7: "OF THE NATURAL AND MARKET PRICE OF COMMODITIES"

Having defined and analyzed the component parts of commodities' prices, Smith turns to definitions and analysis of natural and market prices.

The natural level of a commodity's price (and similarly the natural size of a distributive share – wage, rent, and profit) is that level that is ordinary and customary for that society in the given neighborhood. Here Smith uses "neighborhood" to encompass the extent of the market.

The natural price of a commodity reflects "what it really costs the person who brings it to market … where there is perfect liberty" (*WN*, 72–3). Again his purpose in Book I is to establish a conceptual frame of reference for further analysis. The key to the frame he is constructing here is the phrase "where there is perfect liberty." This is Smith's shorthand for the freedom and thus the fluidity of movement of people and resources that exists in an ideal liberal society.

Market price is the actual price at which a commodity is sold. The market price is determined by the relationship between the "effectual demand" (*WN*, 73) – the quantity actually demanded at the natural price, and the quantity supplied in the market. If the effective demand is equal to the quantity supplied, the market price will equal the natural price. If the effective demand is greater (less) than the quantity supplied, the market price will be higher (lower) than the natural price. Given perfect liberty, as individuals move resources to the advantageous markets (market price greater than natural price) and away from disadvantageous markets (market price below the natural price), the market prices will oscillate around the natural price "to which the prices of all commodities are continually gravitating" (*WN*, 75). The degree of this oscillation will depend on the volatility of the supply and effective demand.

"[Y]et sometimes particular accidents, sometimes natural causes, and sometimes particular regulations of police, may, in many commodities, keep up the market price, for a long time together, a good deal above the natural price"[24] (*WN*, 77). Smith cites as examples: trade or manufacturing secrets, particularly productive land (e.g., a unique vineyard), "exclusive privileges of corporations, statutes of apprenticeship, and all those laws which restrain, in particular employments, the competition" (*WN*, 79). "The price of monopoly is upon every occasion the highest which can be got" (WN, 78).

Here again Smith is both building the foundation for the analysis to follow and framing our minds by anticipating some central issues in that analysis. His reference to "particular accidents, sometimes natural causes, and sometimes particular regulations of police" reflects a constant theme in his narrative: events in humankind are never as simple as straight theory suggests because there are invariably these disturbing forces that affect the dynamics. The real human condition is a messy place.

Smith's interest in theory is as a point of departure for understanding the real course of human events. Thus his analysis builds a theoretical foundation then focuses on how we can represent the actual twists and turns of real human events caused by the inevitable disturbing forces. For example, here he notes that a market price can be sustained at an artificially high level by "exclusive privileges of corporations, statutes of apprenticeship, and all those laws which restrain, in particular employments, the competition." This one line in Book I, chapter 7 becomes a central theme of Books III and IV.

CHAPTER 8: "OF THE WAGES OF LABOUR"

Having defined and analyzed price, Smith turns to an examination of the component parts of price. He begins with wages.

In the rude state before the "appropriation of land and the accumulation of stock, the whole produce of labour belongs to the labourer" (*WN*, 82). From that point of departure Smith quickly transitions to the more advanced and complex case of a world in which the laborer works for "the owner of stock" because "his [(the worker's)] maintenance is generally advanced to him from the stock of the master" (*WN*, 83). In this case "[w]hat are the common wages of labour depends ... upon the contract usually made between those two parties, whose interests are by no means

---

[24] He suggests that, absent institutional constraints, the opposite case of a long-term depressed price is very unlikely because producers would abandon a market in which they could not cover costs. See *WN*, page 79.

the same. The workmen desire to get as much, the masters to give as little as possible" (*WN*, 83). He continues:

> It is not ... difficult to foresee which of the two parties must, upon all ordinary occasions, have the advantage in the dispute, and force the other into a compliance with their terms. The masters, being fewer in number, can combine much more easily; and the law, besides, authorises, or at least does not prohibit their combinations, while it prohibits those of the workmen.... [And further, i]n all such disputes the masters can hold out much longer. (*WN*, 83–4)

Smith's metric of a good society is the condition of the least among the working class. His immediate concern here is that the natural asymmetry of power in labor markets can artificially depress wages.[25] This concern is deepened by his awareness that the political power structure and thus the legal system is often stacked against the workers.[26]

The best situation for workers is the advancing state. In such a world the growing accumulation outstrips the growth of the labor force. This "scarcity of hands occasions a competition among masters who bid against one another" (*WN*, 86), thus raising wages. "It is not, accordingly,

[25] "The high price of labour is to be considered not merely as a proof of the general opulence of Society ... it is to be regarded as ... the very thing in which public opulence properly consists.... National opulence is the opulence of the whole people, which nothing but the great reward of labour ... can give occasion to" (*ED*, 332). Smith's *Early Draft (ED)* of *WN* was, according to Scott (1937), composed prior to his trip to France for the benefit of Charles Townshend (Scott, 318).

[26] "The workmen ... very seldom derive any advantage from the violence of those tumultuous combinations, which, partly from the interposition of the civil magistrate, partly from the superior steadiness of the masters, partly from the necessity which the greater part of the workmen are under of submitting for the sake of present subsistence, generally end in nothing, but the punishment or ruin of the ringleaders" (*WN*, 85). "Whenever the legislature attempts to regulate the differences between masters and their workers, its counsellors are always the masters" (*WN*, 137). See *WN* (643–4) for a classic example of how "[t]he avidity of our great manufacturers" has led to sever oppression of workers and in particular women. More on this in chapter 8. In a 1763 "early draft of *The Wealth of Nations*," as described by William Scott (Scott, 317–9), Smith is much more assertive about the effects of power distortions on distribution in society: "[W]ith regard to the produce of the labour of a great Society there is never any such thing as a fair and equal division. In a Society of an hundred thousand families, there will perhaps be one hundred who don't labour at all, and who yet, either by violence, or by the more orderly oppression of law, employ the greater part of the labour of society than any other ten thousand in it. The division of what remains too, after this enormous defalcation, is by no means made in proportion to the labour of each individual. On the contrary those who labour most get least.... [That being] the poor labourer who has the soil and the seasons to struggle with, and, who while he affords the materials for supplying the luxury of all the other members of the common wealth, and bears, as it were, upon his shoulders the whole fabric of human society, seems himself pressed down below ground by the weight" (*ED*, 327–8).

in the richest countries, but in the thriving ... that the wages of labour are highest" (WN, 87).

In contrast, in a stationary state population growth outstrips growth in accumulation. In such a world "the competition of the labourers and the interests of the masters would soon reduce them [the workers] to this lowest rate which is consistent with common humanity" (WN, 89). It is, therefore, "not the actual greatness of national wealth, but its continual increase, which occasions a rise in the wages of labour.... [And because high wages encourage population growth, t]he most decisive mark of the prosperity of any country is the increase in the number of inhabitants"[27] (WN, 87–8).

What is his best predictor of how any given state will fare given this metric of success?: The "nature of its laws and institutions" (WN, 89).

In Smith's narrative of humankind's evolution there are two kinds of limits. There is the ultimate limit, the ideal liberal society of perfectly ethical (i.e., self-governed) individuals enjoying perfect liberty, making the most for all and doing well for the least. This is the point of reference against which all societies can be compared to determine their level of advancement. Then there is the artificial limit a society imposes on itself by "the nature of its laws and institutions." Smith highlights this in chapter 8 as he compares China, where the laws and institutions (e.g., the monopoly of the rich cited earlier) have caused it to stagnate, with the "present [declining] state of Bengal" where "[w]ant, famine, and mortality" prevail, and then these two cases are compared with the excellent material conditions in British American colonies.

The Bengal and American cases make a particularly stark comparison because they are both run by the British. So to what does Smith ascribe the difference in the conditions of these two British colonies?

The difference between the genius of the British constitution which protects and governs North America, and that of the [British] mercantile company which oppresses and domineers in the East Indies, cannot perhaps be better illustrated than by the different state of those countries. (WN, 91)

Having made his case that the progressive state is made possible by laws and institutions that are just, and that such a state is the best case for workers, Smith reminds us of why this matters:

Is this improvement in the circumstances of the lower ranks of the people to be regarded as an advantage or as an inconveniency to the society? The answer

---

[27] Malthus' work was still a quarter of a century away.

seems at first sight abundantly plain.... [W]hat improves the circumstances of the greater part can never be regarded as an inconveniency to the whole. No society can surely be flourishing and happy, of which the far greater part of the members are poor and miserable. It is but equity, besides, that they who feed, cloath and lodge the whole body of the people, should have such a share of the produce of their own labour as to be themselves tolerably well fed, cloathed, and lodged. (*WN*, 96)[28]

And what is good for workers is good for the state: a "liberal reward for labour ... increases the industry of the common people ... which, like every other human quality, improves in proportion to the encouragement it receives"[29] (*WN*, 99). This industry is encouraged by the freedom a liberal society affords workers to independently better their condition.

Independence is also important because it makes workers less vulnerable to the simplistic hyperbole of a "man of system" (*TMS*, 233) who in difficult times offers simple but appealing solutions to complex problems. The progressive development of liberal society requires thoughtful discourse. Smith believed that the dynamics of an undistorted free market system that improve the lot of labor and make workers more independent contribute to the maturity of workers as participants in this discourse.[30]

His one very significant caveat to this is that the division of labor can become so refined and the work so mindless in the most menial of jobs that these tasks make the lowest ranks of workers "as stupid and ignorant as it is possible for a human creature to become" (*WN*, 782). As we will see in Book V, it is the responsibility of the state to ensure that education ameliorates this tendency and enhances the intellectual engagement of the working class.

The state ... derives no inconsiderable advantage from their instruction. The more they are instructed, the less liable they are to the delusions of enthusiasm and superstition.... They are more disposed to examine, and more capable of seeing through, the interested complaints of faction and sedition, and they are, upon that account, less apt to be misled into wanton or unnecessary opposition to the measures of government. In free countries, where the safety of government depends very much upon the favorable judgment which the people may form of its conduct, it must surely be of the highest importance that they should not be disposed to judge rashly or capriciously concerning it. (*WN*, 788)

---

[28] He notes that "[i]n Great Britain the real recompence of labour ... has increased considerably during the course of the present century ... owing to the peculiarly happy circumstances of the country" (*WN*, 219).

[29] As we will see in Book V, Smith is very big on government managing the alignment of incentives constructively rather than directly intervening to change behavior.

[30] See Weinstein's (2013) very nice work on pluralism and civic discourse in Adam Smith.

In Smith's vision of a properly functioning liberal society it is not the government that makes the nation strong. It is the people. Where the "laws and institutions" are just and the people are "tolerably well fed, cloathed, and lodged," they have the energy, the opportunity, and the incentive to participate vigorously and constructively in the market system and in civil society.

Good wages are both a sign of and a source of progress.

CHAPTER 9: "OF THE PROFITS OF STOCK"

> The rise and fall in profits of stock depend upon the same causes with the rise and fall of the wages of labour, the increasing or declining state of wealth of the society; but those causes affect one and the other very differently.
>
> The increase of stock, which raises wages, tends to lower profit.[31] (*WN*, 105)

Having explained how progress raises wages in chapter 8, in chapter 9 Smith explains the fall in profit rates that comes with progress.

As we saw in chapter 6, if the increased stock generated by the current circuit of production is applied to the next circuit (capital deepening), it can support an ever finer division of labor in that next circuit and in turn can generate greater production. To the degree individuals are parsimonious more accumulated stock will be applied in each successive circuit.

Where there is perfect liberty this accumulated stock flows to its best advantage, the highest rate of profit. As stock crowds into these best return opportunities, this competition drives these advantageous returns down until at some point the returns from alternative opportunities become equally attractive. This diffusion of the available stock across the entire economy continually extends the margins of investment and drives down the rate of profit. The limiting point of this dynamic is

> a country fully stocked in proportion to all the business it had to transact ... [where] the ordinary profit [is] as low as possible.[32]
>
> But perhaps no country has ever yet arrived at this degree of opulence. (*WN*, 111)

---

[31] He cites the difference between England and Scotland as empirical evidence to support this assertion (*WN*, 107).

[32] So too, wages would be low if the country were "fully peopled" and stock not growing (*WN*, 111).

One reason no country has reached this condition is that there are international opportunities for stock to exploit: "The proprietor of stock is properly a citizen of the world, and is not necessarily attached to any particular country" (*WN*, 848–9). At some point, as the opportunities for the domestic employment of stock are being filled and the domestic rate of profit is falling, stock will spill over into the larger international arena. Owners of stock will send it out of the country in search of the most attractive risk-adjusted rate of return.[33] This story of stock and its spilling into ever wider spheres of opportunity is the central theme of Book II: "Of the Nature, Accumulation, and Employment of Stock." Here in Book I, chapter 9 Smith lays the foundation for that analysis.

Chapter 9 begins with a brief exploration of the statutory history of the British rate of interest. In the course of that story Smith weaves in the impact of "religious zeal" against usury in restricting "the legal rate of interest" (*WN*, 106).[34] This then segues into a comparative analysis of interest rates across Europe. His point is that more mature laws and institutions, those that do not impair the ability of "people of good credit" to borrow (*WN*, 106), bring progress that increases the *Wealth of Nations*.

But, as we have seen, progress brings lower interest rates, and lower interest rates bring bitter complaints from the merchants and master-manufacturers, a faction that often has the political wherewithal to reverse this trend[35] – to the benefit of the faction but to the detriment of the nation.[36] In short, where factional interests can capture power, laws and institutions can become significantly distorted.

In China the large capital holders sustain their high profits because the laws and institutions are arranged such that

> though the rich or the owners of large capitals enjoy a good deal of security, the poor or the owners of small capitals enjoy scarce any, but are liable, under the pretence of justice, to be pillaged and plundered at any time by the inferior mandarines, the quantity of stock employed in all the different branches of business

---

[33] Or so it would be if "laws and institutions" allowed. China "neglects or despises foreign commerce" and so it has become stationary before realizing the wealth that "the nature of its soil, climate, and situation might admit of" (*WN*, 112).

[34] Smith's interest in the impact of religion on humankind's evolution is a constant in his work. Later when he turns to the evolution of European universities we see this highlighted again.

[35] He also notes: "A great stock, though with small profits, generally increases faster than a small stock with great profits. Money, says the proverb, makes money. When you have got a little, it is often easy to get more. The great difficulty is to get a little" (*WN*, 110).

[36] High interest rates in Bengal and the British East Indies have "ruined" those countries (*WN*, 111).

transacted within it, can never be equal to what the nature and extent of that business might admit. (*WN*, 112)

Factional manipulation of laws and institutions to ensure high profits, in China or Britain or wherever, distorts the capital market and undermines the wealth of the nation. This issue is central to Smith's presentation regarding British mercantilist policies in Book IV.

Lax or overly restrictive laws and institutions can also have a perverse effect on the capital market. If because of lax enforcement contracts are not secure "[t]he uncertainty of recovering his money makes the lender exact the same usurious interest rate which is usually required from bankrupts" (*WN*, 112). Where the law is unduly restrictive (e.g., usury laws that prohibit interest) interest rates can, ironically, be artificially high. Money *will* be lent, and "[w]hen the law prohibits interest altogether … [the illegally paid interest rate will be raised to cover] the difficulty and danger of evading the law" (*WN*, 112).

Where laws and institutions are properly aligned with good governance, the rate of interest will be declining toward the limiting case in which "it [is] impossible for any but the very wealthiest people to live upon the interest of their money" (*WN*, 113).

Smith applies his theory in these cases to show how his theory works in a real human context. The more richly the theoretical framework is developed, the more fruitfully it can be applied. He completes his theoretical development in Book II. In Book III he applies that theory to a complex historical case to demonstrate the power of the theory to make sense of that history. In Book IV, with his theory established, he debunks the self-serving theoretical assertions that the mercantile faction has imposed on parliament.

CHAPTER 10: "OF WAGES AND PROFIT IN THE DIFFERENT EMPLOYMENTS OF LABOUR AND STOCK"

The opening paragraph of chapter 10 is a capsule image of the dynamics of competition and of the effect of such competition on the allocation of resources and the distribution of returns in the ideal liberal order. In such a society all resources are used to their best advantage (most efficiently) and the returns to those resources are driven to the "ordinary" (*WN*, 118) or natural level – just enough compensation to cover the opportunity cost of a given allocative choice:

The whole of the advantages and disadvantages of the different employments of labour and stock must, in the same neighbourhood, be either perfectly equal or continually tending to equality. If in the same neighbourhood, there was any employment evidently either more or less advantageous than the rest, so many people would crowd into it in the one case, and so many would desert it in the other, that its advantages would soon return to the level of other employments. This at least would be the case in a society where things were left to follow their natural course, where there was perfect liberty, and where every man was perfectly free both to chuse what occupation he thought proper, and to change it as often as he thought proper. Every man's interest would prompt him to seek the advantageous, and to shun the disadvantageous employment. (*WN*, 116)

This is not to suggest that in the ideal case every allocation of a resource will receive the same rate of return. Immediately following this opening paragraph Smith notes that the "[p]ecuniary wages and profit, indeed, are every-where in Europe extremely different according to the different employments of labour and stock" (*WN*, 116).

In Part I of chapter 10 Smith explores the causes of natural (ordinary) differences in the returns to different employments of labor and stock. In Part II he explains those differences that result from artificial impediments created by laws and institutions that distort the natural course of events and thus lead to unnatural differences in the relative returns of different employments of labor and stock.

This distinction between natural and artificial differences in returns turns on Smith's concept of "perfect liberty." In an ideal liberal society individuals are free to choose in a secure and fair market space, thus there are no artificial advantages and so there are no sustained artificially high or low returns.[37] But factional capture of power can create artificial market advantages that in turn generate sustained artificial, unnatural, distributive advantages.

Public and private sources of power are often complements to one another. Recall the "[m]asters [who] are always and every where in a sort of tacit, but constant uniform combination ... sometimes ... to sink the wages of labour below this [natural] rate." When the workers form a "defensive combination" and "clamour" for higher wages, "[t]he masters upon these occasions are just as clamorous upon the other side, and never cease to call aloud for the assistance of the civil magistrate, and the rigorous execution of those laws which have been enacted with so much

---

[37] There are natural cases of returns being "distorted," such as the return to the land of a uniquely valuable vineyard. See my analysis of Book I, chapter 11.

severity against the combinations of servants, labourers, and journey-men" (*WN*, 84–5).

The role of individuals' unbridled self-interests and of factional collusion as threats to progress is a constant theme in Smith's *Inquiry into the Nature and Causes of the Wealth of Nations*.

Part I: "Inequalities [in Wages and Profits] arising from the Nature of the Employments themselves"

What causes variations in wages and profits where there is perfect liberty? Smith cites five factors.

Different employments offer different psychic benefits, "agreeableness or disagreeableness" (*WN*, 116). There are differences in the psychic and pecuniary costs of acquiring the human capital necessary for different employments. There are differences in "the constancy or inconstancy of employment" (*WN*, 116). The degree of trust required often varies. And finally, there is "the probability or improbability of success" (*WN*, 116–17), the risk factor. All five of these affect wages. Only the first and last affect profits.

Having laid out the five conditions that give rise to naturally occurring differences in wages, Smith tells stories that exemplify each of these conditions. His stories are at one and the same time familiar, reflect his theoretical analysis, and validate that analysis.

For example, hunting and fishing are activities that would be very familiar to his audience. These were "the most important employments of mankind in the rude state of society," but in the advanced state they have become "amusements." "In the advanced state of society, therefore, they are all very poor people who follow as a trade, what other people pursue as a pastime.... [This occurs because t]he natural taste for those employments makes more people follow them than can live comfortably by them" (*WN*, 118). Or consider the "keeper of an inn or tavern, who is never master of his own house, and who is exposed to the brutality of every drunkard" (*WN*, 118). It is a dirty business, but this disagreeableness is compensated by pay that is better than most common trades.

As for one who invests in human capital, he must have "replace[d] to him the whole expence of his education, with at least the ordinary profit of an equally valuable capital" (*WN*, 118), and he must be compensated for risk. Smith's discussion of the risk related to investments in human capital offers us a window into his feelings about his own work: "[I]n the liberal professions" the "probability that any particular person shall ever be qualified for the employment to which he is educated ... [is] very uncertain" (*WN*, 122). He initially compares this bet on success to "a perfectly fair lottery, [a zero-sum game in which] those who draw the prizes ought to gain all that is lost by those who draw the blanks" (*WN*, 122). Given the great expense of the investment and the great risk of failure, one would expect the return to be very high in the liberal professions. But it is not so high as this risk factor alone would predict. The reason is twofold. As in most lotteries "the chance of gain is naturally overvalued, [(i.e., the risk is underestimated) a fact] we may learn from the universal success of lotteries"[38] (*WN*, 125). And there is also the fact that a great deal of the benefits are psychic.

> To excel in any profession, in which but few arrive at mediocrity, is the most decisive mark of what is called genius or superior talents. The public admiration which attends upon such distinguished abilities, makes always a part of their reward; a greater or smaller in proportion as it is higher or lower in degree. It makes a considerable part of the reward in the profession of physick; a still greater perhaps in that of law; in poetry and philosophy it makes almost the whole. (*WN*, 123)

This from a professor of Moral Philosophy.

Smith's analysis here in chapter 10, Part I is a sequel to and an enrichment of the "natural price" analysis in chapter 7. If perfect liberty prevails there can be within a given market no sustainable advantage (or disadvantage) in the return to any specific allocation. There can, however, be differences in the natural level of wages and profits across employments due to differences in the nature of the employments.

As noted, while five factors affect relative wages only two of these affect the profits of stock, and the primary natural determinant of differences in profit is variation in risk (*WN*, 127).[39] "The ordinary rate of profit always rises more or less with the risk" (*WN*, 128). This is because an undertaker is always seeking the best *risk-adjusted* rate of return. A higher risk must be compensated by a higher return. The profit of sock

---

[38] "The vain hope of gaining some of the great prize is the sole cause of this demand" (*WN*, 125). He picks up this point of underestimating risk later in developing a story as to why many people underinsure, and why "young volunteers never enlist so readily as at the beginning of a new war" (*WN*, 126).

[39] Smith notes that in cases where a return includes both a wage and a profit the nature of the return can appear muddled to the casual observer. He cites, for example, the fact that "[a]pothecaries profit is become a bye-word, denoting something uncommonly extravagant. This great apparent profit, however, is frequently no more than the reasonable wages of labour.... [Reasonable because h]is reward ... ought to be suitable to his skill and trust" (*WN*, 128–9).

is also constrained by the extent of the market because a more limited market reduces the opportunities for applying one's accumulation.

These two points are central to Smith's analysis of expanding circuits of trade presented in Book II. But before he gets there, Smith has to complete his analysis of distribution by addressing forces that distort it. These forces and the consequent distortions in distribution have a significant impact on a society's ability to accumulate and grow.

Part II: "Inequalities occasioned by the Policy of Europe"

As always, the structure of laws and institutions is never far from the heart of Smith's analysis. In the case of the "Inequalities occasioned by the Policy of Europe," these inequalities are largely the consequence of flawed laws and institutions.

The "policy of Europe, by not leaving things to perfect liberty, occasions other inequalities [beyond the natural ones] of much greater importance" (*WN*, 135). These policies create distributive distortions in three ways. They artificially reduce the amount of labor or stock in a market by limiting access. They artificially bloat the amount of labor or stock in a market by enforcing or over incentivizing that allocation. They obstruct "the free circulation of labour and stock, both from employment to employment and from place to place" (*WN*, 135).

"The exclusive privileges of corporations are the principal means" of artificially reducing the amount of labor or stock in a market by limiting access, thus "restrain[ing] the competition" (*WN*, 135). The laws of apprenticeship in incorporated trades are a classic case in point.

In England the extent of the privilege of incorporation[40] was defined by two important interpretations of "the 5th of Elizabeth": "its operation has been limited to market towns" and the "statute has been limited to those trades which were established in England before the 5th of Elizabeth" (*WN*, 137). With respect to this latter interpretation, he writes that "[t]his limitation has given occasion to several distinctions which, considered as rules of police, appear as foolish as can well be imagined" (*WN*, 137). These regulations are a

manifest encroachment upon the just liberty both of the workman, and of those who might be disposed to employ him. As it hinders the one from working at

---

[40] He includes an interesting note on the etymology of the term *university*, "which indeed is the proper Latin name for any incorporation whatever" (*WN*, 136), and how universities' heritage and structure reflect that origin.

what he thinks proper, so it hinders the others from employing whom they think proper. To judge whether he is fit to be employed, may surely be trusted to the discretion of the employers whose interest it so much concerns. The affected anxiety of the law-giver lest they should employ an improper person is evidently as impertinent as it is oppressive.[41] (*WN*, 138)

The justification of the apprenticeship laws was that they are a means of ensuring that quality work will be brought to the market. But insufficient workmanship "is generally the effect of fraud, and not of inability; and the longest apprenticeship can give no security against fraud. Quite different regulations are necessary to prevent this abuse. The sterling mark upon plate, and the stamps upon linen and woollen cloth, give the purchaser much greater security than any statue of apprenticeship" (*WN*, 138–9).

Government has a responsibility to ensure a fair market. But a responsible government carries out this role by the least intrusive policing (regulations) possible. Overbearing action is often evidence of a motive other than ensuring just interaction among individuals. It can reflect rent-seeking or rent-maintenance behavior.

This is precisely the purpose Smith sees in the apprenticeship laws: it is "to prevent this reduction of price, and consequently of wages and profit [that would come with free and fair competition], by restraining that free competition which would most certainly occasion it, that all corporations, and the greater part of corporations laws, have been established" (*WN*, 140). While apprenticeships serve the master and ultimately the apprentice, they do not serve the market, for by eliminating competition they reduce the incentive for "diligence and attention" by the worker (*WN*, 140), and thus they reduce efficiency and increase the cost of production. If the market distortion caused by apprenticeships was eliminated "the public would be the gainer, the work of all artificers coming in this way much cheaper to the market" (*WN*, 140).

In order to explain the genesis of the power that enables traders and artificers to enjoy the protection of apprenticeship laws Smith returns to a theme he presented earlier in his analysis – collusion.

---

[41] "The property which every man has in his own labour, as it is the original foundation of all other property, so it is the most sacred and inviolable. The patrimony of a poor man lies in the strength and dexterity of his hands; and to hinder him from employing this strength and dexterity in what manner he thinks proper without injury to his neighbour, is a plain violation of this most sacred property" (*WN*, 138).

People of the same trade seldom meet together, even for merriment and diversion, but the conversation ends in a conspiracy against the publick, or some contrivance to raise prices. (WN, 145)

The ability of traders and artificers to collude, and thus their power, derives from their common location in towns. Smith argues that historically "[t]he government of the towns corporate was altogether in the hands of the traders and artificers" (WN, 141). Given this power the various trades allowed one another to establish corporate constraints limiting entry into their trades, making it possible for them to exploit the unorganized people in the countryside.[42]

While in many parts of Europe this power of corporation was the complete prerogative of the town, "[i]n England ... a charter from the king was ... necessary. But this prerogative of the crown seems to have been reserved rather for extorting money from the subject, than for the defence of the common liberty against such oppressive monopolies" (WN, 140).

The consequence of this distortion of power was a distortion of distribution. Towns got a disproportionate share of the social product and thus were able to accumulate much more than the country. But, to the degree there is liberty, markets will ameliorate such distortions. And so it was in this case: the engrossment of accumulation in the towns led to an engorgement of accumulation, and this meant falling profit rates. Smith describes the ensuing dynamic as follows:

It [(the town's accumulated stock), in search of a better risk-adjusted rate of return,] then spreads itself, if I may say so, over the face of the land, and by being employed in agriculture is in part restored to the country, at the expence of which, in a great measure, it had originally been accumulated in the town. That everywhere in Europe the greatest improvements of the country have been owing to such overflowings of stock originally accumulated in towns, I shall endeavour to show hereafter; and at the same time to demonstrate, that though some countries have by this course attained to a considerable degree of opulence, it is in itself necessarily slow, uncertain, and in every respect contrary to the order of nature and of reason. The interests, prejudices, and laws and customs which have given occasion to it, I shall endeavour to explain as fully and distinctly as I can in the third and fourth books of this enquiry. (WN, 145)

---

[42] Farmers, "so dispersed in distant places" (WN, 143), can't collude. They are often seen as roughhewn souls but "after what are called the fine arts, and the liberal professions, ... there is perhaps no trade which requires so great a variety of knowledge and experience" (WN, 143). The farmer's "rank" and "wages" would probably be "superior to those of the greater part of artificers and manufacturers ... if corporation laws ... did not prevent it" (WN, 144).

This brief summary is a rich representation of significant themes in his narrative that, as he notes, will unfold more fully in Books III and IV.

Having explored the perverse effects of apprenticeship as a policy of Europe, Smith turns to subsidies for training that artificially glut a market. He cites as an example the subsidization of education for those who are intended for the clergy[43] and the attendant spillover effect of enhancing the supply in the market for "men of letters"[44] (WN, 148). While this glut is inefficient, Smith sees a positive unintended consequence of the distortion. It reduces the cost of education, in turn expanding access. Because Smith views education as a key tool for building a thoughtful citizenry, more access – whatever the cause of it – is good for society's progress.

The last distorting policy of Europe he identifies is those "absurd laws" (WN, 151) that limit the mobility of labor and stock. Under perfect liberty, resources always move to the best opportunity. Given that transaction costs (including the risk) are normally lowest in the local market, resource holders naturally look at home first for opportunities. But as population and stock expand in this narrow home market, the wage and profit returns decline. At some point, even adjusting for transaction (e.g., transport) costs, the more distant opportunities beckon and so labor and stock begin to spread over the land. Mobility is good for the resource holders because it allows them to better their condition. It is good for the economy because allowing resources to flow to their best advantage increases the nation's productivity.[45] The policies of Europe that artificially restrict labor and stock to a particular neighborhood inhibit resource flows and thus diminish the possibilities for the division of labor, for increased accumulation, and consequently for greater productivity and growth.

A classic example of an artificial constraint on such a free flow is the poor laws: "[I]n England ... it is often more difficult for a poor man to pass the artificial boundary of a parish, than an arm of the sea or a ridge of high mountains, natural boundaries which sometimes separate very distinctly different rates of wages in other countries" (WN, 157). He

---

[43] A subsidy with which Smith had direct experience. Just such a subsidy, The Snell Exhibition, allowed Smith to attend Balliol College, Oxford (WN, 148 fn. 36).

[44] Smith was just such a "spillover." He chose not to enter the clergy and ultimately became a professor.

[45] Smith is describing precisely this flow process when he uses the classic "invisible hand" quotation in Book IV, chapter 2 (WN, 456).

proceeds to explore the history and the perverse effects of poor laws at length.

In the course of discussing the perverse effects of apprenticeship laws on the diligence and industry of town workers, Smith contrasts those workers with the "common farmer," writing that

[t]he common ploughman, though generally regarded as the pattern of stupidity and ignorance, is seldom defective in his judgment and discretion. He is less accustomed, indeed to social intercourse than the mechanick who lives in a town. His voice and language are more uncouth and more difficult to be understood by those who are not used to them.[46] His understanding, however, being accustomed to consider a greater variety of objects, is generally much superior to that of the other, whose whole attention from morning till night is commonly occupied in performing one or two very simple operations. How much the lower ranks of people in the country are really superior to those of the town, is well known to every man whom either business or curiosity has led to converse much with both. (*WN*, 143–4)

This quotation reflects some important characteristics of Smith's method and vision. With respect to method, we hear Smith the empiricist asserting that the way to know your world is to experience it. There are many places in Smith's work where his references to day-to-day life reflect a life rich in observation.[47]

And again we hear his concern with the division of labor creating dullness of mind.

Smith is concerned with the working class both because its well-being is his metric for a good society, and because its maturity is the primary determinant of the stability of a mature, liberal society. The key to progress in the liberal experiment is to exploit the benefits of the division of labor while ensuring that those in the working class approximate the personal maturity of the yeoman farmer. As we will see in Book V, he believes that public education is the policy necessary to make this happen.

And again we see that for Smith being of the "lower ranks" (like the "common ploughman") does not imply being an inferior being. We are, after all, all made from the same coarse clay.

---

[46] Smith views those who write of the rural workers "contemptuously ... [as] very contemptible authors" (*WN*, 143).

[47] In *The Theory of Moral Sentiments* Smith comments on the nature of kids (see, for example, *TMS*, 89, 145, 222, 329, 335). Smith, a bachelor with no kids, seems to me to reflect a rich observation of kids at various ages. I have two of my own, I volunteered two summers in Head Start, and I taught junior and senior high school for six years, so I know something of the species.

As Smith lays out his theory of distribution in chapter 10 his purpose is practical. He is constructing the analytical structure he will use in Book II where he presents his dynamic growth theory and in Book III where he demonstrates the power of that theory in the context of European history. In chapter 11 Smith adds the last piece to his analytical tool kit: rent.

CHAPTER 11: "OF THE RENT OF LAND"

Unlike wages or profits, but like interest, rent is not a return to productive activity. "The rent of land ... is naturally a monopoly price"[48] (*WN*, 161). Here, as is not uncommon, Smith's language suffers a bit. Earlier he contrasted natural price, "the lowest which can be taken ... for any considerable time," and monopoly price, "the highest which can be got"[49] (*WN*, 78–9). Yet this monopoly price, rent, has a natural level – the ordinary level that equally well-cultivated and fertile land in a given neighborhood can command. An unnatural rent would be "the rent of some vineyards in France" – a rent above the level of "equally fertile and equally well-cultivated land in its neighbourhood"[50] (*WN*, 78). Smith's adoption of natural rent is a reflection of his usage of *natural* here as meaning "ordinary."[51] Because even where there is perfect liberty much of the land receives a rent, the ordinary level of that rent is the natural level for that neighborhood.

This ordinary level of rent is, along with the ordinary wages and profits, a component of the natural price of a product. But rent enters into the price in a different way than wages and profits. The latter two are built into the price because together they constitute the cost of production – the cost that must be covered if there is to be sufficient incentive to bring a product to market. Rent on the other hand "depends upon the demand" (*WN*, 162). If demand is sufficient to raise price above the cost of production, "the surplus part of it will naturally go to the rent of the land" (*WN*, 161).[52] In a competitive environment the landlord will extract "the

---

[48] As noted earlier, Smith equates interest with rent as unearned returns (*WN*, 847–8).

[49] In chapter 11 he writes that "the lowest price for which it is possible to bring it [(a commodity)] to market for any considerable time together ... is the price which affords nothing to the landlord, of which rent makes not any component part, but which resolves itself altogether into wages and profit" (*WN*, 231). So he sees rent as part of the natural price in the sense of "ordinary"; he also sees rent as a monopoly price – a part of the price that is not necessary to encourage productive activity.

[50] He returns to this issue and examines it at greater length in Book I, chapter 11, Section b (*WN*, 171–2).

[51] As in "natural or ordinary rate" (*WN*, 46).

[52] What remains is the "smallest share with which the tenant can content himself" (*WN*, 160).

highest [rent] the tenant can afford to pay in the actual circumstances of the land" (*WN*, 160).

Having established the concept of rent and the relationship of rent to price, Smith moves on to his

consideration, first, of those parts of the produce which always afford some rent; secondly, of those which sometimes may and sometimes may not afford rent; and, thirdly, of the variations which, in the different periods of improvement, naturally take place in the relative value of those two different sorts of rude produce, when compared both with one another and with manufactured commodities. (*WN*, 162)

He makes clear in this transition that his analysis of rent is going to be presented in the context of his evolutionary story of humankind's progress. Indeed, the value of the rent concept for Smith's narrative is that "the variations [in the level of rent] which, in the different periods of improvement, naturally take place" offer an indicator of a given society's stage of progress.

Part I: "Of the Produce of Land which always affords a Rent"

To set the scene for this analysis Smith reviews the conditions that determine rent: the "fertility" and the "situation" of the land (*WN*, 163). By *situation* he means the extent of the available market. *Ceteris paribus*, the greater the extent the higher the rent.

The extent of the market is largely a function of transportation costs. "Good roads, canals, and navigable rivers, by diminishing the expense of carriage, put the remotest parts of the country more nearly upon a level with those in the neighbourhood of towns. They are upon that account the greatest of all improvements" (*WN*, 163). As these improvements extend the market, *ceteris paribus*, they increase the level of rent. So, *ceteris paribus*, higher rents are a signal of the progress that is generated when improvements extend the market.

He observes that "not more than fifty years ago ... some of the counties in the neighbourhood of London, petitioned the parliament against the extension of the turnpike roads into the remoter counties" (*WN*, 164). Those in the proximity of London feared that the outlying areas, having cheaper labor, would undercut their position in the London market and thereby reduce rents in the local area. In fact, however, "[t]heir rents have risen, and their cultivation has been improved since that time" (*WN*, 164). As his theory predicts, the extension of the market raised rents.

So what is the dynamic that underlies the rising rents that come with progress? He begins his analysis with the following observation:

A corn field of moderate fertility produces a much greater quantity of food for man, than the best pasture of equal extent. Though its cultivation requires much more labour, yet the surplus which remains after replacing the seed and maintaining all that labour, is likewise much greater. If a pound of butcher's-meat, therefore, was never supposed to be worth more than a pound of bread, this greater surplus would everywhere be of greater value, and constitute a greater fund both for the profit of the farmer and the rent of the landlord. It seems to have done so universally in the rude beginnings of agriculture.

But the relative values of those different species of food, bread and butcher's-meat, are very different in different periods of agriculture. (*WN*, 164)

In the early stage of agriculture the vast majority of land is uncultivated, the domain of free-grazing cattle. Because the cattle eat for "free," butcher's-meat is indeed cheap relative to corn. Smith cites evidence from "Byenos Ayres ... [as] told by Ulloa" (*WN*, 164) to support this assertion.

As population grows some of the previously uncultivated land that had been used for cattle grazing becomes a valuable resource for expanding cultivation of corn for human consumption, thus crowding out the cattle.

By the extension ... of cultivation, the unimproved wilds become insufficient to supply the demand for butcher's-meat [to a growing population]. A great part of the cultivated lands must be employed in rearing and fattening cattle, of which the price, therefore, must be sufficient to pay, not only the labour necessary for tending them, but the rent of the landlord and the profit which the farmer could have drawn from such land employed in tillage [of corn for human consumption]. (*WN*, 165)

As this increased cost of production of cattle feed from cultivated land drives up the market price of cattle, those who own the grazing land can begin to extract a rent for the use of their land. Thus, the emergence of a rent for cattle grazing land is a derivative of the increasing rent on land for cultivation of corn.

The union of Scotland and England (1707), which opened up English markets to cattle from the Scottish highland, had precisely this effect on the rents in the highlands.

It is thus that in the progress of improvement the rent and profit of unimproved pasture come to be regulated in some measure by the rent and profit of what is improved, and these again by the rent and profit of corn. (*WN*, 165)

There are exceptions to this relationship (that agricultural rents are ultimately regulated by the corn rent), but these "peculiar" cases simply serve to prove the rule.[53] For example, if a neighborhood is very heavily populated relative to its hinterland, it makes sense to import corn and let the local land support grazing: "Holland is at present in this situation" (WN, 166). Other examples include land producing "finer fruits" (WN, 170), wine (WN, 171–2), sugar (WN, 173), or tobacco (WN, 174). In each of these cases he identifies the natural or artificial conditions that make for particularly high rents. The natural conditions include a unique soil or climate. Artificial conditions include the case of "laws which at present restrain the free cultivation of the vine" for wine (WN, 171), or the case of "[t]he cultivation of tobacco [which] has … been most absurdly prohibited through the greater part of Europe" in order to make it pass through the customhouse and thus make the collection of taxes easier (WN, 174).

All this is developed to make the basic point that "[e]xcept in peculiar situations" "the rent of the cultivated land, of which the produce is human food [(corn being the staple)], regulates the rent of the greater part of other cultivated land" (WN, 175).

This point is important because the rent of land cultivated for "human food" is Smith's reference point as he explores the topic of rent more deeply.

Part II: "Of the Produce of Land which sometimes does, and sometimes does not, afford Rent"

> Human food seems to be the only produce of land which always and necessarily affords some rent to the landlord. Other sorts of produce sometimes may and sometimes may not, according to different circumstances.
>
> After food, cloathing and lodging are the two great wants of mankind. (WN, 178)

In the rude state with land plentiful relative to population, clothing and lodging are available in "super-abundance" (WN, 178) relative to the demand, but not so food. "[N]inety-nine parts" "of the labour of the whole year" (WN, 180) must be spent on providing sufficient food.[54]

---

[53] Smith's analysis here is empirical and he is careful to assess his sources as he tells the story. For example, citing information on the returns to the sugar planter he adds the caveat: "If this be true, for I pretend not to affirm it," and later he writes, "we are told by Dr. Douglas," but immediately adds the parenthetical remark "(I suspect he has been ill informed)" (WN, 174–5).

[54] "The skins of the larger animals were the original materials of cloathing. Among nations of hunters and shepherds, therefore, whose food consists chiefly in the flesh of those

But when by the improvement and cultivation of land the labour of one family can provide food for two, the labour of half the society becomes sufficient to provide food for the whole. The other half, therefore, or at least the greater part of them, can be employed in producing other things or in satisfying the other wants and fancies of mankind. (*WN*, 180)

Note the closing line "satisfying the other wants and fancies of mankind." As Smith writes shortly thereafter: "The desire of food is limited in every man by the narrow capacity of his stomach; but the desire of the conveniencies and ornaments of building, dress, equipage, and household furniture, seems to have not limit or certain boundary" (*WN*, 181). It is this characteristic of human consumption, combined with the production possibilities that flow from the division of labor, which drives the use of land as humankind evolves. Smith's analysis of rent is his way of tracking and representing this dynamic.

Improvement in food production is the foundation of all other improvements.

Given the "narrow capacity" of our stomach, increased productivity in agriculture makes surpluses possible. These surpluses can support a non-agricultural pool of labor that can be put to work manufacturing "the conveniencies and ornaments ... [that] have not limit or certain boundary." Thus increasing agricultural productivity supports a growing population and with this comes a larger demand for[55] and greater capacity to supply the conveniences and ornaments of life.

As he will explain shortly, the effect of this dynamic on rents is that as society advances nonagricultural rents emerge and eventually surpass agricultural rents. So, *ceteris paribus*, rising nonagricultural rents are a sign of progress.

There are, as always, peculiar exceptions, but these can be understood as consistent with the larger analysis if we identify the sources of the peculiarities. For example, mining rents are peculiar because prices for mined materials are generally determined by scarcity. Rents on the mines are therefore determined relative to the fertility and/or location ("situation") of the mine.[56] This is in contrast to the more general case of surface

---

animals, every man, by providing himself with food, provides himself with the materials of more cloathing than he can wear. If there was no foreign commerce, the greater part of them would be thrown away as things of no value" (*WN*, 178).

[55] "That abundance of food, of which, in consequence of improvement of land, many people have the disposal beyond what they themselves can consume, is the great cause of the demand ... [for] conveniency and ornament" (*WN*, 192).

[56] "Situation" matters more for coal mines and fertility more for "a metalllick mine" because the price of transport in the former case is so much higher (*WN*, 185).

rents, which generally move to a natural level because the quantity can expand to meet the effective demand.

Part III: "Of the Variations in the Proportions between the respective Values of that Sort of Produce which always affords Rent, and of that which sometimes does, and sometimes does not, afford Rent"

The increasing abundance of food, in consequence of increasing improvement and cultivation, [because it supports a larger population] must necessarily increase the demand for every part of the produce of land which is not food, and which can be applied either to use or ornament. In the whole progress of improvement, it might therefore be expected, there should be only one variation in the comparative values of those two different sorts of produce. The value of that sort which sometimes does and sometimes does not afford rent, should constantly rise in proportion to that which always affords some rent.... This accordingly has been the case with most of these things upon most occasions, and would have been the case with all of them upon all occasions, if particular accidents had not upon some occasions increased the supply of some of them in a still greater proportion than the demand. (*WN*, 193)

Smith's brief digression at the end of Part II to explain the nature of rents in mining sets the scene for his major case study in Part III – a long "Digression concerning the Variation in the Value of Silver during the Course of the Four last Centuries." That "Digression" examines the "particular accidents" Smith cites in the opening paragraph of Part III quoted earlier.

"Digression concerning the Variations in the Value of Silver during the Course of the Four last Centuries"

Smith refers to this as a "Digression," but there is much of significance to his analysis imbedded in this digression. As we will see, it is here that he lays the foundation of his more complex analysis of humankind's evolution that he will develop in Books III and IV.

Silver offers a valuable case study for several reasons. It is the commodity most often used as money, it is a commodity that has a global market,[57] and it is the commodity considered by mercantilists – mistakenly in Smith's view – as the essence, with gold, of the wealth of a nation.

---

[57] "The great market for silver is the commercial and civilized part of the world" (*WN*, 194).

Smith divides his analysis of the changing value of silver relative to corn (his long-term metric of value) into three periods: the fourteenth century to 1570, 1570 to 1640, and 1640 to date. In order to establish a point of historical reference for the "corn value" of silver (again, corn being his numeraire of value) he notes that: "From these different facts [(he cites and arranges information from an array of historical sources)], therefore, we seem to have reason to conclude that about the middle of the fourteenth century, and for considerable time before, the average or ordinary price of the quarter of wheat[58] was not supposed to be less than four ounces of silver, Tower-weight" (*WN*, 197).

Then, beginning in the middle of the fourteenth century, the price of silver began to rise. Smith explains this rise as follows: as European societies increased productivity and expanded in population the effective demand for silver outstripped the quantity supplied. But if the value of silver was constant until the fourteenth century and then growth caused it to start rising, what caused the takeoff in growth? Smith writes:

In the end of the fifteenth and the beginning of the sixteenth centuries, the greater part of Europe was approaching towards a more settled form of government than it had enjoyed for several ages before. [(Smith explores the dynamic that led to this condition in Book III.)] The increase of security would naturally increase industry and improvement; and the demand for the precious metals, as well as for every other luxury and ornament would naturally increase with the increase of riches. (*WN*, 199)

Again, we hear a central theme of Smith's moral philosophy that threads its way through his narrative: better laws and institutions mean more security. More security means more growth because it encourages greater accumulation and more investments in productive human or physical capital. More growth means increasing population and in turn more demand, especially (given our limited stomachs) for nonagricultural goods – the ornaments of life.

As Smith tells his story of silver's rise in value, he notes that his assertion that it did indeed rise is contrary to "the opinion … of the greater part of those who have written upon the price of commodities in ancient times" (*WN*, 199). The three reasons he cites for this difference reflect his deep concern for empirical credibility.

---

[58] Smith uses "corn" and "wheat" interchangeably here. Indeed, corn is defined in the OED as "*British* the chief cereal crop of a district, especially (in England) wheat or (in Scotland) oats" http://www.oxforddictionaries.com/us/definition/american_english/corn?q=corn.

First, those other works did not carefully distinguish real from nominal values. Second, in some cases they used data that were sloppily "transcribed" (WN, 201). Third, other works took cases of low prices in ancient times as indicative of average prices, but this is misleading. In those more "turbulent and disorderly societies" prices were more volatile – so while lows may have been very low, the highs may have been very high, leaving the average very difficult to estimate.[59]

Having explained the empirical weaknesses of these contrary analyses, he notes that "at the end of this chapter" he will lay out all of his data so that the reader can review them, and he presents his view on the strength and weakness of these data. He then goes on to defend, yet again, his choice of corn as his metric of value.

Labour ... is the real measure of the value both of silver and of all other commodities.... [However,] we may rest assured, that equal quantities of corn will, in every state of society, in every stage of improvement, most nearly represent, or be equivalent to, equal quantities of labour, than equal quantities of any other part of the rude produce of land. Corn, accordingly, it has already been observed, is, in all the different stages of wealth and improvement, a more accurate measure of value than any other commodity or sett of commodities. (WN, 206)

Smith's concern with value is empirical. He needs an intertemporally consistent, observable measure of value to facilitate his narrative of humankind's evolution as reflected in its history. Corn serves that purpose well.

In the second period of his analysis, 1570 to 1640, there is no empirical debate on the value of silver. All agree it was going down, and the reason is clear.

The discovery of the abundant mines of America, seems to have been the sole cause of this diminution in the value of silver in proportion to that of corn.... [Even though t]he greater part of Europe was, during this period, advancing in industry and improvement ... the increase of the supply [of silver] had, it seems, so far exceeded that of demand, that the value of that metal sunk considerably. (WN, 210–11)

[59] In discussing the work of others exploring historical prices he writes that "[s]uch slight observations ... upon the prices of either corn or of other commodities, would not probably have misled so many intelligent authors, had they not been influenced, at the same time, by the popular notion, that as the quantity of silver naturally increases in every country with the increase of wealth, so its value diminishes as its quantity increases. This notion, however, seems to be altogether groundless" (WN, 207). His concern with the influence of popular notions on philosophical inquiry is most evident in his *History of Astronomy*. See HA (22).

This peculiar accident of "discovery" reversed the natural course of events, but by "about 1636" (WN, 211) this discovery effect was over and the natural course was largely restored.

In his last period of analysis, from 1640, Smith highlights the effect of human events that mitigated or even temporarily reversed the natural course of silver's value – its rise. The three events he cites are the English civil war – which disrupted trade and thus raised the price of corn, the bounty on the exportation of corn – which also raised its price, and the "great debasement of the silver coin" (WN, 212).

And yet, these disturbing forces notwithstanding, the trend was up because "[s]ince the discovery of America, the greater part of Europe has been much improved. England, Holland, France, and Germany; even Sweden, Denmark, and Russia, have all advanced considerably both in agriculture and in manufactures" (WN, 220). Growth in America and the East Indies was also expanding the demand for silver.

Smith uses a lot of data to tell this story. In the course of doing so he punctuates his commentary with comments like "Mr. Gregory King, a man famous for his knowledge in matters of this kind" (WN, 215), or "three very faithful, diligent, and laborious collectors of the prices" (WN, 216), or "and as there seems to be no reason to doubt of the good information of either" (WN, 222), or "[s]everal other very well authenticated, though manuscript, accounts, I have been assured, agree" (WN, 227). This is Smith the empiricist making the case that the history on which he is basing his analysis is a credible history.

Smith also observes in the course of his analysis that "[t]he Spanish colonies are under a government in many respects less favourable to agriculture, improvement, and population than that of the English colonies ... [but] a fertile soil and happy climate, the great abundance and cheapness of land, a circumstance common to all new colonies, is, it seems, so great an advantage as to compensate many defects in civil government" (WN, 221–2).

Again we see the "laws and institutions" thread weaving its way through Smith's analysis of the conditions that encourage or discourage progress. The "genius of the British constitution ... protects and governs North America" (WN, 91) constructively, and with this good government comes progress. In contrast, defects of civil government are at best a drag on progress as in the potentially fruitful Spanish colonies, and at worst can lead to stagnation or decline as in the case of China and Bengal.

"Variations in the Proportion between the respective Values of Gold and Silver ... Grounds of the Suspicion that the Value of Silver still continues to decrease"

While this title suggests that his focus turns to the relative value of gold and silver,[60] Smith's real concern here is the credibility of his analysis.

A reduction of the tax on silver muddled the evidence supporting his assertion that silver has most recently been rising rather than falling because silver demand was growing faster than silver supply.

The silver tax itself is not the issue. Silver is a good choice for taxation because it is "imposed upon one of the most proper subjects of taxation, a mere luxury and superfluity" (WN, 232) and one for which the tax incidence is normally on an unearned income, mine rent.[61] The problem the tax creates for his analysis is that as silver extraction becomes ever more difficult with the exhaustion of easily accessed ore, mining silver "become[s] gradually more expensive in the working" (WN, 232). Assuming the current tax has already extracted all the unearned (rent) returns, this increased cost of production must be "compensated" (WN, 232) by a rise in the price of silver, a reduction in the tax, or some combination of both. What indeed happened was a reduction in the tax. This kept the silver price down, contrary to Smith's assertion that it should be rising with the growth of the European economies. In short, the evidence is muddled by the tax changes, and so he writes

[t]hat, notwithstanding this reduction [in taxes], the value of silver has, during the course of the present century, begun to rise somewhat in the European market, the facts and arguments which have been alleged above, dispose me to believe, or more properly to suspect and conjecture; for the best opinion which I can form upon this subject scarce, perhaps, deserves the name of belief. (WN, 233)

This is a very forthright and honest statement that his assertion is not based on indisputable fact but on his "belief" ... a "conjecture" grounded on: 1) his understanding of events; and 2) his principles, which imply that as a society advances, barring any new discoveries, there will be a rise in the price of precious metals.

---

[60] He rejects "Mr. Meggens's" (WN, 229) assertion that the relative value of gold and silver is determined by the relative quantities in the market because this ignores the demand side. Smith argues that effective demand matters and that, in effect, the elasticities are different for gold and silver. In particular, the value of silver is not driven down fully in proportion to its large supply because the market is more elastic at lower prices.

[61] Here he anticipates his analysis of taxes in Book V.

"Different Effects of the Progress of Improvement upon the real price
of three different Sorts of rude Produce"

Smith explained in the beginning of this chapter that in the rude state of agriculture the vast majority of land is uncultivated, the domain of free-grazing cattle – making the supply of cattle so plentiful that the price of butcher's-meat is very low. As cultivation emerges and advances it absorbs grazing land, initially at least, reducing the supply of cattle. At the same time, the growth in population supported by this expanding cultivation causes the effective demand for butcher's-meat and thus the price of cattle to rise. This rise in price incentivizes the expansion of herds.

This "increase of [cattle] stock and the improvement of [agricultural] land are two events which must go hand in hand" (*WN*, 239), and this connection is central to Smith's analysis of a society's "takeoff." His analysis of this takeoff begins at the point when the rise in the price of cattle makes it worth cultivating some land to produce feed for cattle.

Till the price of cattle ... has got ["so high that it is profitable to cultivate land in order to raise food for them" (*WN*, 237)] ... it seems scarce possible that the greater part, even of those lands which are capable of the highest cultivation, can be completely cultivated. (*WN*, 238)

Why is the "highest cultivation" of land for human consumption constrained until the price of cattle rises sufficiently to justify cultivation of feed for stabled cattle? It is all about the manure:

In all farms too distant from any town to carry manure from it, ... the quantity of well-cultivated land must be in proportion to the quantity of manure which the farm itself produces; and this again in proportion to the stock of cattle it maintains upon it. The land is manured either by pasturing the cattle upon it, or by feeding them in the stable, and from thence carrying out their dung to it. But unless the price of cattle be sufficient to pay both the rent and profit of cultivated land, the farmer cannot afford to pasture them upon it; and he can still less afford to feed them in the stable. It is with the produce of improved and cultivated land only, that cattle can be fed in the stable; because to collect the scanty and scattered produce of waste and unimproved lands would require too much labour and be too expensive. If the price of cattle, therefore, is not sufficient to pay for the produce of improved and cultivated land, when they are allowed to pasture it, that price will be still less sufficient to pay for that produce when it must be collected with a good deal of additional labour, and brought into the stable to them. In these circumstances, therefore, no more cattle can, with profit, be fed in the stable than what are necessary for tillage. But these can never afford manure enough for keeping constantly in good condition, all the lands which are capable of cultivating. (*WN*, 238)

Once the price of cattle (butcher's-meat) rises to a level that justifies allocating land to the cultivation of cattle feed, the economy has reached a tipping point. At that point cattle can be stabled and fed in large, concentrated numbers. This in turn creates a plentiful, concentrated supply of manure that the farmer can easily collect and spread on his fields. Fertilizing the fields significantly increases the productivity of those fields. Achieving this "highest cultivation" makes it possible for the agricultural sector to support a much larger nonagricultural working population.

This could be called Smith's "manure theory of takeoff" because, as he envisions it, for significant growth in manufacturing production to takeoff[62] there must be sufficient production of manure to facilitate the "highest cultivation" that is needed to support a growing population. And, it is this expanding population that creates the increasing demand for and the labor to produce manufactured goods – the focus of unlimited wants.

This threshold effect leads Smith to observe that "[o]f all the commercial advantages ... which Scotland has derived from the union with England ... [the] rise in the price of cattle is, perhaps, the greatest" (*WN*, 239–40). But, he observes, the benefits of union have not spread quickly over the face of the country because the "obstructions to the establishment of a better system ["obstructions" such as endemic poverty that precludes accumulation], cannot be removed but by a long course of frugality and industry" (*WN*, 239). Given these kinds of obstacles, this manure-based takeoff invariably occurs "late ... in the progress of improvement" (*WN*, 241).

Nevertheless, as it unfolds it has a profound impact on "the progress of improvement" (*WN*, 244): The increased population made possible by the increase in agricultural productivity represents an expanding market for manufactured products. This encourages an ever finer division of labor that enhances productivity, increasing the wealth of the nation. Of this dynamic driven by the rise in the price of cattle, Smith writes:

If the compleat improvement and cultivation of the country be, as it most certainly is, the greatest of publick advantages, this rise in the price of all those different sorts of rude produce [(butcher's-meat, poultry, swine, dairy products],[63] instead of being considered as a publick calamity, ought to be regarded as the necessary forerunner and attendant of the greatest of all publick advantages. (*WN*, 245)

---

[62] Manufacturing has much more potential for growth than agriculture because, unlike food consumption, which is limited by the size of our stomachs, the demand for manufactured items is limitless, and because "[t]he nature of agriculture ... does not admit of so many subdivisions of labour ... as manufactures" (*WN*, 16).

[63] Following his analysis of the price of cattle for butcher's-meat, Smith turns to poultry, swine, and dairy products – but butcher's-meat is the key to his growth narrative.

Smith notes that for some rude products this rise in price is not so predictable because of peculiarities of production. He cites, for example, mutton and wool – two jointly produced products that have very different extents of the market.

As he explores this joint production issue, we again see Smith's analysis reflect a concern for careful empiricism, and his continuous highlighting of laws and institutions as a source of distortions in the natural course of events. With respect to empiricism, as he traces the price of wool calculating real and nominal movements Smith cites "many authentick records" from the time of Edward III, but he notes that he was "not able to find any such authentick records concerning the price of raw hides in antient times" (WN, 248–9). As for laws that distort prices, in the case of wool Smith asserts that the "degradation both in the real and nominal value of wool, could never have happened in consequence of the natural course of things. It has accordingly been the effect of violence and artifice" (WN, 248). Laws have, thanks to the political influence of the clothiers, confined domestic wool to the home market and have encouraged competition from other countries. In contrast, tanners have not been so politically effective. Tongue firmly in cheek, Smith writes:

Our tanners ... have not been quite so successful as our clothiers, in convincing the wisdom of the nation, that the safety of the commonwealth depends upon the prosperity of their particular manufacture. They have accordingly been much less favoured. (WN, 250)

"Conclusion of the Digression concerning the Variations in the Value of Silver"

Having made his case that in the natural course of progress the price of most rude provisions will rise but not necessarily all in lock step, Smith applies his analysis to the current (1776) debate about the value of silver. Responding to those who see this rise in provisions as representing a fall in the value of silver, he writes that:

The greater part of the writers who have collected the money prices of things in antient times, seem to have considered the low money price of corn, and of goods in general, or, in other words, the high value of gold and silver, as a proof, not only of the scarcity of those metals, but of the poverty and barbarism of the country at the time when it took place. This notion is connected with the system of political economy which represents national wealth as consisting in the abundance, and national poverty in the scarcity of gold and silver; a system which I shall endeavour to explain and examine at great length in the fourth book of this enquiry. (WN, 255)

Smith is referring here to Mercantilist thought. According to the mercantilists, more (less) precious metal is more (less) wealth for the nation. Smith believes he has established the framework necessary to debunk this mercantilist confusion of metals with wealth. He has made the case that "the real wealth of Europe ... [is] the annual produce of its land and labour ... [and that t]he increase of the quantity of gold and silver in Europe, and the increase of its manufactures and agriculture, are two events which, though they have happened nearly about the same time, yet have arisen from very different causes" (*WN*, 255).

To support his position Smith observes that if the prices of provisions all have the same simple, constant, functional relationship to the quantity of silver, then a change in silver should affect all provisions the same. But as he has just explained theoretically and demonstrated empirically, the prices of different provisions will and, indeed, have increased differently. To debate whether the silver buys less because it is falling or because commodities are rising "is to establish a vain and useless distinction ... The real wealth of a country [is] the annual produce of its land and labour.... [And because] land constitutes by far the greatest, the most important, the most durable part of the wealth of every extensive country" (*WN*, 258), the best metric of material progress is not what is happening to the price of silver but what is happening to the "price" of land: rent.

At this point Smith turns from the narrower question of material progress to the more general question of human progress. Having just established that in the course of material progress the prices of meat, poultry, and other animal-based foods are increasing in varying degrees, how, he asks, does this affect the least among the working class? Does this imply a diminished well-being for the poor? No, says Smith.

As he has explained in his "takeoff" analysis, the extension and improvement of cultivation goes hand in hand with rising animal food prices (e.g., butcher's-meat), but it lowers the prices of vegetable foods. "The circumstances of the poor through a great part of England cannot surely be so much distressed by any rise in the price of poultry, fish, wild-fowl, or venison, as they must be relieved by the fall in that of potatoes" (*WN*, 259). Indeed, with progress comes not only lower vegetable prices, but also, *ceteris paribus*, lower prices for manufactures.

"Effects of the Progress of Improvement upon the real Price of Manufactures"

In a progressing society the price of manufactures will fall as the division of labor increases the productivity of workers:

though, in consequence of the flourishing circumstances of the society, the real price of labour should rise very considerably, yet the great diminution of the quantity [of labor required to produce] will generally much more than compensate the greatest rise which can happen in the price. (*WN*, 260)

Smith has great faith in the productivity gains that come with the ever finer division of labor. His only caveats are the effect on the mental state of workers cited earlier and the possibility of upward pressure on raw commodity prices for manufacture (e.g., "barren timber" (*WN*, 260)). But he is, nevertheless, generally sanguine that increased productivity will reduce cost of production and in turn manufactured product prices. He cites, for example, a watch: "A better movement of a watch, than about the middle of the last century could have been bought for twenty pounds, may now perhaps be had for twenty shillings" (*WN*, 260). And he believes that with the increased productivity, workers' incomes rise.

The net effect of higher incomes and the lower costs of vegetable foods and manufactures is to enhance workers' standard of living.

"Conclusion of the Chapter"

I shall conclude this very long chapter with observing that every improvement in the circumstances of the society tends either directly or indirectly to raise the real rent of land, to increase the real wealth of the landlord. (*WN*, 264)

If the landlords understand their long-term interests they will understand that those interests are at one with the "general interest of the society" and thus "[w]hen the publick deliberates concerning any regulation of commerce or police, the proprietors of land never can mislead it, with a view to promote the interest of their own particular order; at least, if they have any tolerable knowledge of that interest" (*WN*, 265). Unfortunately, however, of the three great orders – those who live by rent, by wages, and by profits – the landlords seem to be least able and least interested in understanding their own interest. Smith ascribes this to the fact that they need not exert themselves or compete in order to enjoy the return that comes to them.

The interests of the worker, like that of the landlord, are "strictly connected with that of society, [but like the landlord] he is incapable either of comprehending that interest, or of understanding its connection with his own" (*WN*, 266). Same malady, but virtually an opposite reason. While for the landlords everything comes so easily that they have no incentive to care, for the workers everything comes with such difficulty that they haven't the time to care, the means to educate themselves if they did care, or the resources to make their voices heard if they did understand and cared to promote their interests.

"His [(the worker's)] employers constitute the third order, that of those who live by profit" (*WN*, 266). These holders of stock, by committing it to the process of production, put into motion the engine of the progress that is always to the benefit of landlords and workers. Ironically they, the holders of stock, are the ones for whom fortune moves inversely with that progress because, as Smith has demonstrated earlier, the rate of profit falls with progress.

The interest of this third order, therefore, has not the same connection with the general interest of the society as that of the other two.

But, he continues, they have the greatest policy influence.

Merchants and master manufacturers are, in this order, the two classes of people who commonly employ the largest capitals, and who by their wealth draw to themselves the greatest share of the publick consideration. (*WN*, 266)

Because the merchants and master manufacturers are constantly engaged in the management of their own interest, they are, unlike the landlords, acutely aware of their interest. Because they are the holders of most of the productive stock of society, unlike the workers they have the means to promote their interest, an interest that

is always in some respects different from, and even opposite to, that of the publick. To widen the market and to narrow the competition, is always the interest of the dealers. To widen the market may frequently be agreeable enough to the interest of the publick; but to narrow the competition must always be against it, and can serve only to enable the dealers, by raising their profits above what they naturally would be, to levy, for their own benefit, an absurd tax upon the rest of their fellow-citizens. The proposal of any new law of regulation of commerce which comes from this order, ought always to be listened to with great precaution, and ought never to be adopted till after having been long and carefully examined, not only with the most scrupulous, but with the most suspicious attention. It comes from an order of men, whose interest is never exactly the same with that of the publick, who have generally an interest to deceive and even to oppress the publick, and who accordingly have, upon many occasions, both deceived and oppressed it. (*WN*, 267)

CONCLUSION

This warning reflects Smith's purpose and his growing concern. His purpose is to represent the process that has led and, if unencumbered, can continue to lead to progress for humankind in general, and for the British people in particular. His concern is with those laws and institutions in general and those in Britain in particular that impede that progress. This concern will be the focus of Book IV. But before he can get to that issue, he has to complete his model and establish its credibility.

Book I has established the foundation of his model. It has laid out Smith's terms and principles, and it has explained the conditions that lead from the nascent agricultural stage to the takeoff of commercial society.

Book II presents Smith's analysis of the dynamics of material progress in the commercial stage including the roles of accumulation, productive and unproductive labor, money, and capital flows that, if unencumbered by perverse laws and institutions, can lead to growth and the progressively greater wealth of the nation.

In Book III he makes the empirical case for his model.

3

The Wealth of Nations: Books II and III

Book II
Of the Nature, Accumulation,
and Employment of Stock

Having, in Book I, set the stage for his analysis of the dynamic that drives the engine of material progress in commercial society, in Book II Smith turns to that dynamic.[1]

Progress is driven by the continuous reinvestment of stock into circuits of production that put productive labor to work. Capital is that portion of accumulated stock that is allocated to these circuits. To the degree that parsimony grows this capital stock with each circuit, the division of labor is refined, productivity is enhanced, and there is growth in the wealth of the nation.

Money plays a crucial role in this dynamic. Smith examines the forms and functions of money, discusses the role and challenges of the banking system in a commercial system, and explains how a well-regulated paper currency can facilitate the expansion of trade.

The division of labor is limited by the extent of the market, so to justify capital deepening that leads to an ever finer division of labor and increasing productivity, the market must be expanding. In Smith's analysis the market grows through a process of the sequential widening of the circuits of trade. It is this dynamic of capital flowing into ever expanding circuits that drives the engine of material progress in commercial society.

"INTRODUCTION"

In the first, rude state, of humankind's evolution human beings live hand to mouth. There is no division of labor, no surplus, no accumulation.

---

[1] For an interesting analysis of Smith's growth theory see Spengler (1959A and 1959B).

The progress of opulence, humankind's material progress, begins with the emergence of private surpluses that allow personal accumulation. This accumulation is necessary for the division of labor because the division of labor is predicated on exchange – and one must have a "stock sufficient to maintain him ... till he has not only completed, but sold" his product (*WN*, 277).

> As the accumulation of stock must, in the nature of things, be previous to the division of labour, so labour can be more and more subdivided in proportion only as stock is previously more and more accumulated. (*WN*, 277)

A "more subdivided" division of labor means greater productivity. Greater productivity generates larger surpluses. With larger surpluses greater accumulation is possible. If this accumulation is used to improve and/or increase the capital stock this makes possible an ever finer division of labor. This generates further improvements in productivity. Increased productivity means greater surpluses ... increased accumulation ... more and better capital stock ... ever greater productivity ... and so it can go with capital and wealth expanding in each round of this circuit.[2] Book II is about this central role the capital stock plays in the *Causes of the Wealth of Nations*.

CHAPTER 1: "OF THE DIVISION OF STOCK"

In the rude state each man initially accumulates simply to smooth the pattern of his consumption. "He seldom thinks of deriving any revenue from it" (*WN*, 279). As a man's stock grows beyond the level necessary to cover any contingencies in life "he naturally endeavours to derive a revenue from the greater part of it" (*WN*, 279). At that point

> [h]is whole stock ... is distinguished into two parts. That part which, he expects, is to afford him ... revenue, is called his capital. The other is that which supplies his immediate consumption.[3] (*WN*, 279)

Capital can take two forms. Circulating capital leaves the hand of its owner and changes "shape" (*WN*, 279) as it passes through the circuit of

---

[2] In effect capital is in a self-expanding circuit. Whether or not this is where Marx learned this notion of capital as self-expanding value, it was certainly available to him in Smith. As will be shown later in this chapter, the concept of capital flowing in circuits that have different velocities is central to Smith's story of a society's material growth.

[3] "[I]mmediate consumption" can be a misleading term. Smith writes of dwelling houses that "[t]hough the period of their consumption ... is more distant, they are still as really stock reserved for immediate consumption as either cloaths or household furniture" (*WN*, 281–2).

production. For example, the capital that goes into manufacturing a shirt is transformed as it travels the circuit of production from money, to raw cotton and wages, to fabric and wages, to a shirt, to money again. Fixed capital is instrumental in the circuit of production, but its physical form and owner are constant. For example "the improvement of land [or] ... useful machines and instruments of trade yield a revenue or profit without changing masters, or circulating any further" (WN, 279).

Smith is careful to distinguish between a micro and macro conception of capital. What is capital to the individual may not be capital to the nation. Stock that generates revenue for the individual who owns it but does not generate a social product that can be reinvested in the next circuit of production is not capital in Smith's analysis. Rental property, for example, generates private revenue but is not capital for society:

> Though a house ... may yield a revenue to its proprietor, and thereby serve in the function of capital to him, it cannot yield any to the publick, nor serve in the function of a capital to it, and the revenue of the whole body of people can never be in the smallest degree increased by it. (WN, 281)

Stock is only capital if its use generates wealth for the nation that is thrown back into the expanding circuit of production.

Fixed capital includes "useful machines and instruments of trade which facilitate and abridge labour," "improvements of land," buildings that are let for rent but that produce revenue above and beyond the net rent "such as shops, warehouses, workhouses, farmhouses," and "capital fixed and realized ... in his person" (human capital) (WN, 282).

Circulating capital "is composed ... of four parts: First of money by means of which all the other three are circulated and distributed to their proper consumers" (WN, 282). The other three parts are different forms of inventory: provisions that will support labor, the materials of production (both raw and intermediate), and the finished products awaiting sale.

Capital fuels the engine of growth, but growth is not an end in itself. The goal of growth is to enhance material well-being: "To maintain and augment the stock of which may be reserved for immediate consumption, is the sole end and purpose of both the fixed and circulating capital" (WN, 283). In order to accomplish this the various forms of the capital stock, generally owned by different individuals, must be put to work in concert.

Markets make it possible for independent owners of interdependent parts of the capital stock to make the exchanges necessary to accomplish this. Within this market nexus money capital plays an instrumental role in facilitating these exchanges efficiently.

Individuals' participation in this market nexus depends on their confidence that there is "tolerable security" in the system:

In all countries where there is tolerable security, every man of common understanding will endeavour to employ whatever stock he can command in procuring either present enjoyment or future profit.... A man must be perfectly crazy who, where there is tolerable security, does not employ all the stock which he commands. (*WN*, 284–5)

Here again Smith weaves a larger theme of his moral philosophy into his narrative of *The Wealth of Nations*. The success of a society, in this case the success of a society's capital markets, depends significantly on the degree to which the people of that society feel secure.

In those unfortunate countries, indeed, where men are continually afraid of the violence of their superiors,[4] they frequently bury and conceal a great part of their stock in order to have it always at hand to carry with them to some place of safety, in case of their being threatened with any of those disasters to which they consider themselves as at all times exposed. (*WN*, 285)

Anticipating his historical analysis in Book III, Smith cites the period of feudal government in Europe as such a time and place. Insecurity in those days led so many people to bury treasure that the laws of the time explicitly granted to the sovereign the rights to any treasure trove that was discovered.

Having defined the conditions necessary for capital to circulate in the production system, Smith examines the instrumental role of money in this circulation in more detail.

CHAPTER 2: "OF MONEY CONSIDERED AS A PARTICULAR BRANCH OF THE GENERAL STOCK OF THE SOCIETY, OR OF THE EXPENCE OF MAINTAINING THE NATIONAL CAPITAL"

Smith begins chapter 2 by reviewing the components of commodity prices that he laid out in Book I: wages, profit, and rent. He then transitions from a micro to a macro perspective by pointing out that as with the micro price of a commodity, so too the macro functional distribution of society can be resolved into and analyzed in these three parts. For example, "as in the rent of a private estate we distinguish between the

---

[4] Recall the case of China from Book I.

gross rent and neat [(net)] rent, so may we likewise in the revenue of all the inhabitants of a great country" (*WN*, 286).

For the landlord the net rent is what is left over when all the costs of maintaining the estate are deducted from the gross rent. "His real wealth is in proportion, not to this gross, but to his neat rent" (*WN*, 286). Similarly, for the nation, the net revenue from the "whole annual produce" is what remains free for immediate consumption or for further augmenting the capital stock, *after* maintaining and/or replacing the existing fixed and circulating capital stock.

If fixed capital is simply maintained or replaced, its productivity remains the same in the next circuit of production. If fixed capital is improved, its productivity increases, and so too net revenue:

In manufacturers the same number of hands, assisted with the best machinery, will work up a much greater quantity of goods than with more imperfect instruments of trade.... It is upon this account that all such improvements in mechanicks, as enable the same number of workmen to perform an equal quantity of work, with cheaper and simpler machinery than had been usual before, are always regarded as advantageous to every society. (*WN*, 287)

Fixed capital is instrumental in production but it is not a part of the revenue of that production.

In this respect fixed capital is different from three parts of circulating capital (provisions, materials, and finished work), but it is very similar to one: money. "The fixed capital, and that part of the circulating capital which consists of money ... bear a very great resemblance to one another" (*WN*, 288). Money, as with fixed capital, is not part of the revenue of production. Both are, however, instrumental in producing that revenue. In the case of money ...

The great wheel of circulation is altogether different from the goods which are circulated by means of it. The revenue of the society consists altogether in those goods, and not in the wheel which circulates them. In computing either the gross or neat revenue of any society, we must always, from their whole annual circulation of money and goods, deduct the whole value of the money, of which not a single farthing can ever make any part of either....

Money, therefore, the great wheel of circulation, the great instrument of commerce, like all other instruments of trade [(fixed capital)], though it makes a part and a very valuable part of the capital, makes no part of the revenue of the society to which it belongs; and though the metal pieces of which it is composed, in the course of their annual circulation, distribute to every man the revenue which properly belongs to him, they make themselves no part of that revenue. (*WN*, 289, 291)

As money is like fixed capital in that it is only instrumental; it is also like fixed capital in that to the degree it can function more efficiently the revenue, and thus the wealth of the nation, is enhanced. This point brings Smith to an analysis of paper money because, properly managed, paper money can make the use of money more efficient.

"[C]irculating notes of banks and bankers ... [are the] best known" form of paper money (*WN*, 292). Where there is full "confidence in the fortune, probity, and prudence" (*WN*, 292) of the issuers these notes can become the basis for a fractional reserve system: if "twenty thousand pounds of gold and silver [are sufficient reserves 'for answering occasional demands' on one hundred thousand pounds worth of paper notes in circulation, then that twenty thousand can] perform all the functions which a hundred thousand [of specie] could otherwise have performed" (*WN*, 293).

Scaling his case up, Smith analyzes the situation in which a million pounds sterling is just sufficient to service what he refers to as the nation's domestic "channel of circulation" (*WN*, 293). If 200,000 of this sterling was held in reserve to support a million pounds paper, the money supply of the nation would be 1,800,000 pounds. He continues:

One million we have supposed sufficient to fill that [domestic] channel. Whatever, therefore, is poured into it beyond this sum, cannot run in it, but must *overflow*.... Eight hundred thousand pounds ... must *overflow*, that sum being over and above what can be employed at home, it is too valuable to be allowed to be idle. It will, therefore, be sent abroad, in order to seek that profitable employment which it cannot find at home. (*WN*, 293–4, emphasis added)

It is not the paper that will travel abroad because paper notes will be discounted in foreign markets. It is the gold and silver that will flow out. Is this a bad thing? Only if the money brings home "goods as are likely to be consumed by idle people who produce nothing" (*WN*, 294). It seems more likely to Smith, however, that this overflow will pour into more productive channels: either purchasing goods in one country for sale in another, the carrying trade, or purchasing goods "destined for the employment of [domestic] industry" (*WN*, 295).

By freeing up money capital in specie form for more distant opportunities (the carrying trade or procuring materials from other nations for domestic industry to finish and export), paper money extends the market. In doing so it functions, like fixed capital, as a catalyst for production, enhancing the efficiency of the production system without itself being transformed. Those who hold this financial capital will, in pursuit of their own self-interest, pour it into whichever channel is most productive, thereby contributing to the increasing wealth of the nation.

Smith claims that "[t]he effects [of the 'erection of new banking companies' in Scotland during the preceding twenty five to thirty years] ... have been precisely those above described" (*WN*, 297). As evidence of this he cites information he has "heard" of tremendous increases in Scottish trade. But he adds the caveat: "Whether the trade ... has really increased in so great a proportion, during so short a period, I do not pretend to know.... That the trade and industry of Scotland, however, have increased very considerably during this period, and that the banks have contributed a good deal to this increase, cannot be doubted" (*WN*, 297). Typical of Smith the empiricist, as he offers his evidence he is careful to assess its accuracy.

Drilling into this financial system, Smith explains how "discounting bills of exchange" and "cash accounts" work (*WN*, 298, 299), he describes the path of circulation (*WN*, 299), and he contrasts the benefits of the flexible Scottish system with that with which a London merchant must deal (*WN*, 300). While lauding the advantages that can be generated by the issue of paper currency, he also appreciates the dangers of such an issue. "Should the circulating paper exceed the" "value of the gold and silver, of which it supplies the place" (*WN*, 301, 300), this could ultimately lead to "a run upon the banks" (*WN*, 301).

Short of a run, over issuing of paper by banks increases the cost of maintaining the paper and decreases the benefit of doing so. Unfortunately banks are far too often guilty of such an over issue. He cites the experience of the Bank of England and Scottish banks as examples of the inefficiencies that come with having to meet demands for repayment when the means of repayment are not in the coffers of the bank.

Smith traces this problem to the banks dealings with "bold projectors" (*WN*, 304) who, unlike sober businessmen, are constantly drawing more out of the bank than they are paying back. When dealing with the sober businessmen "[t]he coffers of the bank ... resemble a water pond, from which, though a stream is continually running out, yet another is continually running in, fully equal to that which runs out; so that, without any further care or attention, the pond keeps always equally, or very near equally full. Little or no expense can ever be necessary for replenishing the coffers of such a bank" (*WN*, 304). The projectors, on the other hand, drain the bank of reserves, which forces the bank to purchase reserves at high prices in order to cover the increased demand that comes when its paper issue is out of balance.

Smith goes on to describe a classic scam that unscrupulous projectors have employed in order to gain access to the capital when banks became reticent to lend. Failing to get what they needed from the banks by legitimate means, these projectors resorted to "[t]he practice of drawing and re-drawing" (WN, 308). Smith writes that while this practice is "well known to all men of business … this book may come into the hands of many people who are not men of business … [so] I shall endeavour to explain it as distinctly as I can" (WN, 309).

This is indicative of Smith's sense of purpose. He is writing as a moral philosopher, but he is also writing for an audience living in the 1770s in Great Britain, and he wants to address practical policy issues of the day. This practical agenda becomes especially clear in Books IV and V.

He explains that drawing and redrawing bills of exchange is a process of rolling over notes among different banks, in effect taking out new debt to cover payments on old debt. Two people can dupe banks into valuing otherwise valueless paper by "drawing and re-drawing upon one another … [and] discount[ing] their bills sometimes with one banker, and sometimes with another" (WN, 311). A "great circle of projectors" can dupe banks even more effectively by making the scheme even more opaque. In such a scheme it is "as difficult as possible to distinguish between a real or fictitious bill of exchange; between a bill drawn by a real creditor upon a real debtor, and a bill for which there was properly no real creditor but the bank which discounted it; nor any real debtor but the projector who made use of the money" (WN, 312).

Once a bank is duped into the process it is very difficult to free itself from this web the projectors have spun. Refusing to loan more can bring the scheme crashing down, bringing the bank down with it. When in England and Scotland the banks tried to "gradually … get out of the circle" (WN, 312) by slowly withdrawing credit, there was a clamor from projectors that the banks were undermining the business of the country.

Smith describes the "solution" that emerged as follows: "In the midst of this clamour and distress, a new bank was established in Scotland [the Ayr Bank] for the express purpose of relieving the distress of the country…. This bank was more liberal than any other had ever been" (WN, 313). What unfolded was ironic and tragic.

The fresh line of credit from Ayr Bank allowed other banks to get out from under their bad loans. But this infusion of credit also "enabled them [(the projectors)] to carry on their projects for about two years longer than they could otherwise have done … so that when the ruin came, it fell so much heavier, both upon them and upon their creditors" (WN, 315).

The Ayr Bank crisis[5] was only the most recent example of the dangers of excess paper. Smith cites John Law's "Mississippi scheme [as the classic example of capital market folly, calling it] the most extravagant project both of banking and stock-jobbing that, perhaps, the world ever saw" (*WN*, 317).

A lesson Smith takes from these fiascos is that the private capital market is more efficient when it is less concentrated. Large lending enterprises cannot know their borrowers as well as small lenders who serve their immediate communities. The "bank which lends money, perhaps, to five hundred different people, the greater part of whom its directors can know very little about, is not as likely to be more judicious in the choice of its debtors, than a private person who lends out his money among a few people whom he knows, and in whose sober and frugal conduct he thinks he has good reason to confide" (*WN*, 316). Banking is based on trust, and trust has a more secure foundation in private markets when the banker and the borrower are more directly visible to one another, when transactions are transparent.

Smith then turns his attention to the unique role of the Bank of England: "It acts, not as an ordinary bank, but as a great engine of state" (*WN*, 320). Public trust in the bank is based on the warrant of the British government so "[t]he stability of the bank of England is equal to that of the British government" (*WN*, 320). Whether it be the Bank of England or a private bank, according to Smith one principle underlies the contribution of a banking system to enhancing the wealth of a nation: it facilitates the mobility of financial capital.

It is not by augmenting the capital of the country, but by rendering a greater part of that capital active and productive than would otherwise be so, that the most judicious operations of banking can increase the industry of a country.... The judicious operations of banking, by substituting paper in room of a great part of ... [the nation's stock of] gold and silver, enables the country to convert a great part of this dead stock into active and productive stock; into stock that produces something for the country. The gold and silver money which circulates in any country may very properly be compared to a highway, which, while it circulates and carries to market all the grass and corn of the country, produces itself not a single pile of either. The judicious operations of banking, by providing, if I may be allowed so violent a metaphor, a sort of wagon-way through the air; enable the country to convert, as it were, a great part of its highways into green pastures and corn fields, and thereby to increase very considerably the annual produce of its land and labour. The commerce and industry of the country, however, it must be acknowledged, though they may

---

[5] For a brief synopsis of the crisis see Rockoff (2013).

be somewhat augmented, cannot be altogether so secure, when they are thus, as it were, suspended upon the Daedalian wings of paper money, as when they travel about upon the solid ground of gold and silver. (*WN*, 320, 321)

Having laid out the virtues of a judicious use of paper money in the banking system and the main danger of such activity – lack of judiciousness – Smith examines other potential pitfalls in such a system.

If in a time of war an enemy captures the reserves that support the circulating paper, confidence in the monetary system will be destroyed, disrupting the nation's ability to carry on public and private exchanges.

There is also an issue regarding the appropriate denominations of paper currency. Wholesale trade can be transacted with bills of large denomination because the transactions are themselves large. Retail trade, being generally small transactions, requires smaller denominations. These small denominations are problematic because they can be issued by small, unscrupulous banks that do not hold adequate reserves. A collapse of these small banks can lead to "a very great calamity to many poor people" who hold these bills (*WN*, 323). Noting that "[p]aper money may be so regulated, as ... to confine itself very much to the circulation between the different [wholesale] dealers" (*WN*, 322), Smith asserts that this is precisely what should be done.

Is such a government intervention warranted? Isn't this intervention a violation of natural liberty?

Such regulations may, no doubt, be considered as in some respect a violation of natural liberty. But those exertions of the natural liberty of a few individuals, which might endanger the security of the whole society, are, and ought to be, restrained by the laws of all governments; of the most free, as well as of the most despotical. The obligation of building party walls, in order to prevent the communication of fire, is a violation of natural liberty, exactly of the same kind with the regulations of the banking trade which are here proposed. (*WN*, 324)

Smith values liberty. The raison d'être of his moral philosophy is to describe and to contribute to the ever closer approximation of what he envisions as the human prospect: an ideal liberal society. But given that we are not angels, this ideal can only be approximated. As a consequence:

Every system of positive law may be regarded as a more or less imperfect attempt towards a system of natural jurisprudence [(the ideal system of law)].... In no country do the decisions of positive law coincide exactly, in every case, with the rules which the natural sense of justice would dictate. Systems of positive law, therefore, though they deserve the greatest authority, as the records of the sentiments of mankind in different ages and nations, yet can never be regarded as accurate systems of the rules of natural justice. (*TMS*, 340–1)

We live in an imperfect, messy world. Given the freedom to do so, some individuals will exploit opportunities for private gain by pursuing socially destructive behaviors like the unsustainable issue of small bills. In order to protect the community from such unscrupulous actors, government must police that behavior.

Smith believes that, given the policing policies he proposes, the use of paper money can facilitate economic growth. But what about inflation? "The increase of paper money, it has been said, by augmenting the quantity ... necessarily augments the money price of commodities" (*WN*, 324). He asserts that it need not be so and he cites the Scottish experience to support his contention. Prices have not risen with the expansion of paper in Scotland. Indeed, they have fallen. The only exception came in "1751 and in 1752, when ... there was a very sensible rise in the price of provisions, owing, probably, to the badness of the seasons, and not to the multiplication of paper money" (*WN*, 325).

The perverse effect of paper money on prices is not inherent in the concept. It is a function of a corrupt execution of the issue. He cites the American colonies as examples of this corruption. There the issue was "government paper, of which the payment was not exigible till several years after it was issued [(so it is inherently discounted)] ... [but which was, by law] a legal tender of payment for the full value for which it was issued" (*WN*, 326). This abuse of paper money was "an act of such violent injustice, as has scarce, perhaps, been attempted by the government of any other country which pretended to be free" (*WN*, 326). He agrees with the "honest and downright Doctor Douglas ... [that] it was, a scheme of fraudulent debtors to cheat their creditors" (*WN*, 326).

Here again we hear a theme that weaves its way through Smith's moral philosophy. Factions can and do use government to implement schemes to defraud and cheat the public. Government can be a tool for destructive policy, as in this case, or it can be a tool for constructive policy as in the parliament's response to these colonial abuses: the elimination of the colonies' right to issue legal tender.

Smith's principles for a good private banking system are: paper issued by banks should be of large denominations, and it must be payable immediately and unconditionally in full upon demand. This will ensure the security of the public. Competition among banks is desirable and transparency in the relationship between a bank and its customers is too, so small is beautiful. Such a system is more agile, more secure, and more responsive to customers. It is also less vulnerable to catastrophic consequences of a single bank's imprudence. "In general, if any branch of trade, or any division of labour, be advantageous to the publick, the freer and more general the competition, it will always be the more so" (*WN*, 329). With these standards in place the private banks serve the community with their paper issue.

Financial capital facilitates the allocation of stock. But how do we distinguish a productive from an unproductive allocation?

CHAPTER 3: "OF THE ACCUMULATION OF CAPITAL, OR OF PRODUCTIVE AND UNPRODUCTIVE LABOUR"

There is one sort of labour which adds to the value of the subject upon which it is bestowed: There is another which has no such effect. The former, as it produces value, may be called productive; the latter, unproductive labour. (*WN*, 330)

To understand the distinction between productive and unproductive labor it is useful to remember how Smith distinguished between two uses of stock: for consumption and as capital.

The difference between that part of the stock that *is capital* and that part of the stock that *is not capital* does not turn on whether it is put to good use. One's home is useful. It keeps a family warm, safe, and dry. It is not, however, in Smith's terms, capital because as it is used it does not produce the means to restore itself much less yield additional revenue. The machinery in one's workhouse is also useful, and *it is capital* because through its application it produces the means to restore itself and it can contribute to generating an additional yield.

The distinction between productive and unproductive labor turns on this same point. The difference between productive and unproductive labor lies not in whether the labor produces something useful. It lies in the sustainability of that production. Productive labor generates the means to restore itself for the next circuit of production, and it can add to the stock available for further production. Unproductive labor does not.

A soldier does useful work; he defends the nation. But his labor does not produce the means to restore himself in the next circuit of production, so his is unproductive labor.

The sovereign, for example, with all the officers both of justice and war who serve under him, the whole army and navy, are unproductive labour.... In the same class must be ranked, some both of the gravest and most important, and some of the most frivolous professions: churchmen, lawyers, physicians, men of letters of all kinds [(Smith's own work)]; players, buffoons, musicians, opera-singers, opera-dancers, &c. (*WN*, 330–1)

A blacksmith or a farmer or a mechanic also does useful work, and because he does produce the means to restore himself for the next circuit of production, he is doing productive labor.

This distinction between productive and unproductive labor is central to the analysis in his *Inquiry into the Nature and Causes of the Wealth of Nations* for "the whole annual produce, if we except the spontaneous productions of the earth ... [is] the effect of productive labour" (*WN*, 332). While productive labor contributes to the increasing wealth of the nation, unproductive labor diminishes it by using up product that it does not replace. Connecting terms, capital is that share of the stock allocated to productive labor.

Upon the completion of each circuit of production, the stock generated by that circuit is allocated to either productive or unproductive labor. If the portion allocated to productive labor, that is, used as capital in the subsequent circuit, restores the capital stock used up in the previous circuit and adds to (or enhances) that stock of capital, the wealth of the nation will grow. If the portion used as capital is not sufficient to restore the stock used up in the previous circuit, the wealth of the nation will decline.

In "opulent countries" (*WN*, 334) the capital stock is very large, and thus the share of the gross product that must go to restoring that capital stock is very large relative to the additional yield. In a growing commercial society this implies that a large proportion of labor is going to productive employment. Smith contrasts this current state of the "opulent countries of Europe" with their situation in feudal times, when "a very small portion of the [gross] produce was sufficient to replace the capital employed" (*WN*, 334).

In those earlier times, given the predilections of men and given the lack of opportunities for productive investments, the share of gross product expended on unproductive labor was very large. The lords used most of their stock to support courtiers, retainers, and tenants – individuals dependent on the lord for their livelihood.

Dependence is destructive.

In feudal society those many who were dependent on the lord were "in general idle, dissolute, and poor" (*WN*, 335). "It is better, says the proverb, to play for nothing, than to work for nothing" (*WN*, 335). The only engaged members of the working class of those days were in the "mercantile and manufacturing towns" where men were employed by capital – that is employed as productive labor, rather than as unproductive labor living off of revenue without replacing it (*WN*, 335).

"The proportion between capital and revenue ... seems every where to regulate the proportion between industry and idleness. Wherever capital predominates, industry prevails: wherever revenue, idleness" (WN, 337). Ultimately all production becomes someone's consumption; the crucial question for the progress of the wealth of nations is: Who is doing the consuming?

What is annually saved is as regularly consumed as what is annually spent, and nearly at the same time too; but it is consumed by a different set of people. (WN, 337–8)

If the consumption is sustaining productive labor, the stock consumed will be replenished and the wealth of the nation will grow with that labor's increasing productivity. If the consumption is that of unproductive labor employed to satisfy the immediate needs and desires of others (e.g., courtiers and retainers), the wealth of the nation is dissipated.[6]

The key to the progress of opulence lies in expanding the capital stock and in turn the productive labor of the nation. So how is this accomplished? "Capitals are increased by parsimony, and diminished by prodigality and misconduct.... Parsimony, and not industry, is the immediate cause of the increase of capital. Industry, indeed, provides the subject which parsimony accumulates. But whatever industry might acquire, if parsimony did not save and store it up, the capital would never be the greater" (WN, 337).

Here we hear Smith the moral philosopher identifying another key element among the *Causes of the Wealth of Nations*. It is a moral element: parsimony. Parsimony is an expression of prudence. Prudence is a mature characteristic of self-love, one of Smith's moral sentiments. In his *Theory of Moral Sentiments* Smith writes that the prudent man demonstrates a "steadfastness of ... industry and frugality, in his steadily sacrificing the ease and enjoyment of the present moment for the probable expectation of the still greater ease and enjoyment of a more distant but more lasting period of time" (TMS, 215). But while parsimony is necessary for the growth of the wealth of nations, it is not sufficient. The sentiments must be in proper balance: self-love must move men to action, and justice must ensure that those actions are constructive. Morals matter to the progress of opulence.

---

[6] This "what is saved ... " quotation is often cited (see, for example, Baumol, 1999) as Smith's anticipation of Say's Law (supply creates its own demand), but in context it is clear that this is not his meaning.

Only a free, secure, independent people have the incentive to work hard, the confidence to safely accumulate capital, and the freedom to seize opportunities presented by markets. Only an ethically mature citizenry has the prudence to be parsimonious and thus to grow the capital stock of the nation, and only such an ethical citizenry has a commitment to the justice that secures that accumulation. Only a nation with an expanding accumulation of capital stock will enjoy the progress of opulence, for it is an expanding stock of capital employing a growing number of productive laborers in a free and fair market nexus that is the main cause among the *Causes of the Wealth of Nations*.

One can hear the moral standing of parsimony in Smith's commentary on frugality and prodigality:

By what the frugal man annually saves, he not only affords maintenance to an additional number of productive hands, for the ensuing year, but ... he establishes as it were a perpetual fund for the maintenance of an equal number in all times to come....

The prodigal ... [b]y not confining his expense within his income ... encroaches upon his capital.... [H]e pays the wages of idleness with those funds which the frugality of his forefathers had, as it were, consecrated to the maintenance of industry. By diminishing the funds destined for the employment of productive labour, he necessarily diminishes, so far as it depends upon him, the quantity of that labour which adds a value to the subject upon which it is bestowed, and consequently, the value of the annual produce of the land and labour of the whole country, the real wealth and revenue of its inhabitants. (*WN*, 338, 339)

At least the prodigal who consumes domestic products keeps that specie in the nation, doesn't he? No, says Smith. Prodigality diminishes the capital stock with each circuit, and as a consequence the productive capacity of the nation is diminished. With less being produced domestically, specie "will, in spite of all laws and prohibitions, be sent abroad, and employed in purchasing consumable goods which may be of some use at home" (*WN*, 340).

Prodigality brings decline and, contrary to mercantilist logic (here he anticipates his analysis of Mercantilism in Book IV), "[t]he exportation of gold and silver is, in this case, not the cause, but the effect of ... [this] declension" (*WN*, 340). In contrast, parsimony expands the capital stock and thus the production of the economy. This increase in goods "will require a greater quantity of money to circulate them. [Specie will flow in.] ... The increase of those metals will in this case be the effect, not [as mercantilists argue] the cause, of the publick prosperity" (*WN*, 340).

In an ideal world naturally parsimonious individuals would provide the constantly expanding supply of capital that would take the nation down the most fruitful path. But in reality human frailty impedes that path. We are not all naturally parsimonious. Here, as in many other cases, Smith believes that, happily, nature provides a second best path to progress through the unintended consequences of individuals' actions. We need not depend on the parsimony of individuals to realize the necessary accumulation for growth. Nature has instilled in each of us a desire for "bettering our condition … [and this desire encourages accumulation because a]n augmentation of fortune is the means by which the greater part of men propose and wish to better their condition" (*WN*, 341).

Smith is sanguine with respect to private accumulation increasing the capital stock. Individuals' prodigality and those who foolishly sink capital into "injudicious and unsuccessful project[s]" (*WN*, 341) certainly do reduce the capital stock. But given the desire of most individuals to better their condition, and given that as society matures so too do individual ethics including prudence, Smith believes that the net effect of individuals' behavior on the capital stock is progressively more positive. The real danger to the capital stock, and thus to the progress of opulence of the nation, lies in not individual prodigality, but in government prodigality.

Great nations are never impoverished by private, though they sometimes are by publick prodigality and misconduct. The whole, or almost the whole publick revenue, is in most countries employed in maintaining unproductive hands. Such are the people who compose a numerous and splendid court, a great ecclesiastical establishment, great fleets and armies, who in time of peace produce nothing, and in time of war acquire nothing which can compensate the expense of maintaining them, even while the war lasts. (*WN*, 342)

The progress of great nations is due to the "frugality and good conduct of individuals" (*WN*, 342) who given their parsimony and their desire to better their condition accumulate capital at a rate sufficient to offset the perverse effects of prodigal individuals and of the government.

Smith sums up his analysis of accumulation, capital stock, and productive labor as follows:

The annual produce of the land and labour of any nation can be increased in its value by no other means, but by increasing either the number of its productive labourers, or the productive power of those labourers who had before been employed. The number of its productive labourers, is it evident, can never be much increased, but in consequence of an increase of capital, or of the funds destined for maintaining them. The productive powers of the same number of labourers cannot be increased, but in consequence either of some addition and improvement to those machines and instruments which facilitate and abridge labour; or of a more proper division and distribution of employment. In either case an additional capital is almost always required. (*WN*, 343)

Having described the elements that contribute to the progress of opulence, Smith turns to a brief empirical example of this progress unfolding. He begins, however, with a caveat. Because the progress of opulence made possible by accumulation, increased capital stock, and an increase in productive labor "is frequently so gradual, that, at near periods, the improvement is not ... sensible" (*WN*, 343) or may even be overshadowed by short-term declines caused by peculiar events, it is necessary to "compare the state of the country at periods somewhat distant from one another" (*WN*, 343).

Again, classic Smith. His purpose is to represent the invisible connecting principles that, given human nature, guide the evolution of humankind. This is a *long view*.

In his narrative he explains how things would go if unimpeded by the distortions of human frailty, and then he expands the story to describe how these frailties distort, impede, or even reverse what would otherwise be the natural flow of events. His standard for the credibility of his analysis is: Can it efficiently and effectively explain both the long view of history and the twists and turns that characterize the day-to-day, month-to-month, and year-to-year realities of life?[7]

The long historical view provides Smith his empirical test. In this case he demonstrates that the long flow of British history seems consistent with his analysis of the dynamics of growth.

"The annual produce of the land and labour of England" (*WN*, 344) is certainly more than it was a century ago, a century ago it was greater than it had been a century before that, and even then it was greater than at the time of the Norman conquest. In short, over the long term England's wealth has been growing. This in spite of public and private prodigality, wars, and civil unrest, all of which impede the growth of capital and much of which has been due to the government.[8]

---

[7] "To form a right judgment of it, indeed, we must compare the state of the country at periods somewhat distant from one another. The progress is frequently so gradual, that, at near periods, the improvement is not [sensible]" (*WN*, 343).

[8] He is particularly keen to point out the immense cost of "four French wars" (1688, 1702, 1742, 1756) for which "the nation has contracted more than a hundred and forty-five million of debt" (*WN*, 345). This particular example anticipates his scathing attack on Mercantilism, for he blames this public profligacy on the political power of those private interests: "For the sake of that little enhancement of price which this monopoly might

But though the profusion of government must, undoubtedly, have retarded the natural progress of England toward wealth and improvement, it has not been able to stop it.... In the midst of all the exactions of government, ... capital has been silently and gradually accumulated by the private frugality and good conduct of individuals, by their universal, continual, and uninterrupted effort to better their condition. It is this effort, protected by law and allowed by liberty to exert itself in the manner that is most advantageous, which has maintained the progress of England towards opulence and improvement in almost all former times, and which, it is to be hoped, will do so in all future times. (WN, 345)

Consider Smith's conception of civil government as represented in this quotation. He begins by castigating the "profusion of government" for retarding natural progress. Two sentences later he attributes the private accumulation that more than offsets "the exactions of government" to the fact that the pursuit of a better life is "protected by law and allowed by liberty." This law and this liberty are also a function of civil government. Not all governments afford such security and freedom. Indeed, Smith writes that among the nations of his day Great Britain has enjoyed the greatest progress because, all of its foolish wars and regulations notwithstanding, it enjoys the best government humankind has produced to date:

That security which the laws in Great Britain give to every man that he shall enjoy the fruits of his own labour, is alone sufficient to make any country flourish, notwithstanding these [mercantile impediments] and twenty other absurd regulations of commerce.... The natural effort of every individual to better his own condition, when suffered to exert itself with freedom and security, is so powerful a principle, that it is alone, and without any assistance, not only capable of carrying on the society to wealth and prosperity, but of surmounting a hundred impertinent obstructions with which the folly of human laws too often incumbers its operations.... In Great Britain industry is perfectly secure; and though it is far from being perfectly free, it is as free or freer than in any other part of Europe. (WN, 540)

In Smith's narrative civil government is instrumental. It can be constructive or destructive, or some combination thereof. To the degree that its constructive dimensions are more powerful than its destructive dimensions it contributes to progress. So, on the one hand, there are factions that distort British government policy and squander the nation's

---

afford our producers, the home-consumers have been burdened with the whole expense of maintaining and defending that empire. For this purpose, and for this purpose only, in the last two wars, more than two hundred millions have been spent, and a new debt of more than a hundred and seventy millions has been contracted over and above all that had been expended for the same purpose in former wars" (WN, 661).

resources for the sake of their own private interests. On the other hand, the British system of government, in particular its common law and its courts, affords individuals the freedom and security that encourage capital accumulation and innovation.

Constructive systems of law, the topic he explored in his *Lectures on Jurisprudence*, afford individuals independence and security. These constructive laws are nurtured by and they nurture mature citizenship, the topic he explores in his *Theory of Moral Sentiments*. Citizens who enjoy freedom and security invest in their future by accumulating capital. Accumulating capital grows the economy, and to the degree the reach of the well-being that this growth creates is inclusive, more and more citizens buy into the common standards of civic ethics. This facilitates the maturation of social and political institutions. Smith's narrative on the progress of opulence, of *The Nature and Causes of the Wealth of Nations*, is a part of a larger narrative on humankind's progress and its prospect.

One thing is clear about the relationship Smith envisions between government and the economy. The government should not micro manage: "It is the highest impertinence and presumption … in kings and ministers, to pretend to watch over the economy of private people" (*WN*, 346).

Having developed the role of capital in the progress of opulence, Smith explores the dynamic that determines where capital flows.

CHAPTER 4: "OF STOCK LENT AT INTEREST"

Smith refers to those who lend stock at interest as "the monied interest" (*WN*, 351). He is careful to note that, while it is money that exchanges hands, "what the borrower really wants, and what the lender really supplies him with, is, not the money, but the money's worth" (*WN*, 351). Unlike the landed interests or the trading interests or the manufacturing interests, the monied interests do not employ their own capital. They lend "to another those capitals which … [they] do not care to employ themselves" (*WN*, 351). The terms of such a loan require that the borrower return the full portion borrowed, "the repayment," and in addition "a smaller portion, called the interest" (*WN*, 352).

As the general stock of capital in a nation grows, so too does the stock of capital available for loan from the monied interests. "As the quantity of stock to be lent at interest increases, the interest, or the price which must be paid for the use of that stock necessarily diminishes … [because a]s capitals increase … [i]t becomes gradually more and more difficult to find within the country a profitable method of employing any new capital" (*WN*, 352–3). This gives rise to a "competition between different capitals" (*WN*, 353), a competition that unfolds in both the product and the factor markets.

On the product side, the competition is over market share and the only way to succeed or even survive is "by dealing upon more reasonable terms" (*WN*, 353). This becomes one jaw of a vise that squeezes profit and in turn interest rates: "He must not only sell what he deals in somewhat cheaper, but in order to get it to sell, he must sometimes buy it somewhat dearer" (*WN*, 353). That "buying dearer" is the other jaw that squeezes the return to capital: competition in the factor market. In particular, capitals must compete with one another for the available labor. "Their competition raises the wages of labour, and sinks the profits of stock.... [W]hen the profits which can be made by the use of capital are in this manner diminished, as it were, at both ends [(in the product and factor markets)], the price which can be paid for the use of it, that is, the rate of interest, must necessarily be diminished with them" (*WN*, 353). Like net rent, interest is "a monopoly price" (*WN*, 161). Its diminution reduces unearned income without reducing the incentive for industry.

What Smith has just described is a natural course of events in a fair and free market: expanding capital stock leads to a "competition between the different capitals" (*WN*, 356), which causes profit rates to fall and wage rates to rise, which together squeeze interest rates. This analysis provides him with a framework for cross-national comparisons of market maturation. His work predicts that when comparing two nations the one that has progressed more will exhibit lower profit and interest rates and higher wages, and that there must be a sociopolitical difference between these two nations that explains this difference. He presented just such a comparison in Book I, chapters 8 and 9.

"Since the time of Henry VIII. the wealth and revenue of the country [England] have been continually advancing.... The wages of labour have been continually increasing during the same period, and in the greater part of the different employments of trade and manufactures the profits of stock have been diminishing" (*WN*, 106). In contrast, "[t]he poverty of the lower ranks of people in China far surpasses that of the most beggarly nations in Europe" (*WN*, 89). In China the "oppression of the poor ... [has] establish[ed] the monopoly of the rich, who, by engrossing the whole trade to themselves ... [are] able to make very large profits. Twelve per cent. accordingly is said to be the common interest on money in China, and the ordinary profits of stock must be sufficient to afford this large interest"⁹ (*WN*, 112).

Smith is not simply demonstrating that England has greatly surpassed China in the progress of market maturation. He is highlighting why England has made more progress. It is all about "laws and institutions" (*WN*, 111). Recall "[t]hat security which the laws in Great Britain give to every man that he shall enjoy the fruits of his own labour" (*WN*, 540), and contrast that with the "different laws and institutions [of China] ... a country ... where, though the rich or owners of capitals enjoy a good deal of security, the poor or the owners of small capitals enjoy scarce any, but are liable, under pretence of justice, to be pillaged and plundered at any time" (*WN*, 112).

The *Wealth of Nations* is not simply a function of markets. It depends mightily on the system of laws and institutions that determine the degree of justice within which markets function.

Having presented his analysis of stock lent at interest, Smith briefly reviews Hume's demonstration that Locke, Law, and Montesquieu were wrong to associate the real interest rate with the quantity of money. The confusion derives from a lack of care in distinguishing real from nominal changes.

Chapter 4 closes with a discussion of usury laws.

Smith argues that usury laws are perverse. They do not eliminate lending; they simply add a risk premium to the rate of interest. But while he is against outlawing interest, he is not against fixing a legal rate ceiling so long as that ceiling is "not too much above the lowest market rate" (*WN*, 357).

His advocacy for a rate ceiling reflects his concern that the combination of projectors who have an unrealistic estimation of their probability of success ("their golden dreams" (*WN*, 310)) and banks that are too big to accurately assess the integrity of their borrowers will lead to artificially high interest rates as the projectors outbid the more sober investors for the available capital.

If the legal rate of interest in Great Britain, for example, was fixed so high as eight or ten percent, the greater part of the money which was to be lent, would

⁹ To put this Chinese number in perspective, Smith writes shortly after that "In a country where the ordinary rate of clear profit is eight or ten per cent., it may be reasonable that one half of it should go to interest, wherever business is carried out with borrowed money" (*WN*, 114). Thus the interest would be 4 to 5 percent. In Holland, the country that is closest to having "acquired its full complement of riches ... the ordinary rate of clear profit ... is very small, so that usual market rate of interest which could be afforded out of it, would be so low as to render it impossible for any but the very wealthiest people to live upon the interest of their money" (*WN*, 113).

be lent to prodigals and projectors, who alone would be willing to give this high interest. Sober people, who will give for the use of money no more than a part of what they are likely to make by the use of it, would not venture into the competition. (*WN*, 357)

As we have seen in the case of banks being duped by schemes for drawing and redrawing bills of exchange, this does occur. "Where the legal rate of interest ... is fixed but a very little above the lowest market rate, sober people are universally preferred, as borrowers, to prodigals and projectors"[10] (*WN*, 357).

CHAPTER 5: "OF DIFFERENT EMPLOYMENTS OF CAPITALS"

Having established the central role of capital in the progress of opulence and the nature of its return, Smith turns his attention to the different ways capital can be employed in circuits of production.

Capital can be productively committed to four employments:

- "procuring the rude produce" (farmers and miners);
- "manufacturing" (mechanics and manufacturers);
- "transporting" or wholesaling (merchants); and
- "dividing" or retailing (retailers) (*WN*, 360).

Of particular interest is the employment of capital in agriculture and in transport. Agriculture is, for reasons explained shortly, a uniquely productive application of capital. Transport is, as we will see, significant because it affords capital holders options beyond the domestic market and thus makes possible expanded circuits that extend the market.

Each of the four employments of capital is "necessary" (*WN*, 360) to the operation of the other (a supply chain argument), but they have different productivities. He rejects the "prejudices of some political writers against [the productive value of the work of] shopkeepers and tradesmen ... [as] altogether without foundation" (*WN*, 361). Their service allows individuals to live with small stocks thereby not tying up lots of personal resources in inventories. Proposals to "tax them, or to restrict their numbers ... [so] that they can never be multiplied" (*WN*, 361) are entirely misguided. "Their competition ... can never hurt either the

---

[10] Again, as with the denomination of bills (*WN*, 324), we hear Smith calling for regulation. In this case his advocacy of the regulation of interest rates is, no doubt, also a function of his view that interest is, like rent, a monopoly price (*WN*, 847–8).

consumer, or the producer; on the contrary, it must tend to make the retailers both sell cheaper and buy dearer" (*WN*, 362).

As for agriculture: "No equal capital puts into motion a greater quantity of productive labour than that of the farmer ... [because i]n agriculture ... nature labours along with man.[11] ... [Farmers' labors at] planting and tillage frequently regulate more than they animate the active fertility of nature; after all their labour, a great part of the work always remains to be done by her" (*WN*, 363). It is this labor of nature that occasions a "natural" return in agriculture beyond the profits of stock, the return that is extracted by the landlord as rent. Because of this contribution by nature, "[o]f all the ways in which a capital can be employed ... [agriculture] is by far the most advantageous to the society" (*WN*, 364).

In manufacturing "nature does nothing; man does all" (*WN*, 364). But while the capital of the farmer may be more productive, the capital of the merchant is more mobile: "The capital of a wholesale merchant ... seems to have no fixed or necessary residence anywhere, but may wander about from place to place, according as it can either buy cheap or sell dear" (*WN*, 364).

In introducing this concept of mercantile capital as mobile, Smith continues to develop a very important thread in his narrative. Recall the virtue of paper money is that it frees up bullion to pursue opportunities in more extended markets. As he explained in chapter 2, when the domestic "channel of [capital] circulation" (*WN*, 293) is full it will "*overflow* ... [Money capital will] be sent abroad, in order to seek that profitable employment which it cannot find at home" (*WN*, 293–4, emphasis added). It is the merchants' capital that travels.

This mobility of merchant capital plays a central role in Smith's analysis. If he is to persuasively represent the invisible connecting chain that has given rise to the progress of opulence in the long course of history, he must convincingly describe the order of events in which that progress would naturally unfold. Because capital is the fuel for the engine of progress and because, if unencumbered, it flows to its best advantage, the logical way to present the stages of the progress of opulence is to follow the natural course of capital flow.

That natural flow would, he asserts, unfold as follows: the first employment of capital will be in agriculture for, as he has just explained, this is the most productive application of capital.[12] As the capital stock applied

---

[11] Even "his labouring cattle, are productive labourers" (*WN*, 363).

[12] He cites the American colonies as evidence of this: "It has been the principal cause of the rapid progress of our American colonies towards wealth and greatness, that almost their whole capitals have hitherto been employed in agriculture" (*WN*, 366).

to agriculture grows the rate of profit in that employment falls. When the conditions necessary for takeoff (as described in Book I) are realized capital will spill over into manufacturing.

Again, now in manufacturing, capital deepens. Again, the rate of profit falls.

At some point this falling rate of return will cause capital to spill over into the wholesale trade. Smith subdivides this wholesale trade into three branches:

- "home trade" – all within the domestic market;
- "foreign trade of consumption" – between the domestic and a foreign market; and
- "the carrying trade" (*WN*, 368) – between two foreign markets.

Smith distinguishes these three branches of wholesale trade along three dimensions. Two of these are the amount of domestic productive labor employed and the rapidity of the capital's circulation (i.e., the velocity of the circuit).[13]

Comparing the home and the foreign trade of consumption with respect to the amount of domestic productive labor they respectively employ, Smith identifies the former as more advantageous to the nation. In the home circuit all of the capital is engaged in employing domestic productive labor, while in foreign trade only half is. With respect to relative velocity of these two circuits he writes:

[T]he returns of the foreign trade of consumption are very seldom so quick as those of the home-trade. The returns of the home-trade generally come in before the end of the year, and sometimes three or four times in the year. The returns of the foreign trade of consumption seldom come in before the end of the year, and sometimes not till after two or three years. A capital, therefore, employed in the home-trade will sometimes make twelve operations [(circuits)], or be sent out and returned twelve times, before a capital employed in the foreign trade of consumption has made one. If capitals are equal, therefore, the one will give four and twenty times more encouragement and support to the industry of the country than the other. (*WN*, 368–9)

He goes on to note that a "round-about foreign trade of consumption," like the famous triangle trade with the American colonies, is even

---

[13] As we will see, in Books III (see *WN*, 377–9) and IV (see *WN*, 628–9) Smith introduces and develops one more consideration that reinforces the order of priority: risk of capital loss. It is most commonly the case that the closer capital stays to home the less risky so, *ceteris paribus*, home is less risky than foreign trade in consumption, is less risky than carrying trade.

slower than normal foreign trade. This reference is important because it anticipates the argument he will make in Book IV about the foolishness of the mercantilist policies that force British capital into that "one great [round-about] channel" (*WN*, 604).

The carrying trade has the slowest velocity and uses capital to support the least domestic productive labor (the products being transported are all being produced by foreign workers), so while it does generate revenue this last circuit is the least beneficial to the wealth of the nation.

Each of these different branches of trade ... is not only advantageous, but necessary and unavoidable, when the course of things without constraint or violence, naturally introduces it. (*WN*, 372)

Given the high velocity of that inner circuit the best returns are to be had in the home trade, so capital will initially stay home. This is good for the nation: "The capital ... employed in the home-trade of any country will generally give encouragement and support to a greater quantity of productive labour in that country, and increase the value of its annual produce more than an equal capital employed in the foreign trade" (*WN*, 371).

As the stock of the capital in the domestic economy increases and the rate of profit in that home circuit falls, the returns from the foreign trade become attractive. At that point capital will spill into this wider circuit as the interests of the merchant holders of this mobile capital compel them to seek these now relatively attractive returns.[14]

"[T]he capital employed in this latter [foreign] trade has ... [an] advantage [(greater velocity)] over equal capital employed in the carrying trade" (*WN*, 371–2). But again, as the capital stock in foreign trade increases the rate of profit falls. At some point the level of capital in the first two circuits of trade is high enough, and thus the rate of profit low enough, that "the surplus part of it naturally disgorges itself into the carrying trade" (*WN*, 373).

Based on this analysis of natural progress Smith rejects the mercantilists' argument that the nation should subsidize their carrying trade enterprises. The motive that drives their argument is transparent. They enjoy a monopoly in the carrying trade so subsidizing it serves their self-interest. They could not care less about the nation's interest:

---

[14] "By opening a more extensive market for whatever part of the produce of their labour may exceed the home consumption, it encourages them to improve its productive powers, and to augment its annual produce to the utmost, and thereby to increase the real revenue and wealth of the society" (*WN*, 447).

The carrying trade is the natural effect and symptom of great national wealth; but it does not seem to be the natural cause of it. Those statesmen who have been disposed to favour it with particular encouragements, seem to have mistaken the effect and symptom for the cause....

The consideration of his own private profit, is the sole motive which determines the owner of any capital to employ it either in agriculture, in manufactures, or in some particular branch of the wholesale or retail trade. The different quantities of productive labour which it may put into motion, and the different values which it may add to the annual produce of the land and labour of the society, according as it is employed in one or other of those different ways, never enter into his thoughts. (*WN*, 373–4)

Smith's analysis in Book II can be summarized briefly as follows.

Productive labor is the source of the wealth of a nation. That share of the accumulation that is allocated to the capital stock determines the resources available to employ productive labor. Given laws and institutions that ensure liberty and justice for all, secure and independent citizens seeking to better their condition will accumulate capital stock and allocate it to the productive activity that offers the best advantage. The natural flow of that capital will be first into agriculture, then into manufacturing, then into subsequent circuits of trade: home, foreign consumption, carrying. This dynamic is consistent with the production of the greatest wealth for the nation, for this flow, while motivated by the self-interest of the participants, always takes capital to its most productive allocation – the allocation employing the most productive labor. It is this narrative in Book II that underlies the most famous of all lines in *The Wealth of Nations* (found in Book IV):

As every individual … endeavours as much as he can both to employ his capital in the support of domestick industry, and so to direct that industry that its produce may be of the greatest value; every individual necessarily labours to render the annual revenue of society as great as he can. He generally, indeed, neither intends to promote the publick interest, nor knows how he is promoting it. By preferring the support of domestick to that of foreign industry, he intends only his own security; and by directing that industry in such a manner as its produce may be of the greatest value, he intends only his own gain, and he is in this, as in many other cases, *led by an invisible hand* to promote an end which was no part of his intention. (*WN*, 456, emphasis added)

Based on Books I and II, we can describe the path that the progress of opulence would follow if it were natural, that is, undistorted, as follows: it would begin in the countryside with agriculture, grow into the towns with manufacturing, and finally extend into ever expanding geographic realms through international trade. This framework in place,

Smith ends Book II with the observation that events in Europe have not in fact followed this natural path, and his model can explain why.

> What circumstances in the policy of Europe have given the trades which are carried on in towns so great an advantage over that which is carried on in the country, that private persons frequently find it more for their advantage to employ their capitals in the most distant carrying trades of Asia and America, than in the improvement and cultivation of the most fertile fields in their own neighborhood, I shall endeavour to explain at full length in the following two books. (*WN*, 374–5)

In Book III Smith explores a complex historical case in order to demonstrate the power of his analysis:

- He explains the unnatural twists and turns that we observe in the course of this history as being the consequence of distorting laws and institutions that were established over the course of European history, and ...
- He demonstrates that, these twists and turns notwithstanding, in the *long view* of history his analysis that the natural power of progress, driven by individuals' desire to better their condition and embodied in the maturation of laws and institutions, will prevail is validated.

Book III
"Of the different Progress of Opulence in different Nations"

CHAPTER 1: "OF THE NATURAL PROGRESS OF OPULENCE"

Smith begins Book III by laying out the "general rule" (*WN*, 377) of "the progress of opulence" that he developed in Books I and II:

The material progress of human society begins in the place where the essentials of human life are produced, agriculture. Only when that foundation is sufficient to generate a surplus can manufacturing of goods for "conveniency and luxury" (*WN*, 377) be undertaken. Therefore, geographically, natural progress begins in the countryside where food is produced and then, when a sufficient surplus is generated, proceeds to the towns where concentrations of people supported by the agricultural surplus make possible the finer division of labor necessary for manufacturing. Both domains benefit from the exchange of surpluses.

The great commerce of every civilized society, is that carried on between the inhabitants of the town and those of the country.... The gains of both [from this trade] are mutual and reciprocal, and the division of labour is in this, as in all other cases, advantageous to all the different persons employed in the various occupations. (*WN*, 376)

Variations on this pattern do occur because some towns can reach beyond the immediate locale for sources of subsistence (e.g., port towns), but while there are "considerable variations" (*WN*, 377), they form "no exception to the general rule" (*WN*, 377).

This brief review of the analysis he has presented in Books I and II on the emergence of surpluses in agriculture and the flow of capital into manufacturing and then trade brings Smith to the role of risk as a consideration in the allocation of capital. Given "the natural inclinations of man" (WN, 377) to be risk averse:

Upon equal, or nearly equal profits, most men will chuse to employ their capitals rather in improvement and cultivation of land, than either in the manufactures or in foreign trade. The man who employs his capital in land, has it more under his view and command, and his fortune is much less liable to accidents than that of the trader, who is obliged frequently to commit it, not only to the wind and the waves, but to the more uncertain elements of human folly and injustice, by giving great credits in distant countries to men with whose character and situation he can seldom be thoroughly acquainted. The capital of the landlord, on the contrary, which is fixed in the improvement of land, seems to be as well secured as the nature of human affairs can admit of.[15] ... In seeking employment of a capital, manufactures are, upon equal or nearly equal profits, naturally preferred to foreign commerce, for the same reason that agriculture is naturally preferred to manufactures. (WN, 377–8, 379)

Thus, because of both the productivity differentials he has outlined in Book II and the risk differential just described:

[a]ccording to the natural course of things ... the greater part of capital of every growing society is, first, directed to agriculture, afterwards to manufactures, and last of all to foreign commerce. (WN, 380)

Or, so it would be:

had human institutions ... never disturbed the natural course of things (WN, 378) ...
     But though this natural order of things must have taken place in some degree in every ... society, it has, in all the modern states of Europe been, in many respects, entirely inverted. (WN, 380)

The "natural course" of human progress is Smith's reference point. But, given human frailty, humankind's evolution is never "natural." It is inevitably distorted, and on occasion even "inverted," by perverse structures of social, political, and economic institutions. So any meaningful analysis of humankind's evolution must systematically address institutional distortions.

To this end, Smith's narrative in Book III explains how, contrary to the natural course, institutional constructs in Europe after the fall of Rome[16]

---

[15] Smith also notes the "pleasures of country life": "The beauty of the country, ... the tranquility of the mind which it promises, and wherever the injustice of human laws do not disturb it, the independency which it really affords" (WN, 378).

[16] The editors of WN note that "[i]n both the LJ(A) and LJ(B) Smith dealt at some length with the rise, progress, and decline of Greece and Rome. The argument then offered a version of events outlined in the following chapters of this Book, treating these events as

caused towns to progress before the country; and how, often because of unintended consequences as individuals sought to better their condition, those constructs evolved such that the progress of the country followed.

By demonstrating that the analysis he has presented in Books I and II can offer a compelling explanation of a significant historical (long view) case, as well as the unnatural twists and turns along the way, Smith seeks to convince his reader of the plausibility of his analysis and thereby to persuade the reader that his analysis warrants serious consideration.[17]

CHAPTER 2: "OF THE DISCOURAGEMENT OF AGRICULTURE IN THE ANTIENT STATE OF EUROPE AFTER THE FALL OF THE ROMAN EMPIRE"

Smith describes the "antient State of Europe after the Fall of the Roman Empire" as one in which "[t]he rapine and violence which the barbarians exercised against the antient inhabitants ... [left the] towns ... deserted, and the country ... uncultivated" (*WN*, 381). As a result, "the western provinces of Europe, which had enjoyed a considerable degree of opulence under the Roman empire, sunk into the lowest state of poverty and barbarism" (*WN*, 381–2).

Into this vacuum stepped "a few great proprietors" who "engrossed" the land. In order to secure these holdings "[t]he law of primogeniture ... [and] of entails" precluded the subdivision of these large parcels. These laws are a clear violation of the "natural law of succession [which] divides it [(the land)] ... among all the children of the family" (*WN*, 382), but under the circumstances Smith believes these laws were necessary. In a world of chaos, a source of order is desired. "In those disorderly times, every great landlord was a sort of petty prince. His tenants were his subjects.... The security of a landed estate, therefore, the protection which its owner could afford those who dwelt on it, depended upon its greatness" (*WN*, 383). Entail and primogeniture ensured that "power and consequently ... security" (*WN*, 383) could be seamlessly passed on from generation to generation.

This is by no means an ideal order in Smith's view. But he is not a "man of system" who believes that the ideal world can be constructed *de*

---

parts of a single historical argument ranging from the foundation of Greek civilization to the English Revolution Settlement" (*WN*, 381 fn 1).

[17] See Campbell for the importance to Smith of addressing seeming "irregularities" as "crucial tests" of his analysis. (Campbell, 564–5).

novo at any time in any place.[18] The ideal can only emerge from a process within which laws and institutions evolve toward a system of liberty and justice for all. In the course of this evolution, the laws and institutions of a given age and place must be consistent with the circumstances of that age and place if that society is to function.[19] For Smith, the laws of entail and primogeniture were consistent with the need to fill a power vacuum in Europe after the fall of Rome. Given that the alternative was chaos, they made sense.

For Smith the evolutionist, the problem with such laws is that while they are appropriate for the time and place in which they emerge, these "[l]aws frequently continue in force long after the circumstances, which first gave occasion to them, and which could alone render them reasonable are no more" (*WN*, 383). Such impediments are inevitable obstacles to any society's evolutionary progress because self-serving customs and factional interests tend to ossify the extant institutional structure.

But in the chaos that followed the end of the Roman Empire security needed to be established, and the power the great lords seized by engrossing the land offered the people some security. These lords were not, however, by ability or inclination "great improvers" (*WN*, 385). And "[i]f little improvement was to be expected from such great proprietors, still less was to be hoped for from those who occupied the land under them" (*WN*, 386).

The "tenants at will ... were all or almost all slaves"[20] (*WN*, 386). "Whatever work he [a slave] does beyond what is sufficient to purchase his own maintenance, can be squeezed out of him by violence only, and by no interest of his own" (*WN*, 387–8). For this reason, slavery is, according to Smith, the least productive of all labor.[21] It only exists

---

[18] "Some general, and even systematical, idea of the perfection of policy and law, may no doubt be necessary for directing the views of the statesman. But to insist upon establishing, and upon establishing all at once and in spite of all opposition, every thing which that idea may seem to require, must often be the highest degree of arrogance. It is to erect his own judgment into the supreme standard of right and wrong. It is to fancy himself the only wise and worthy man in the commonwealth, and that his fellow-citizens should accommodate themselves to him and not he to them" (*TMS*, 234).

[19] For example, opening up markets in a nation that has no culture of property rights or justice in exchange is problematic. It is not unlikely that in such a context theft and fraud will be epidemic, and as Smith expresses elsewhere (*LJA*, 332), policing in that context is hopeless – either the number of police will be insufficient to police this unbridled totally free people or the large force necessary will undermine the freedom of that people.

[20] "[B]ut their slavery was of a milder kind than that known among ... our West Indian colonies" (*WN*, 386).

[21] Smith notes that only the incredibly high profit production of sugar and tobacco in the colonies returns enough to support "the expence of slave-cultivation" (*WN*, 389).

because "[t]he pride of man makes him love to domineer ... [and it is only sustainable where] the nature of the work can afford it" (*WN*, 388).

Smith briefly traces the evolution, "though by very slow degrees," of the European agricultural workers from slaves who had no interest in the produce of the land, to metayers who had a shared but insecure interest in the fruits of their labor, to freehold farmers who paid a "rent certain" (*WN*, 391) and who therefore, to the degree their lease was secure, had an interest in the land's productivity. This last case of independence and security is by far the most productive arrangement.

With each successive step to more independence and security, there was more of an incentive to improve the land. This story of "so important a revolution" is, according to Smith, "one of the most obscure points in modern history" (*WN*, 389). Its importance to Smith is that it represents an historical case that supports a theme of his narrative: where laws and institutions ensure the freedom and security of individuals, there is greater incentive for initiative and innovation. "Those laws and customs so favourable to the yeomanry, have perhaps contributed more to the present grandeur of England than all their boasted regulations of commerce taken together"[22] (*WN*, 392).

Reflecting on his own day, he cites examples of institutional "discouragements [(e.g., the French "taille")] ... [because of which] little improvement could be expected from the occupiers of land" (*WN*, 395). Then, returning to his narrative on Europe after the fall of Rome, he sets the scene by observing that "[t]he antient policy of Europe was[, because of perverse institutional conditions] ... unfavourable to the improvement and cultivation of land" (*WN*, 396), and for this reason the course of progress was "inverted." It began in the towns.

CHAPTER 3: "OF THE RISE AND PROGRESS OF CITIES AND TOWNS, AFTER THE FALL OF THE ROMAN EMPIRE"

The towns were "inhabited by tradesmen and mechanicks" (*WN*, 397) whose livelihood depended on peddling goods for sale in the country. But in the chaos that ensued after Rome's fall, as they transported goods around the countryside traders were liable to taxes at every turn. This severely limited the extent of their market, and consequently

---

[22] Smith expresses immense respect for the yeoman farmer in Book I, chapter 10, Part c (*WN*, 143).

townspeople were initially "very nearly in the same state of villanage with the occupiers of land in the country" (*WN*, 397).

A process began to unfold, however, that afforded traders in towns growing security and independence long before those who tilled in the country.

Sometimes the king, sometimes a great lord who had, it seems, upon some occasions, authority to do this, would grant to particular traders ... a general exemption from such ["passage"] taxes [that were such an onerous impediment to trade]. Such traders, though in other respects of servile, or very nearly of servile condition, were upon this account called Free-traders. They in return usually paid to their protector a sort of annual poll-tax.[23] ... But how servile soever may have been originally the condition of the inhabitants of the towns, it appears evidently, that [starting from this first step] they arrived at liberty and independency much earlier than the occupiers of the country. (*WN*, 398–9)

The collection of poll-taxes for the king was usually farmed out, the king receiving "rent certain" payments (*WN*, 399) from individuals via the collector. Over time the burghers of the town became the agents for collecting and paying these fees for the entire town. This gave the town flexibility in determining assessments and freedom "from the insolence of the king's officers" (*WN*, 400).

This relationship between the king and the towns evolved from an intermittently recontracted term payment into a perpetual fixed payment for a perpetual set of privileges.

The payment having thus become perpetual, the exemptions, in return for which it was made, naturally became perpetual too. Those exemptions ... could not afterwards be considered as belonging to individuals as individuals, but as burghers of a particular burgh.[24] ... Along with this grant ... [privileges] that they might give away their own daughters in marriage, that their children should succeed them, and that they might dispose of their own effects by will, were generally bestowed upon the burghers of the town to whom it was given.... [In this process] they now, at least, became really free in our present sense of the word Freedom.[25] (*WN*, 400)

---

[23] Smith cites "the very imperfect accounts" of the Domesday Book to support this story (*WN*, 388). This kind of caveat is a consistent element in Smith's presentation. He is not an historian, and he at least tries to be forthright in his use of history.

[24] "[W]hich, upon this account was called a Free-burgh" (*WN*, 400).

[25] Smith writes in this context: "Whether such privileges had before been usually granted along with the freedom of trade, to particular burghers, as individuals, I know not. I reckon it not improbable that they were, though I cannot produce any direct evidence of it" (*WN*, 400). This caveat reflects Smith's respect for empirical evidence, and also his style as a moral philosopher telling a story as opposed to an historian. He cites the gap,

Smith continues: "Nor was this all" (*WN*, 400). He goes on to describe many more elements of self-governance, including the burghers' "authority to compel their inhabitants to act according to some certain plan or system" that made possible "regular government ... [and the establishment of a] voluntary league of mutual defence" among towns (*WN*, 402). In effect the kings had "voluntarily erected a sort of independent republicks in the heart of their own dominions" (*WN*, 401).

Why, Smith poses the question, would a king do this? The answer lies in the political struggle between the kings and the lords. In this age a king did not have the power to control the lords, so the towns were at the mercy of the great lords. The lords looked down on the burghers as lesser beings, were galled by any wealth the burghers accumulated, and preyed upon them whenever they could.

The lords despised the burghers.... The burghers naturally hated and feared the lords. The king hated and feared them [(the lords)] too; but though he perhaps might despise [the burghers as inferiors], he had no reason either to hate or fear the burghers. Mutual interest, therefore, disposed them to support the king, and the king to support them against the lords. They were the enemies of his enemies, and it was his interest to render them as *secure and independent* of those enemies as he could. (*WN*, 402, emphasis added)

Only in league with one another could towns muster enough power to be formidable to a great lord. By offering the towns the opportunity to establish independent, regular government under a magistrate, the king empowered the towns to form such alliances for their own security and for his support. As empirical evidence of this incentive for coalition building between kings and towns, Smith cites evidence that "[t]he princes who lived upon the worst term with their barons, seem accordingly to have been the most liberal in grants of this kind to their burghs"[26] (*WN*, 402).

A consequence of this alliance was the independence and security that nurtures the progress of opulence:

Order and good government, and along with them the liberty and security of individuals, were, in this manner, established in cities at a time when the occupiers of land in the country were exposed to every sort of violence. But men in this defenceless state naturally content themselves with their necessary subsistence;

and moves on with the story. It is this exact attitude toward history that allows him to indulge in "conjectural history."

[26] He explores some of the European examples, noting that where kings were especially weak, "as in Italy and Switzerland, ... the towns became independent republicks" while in England and France "the representation of the burghs in the states general" can be traced to this alliance with the king against the lords (*WN*, 403, 404).

because to acquire more might only tempt the injustice of their oppressors. On the contrary, when they are secure of enjoying the fruits of their industry, they naturally exert it to better their condition, and to acquire not only the necessaries, but the conveniencies and elegancies of life. That industry, therefore, which aims at something more than necessary subsistence, was established in cities long before it was commonly practised by the occupiers of land in the country. (*WN*, 405, emphasis added)

This history represents a distortion of the "natural course" of progress – and that is precisely Smith's point. His case for the persuasiveness of the connecting principles he has presented lies in his ability to effectively demonstrate that, twists and turns of human events notwithstanding, over the long view of history the natural course of humankind driven by chance, circumstance, and the intended and unintended consequences of human actions has brought forth maturing laws and institutions and in turn progress.

This progress is not monotonic. There are inevitable distortions that impede and even invert the natural course. These distortions can generally be attributed to factional interests that create perverse institutional constructs.

This progress is not the product of human wisdom. History reveals the importance of unintended consequences of human actions as a prime mover in this process. Nevertheless, over the long term, the twists and turns of human events notwithstanding, his analysis suggests that given natural selection "[o]rder and good government" will emerge and with this the wealth of nations grows.

In this European case progress ultimately did prevail. Because of chance, circumstance, and the unintended or intended consequences of human action, government provided more independence and security, increasing the incentive for individuals to accumulate capital and to invest and innovate with that capital in order to better their condition. As people do so, with no such intention, they contribute to the growth of the wealth of the nation. *Ceteris paribus*, wealthier nations are stronger, better able to defend themselves and to provide a foundation for further progress.

It was the self-interests of the king and the burghers, not any intent on their part to bring progress to society, that led to an alliance that provided towns the independence, the security, and the regular government that encouraged accumulation and growth.

Initially, the great lords' power was maintained in the countryside, resulting in continued dependence, insecurity, and oppressive government. This destroyed any incentive to work or accumulate. Indeed, "[w]hatever stock ... accumulated in the hands of the industrious part of the inhabitants of the country, naturally took refuge in cities, as the only sanctuaries in which it could be secure to the person who acquired it" (WN, 405).

But Smith's narrative does not end here.

The initial demand by those in the countryside for the manufactured goods from the towns was for the common clothing and furnishings suitable for the working people of the country. Such items need to be produced domestically because they are too bulky and cheap to warrant carriage from a distant market. Foreign trade only emerged once the home market generated commodities that were marketable in exchange for more refined foreign goods.[27] Most early European foreign trade largely consisted of "importing the improved manufactures and expensive luxuries of richer countries ... eagerly purchased [by the lords] ... with great quantities of the rude produce of their own lands" (WN, 406–7).

These fineries were the first items of distant trade "[f]or ... in small bulk it [(the refined product, such as 'a piece of fine cloth')] frequently contains the price of a great quantity of rude produce" (WN, 409). A town situated "near either the sea-coast or the banks of a navigable river" (WN, 405) was naturally first to engage in this distant trade because the access to that trade was significantly less costly. As the European demand for these fineries expanded, the market in Europe became sufficiently extensive to support manufacturing of fineries in European towns for domestic sale.

This historical course – towns growing with trade even as the country stagnated under the oppression of the lords – is an inversion of natural progress. So how did progress come to the country?

CHAPTER 4: "HOW THE COMMERCE OF THE TOWNS CONTRIBUTED TO THE IMPROVEMENT OF THE COUNTRY"

The country benefited from this success of the towns, first and foremost because the towns provided an expanding market for the produce of the country. This "gave some encouragement to industry and improvement" in the country (WN, 411). The country also benefited from the movement of merchants into the country. "Merchants are commonly ambitious of

---

[27] There are certainly peculiar exceptions. For example it was an artificial stimulus that encouraged the foreign trade of "Venice, Genoa, and Pisa" when they served "commissaries" to the crusaders (WN, 406).

becoming country gentlemen, and when they do, they are generally the best of all improvers" (*WN*, 411). They see their accumulation as capital stock that should return a profit, so they invest in the land and improve it.

Thirdly, and lastly, commerce and manufactures gradually introduce *order and good government*, and with them, the liberty and security of individuals, among the inhabitants of the country, who had before lived almost in a continual state of war with their neighbours, and of servile dependency upon their superiors. This, though it has been the least observed, is by far the most important of all their effects. Mr. Hume is the only writer, who, so far as I know, has hitherto taken notice of it. (*WN*, 412, emphasis added)

Smith is very proud of his analysis of the natural market process: the division of labor and exchange of surpluses through markets, the importance of the extent of the market in limiting how much this division of labor can be refined, the role of capital accumulation in determining how extensively this infrastructure of production can be developed, and the natural inclinations and propensities in humans that drive this process of expanding markets and thus the progress of opulence with no intent nor anyone in charge.

But he is equally proud of his analysis of the unnatural course of human history and of his ability to offer a plausible explanation of that unnatural path based on his analysis of the evolution of the laws and institutions of society – an evolution naturally distorted by the human frailty that leads to what in the modern literature is called rent-seeking and rent-maintenance behavior.[28] In the quotation just cited, he asserts that, aside from his dearest friend, David Hume, he alone has highlighted this "most important" relationship between the progress of opulence and the evolution of laws and institutions as he inquires into the nature and causes of the wealth of nations.

The Wealth of Nations is not an analysis of the one path that all nations must take to progress. There are common principles that underlie the process of societal evolution (laws and institutions that ensure independence and security), but the specifics of any particular nation's evolution are a function of the peculiar geographic circumstances of that nation and the intended and unintended consequences of the choices made by the individuals living in that time and place. In his analysis of the emerging progress of Europe after the fall of Rome, that progress is propelled in significant ways by the unintended consequences of the greed and material fetishes of the lords.

---

[28] See Buchanan, Tollison, and Tullock (1980).

In the wake of Rome's decline lords lorded over both town and country. There was "neither foreign commerce, nor any of the finer manufactures, [so] a great proprietor, having nothing for which he can exchange the greater part of the produce of this lands which is over and above the maintenance of the cultivators, consumes the whole in rustick hospitality at home" (WN, 412–13). In Smith's terms, all of the accumulation went to the maintenance of unproductive, dependent labor.

For example, "[t]he great earl of Warwick is said to have entertained every day at his different manors, thirty thousand people; and though the number here may have been exaggerated, it must, however, have been very great to admit of such exaggeration" (WN, 413). Again we see Smith's use of history. He regularly cites evidence from history with caveats about its absolute accuracy, but as indicative of what he believes was the spirit of the occasion.

Whatever the accuracy of his history, the point of Smith's description of the lords' conspicuous consumption in these early days is clear. There was stagnation in those days because virtually all accumulation went into consumption rather than capital stock, and because dependence eliminated any incentive for workers to exert themselves. The lords determined what was law, enforced that law, and judged any question of law for all who lived under them. The lords had the loyalty of an army of dependents that made up their militias. The lords had real power and the king was "in those ancient times ... little more than the greatest proprietor in his dominions" (WN, 415).

In these early days the authority of the lords was based on allodial, not feudal law. "That authority and those jurisdictions all necessarily flowed from the state of property and manners [of the age.] ... The introduction of the feudal law, so far from extending, may be regarded as an attempt to moderate the authority of the great allodial lords" (WN, 416–17) vis-à-vis the king, and to bring some regularity and with it some semblance of order and good government. But it was too weak a system to undermine the power of the lords. Ironically, it was only their own greed and their fetishes for material things in the context of an expanding market system in the towns that diminished the lords' power over men:

[W]hat all the violence of the feudal institutions could never have effected, the silent and insensible operation of foreign commerce and manufactures gradually brought about. These gradually furnished the great proprietors with something for which they could exchange the whole of their surplus produce of their lands, and which they could consume themselves without sharing it wither with tenants or retainers. All for ourselves, and nothing for the other people, seems, in every age of the world, to have been the vile maxim of the masters of mankind.... For a pair of diamond buckles perhaps, or for something as frivolous and useless, they exchanged the maintenance, or what is the same thing, the price of the maintenance of a thousand men for a year, and with it the whole weight and authority which it could give them.... [A]nd thus, for the gratification of the most childish, the meanest and the most sordid of all vanities, they gradually bartered their whole power and authority.[29] (*WN*, 418)

It was this invasion by markets and the fineries that those markets brought that ultimately made possible the development of secure independence among the country workers that workers in the towns were already enjoying.

Markets are very opportunistic. Those selling fineries found a ready market in the vain, rich, selfish lords of the country. The more the lords engaged in this market exchange, the less of their produce went to supporting the unproductive labor of their dependents. The fewer dependents they had, the smaller the loyal following that made up their military power base. As Smith describes it, the lord who had once supported 10,000 dependents with the surplus of his estate now through the market supported a fraction of the subsistence of a much larger number of workers.

In the market nexus many workers contribute to supplying the fineries that the lord purchases, but no one of these workers depends on that lord alone, for each is producing not for a single lord but for the market in which that lord is but one customer. "Though he [the lord] contributes, therefore, to the maintenance of them all, they are all more or less independent of him, because generally they can all be maintained without him" (*WN*, 420). This process led not only to the lord supporting more independent workers in the larger market nexus, but also more independence of the workers in his own country domain.

To buy in the market, the lords needed to produce for the market. This transformed the relationship between the lord and his tenants. He needed to use his accumulation for productive rather than unproductive labor and this meant supporting fewer tenants working larger plots of land, so the sizes of the "[f]arms were enlarged" (*WN*, 420).

Always seeking to better his condition, the lord desired ever greater rents from these larger farms so that he could buy more baubles. "His tenants could agree to this upon one condition only, that they should be secured in their possessions, for such a term of years as might give them time to recover with profit whatever they should lay out in the

---

[29] Smith draws a parallel between this decline of the lords and the decline of the Roman clergy later in Book V (*WN*, 803).

further improvement of the land. The expensive vanity of the landlord made him willing to accept of this condition; and hence the origin of long leases" (*WN*, 421). And with long leases came independence and security:

A regular government was [thus] established in the country as well as in the city, nobody having sufficient power to disturb its operations in the one, any more than in the other (*WN*, 421).

With this independence and security came the real opportunity for the workers to better their condition. They could achieve this by working hard, saving, investing in improvements, and building their capital stock by reinvesting that capital in successive circuits of production,[30] all of which contributes to the growing wealth of the nation.

It was thus that that "the Commerce of the Towns contributed to the Improvement of the Country" (*WN*, 411).

A revolution of the greatest importance to the publick happiness, was in this manner brought about by two different orders of people, who had not the least intention to serve the publick. To gratify the most childish vanity was the sole motive of the great proprietors. The merchants and artificers, much less ridiculous, acted merely from a view to their own interest, and in pursuit of their own pedlar principle of turning a penny wherever a penny was to be got. Neither of them had either knowledge or foresight of that great revolution which the folly of the one, and the industry of the other, was gradually bringing about.... This order [(growth from town to country)], however, being contrary to the natural course of things, is necessarily both slow and uncertain. (*WN*, 422)

---

[30] Smith observes as a side note: "It does not, perhaps relate to the present subject, but I cannot help remarking it, that very old families, such as have possessed some considerable estate from father to son for many successive generations, are very rare in commercial countries." He contrasts this condition with less commercial societies. He suggests that this diffusion of wealth is a natural process that occurs in commercial countries "in spite of the most violent regulations of law to prevent this dissipation" (*WN*, 422). It is clearly a process Smith believes is consistent with a healthy commercial society. He's already made the case that "a man born to a great fortune, even though naturally frugal, is very seldom capable" (*WN*, 385). He proceeds here to demonstrate that the North American colonies are growing incredibly rapidly and he attributes this, at least in part, to the diffusion of the land among a large number of small proprietors, each of whom, because he "knows every part of his little territory, ... views it with all the affection which property, especially small property, naturally inspires, and who upon that account take pleasure not only in cultivating but in adorning it, is generally of all improvers the most industrious, the most intelligent, and the most successful" (*WN*, 423). Entail and primogeniture preclude this "small is beautiful" reality in Europe.

Again and again, we hear this theme in Smith: wherever the laws and institutions of a society evolve – through chance, circumstance, and the unintended and intended consequences of human action – so as to enhance individuals' independence and security, individuals will pursue that opportunity to better their condition and the society's progress of opulence will flow from that pursuit.

Because the status quo of laws and institutions inevitably serves some faction of society, this evolution is, as Smith puts it, "necessarily both slow and uncertain" (*WN*, 422). But, nevertheless, nature prevails, so the course of humankind's history has been through four stages of progress.

Having described how, seemingly against all odds, progress emerged in Europe after the fall of Rome, Smith notes that where the legal artifacts of the past (e.g., entail and primogeniture) are still the law that progress has been impeded. Where chance and circumstance have been kind, and wise leadership has been enjoyed, progress has been most significant. This, for Smith, is the case of England:

England, upon account of the natural fertility of the soil, of the great extent of the sea-coast in proportion to that of the whole country, and of the many navigable rivers which run through it, and afford the conveniency of water carriage to some of the most inland parts of it, is perhaps as well fitted by nature as any large country in Europe, to be the seat of foreign commerce, of manufactures for distant sale, and of all the improvements which these can occasion. From the beginning of the reign of Elizabeth too, the English legislature has been particularly attentive to the interests of commerce and manufactures. (*WN*, 424)[31]

But it is not these artificial trade advantages serving the "interests of commerce and manufacturers" (a "monopoly against their countrymen" (*WN*, 425)) that account for England's progress. If anything, they are an impediment. "[W]hat is of much more importance than all of them ... [is that] the yeomanry of England are rendered as secure, as independent, and as respectable as law can make them" (*WN*, 425).

Other countries (Smith cites France, Spain, and Portugal) had great wealth from trade long before England. But wealth based on trade is a fickle foundation for long-term progress. First of all, "[a] merchant, is has been said very properly, is not necessarily the citizen of any particular country"[32] (*WN*, 426). So merchants' capital is not a dependable

---

[31] Agriculture there has also been favored by the legislature with protections such as the corn laws.

[32] As Smith explained back in Book II, chapter 5, it is the merchants' capital that is the mobile capital (*WN*, 364). This mobility becomes an issue when Smith discusses taxing

foundation for long-term progress. Also, the kinds of infrastructure merchants invest in are much more likely to be destroyed in a war, so again merchant capital is problematic as a long-term foundation for progress. In contrast, agriculture capital is invested in the land so it cannot leave, and those investments are much less vulnerable to the destruction of a war. For these reasons "the more solid improvements of agriculture ... [are a] much more durable" foundation for progress (*WN*, 427).

But first and foremost, it is the laws and institutions that protect the independence and security of those who work the land that explains both the success of Britain and the durability of that success: "It is now more than two hundred years since the beginning of the reign of Elizabeth, a period as long as the course of human prosperity usually endures" (*WN*, 425).

A deep concern of Smith's is that this period of prosperity in Britain is at risk because of the misguided and self-serving principles of the mercantile system, principles that are currently (1776) directing much of British policy. In Book IV Smith turns his attention from the past to his present, exploring the current alternative "Systems of Political Œconomy" (*WN*, 428) with a special focus on the mercantile system and its perverse character.

interest. Because the merchants' capital can flee, it is hard to impose an effective tax on interest (*WN*, 848).

4

The Wealth of Nations: Book IV

Of Systems of Political Economy

Having, in Books I and II, laid out his analysis of the progress of opulence, and having in Book III offered empirical evidence that his analysis is a valuable tool for understanding the actual course of human history, in Book IV Smith examines the strengths and weaknesses of the contemporary, competing models of political economy: the Mercantile system and Physiocracy.

"INTRODUCTION"

> Political œconomy, considered as a branch of the science of a statesman or legislator, proposes two distinct objects; first, to provide a plentiful revenue or subsistence for the people, or more properly to enable them to provide such a revenue or subsistence for themselves; and secondly, to supply the state or commonwealth with a revenue sufficient for the publick services. (*WN*, 428)

This statement reflects three central principles in Smith's moral philosophy.

His assertion that the *proper* role of the "statesman or legislator" is not to provide for the people but rather "to enable them to provide ... for themselves" reflects his deeply held conviction that the secure independence afforded by "the liberal plan of equality, liberty and justice" (*WN*, 664) empowers people.

Citing as one of the "objects" of political economy the realization of a "*plentiful* revenue or subsistence for the people" (emphasis added) reflects his belief that the well-being of the general population is the metric of a good society.

And finally, that a system of political economy must "supply the state or commonwealth with a revenue sufficient for the publick services" reflects his view that there is a role for the state in society. This anticipates Book V, "Of the Revenue of the Sovereign or Commonwealth," in which he examines the role of the state and how that role should be optimally financed.

His "Introduction" continues: "The different progress of opulence in different ages and nations, has given occasion to two different systems of political œconomy ... the system of commerce ... [and] that of agriculture" (*WN*, 428). In Book IV he examines these systems of political economy.

CHAPTER 1: "OF THE PRINCIPLE OF THE COMMERCIAL, OR MERCANTILE SYSTEM" (THE HISTORY)

In order to frame the logic of "the commercial, or mercantile system," Smith cites the "popular notion" that "wealth consists of money" (*WN*, 429) and that "[t]o grow rich is to get money" (*WN*, 429).

The mercantilist view of the wealth of a nation is a simple extrapolation of this popular usage: "A rich country, in the same manner as a rich man, is supposed to be a country abounding in money" (*WN*, 429). Following from this extrapolation, the initial mercantilist policy imperative was to accumulate and hoard bullion.

Indicative of this national obsession with money as wealth was the focus of European exploration in the Americas: "[T]he first enquiry of the Spaniards, when they arrived upon any unknown coast, used to be, if there was any gold or silver to be found in the neighbourhood?" (*WN*, 429).

The available evidence seemed to support this view that more money means greater wealth for the nation: the Dutch, for example, seemed to be achieving power by accumulating money.[1] And not only did the evidence seem to support this view, it enjoyed the imprimatur of philosophical legitimacy: John Locke endorsed it.[2]

But what was in the work of Locke a philosophical system of political economy became over time, according to Smith, a philosophical guise for

---

[1] Smith notes that mercantilism only makes sense in a multinational context. Even those who held these views recognized that a nation in isolation had no need to hoard money if there were no other nations with which to trade (*WN*, 430–1).

[2] See *LJA* (381).

the advancement of mercantile interests.[3] And with this transformation came an adjustment in the mercantilist policy prescriptions.

Hoarding bullion did not serve the interests of merchants: "When those countries became commercial, the merchants found this prohibition [on exporting bullion], upon many occasions, extremely inconvenient. They remonstrated, therefore, against this prohibition as hurtful to trade" (*WN*, 431). The mercantilists made the case that by using domestic stocks of bullion to buy raw materials to be worked up for re-export, "and [then these finished products] being ... sold at a large profit, might bring back much more treasure than was originally sent out to purchase them" (*WN*, 431). In short, the prohibition of bullion export undermined the very objective of mercantilism: accumulating monetary wealth.

With this strategic adjustment mercantilism took on a new form: the wealth of the nation was still measured in bullion, but the key to growing that wealth was not hoarding bullion, it was a positive trade balance. Prohibiting bullion exports put domestic traders at a disadvantage in the international marketplace because "the merchant who purchased a bill upon the foreign country [was] ... obliged to pay the banker who sold it, not only for the natural risk, trouble and expense of sending the money thither, but for the extraordinary risk arising from [evading] the prohibition" (*WN*, 432). This additional risk premium hurt the trade balance and caused bullion to leave the country, an unintended consequence of the policy meant to protect and grow the nation's stock of bullion.

"Those arguments were partly solid and partly sophistical" (*WN*, 433). The mercantilists were correct in saying that using bullion in trade "might frequently be advantageous to the country" (*WN*, 433) and that a prohibition is impossible to enforce completely given the incentive of profits to be made in trade. "But they were sophistical in supposing, that either to preserve or to augment the quantity of those metals required more the attention of government, than to preserve or to augment the quantity of any other such useful commodities, which the freedom of trade, without any such attention, never fails to supply in the proper quantity" (*WN*, 433).

The merchants inherited a philosophy of political economy from Locke and others, but their purpose was not philosophical – it was profit.

---

[3] While "mercantilist doctrine stressed the importance of national economic interests, it also contained implicitly the potential disharmony between particular commercial groups, individual merchants, and classes on one hand, and the welfare of the commonwealth as a whole, on the other" (Kammen, 41). See Evensky (2005, chapter 8) for more detail on this transformation.

They used sophistry to make the case for their position, and they were very successful in doing so because they took advantage of an asymmetry of information. Their case about trade was

by merchants to parliaments, and to the councils of princes, to nobles, and to country gentlemen; by those who were supposed to understand trade, to those who were conscious to themselves that they knew nothing about the matter. That foreign trade enriched the country, experience demonstrated to the nobles and country gentlemen, as well as to the merchants; but how, or in what manner, none of them knew well. The merchants knew perfectly in what manner it enriched themselves. It was their business to know it. But to know in what manner it enriched the country, was no part of their business. This subject never came into their consideration, but when they had occasion to apply to their country for some change in the laws relating to foreign trade. It then became necessary to say something about the beneficial effects of foreign trade, and the manner in which those effects were obstructed by the laws as they then stood. To the judges who were to decide the business, it appeared a most satisfactory account of the matter. (WN, 434)

When sophistry failed the merchants used their resources to exercise raw political power, imposing their policies on the nation. As a consequence, "in our own country and in our own times," the economic policies of the nation are guided by the merchants of the nation. Indeed, "[t]he title of Mun's book, England's Treasure in Foreign Trade, became a fundamental maxim in the political œconomy, not of England only, but of all other commercial countries" (WN, 434–5).

Given mercantilist's self-serving emphasis on pursuing a positive trade balance, the home trade, that inner circuit of trade "in which [(following Smith's analysis of the circuits of trade in Book II)] an equal capital affords the greatest revenue, and creates the greatest employment to the people of the country, was considered as subsidiary only to foreign trade" (WN, 435). The consequence was a significant distortion from the optimal flow of capital.

In pursuit of private profit, public progress was diminished.

CHAPTER 1: "OF THE PRINCIPLE OF THE COMMERCIAL, OR MERCANTILE SYSTEM" (CONTINUED)

Having presented his narrative on the emergence of mercantilism, Smith attacks its logic.

First target: the initial naïve notion that the government should and could control bullion flows.

Given its "small bulk and great value" bullion is the easiest of all commodities to trade. Thus "with perfect security ... the freedom of trade" will ensure that stocks of bullion will flow, according to "effectual demand," to the market where it can be put to the best advantage (*WN*, 435). Where the supply of gold and silver in "any country exceeds the effectual demand, no vigilance of government can prevent their exportation"[4] (*WN*, 436). It is, after all, not only easy to trade bullion, it is easy to smuggle it. Smith cites the fairly stable international price parity of gold and silver as empirical evidence of the easy flow of bullion in spite of restrictions. In contrast, the prices of bulkier, more easily restricted commodities "fluctuate continuously" (*WN*, 437). And, he adds, why worry about the amount of bullion in the nation? Unlike most other commodities there is, as he has explained in Book II, a reasonable substitute for bullion: paper.

A well regulated paper money will supply it [(the exchange needs of the nation)], not only without any inconveniency, but, in some cases, with some advantages. Upon every account, therefore, the attention of government never was so unnecessarily employed, as when directed to watch over the preservation or increase of the quantity of money in any country. (*WN*, 437)[5]

Certainly an individual feels wealthier with more money in his pocket "because money is the known and established instrument of commerce, for which every thing is readily given in exchange" (*WN*, 438). "It is[, however,] not for its own sake that men desire money, but for the sake of what they can purchase with it" (*WN*, 439). As a nation, all there is to buy is that which comes from the "annual produce of ... [the] land and labor" (*WN*, 439). Individuals may see money as wealth, but for a nation it is the produce of the land and labor that constitutes its wealth.

As for the notion that, being more durable than, for example, wine, bullion is a medium meant for hoarding wealth, Smith says this is absurd. "Gold and silver, whether in the shape of coin or of plate, are utensils, it must be remembered, as much as the furniture of the kitchen" (*WN*, 440). Pots and pans are also more durable than wine. Would we hoard more of these utensils than we could ever hope to use rather than exchanging

---

4 For example: "All the sanguinary laws of Spain and Portugal are not able to keep their gold and silver at home" (*WN*, 436).

5 The "complaint, ... more common than" any other, that money is too scarce is not a function of too little money, but of irresponsible use of credit (*WN*, 437). The demand for credit is indeed keen when "bold projectors" (*WN*, 304) draw more out of the bank than they can pay back. But the problem here lies not in the quantity of currency, but in the people and their choices.

some for wine? No. We stock our kitchen with utensils based on the need we have for their services, and so it should be with bullion.

Regarding the argument that hoarding bullion is essential for national defense – quite to the contrary:

> It is not always necessary to accumulate gold and silver, in order to enable a country to carry on foreign wars.... Fleets and armies are maintained, not with gold and silver, but with consumable goods. The nation which, from the annual produce of its domestick industry ... has the wherewithal to purchase those consumable goods in distant countries, can maintain foreign wars there. (WN, 440–1)

He points out that during "[t]he last French war" (WN, 441–2) there was no treasury accumulation to cover the costs of large expenditures overseas, and yet there was no scarcity of funds to cover domestic needs, concluding that "[t]he enormous expence of the late war, therefore, must have been chiefly defrayed, not by the exportation of gold and silver, but by that of British commodities of some kind or other" (WN, 443). Indeed, "during the war ... [manufacturers] have a double demand upon them" (WN, 444), the normal demand for what has "usually been consumed in the country" and the added demand for "provisions for the army" (WN, 444). As a consequence,

> [i]n the midst of the most destructive foreign war ... the greater part of manufactures may frequently flourish greatly; and, on the contrary, they may decline on the return to peace. They may flourish amidst the ruin of their country, and begin to decay upon the return to its prosperity. (WN, 444–5)

Mercantilist rhetoric is only nominally about concerns for national security or growing the wealth of the nation. Its real agenda is factional power and private advantage.

The mercantilists have sold the nation a bill of goods. The wealth of the nation is not served by treating trade as a zero-sum game in which we "win" by generating a positive trade balance. It is productive labor that generates the nation's wealth. Free and fair trade facilitates the development of productive labor by expanding the extent of the market:

> The importation of gold and silver is not the principal, much less the sole benefit which a nation derives from its foreign trade. Between whatever places foreign trade is carried on, they all of them derive two distinct benefits from it. It carries out that surplus part of the produce of their land and labour for which there is no demand among them, and brings back in return for it something else for which there is a demand. It gives a value to their superfluities, by exchanging them for something else, which may satisfy a part of their wants, and increase their enjoyments. By means of it, the narrowness of the home market does not hinder the division of labour in any particular branch of art or manufacture from

being carried to the highest perfection. By opening a more extensive market for whatever part of the produce of their labour may exceed the home consumption, it encourages them to improve its productive powers, and to augment its annual produce to the utmost, and thereby to increase the real revenue and wealth of the society. (*WN*, 446–7)

Of all the policies the mercantilists have imposed on the nation, the most perverse have been the establishment and maintenance of colonies with which trade has been managed in order to source raw materials and vent surplus. Exploration opened up significant new opportunities for trade, but by establishing colonies and colonial policies designed for their advantage the mercantilists undermined the fruitfulness of those opportunities.

In the case of the Americas the golden opportunities lay not in the gold and silver to be found, or in the markets that could be managed, but in the extension of the market: "By opening a new and inexhaustible market to all the commodities of Europe, it [(the Americas)] gave occasion to new divisions of labour and improvements of art" (*WN*, 448).

The opportunities were even greater in the East because those nations (China, Indostan, Japan) were much more advanced than those of America (Mexico, Peru), and thus more ripe for constructive engagement and mutual benefit. But "Europe ... has hitherto derived much less advantage from its commerce with the East Indies, than from that with America" (*WN*, 448–9). In the East nations followed the Dutch mercantilist example, "vest[ing] their whole East India commerce in an exclusive company [which established restraints on this trade in order to monopolize it. As a result,] ... no great nation in Europe has ever yet had the benefit of a free commerce to the East Indies" (*WN*, 449).

Mercantilism was the prevailing system of thought in the age of colonization, so ...

it necessarily became the great object of political œconomy to diminish as much as possible the importation of foreign goods for home-consumption, and to increase as much as possible the exportation of the produce of domestick industry. Its two great engines for enriching the country, therefore, were restraints upon importation, and encouragements to exportation. (*WN*, 450)

High duties and prohibitions became the tools to limit importation, while "[e]xportation was encouraged sometimes by drawbacks, sometimes by bounties, sometimes by advantageous treaties of commerce with foreign states, and sometimes by the establishment of colonies in distant countries" (*WN*, 450).

CHAPTER 2: "OF RESTRAINTS UPON THE IMPORTATION FROM FOREIGN COUNTRIES OF SUCH GOODS AS CAN BE PRODUCED AT HOME"

With restraints on importation "the monopoly of the home-market is more or less secured to the domestic industry employed in producing them" (*WN*, 452). Citing several examples, Smith suggests that those "not well acquainted with the laws of the customs" (*WN*, 452) would be very surprised at how many such monopolies exist in Great Britain.

There is no doubt that the effect of this policy is to channel capital into the advantaged industries and in turn to increase their production. The question remains: Is this good for the nation? No, says Smith, because it distorts the natural flow of capital.

In any given cycle of production there is only so much capital to allocate; "[n]o regulation of commerce" (*WN*, 453) can change this. Writing in terms that anticipate his famous "invisible hand" passage, Smith asserts:

It can only divert a part of it into a direction into which it might not otherwise have gone; and it is by no means certain that this artificial direction is likely to be more advantageous *to the society* than that which it would have gone of its own accord.

Every individual is continually exerting himself to find out the most advantageous employment for whatever capital he can command. It is his own advantage, indeed, and not that of the society, which he has in view. But the study of his own advantage naturally, or rather necessarily leads him to prefer that employment which is most advantageous to the society. (*WN*, 453–4, emphasis added)

There is no need to protect the home market to ensure that it gets it proper share of capital. If the home market is the optimal allocation of capital, capital will flow there of its own accord. Indeed, as the inner, quickest, and most secure circuit the home trade will fill with the capital it warrants before capital seeks other options.

Home is ... the center, if I may say so, round which the capitals of inhabitants of every country are continually circulating. (*WN*, 455)

He has laid out this analysis already in Book II: in the natural course of events as this most secure and quickest circuit fills, the rate of profit falls. At some point the merchant finds attractive opportunities for his capital in the second circuit of capital, the foreign trade of consumption. And finally as that second circuit fills, capital spills into the slowest-velocity, least-secure circuit – the carrying trade.

His analysis of natural capital flows demonstrates that unfettered capital finds its best advantage quite effectively. Thank you ever so much for your concern about our nation's well-being, Mr. Mercantilist, but there is no need for government to manage or manipulate the flow of capital. The natural flow serves the nation most effectively for the incentives always attract it to the place where it sets into motion the most productive labor. He concludes this point with that most famous of Smithian passages:

As every individual ... endeavours as much as he can both to employ his capital in the support of domestick industry, and so to direct that industry that its produce may be of the greatest value; every individual necessarily labours to render the annual revenue of society as great as he can. He generally, indeed, neither intends to promote the publick interest, nor knows how he is promoting it. By preferring the support of domestick to that of foreign industry, he intends only his own security; and by directing that industry in such a manner as its produce may be of the greatest value, he intends only his own gain, and he is in this, as in many other cases, led by an invisible hand to promote an end which was no part of his intention. (*WN*, 456)

The national leader who presumes that he can optimally micro manage the flow of capital is arrogant and destructive. Granting merchants monopolies in the market is, in effect, to do just that because capital is diverted from its natural course in order to exploit the unnatural advantages these monopolies create.

"The taylor does not attempt to make his own shoes, the shoemaker ... his own clothes, ... [and t]he farmer attempts to make neither" (*WN*, 456–7). They each work at their "advantage" (*WN*, 457) and purchase the other necessaries with their surplus. "What is prudence in the conduct of every private family, can scarce be folly in that of a great kingdom" (*WN*, 457). As with families so too as nations, each should "seek the advantageous, and to shun the disadvantageous employment" (*WN*, 116), dividing up the labor and exchanging surpluses to mutually benefit from the gains from trade. Freedom facilitates this flow.

Just as perverse as regulations that artificially direct capital into domestic circuits producing commodities that could have been purchased more cheaply abroad are those that direct capital away from the domestic circuit. They too distort the flow of capital from "its natural course" (*WN*, 457) and reduce the productive power of the nation. Even policies designed to spur nascent industries are a distortion, for the optimal growth path is most likely to be pursued when "both capital and industry [have] been left to find out their natural employments" (*WN*, 458).

Smith's concern here, as always, is long-term growth. He laid out his growth theory based on capital accumulation and circulation in Book II. Here he writes that but for the distorting mercantile policies "[i]n every period its [(the nation's)] revenue might have been the greatest which its capital could afford, and both the capital and revenue might have been augmented with the greatest possible rapidity" (*WN*, 458).

Returning to the source of these "restraints upon the importation from foreign countries of such goods as can be produced at home," Smith notes that "[m]erchants and manufacturers are the people who derive the greatest advantage from this monopoly of the home market" (*WN*, 459).

One might imagine that at least with respect to agricultural goods (live cattle, corn, and salt provisions)[6] it would be the "country gentleman and farmers" (*WN*, 461) pushing for trade advantages. But in fact the clamor for policies that offer bounties on these items in years of plenty and encourage importation in years of scarcity comes not from the country gentleman and farmers. It comes from the merchants who, absent these policies, would enjoy less shipping business.

Smith writes of the country gentleman and farmers that they "are, to their great honor, of all people, the least subject to the wretched spirit of monopoly," in part because their very dispersion makes collusion difficult. In contrast, the

merchants and manufacturers, who being collected in towns, and naturally accustomed to that exclusive corporation spirit which prevails in them,[7] naturally endeavour to obtain against all their countrymen, the same exclusive privilege which they generally possess against the inhabitants of their respective towns. They accordingly seem to have been the original inventors of those restraints upon the importation of foreign goods, which secure to them the monopoly of the home-market. (*WN*, 462)

Under the guise of enhancing the wealth of the nation, the mercantilists advocate for a trading system that serves themselves. Given a lack of clear understanding of their own interests and deferring to the "expertise" of the merchants, the country gentlemen and farmers joined the mercantilists in supporting policies to manage trade.

There are only "two cases" (*WN*, 463) in which this might make sense.

[6] In the course of this discussion he writes: "The small quantity of salt provisions imported from Ireland since their importation was rendered free, *is experimental proof* that our graziers have nothing to apprehend from it" (*WN*, 460–1, emphasis added). Again we see Smith's commitment to empiricism.

[7] Smith examines and explains the *quid pro quo* between king and towns that led to this corporate spirit in Book II, chapter 3.

One is "for the defence of the country ... [While monopoly reduces domestic opulence, defense is more important than opulence.] The act of navigation, therefore, very properly endeavours to give sailors and shipping of Great Britain the monopoly of the trade of their own country" (WN, 463) in order to ensure sufficient manpower and vessels for the navy when the need arises.

Noting that these navigation acts were aimed at the Dutch for whom Britain felt "the most violent animosity" (WN, 464), he writes:

> It is not impossible, therefore, that some of the regulations of this famous act may have proceeded from national animosity. They are as wise, however, as if they had all been dictated by the most deliberate wisdom. (WN, 464)

Classic Smith: in the course of institutional development, good outcomes sometimes flow from the unintended consequences of bad motives.

A second case that makes sense is a tax on a foreign good that is a suitable substitute for a domestic good that is itself being taxed. This is simply a matter of fair play. Untaxed foreign goods should not be allowed to compete with a taxed domestic good. Some individuals, however, take this logic too far. They assert that any domestic tax raises the domestic cost of living, in turn the cost of labor, and ultimately the domestic cost of production. As a result they argue for a tax on all imports to compensate for this effect of domestic taxes.

Smith raises doubts about the premise here, saying he will return to the effect of taxes on cost of production in Book V. But no matter the premise, he rejects the logic for two reasons: first, the size of the effect, if any, is too difficult to measure, so setting such a tax is pure guesswork. Second, if such taxes were imposed on the necessaries of life, the effect would be to further impoverish the poorest workers for they will bear the burden most harshly. Any policy that would unduly burden them is, by his standards of a good society, perverse.

There are two other cases for taxing imports that at least warrant consideration. One is retaliation for obstructive barriers imposed by another nation: "Revenge ... dictates retaliation, and ... [n]ations ... seldom fail to retaliate" (WN, 467). But such actions are often advocated by those who will enjoy the advantage that comes with retaliation; they are then protectionism in disguise.

France has been a leader in protectionism because "Mr. Colbert, ... notwithstanding his great abilities, seems in this case to have been imposed upon by the sophistry of the merchants and manufacturers, who are always demanding a monopoly against their countrymen"

(*WN*, 467). Such policies were, at least in part, the cause of war with the Dutch in 1672, and their amelioration was part of the price of peace in 1678. "It was about the same time that the French and English began mutually to oppress each other's industry ... [and t]he spirit of hostility ... has subsisted between the two nations ever since" (*WN*, 467–8).

Retaliatory tariffs may be worthwhile if there is reasonable expectation that the result will be a de-escalation. But absent that, such retaliation makes no sense because the punishment aimed at one's enemy is in fact an effective tax imposed on all at home.

Smith notes that if after a long period of mutual oppression of trade cooler heads prevail and a new regime is proposed that opens up trade, such a change should be done gradually. The structure of the economy in both countries has been based on protection and a rapid adjustment to free trade would mean dramatic and painful adjustments for many workers:

Humanity may in this case require that the freedom of trade should be restored only by slow gradations, and with a good deal of reserve and circumspection. (*WN*, 469)

Again we hear Smith's fundamental concern that workers be treated in a humane fashion as the world is shaped by those in power. We also hear Smith the system builder rejecting the simple solutions of the "man of system" who would immediately impose the dictates of his system in any context.[8] For Smith, thoughtful general principles should guide policy, but policy must be shaped to accommodate current realities. Apropos of this, returning to the advisability of retaliation in trade he notes that to play this geopolitical game requires a keen mind well-tuned to intricacies of current political dynamics:

To judge whether such retaliations are likely to produce [the desired] ... effect, does not, perhaps, belong so much to the science of a legislator, whose deliberations ought to be governed by general principles which are always the same, as to the skill of that insidious and crafty animal, vulgarly called a statesman or politician, whose councils are directed by the momentary fluctuations of affairs. (*WN*, 468)

This reflects Smith's conception of history, of philosophy, and of his role as a moral philosopher. At one level history represents a record of a series of short-term, often chaotic "momentary fluctuations." This is the realm of politics. But underlying these apparently chaotic movements are "general principles" that can be discerned from the long flow of history.

---

[8] See *TMS* (232–4).

Informed by the moral philosopher who has studied this history and has culled from it the general principles of constructive arrangements that encourage progress, the science of a legislator can help the statesman to shape more constructive institutions for a society and thus enhance the probability of its progress. The raison d'être of *The Wealth of Nations* in particular and of Smith's work more generally is to make such a contribution as a moral philosopher.

While adjustments from constrained trade to free trade can be very disruptive if done too quickly, they should be made. Free markets are very adaptive, so while some dislocation is inevitable, with freedom and security comes progress.

Smith cites as a case in point of adaptive markets the economy's adjustment to "the reduction of the army and navy at the end of the late war" (*WN*, 469). The numbers thrown into the labor market were huge relative to the size of that market, but "[n]ot only no great convulsion, but no sensible disorder arose from so great a change in the situation of more than a hundred thousand men" (*WN*, 470). The market absorbed the labor of these former soldiers and sailors because by law[9] they were free to flow to their best advantage. This should serve as a model:

Let the same natural liberty of exercising what species of industry they please be restored to all his majesty's subjects ... that is, break down the exclusive privileges of corporations, and repeal the statute of apprenticeship ... and add to these the repeal of the law of settlements ... and neither the publick nor the individuals will suffer much more from the occasional disbanding some particular classes of manufacturers, than from that of soldiers. (*WN*, 470–1)

Unfortunately, the clamor about the dislocations that would result from such free and unfettered markets comes from the loud and powerful voices of those who benefit from the status quo. Given the power of these voices, free and unfettered markets are very unlikely:

To expect, indeed, that the freedom of trade should ever be entirely restored in Great Britain, is as absurd as to expect that an Oceana or Utopia should ever be established in it. Not only the prejudices of the publick, but what is much more unconquerable, the private interests of many individuals, irresistibly oppose it. (*WN*, 471)

Foremost among these interested individuals are the members of the mercantile faction. They "enflame their workmen, to attack with violence

---

[9] "Soldiers and seamen ... when discharged from the king's service are at liberty to exercise any trade, within any town or place of Great Britain or Ireland" (*WN*, 470).

and outrage the proposers of any such regulation" (*WN*, 471) that would reduce their market advantages. And they use the returns from the monopoly advantages they enjoy to influence and even shape the political process:

This monopoly has so much increased the number of some particular tribes of them, that, like an overgrown standing army, they have become formidable to the government, and upon many occasions intimidate the legislature. The member of parliament who supports every proposal for strengthening this monopoly, is sure to acquire not only the reputation of understanding trade, but great popularity and influence with an order of men whose numbers and wealth render them of great importance. If he opposes them, on the contrary, and still more if he has authority enough to be able to thwart them, neither the most acknowledged probity, nor the highest rank, nor the greatest publick services can protect him from the most infamous abuse and detraction, from personal insults, nor sometimes from real danger, arising from the insolent outrage of furious and disappointed monopolists. (*WN*, 471)

CHAPTER 3: "OF THE EXTRAORDINARY RESTRAINTS UPON THE IMPORTATION OF GOODS OF ALMOST ALL KINDS, FROM THOSE COUNTRIES WITH WHICH THE BALANCE IS SUPPOSED TO BE DISADVANTAGEOUS"

Part I: "Of the Unreasonableness of those Restraints even upon the Principles of the Commercial System"

A basic tenet of the mercantile system[10] is that it is appropriate "[t]o lay extraordinary restraints upon the importation of goods of almost all kinds, from those particular countries with which the balance of trade is supposed to be disadvantageous" (*WN*, 473). This policy, born of "national prejudice and animosity" (*WN*, 474), is, according to Smith, "unreasonable ... even upon the principles of the commercial system" itself (*WN*, 474).

The policy suffers from two basic flaws. First, the bilateral mentality that underlies it obscures the multilateral reality of trade. It might well be that a nation's optimal global trade position includes a deficit

---

[10] Note: For consistency I use "mercantile system" while up to this point Smith is referring to the "commercial system." For reasons outlined later, he shifts to "mercantile system" in later chapters.

with one country among its many trading partners. Second, the whole logic depends on a political arithmetic that may be quite problematic. The "custom-house books and the course of exchange" (*WN*, 475) are notoriously inaccurate and thus a poor basis for gauging the trade balance. This problem stems from the fact that the multilateral nature of credit makes bilateral credit conditions a poor measure of trade activity, and differences in mint standards and practices among countries can make measuring the real value of transactions between nations problematic.

In a long "Digression concerning Banks of Deposit, particularly concerning that of Amsterdam," Smith examines the history of Amsterdam as a classic case in the creation of "bank money" (*WN*, 482) to demonstrate that "exchange between countries which pay in what is called bank money, and those which pay in common currency, should generally appear to be in favour of the former" (*WN*, 488). This is so because bank money maintains its value more securely than common currency.

Part II: "Of the Unreasonableness of those extraordinary Restraints upon other Principles"

Having demonstrated that even if we accept the principles of the mercantile system effectively implementing policies to generate a trade surplus are problematic, Smith returns to his assault on the mercantile principles themselves.

His point is clear and concise.

Trade is not a zero-sum game. Treating it as a zero-sum game and implementing policies to "win" at the trade game can turn it into a negative-sum game. At its best, trade that is free, unfettered, and fair is a positive-sum game:

Nothing ... can be more absurd than this whole doctrine of the balance of trade, upon which, not only these restraints, but almost all other regulations of commerce are founded. When two places trade with one another, this doctrine supposes that, if the balance be even, neither of them either loses or gains; but if it leans in any degree to one side, that one of them loses and the other gains in proportion to its declension from the exact equilibrium. Both suppositions are false. A trade which is forced by means of bounties and monopolies, may be, and commonly is disadvantageous to the country in whose favour it is meant to be established.... But that trade which, without force or constraint, is naturally and regularly carried on between any two places is always advantageous, though not always equally so, to both. (*WN*, 488–9)

This gain, he is careful to note, is measured in production, not bullion.

The web of trade connections is so very complex that tracing the ultimate source of gains from trade is very difficult, but there are mutual gains: "No goods are sent abroad but those for which the demand is supposed to be greater abroad than at home, and of which the returns consequently, it is expected, will be of more value at home than the commodities exported" (WN, 491). As the value of the nation's production is augmented by this exchange, so too is its capital stock and thus too its capacity for growth in the progress of opulence. Free trade, therefore, enhances the wealth of the nation. Unfortunately:

nations have been taught that their interest consisted in beggaring all their neighbours. Each nation has been made to look with an invidious eye upon the prosperity of all the nations with which it trades, and to consider their gain as its own loss. Commerce, which ought naturally to be, among nations, as among individuals, a bond of union and friendship, has become the most fertile source of discord and animosity. The capricious ambition of kings and ministers has not, during the present and the preceding century, been more fatal to the repose of Europe, than the impertinent jealousy of merchants and manufacturers.[11] The violence and injustice of the rulers of mankind is an ancient evil, for which, I am afraid, the nature of human affairs can scarce admit of a remedy. But the mean rapacity, the monopolizing spirit of merchants and manufacturers, who neither are, nor ought to be the rulers of mankind, though it cannot perhaps be corrected, may very easily be prevented from disturbing the tranquility of any body but themselves. (WN, 493)

"[T]he interested sophistry of merchants and manufacturers [has] confounded the common sense of mankind [when in fact t]heir interest is … directly opposite to that of the great body of the people" (WN, 494). As a consequence Europe is burdened by a system of restraints on trade that reduces the wealth of each nation and pits nation against nation.

As an example of this absurdity Smith cites the British trade relationship with France. It is adversarial and includes many mutual restraints. Referencing his extent of the market and his circuits of trade analyses, Smith asserts:

France[, being very large and very near,] … could afford a market at least eight times more extensive, and, on account of the superior frequency of the returns, four and twenty times more advantageous, than that which our North American colonies ever afforded. The trade of Great Britain would be just as advantageous to France. (WN, 496)

---

[11] John Maynard Keynes expresses something similar in his "Concluding Notes on the Social Philosophy Towards Which the General Theory Might Lead" (Keynes, 381–3).

But there is a natural wariness of a strong, wealthy, close neighbor, for such is a potentially formidable opponent. The mercantilists on both sides of the Channel have exploited this fear, announcing "with all the *passionate confidence of interested falsehood*, the certain ruin of each, in consequence of that unfavorable balance of trade, which, they pretend, would be the infallible effect of an unrestrained commerce with the other" (*WN*, 496, emphasis added).

These mercantile interests have been heard again and again across Europe, predicting doom and gloom if trade were freed and the balance of trade was not attended to, but those that have adopted a free trade policy, "instead of being ruined ... have been enriched by it" (*WN*, 497).

If there is a balance that nations should be concerned about, it is not the balance of trade, it "is the balance of the annual produce and consumption" (*WN*, 497). If nations produce more than they consume, capital stock grows. It is a growing capital stock that fuels the ever finer division of labor and in turn grows *The Wealth of Nations*.

A Digression for Context on Smith's Unfolding Narrative in Book IV

It is worthwhile to pause here and reflect on Book IV's narrative in the context of events that were unfolding as Smith completed *The Wealth of Nations* because that context has a significant impact on the evolution of Book IV – particularly on the chapters to come – as Smith drafts the first edition of *WN*.

At this point in his Book IV narrative Smith has already spent a great deal of ink attacking the mercantile system's principles. His purpose is, however, not simply to expose mercantilism's theoretical errors. Smith is determined to demonstrate that the mercantilists have sold the British nation on a "golden dream" (*WN*, 947) – but it is fool's gold. It is a policy program predicated on the promise of immense national wealth from a colonial empire, but it is in fact a self-serving program for mercantilists' benefit at the nation's expense.

In the chapters that follow we will see that as he was developing the original version of Book IV, and in his subsequent revision to Book IV, the harshness of his criticism grows. To understand why, it is useful to consider the evolving context that is shaping Smith's evolving view of mercantilism.

In his *Lectures on Jurisprudence*, which Smith delivered as a professor at Glasgow during the 1762–3 and 1763–4 sessions (hereafter LJA and LJB respectively),[12] he refers to the "system" of Mun to which Locke had given "a more philosophical air" (*LJA*, 381; see also *LJB*, 508). He mentions the merchants in these lectures, but theirs is only a cameo appearance[13] related to their desire to export bullion "under certain regulations and directions" (*LJA*, 385): "[Upon Parliament's decision to] prohibit the exportation of money ... The merchants ... complained of this hardship, and were then allowed to export money to a small extent" (*LJB*, 509).

At that time, his concern with the mercantile system was that the pursuit of a positive trade balance distorts the flow of money and thus undermines its value as a tool of commerce:

Tis not in money that opulence consists, ... it consists in the abundance of the necessarys and conveniences of life and the industry of the people; money is only beneficiall in circulating of these. (*LJA*, 378) ...

[Thus] regulations [on money] are ... prejudiciall as far as they take effect, for they endeavour to throw more into the channel of circulation than is naturally proper. (*LJA*, 386)

When he gave these lectures, mercantilism was not a major concern for Smith.

At the end of 1763, having accepted Charles Townshend's offer to tour Europe as the tutor to the Duke of Buccleuch (Ross, 196), Smith left his position at Glasgow and traveled with the Duke to France. That year, 1763, is a significant year for British trade policy:

[Starting in] 1763 ... [mercantile] interests ... so dominated politics that men observed that mercantilism had changed from the control of trade in the interest of national policy, to the control of national policy in the interest of trade.... The increasing importance of Parliament [and its "factionalized and undisciplined party system" (Kammen, 97)] seemed to encourage efforts by powerful groups seeking to influence regulation by political pressure. (Kammen, 75, 95)

So just as Smith and the Duke were leaving for France, the political power of the mercantile interests in parliament was expanding.

It was in Paris that Smith first got a close-up view of a powerful mercantile policy in practice:

[12] "LJ(A) owes its origin to Adam Smith's Jurisprudence course as it was delivered in 1762–3, and LJ(B), in all probability, to that course as it was delivered in 1763–4" (Meek, Raphael, and Stein, 22). For more on the timing see Meek et. al (7–8).

[13] Similarly, the mercantile monopolies, most especially the East India Company, that become the focus of his scathing pen are only briefly mentioned in *LJA* (363) and *LJB* (497) as examples of monopolies. They are cited along with those paragons of evil the "butchers, brewers, [and] bakers" (*LJA*, 363) who collude through corporations.

The French [system was] ... particularly forward to favour their own manufactures by restraining the importation of such foreign goods as could come into competition with them. In this consisted a great part of the policy of Mr. Colbert, who, notwithstanding his great abilities, seems in this case to have been imposed upon by the sophistry of merchants and manufacturers, who are always demanding a monopoly against their countrymen. (*WN*, 467)

After three years on the Continent and a brief stay in London, Smith returned to his hometown, Kirkcaldy, Scotland, "to be with his mother and cousin" (Ross, 227). His compensation for escorting the Duke on this educational tour was a very comfortable "annuity" for life (Ross, 231). Smith was now a man of independent means.

In 1767 he arrived in Kirkcaldy with "[w]riting *WN* ... on his mind" (Ross, 227). His time his own, work on this project began in earnest.

In Kirkcaldy Smith was far from the center of political gravity in Britain. He was, in modern U.S. political vernacular: "outside the Beltway" – indeed, he was way outside the Beltway.

It is over 400 miles from London to Kirkcaldy. Given that the only source of news from London was travelers or mail and that the trip was long and arduous,[14] news did not travel fast and the news that did arrive was very fragmented. Smith was at a great informational distance from the "inside the Beltway" realities of London, including the growing influence of mercantilists that Kammen described earlier.

On 3 September 1772 Smith wrote to Sir William Pulteny that "[m]y book would have been ready for the Press by the beginning of this winter; but for interruptions ... [that] will oblige me to retard its publication for a few months longer" (*Correspondence*, 164). As 1772 came to a close he was ready to publish. But in fact publication took not "a few months longer" but a few years longer. Why?

Smith arrived in London in early 1773, manuscript in hand. He quickly integrated into the intellectual society of the city (Ross, 250–2). What he encountered was a keen debate about colonial policy. With a front row seat to the unfolding disintegration of the British colonial enterprise,

---

[14] "[B]y 1750 the Flying Stage Wagon had come into being, which progressed much more speedily [than a traditional stage wagon] as it changed horses all along the route. They could travel well in excess of the wagon speed of three miles an hour and the Alton and Farnham Machine of 1750 could accomplish a journey of forty-seven miles in one day by starting / at six o'clock in the morning and reaching its destination the same night. In 1754 the merchants of Manchester started a flying coach with the advertisement stating, 'incredible as it may appear, this coach will actually (barring accidents) arrive in London in four days and a half after leaving Manchester" (Sparkes, 38–9).

Smith spent several years in London transforming Book IV to more fully reflect the perverse nature of this costly enterprise.

There are numerous references in Book IV of the original 1776 edition[15] to dates, laws, and events post-1773. Clearly, after arriving in London in 1773, Smith was reworking his book. Just as clearly, as we will see, these changes reflect the fact that he was growing ever more angry about the power wielded by the self-serving mercantile faction and more concerned about the destructive consequences of its policy regime for Britain.

In an interesting shift in usage, what Smith refers to most often as the "commercial system" in the first part of Book IV becomes more often the "mercantile system" in the latter part where he does the most revising. This reflects his reworking of the latter part to express his growing focus on the mercantilist faction as the source of the destructive policies he refers to as the mercantile system.

The first edition of *The Wealth of Nations* was finally published on 9 March 1776. In 1777 Smith pursued a position as a commissioner of customs.

Following the death in 1777 of Archibald Menzies, one of the Commissioners, Smith announced his candidacy to Strahan [(his well-connected publisher located in London)] on 27 October 1777, and asked him to find out how matters stood at the Treasury Board, claiming, however: "I am not apt to be over-sanguine in my expectations." (Ross, 306)

Clearly Smith desired the position.

Why would a man with a very comfortable annuity pursue such a position? "Financial inducement could not have been a strong factor ... [because] he offered to give up the pension ... he held from [the Duke of] Buccleuch on receiving the Customs appointment" (Ross, 306).[16] I believe Smith desired the position for the insider's perspective on the customhouse that being a commissioner would afford him.[17] Customs

---

[15] R. H. Campbell and A. S. Skinner, general editors, and W. B. Todd, textual editor of *Wealth of Nations* published as a part of the Oxford Press' *Glasgow Edition of the Works and Correspondence of Adam Smith*, deserve the undying gratitude of any Smith scholar for their incredibly valuable notations that allow the reader to determine what revisions were done and when they were done.

[16] "Smith appears to have initiated the process by which he received his appointment and expressed excitement concerning the job, emphasizing in this correspondence not the financial aspect (the position paid £600 per annum) but his interest in the job itself" (Anderson, Shughart, and Tollison, 743).

[17] Indicative of the value of this inside perspective, he writes in his 1784 revision: "The variety of goods of which the importation into Great Britain is prohibited, either absolutely,

oversaw the very issues on which he was now so keenly focused: trade in general and mercantilist policies in particular.

Whatever Smith's reason for pursuing the position, he received it and his experience in customs clearly informed his revisions to the 1784 edition of *The Wealth of Nations*: these are by far the most significant revisions he makes to the work. In the Advertisement to the 1784 edition he writes:

I have made several additions, particularly to the chapter upon Drawbacks, and to that upon Bounties; likewise a new chapter entitled, *The Conclusion of the Mercantile System.* (WN, 8)

With this context in mind, we now turn to those significantly revised chapters and his new chapter.

CHAPTER 4: "OF DRAWBACKS"

Chapter 4 begins: "Merchants and manufacturers are not contented with the monopoly of the home market, but desire likewise the most extensive foreign sale for their goods" (WN, 499). Because their own government has no control in those foreign markets, the only way to create an advantage there is by domestic policies that subsidize, or at the least do not penalize, sales in those foreign markets.

"Drawbacks seem to be the most reasonable [of these. They] ... allow the merchant to draw back upon exportation, either the whole or part of whatever excise or inland duty is imposed upon domestick industry" (WN, 499). As such they do not distort the flow of capital; they simply eliminate any distortion that a duty might cause:

They tend not to overturn that balance which naturally establishes itself among all the various employments of the society; but to hinder it from being overturned by the duty ... [and thus they] preserve, what it is in most cases advantageous to preserve, the natural division and distribution of labour in the society. (WN, 499)

Chapter 4 goes on to explore issues related to drawbacks in particular and regulation more generally.

Smith emphasizes that regulation is only as effective as its enforcement. In the case of trade regulations the effectiveness of enforcement is inversely related to the porousness of the borders. So "[i]n a country of so extensive a coast as our North American and West Indian colonies,

or under certain circumstances, greatly exceeds what can easily be suspected by those who are not well acquainted with the laws of the customs" (WN, 453).

where authority was always so very slender" (*WN*, 502), trade regulation was very difficult and smuggling was the norm.[18] For example, Madeira wine comes from an island well off the coast so it was easy for colonial ships to avoid duties on this wine.

His position on drawbacks is that if they level the playing field in free trade they make sense. However, those that simply fill the pockets of monopolists because the goods would have been shipped in any case, as was the case with "exportation of European goods to our American colonies" (*WN*, 504), are a distortion.

CHAPTER 5: "OF BOUNTIES"

In effect a bounty "pay[s] them [(foreigners)] for buying" our goods (*WN*, 505). It is "pretended" by those who advocate the "mercantile system" that bounties enable our domestic manufacturers to sell cheap overseas, thereby encouraging more industry at home and "enrich[ing] the whole country" (*WN*, 505). But such an encouragement actually perversely distorts the behavior of the merchant.

If the free market does not offer him "a price which replaces to him, with the ordinary profits of stock, the whole capital employed" (*WN*, 505), this is a valuable signal that he should redirect his capital to other pursuits. A bounty, by distorting this signal, encourages an artificially expanded supply. It is, in effect, a subsidy that covers that part of the capital expenditure not compensated by the market price.

"[E]very operation [of this encouragement] eats up a part of the capital employed in it.... [I]f all other trades resembled it, there would soon be no capital left in the country" (*WN*, 505). Policies that systematically reduce the capital stock of the country impoverish the nation.

Bounties not only waste capital, they force trade into "a channel much less advantageous than that in which it would naturally run" (*WN*, 506). Smith examines the corn bounty as example of such a distortion.

An "ingenious and well-informed" (*WN*, 506) supporter of the mercantile system has demonstrated that this bounty led to a greater value of corn being exported than imported. This is not however, Smith notes, the full measure of the effect.

By encouraging exports the bounty tends to raise the domestic price of corn. In good years the bounty adds extra encouragement to the

---

[18] This is past tense because it is part of a 1784 addition, referring to events "[b]efore the revolt of our North American colonies" (*WN*, 500).

natural vent of the surplus, thus keeping domestic prices unnaturally high. With less of the surplus on hand from those good years, when bad years come there is less stored corn to meet demand, pushing up the price. Thus the bounty imposes a double tax. The first is the one that must be collected to cover the cost of the bounty itself. The "second tax, ... by much the heaviest of the two" (WN, 508), is the higher domestic price that all must pay for corn. "So very heavy a tax upon the first necessary of life must either reduce the subsistence of the labouring poor, or it must occasion some augmentation in their pecuniary wages" (WN, 508).

Either possibility harms the economy.

If it is the former "it must reduce the ability of the labouring poor to educate and bring up their children ... [and it] tends to restrain the population" (WN, 508). A progressively larger, more well-educated population is of all the resources of society, for Smith, the most productive. So "reducing the subsistence of the laboring poor" is a significant negative effect of a corn bounty.

If the effect is to artificially raise workers' wages, this will "reduce the ability of the employers of the poor, to employ so great a number as they otherwise might do, and must, so far, tend to restrain the industry of the country" (WN, 508). Thus the effect of the corn bounty is "in the long run, rather to diminish, than to augment, the whole market and consumption of corn" (WN, 509).

But doesn't this rise in price caused by the bounty encourage more domestic production?

No: "It is not the real, but the nominal price of corn, which can in any considerable degree be affected by the bounty" (WN, 509). This is so because "the money price of corn regulates that of all other home-made commodities" (WN, 509).

Corn price is the foundation of input prices across the economy because, as the basis of subsistence, corn price significantly influences labor costs. Corn price also significantly influences the cost of the rude produce of the land because corn price ultimately determines, as he demonstrates in Book I, the entire rent structure on the land. Thus, as corn price rises so does the cost of production and in turn the price level, making any rise in corn only nominal in value.

This inflationary effect, the rise in nominal or money prices, is in effect a "degradation in the value of silver" (WN, 510). If silver falls because of increased fertility of mines and there are not distortions in the global trading system, the effect is of no great consequence because the price level and the means of purchasing rise together. But if silver falls in a particular country because of "political institutions of a particular country," as is the case of the corn bounty, then the effect can be "a matter of great consequence." It can "make every body really poorer" (*WN*, 510).

Spain and Portugal, as the "proprietors of the mines" (*WN*, 510), sought, following mercantilist principles, to restrict the flow of bullion out of their borders. But "[w]hen you dam up a stream of water, as soon as the dam is full, as much water must run over the dam-head as if there was no dam at all" (*WN*, 511). And so it has been for Spain and Portugal. "[B]y all accounts, notwithstanding these restraints, [the flow of bullion out is] very near equal to the annual importation" (*WN*, 512).

Restraints do not stem the flow, but they do have a dramatic perverse effect. The level behind the dam is much higher than that outside the dam. The higher the dam the greater the difference. For Spain and Portugal this deep domestic pool of gold and silver has meant artificially high prices inside and artificially low prices outside of the country. As a result, imports are in artificially high demand and domestic production is severely discouraged. Eliminate the dam and domestic industry would begin to thrive.

"The [British] bounty upon the exportation of corn necessarily operates exactly in the same way as this absurd policy of Spain and Portugal" (*WN*, 514). So who benefits from this bounty? "The corn merchants" do for it increases the activity of their trading business in both good and bad years (*WN*, 514).

"Our country gentlemen, when they imposed the high duties on the importation of foreign corn, ... and when they established the bounty, seem to have imitated the conduct of our manufacturers" (*WN*, 515). But their design was ill informed because "they did not act with that compleat comprehension of their own interest" (*WN*, 516). Corn is a unique commodity. It is central to the production system of the economy and thus underlies the price structure. Unlike other producers who can capture the benefits of a monopoly on home trade, a monopoly on corn production only begets nominal, not real returns.

As with many other proposals from "our merchants and manufacturers" (*WN*, 516), this regulation suffers from the "general objection which can be made of all the different expedients of the mercantile system; the objection of forcing some part of the industry of the country into a [trade] channel less advantageous than that which it would run of its own accord" (*WN*, 516), thus reducing the wealth of the nation.

If one really wanted to increase production of a particular commodity the appropriate bounty would be on production, not on export. But this is not the kind of bounty one normally sees and the reason is clear. It is export bounties that serve the mercantile interests. Indeed, "[o]f all the expedients of the mercantile system ... it is this one of which they are fondest" (*WN*, 517).

There may be some constructive applications of a bounty on production. For example, the case is made that the bounty benefiting fisheries contributes to national defense. It is said to create a readily available pool of nautical expertise for the navy in the case of war. But in actual practice the fisheries bounty policy has not worked well. As an example of this policy done badly, in additions largely to the third edition (1784), he examines the "herring buss bounty" (*WN*, 519) at length. Clearly well informed by his years in the customhouse,[19] he explains why this bounty is at best perverse and at worst a scam, to wit:

[T]he bounty to the white herring fishery is a tonnage bounty; and is proportioned to the burden of the ship, not to her diligence or success in the fishery; and it has, I am afraid, been too common for vessels to fit out for the sole purpose of catching, not the fish, but the bounty. (*WN*, 520)

Smith concludes chapter 5 with a long "Digression concerning the Corn Trade and Corn Laws." It begins:

I cannot conclude this chapter concerning bounties, without observing that the praises which have been bestowed upon the law which establishes the bounty upon the exportation of corn ... are altogether unmerited.... The great importance of this subject must justify the length of the digression. (*WN*, 524)

The narrative he presents in this digression is a synthesis of his argument for free trade and against mercantile policy in the context of the corn laws. To structure his analysis he explains that "[t]he trade of the corn merchant is composed of four different branches" (*WN*, 524)

- "the inland dealer";
- "the merchant importer for home consumption";
- "the merchant exporter of home products for foreign consumption"; and
- "the merchant carrier, or of the importer of corn in order to export it again."

---

[19] At one point he actually cites lack of customhouse data for his inability "to speak with much precision" (*WN*, 521).

He begins with the inland dealer. "It is in his interest to raise the price of his corn as high as the real scarcity of the season requires, and it can never be his interest to raise it higher" (*WN*, 524). Some see this as price gouging. Smith sees it as a very constructive market signaling and allocation process.

Corn, as with capital, flows to the place it is needed most when the flow is regulated least. The key to this dynamic is price signaling. Price adjustments will signal the "real scarcity of the season" (*WN*, 524) and corn will flow accordingly. In response to scarcity, price will rise, encouraging frugality and thereby allowing the limited supply to serve the population longer. Echoing his famous invisible hand image, Smith writes that "[w]ithout intending the interest of the people, he [(the inland dealer)] is necessarily led, by a regard to his own interest," to price corn in a way that serves the long-term interest of the people (*WN*, 525).

Clearly, if the corn crop is monopolized by "one great company," then the people can be grossly exploited. Such a monopoly could do "as the Dutch are said to do with the spiceries of the Molluccas, to destroy or throw away a considerable part of it, in order to keep up the price of the rest. But it is scarce possible, even by violence of law, to establish such an extensive monopoly with regard to corn" (*WN*, 525). There are so many growers scattered so widely that collusion for market control is virtually impossible.

The superiority of the price allocation system to a government-controlled system is reflected in the fact that "famine has never arisen from any other cause but the violence of government attempting, by improper means, to remedy the inconveniences of a dearth" (*WN*, 526). For example, government price ceilings meant to "remedy the inconveniences of a dearth" (*WN*, 527) remove the price incentive to restrain consumption, causing a dearth to become a famine.

He appreciates that it is difficult for government to avoid this intervention. "In years of scarcity the inferior ranks of the people impute their distress to the avarice of the corn merchant, who becomes the object of hatred and indignation" (*WN*, 527). There is inevitably a popular call for government to force the merchant to sell more cheaply. But the corn merchant is simply responding to market conditions. If not allowed to do so he could be ruined.

Smith blames "[t]he ancient policy of Europe" (*WN*, 528) for institutionalizing suspicion of the corn merchant. To eliminate this middle man, that policy made it illegal for anyone but the farmer to sell the grain. This is ironic because in these same times the manufacturers of the towns, being prohibited from selling directly to the public, were forced to sell to shopkeepers. Both constraints are market distortions. The division of labor applies to the process of marketing just as well as it does to production. Left to natural forces the market will determine the appropriate structure for the marketing process.

The law which prohibited the manufacturer from exercising the trade of a shop-keeper, endeavoured to force this division in the employment of stock to go on faster than it might otherwise have done. The law which obliged the farmer to exercise the trade of a corn merchant, endeavoured to hinder him from going on so fast. Both laws were evident violations of natural liberty, and therefore unjust; and they were both too as impolitick as they were unjust. It is the interest of every society, that things of this kind should never either be forced or obstructed.... [T]he law ought always to trust people with the care of their own interest, as in their local situations they must generally be able to judge better of it than the legislator can do. (*WN*, 530–1)

All such distortions cause an inefficient allocation of capital. Left to determine the proper structure for marketing, the farmer and the manufacturer would allocate their capital most efficiently. If farmers were freed to deal with corn merchants, given that agricultural production is the foundation of all other production, "it is not perhaps very easy to imagine how great, how extensive, and how sudden would be the improvement which this change of circumstances would alone produce upon the whole face of the country" (*WN*, 532).

The existing laws reflect "two very absurd popular prejudices" (*WN*, 533).

First, the notion that corn will be engrossed assumes an ability to collude that, given the number of growers, is not possible.

Second, "that there is a certain price at which corn is likely to be forestalled, that is, bought up in order to be sold again soon after in the same market, so as to hurt the people" (*WN*, 533). This kind of speculation in corn may indeed occur, but it is risk taking that actually serves the public. If the speculator is correct, the effect of the unfolding shortage is ameliorated by that share that is forestalled and then later brought to the market. Thus, "instead of hurting the great body of the people, he renders them a most important service" (*WN*, 533). If he is wrong, he loses but not the people. Apropos of the division of labor logic, the corn merchant, given his personal "interest," "knowledge," and "ability" in the market (*WN*, 534), is most likely to study the market carefully and make the best judgments as to when to forestall some share of the crop and when not to.

Smith compares what he considers the irrational "popular fear of engrossing and forestalling ... to the popular terrors and suspicions of witchcraft" (*WN*, 534). Both superstitions are encouraged by the laws that brand the subjects of the laws as evildoers. He cites as evidence of this the fact that the repeal of the witchcraft law ended the "prosecutions against witchcraft, which put it out of any man's power to gratify his own malice by accusing his neighbour of that imaginary crime, seems effectually to have put an end to those fears and suspicions, by taking away the great cause [(the law)] which encouraged and supported them" (*WN*, 534), and so too it would be if laws against engrossing and forestalling were repealed.

This commentary on witchcraft reflects Smith's view that the system of laws not only polices citizens, it also reflects extant cultural values, reinforces those values, and inculcates those values in emerging generations of citizens.[20] Thus the evolution of a society's values and its laws go hand in hand.

In the course of his commentary on the corn laws and the optimal legal environment for production, in order to emphasize the importance of home production he cites statistics on how small a proportion of domestic needs is supplied by imports. Having cited the data he notes that "I have no great faith in political arithmetick, and I mean not to warrant the exactness of either of these computations" (*WN*, 534–5). For Smith the most compelling data are those culled from a long view of history.

Having addressed at length the issues relating to the inland dealer, Smith writes that "[a] very few words will sufficiently explain all I have to say concerning the other three branches of the corn trade" (*WN*, 535).

If the importer for home consumption were free to carry on that trade as he saw fit, the supply would expand and the price of corn would fall. Because a socially defined subsistence is based on corn as the numeraire, the fall in the nominal price of corn would not imply a fall in its real value. This fall would, however, have a positive effect on the production of other commodities, for it would lower their money price giving "industry of the country ... some advantage in all foreign markets" (*WN*, 535). An advantage in foreign markets would expand the number of productive hands in the country, in turn expanding the demand for corn and

---

[20] He writes later that "what forms the character of every nation ... [is] the nature of their government" (*WN*, 586). See *Adam Smith's Moral Philosophy* (Evensky, 2005, chapter 3) for more detail on this.

encouraging its production. As always, the theme here is that freedom of trade is the best environment for the progress of opulence.

The exporter for foreign consumption should also be free to ply his trade. Such export "certainly does not contribute directly to the plentiful supply of the home market. It does so, however, indirectly" (*WN*, 537). The logic here is taken directly from his analysis of circuits of trade in Book II. Surpluses, whether they be capital or commodities, must have vent or the growth of the system is constrained. In this case being able to export corn allows greater improvement and cultivation in agriculture. "The prohibition of exportation limits the improvement and cultivation to what the supply if its own inhabitants requires" (*WN*, 537).

Current British law is, according to Smith, impeding the progress of opulence. By offering bounties to encourage exports and imposing prohibitions to limit imports, the law is nominally meant to encourage domestic production. Instead, the law creates an unstable market vulnerable to sever dearth. "[T]emporary laws [suspending the existing structure] ... to which Great Britain has been obliged so frequently to have recourse, sufficiently demonstrate the impropriety of her general system" (*WN*, 538).

"Were all nations to follow the liberal system of free exportation and free importation ... [this would be] the most effectual preventative of a famine" in any nation, for corn would flow to its greatest need as signaled by the price (*WN*, 538). But a small country cannot risk liberalization if a larger neighboring nation is following foolish mercantile policies. If that larger nation suffers a dearth, the liberalizing small nation could experience such a dramatic outflow of corn that it too would suffer from its neighbor's mistakes. Only "such great countries as France or England" (*WN*, 539) can take the lead in liberalization.

Returning to his theme that many trade restrictions are based on government responsiveness to the irrational impressions of the public, Smith compares "laws concerning corn ... to the laws concerning religion" (*WN*, 539). In both cases, the issue lies so close to the heart of people's concerns, "their subsistence in this life, or to their happiness in a life to come, that government must yield to their prejudices ... [and so we] seldom find a reasonable system established with regard to either" (*WN*, 539).

Turning finally to "[t]he trade of the merchant carrier" (*WN*, 539), Smith demonstrates the value of this role. The carrier keeps a warehouse of corn. While it is not his intention to sell locally, he has no aversion to doing so and his is a ready supply in case of a need. But this trade has been "in effect prohibited in Great Britain" (*WN*, 540) by high duties that make importation prohibitively expensive. Here again the progress of opulence in Britain is impeded by regulations that limit the freedom of supply chain development for trade.

Given all these absurd regulations, how is it possible that Great Britain is, by Smith's own account, the most prosperous nation in the world? This progress dates from after the implementation of these very regulations. Is this evidence of causation? Have these regulations actually contributed to this progress? Smith addresses this issue directly, and his answer is a resounding: No!

The improvement and prosperity of Great Britain, which has been so often ascribed to those laws, may very easily be accounted for by other causes. That security which the laws in Great Britain give to every man that he shall enjoy the fruits of his own labour, is alone sufficient to make any country flourish, notwithstanding these and twenty other absurd regulations of commerce; and this security was perfected by the revolution, much about the same time that the bounty was established. The natural effort of every individual to better his own condition, when suffered to exert itself with freedom and security, is so power-ful a principle, that it is alone, and without any assistance, not only capable of carrying on the society to wealth and prosperity, but of surmounting a hundred impertinent obstructions with which the folly of human laws too often incumbers its operations; though the effect of these obstructions is always more or less either to encroach upon its freedom, or to diminish its security. In Great Britain industry is perfectly secure; and though it is far from being perfectly free, it is as free or freer than in any other part of Europe. (*WN*, 540)

...

[In contrast, i]ndustry [in Spain and Portugal] ... is neither free nor secure, and the civil and ecclesiastical governments ... [there] are such as would alone be suf-ficient to perpetuate their present state of poverty, even though their regulations of commerce were as wise as the greater part of them are absurd and foolish. (*WN*, 541)

These assertions reflect Smith's larger moral philosophical vision. We can, as he has been doing, analyze and critique the regulations of com-merce, pointing out how they can encourage or discourage trade and in turn the progress of opulence. But the foundation of *The Wealth of Nations* and ultimately of the well-being of the people lies not on the civil governmental superstructure that regulates trade; it lies in a constitution of government that ensures the freedom and security of each individual. Civil government, that set of political institutions that establishes and enforces the superstructure that regulates market intercourse can, as it has in Britain, distort things royally. But so long as the civil government's constitution embodies and enforces a system of civil society that protects individuals from the abuse of government and/or factional interests, that government is playing a constructive role in human progress.

Smith's moral philosophy is all about that progress. He explores history in order to understand and represent the principles that guide progress for his purpose is to contribute to that progress. Great Britain has, he believes, enjoyed the most progress of any nation to date thanks to the freedom and security its government affords its people.

In Smith's analysis government is not inherently good or evil. It is instrumental. Its laws and regulations are a poor proxy for that government that regulates an ideal human order, self-government based a common set of civic ethics accepted and adhered to by all citizens. But where people are not perfect, proxies can be helpful. Approaching that ideal requires an evolving constitution of civil government that enforces and inculcates ever more constructive rules of order. The closing words of chapter 5 reflect this larger moral philosophical vision of Smith:

With all its [(the current British constitution's)] imperfections, however, we may perhaps say of it what was said of the laws of Solon, that, though not the best itself, it is the best which the interests, prejudices, and temper of the times would admit of. It may perhaps in due time prepare the way for a better. (*WN*, 543)

CHAPTER 6: "OF TREATIES OF COMMERCE"

The mercantilist rationale behind "treaties of commerce" is that if a nation can negotiate a trade *quid pro quo* that generates a positive trade balance, by mercantilist standards that is a deal worth making. They cite as an example the "treaty of commerce between England and Portugal, concluded in 1703" (*WN*, 546).

That treaty allowed previously prohibited woolen products of England to gain access to Portugal on the same terms as all other imports, and in return Portuguese wine would pay "only two-thirds of the duty, which is paid for those of France" (*WN*, 547). The advertised benefit to England was that Portugal, controlling the mines of Brazil, had a glut of gold and, for reasons explained earlier (*WN*, 511–12), this would open the spigot for a flow of gold out of Portugal and into England.

Smith's response to this argument is that while the trade generated by this treaty may indeed bring gold into England, England has no use for so much gold. A small share might be used for plate and coinage, but most will leave again in search of commodities that it can purchase. By artificially forcing trade into this roundabout circuit the productive value of the capital involved is reduced. Capital is most productive when it travels in a natural course. Any artificial distortion of this natural flow reduces the "annual produce" (*WN*, 548).

Having made this point, chapter 6 ends with a lengthy analysis of coinage issues. In particular he notes the negative consequences of Britain not requiring a modest seignorage for coining bullion. This analysis seems to hang by itself in the flow of the narrative. Indeed, at the end of this exposition Smith writes:

Some of the foregoing reasonings and observations might perhaps have been more properly placed in those chapters of the first book which treat of the origin and use of money.... But as the law for the encouragement of coinage derives from its origin from those vulgar prejudices which have been introduced by the mercantile system; I judged it more proper to reserve them for this chapter. (*WN*, 555)

The mercantilists do not miss an opportunity to exploit the system: "Nothing could be more agreeable to the spirit of that system than a sort of bounty upon the production of money, the very thing which, it supposes, constitutes the wealth of every nation" (*WN*, 555).

CHAPTER 7: "OF COLONIES"

By far the longest chapter in Book IV, Smith's exposition on colonies brings him to the heart of his argument against the most destructive manifestation of the mercantile system. Among the many mercantile contrivances, the case for maintaining the colonies is to Smith the most absurd. Of all those contrivances the cost of the colonies has been the most severe in lost productivity, in blood, and in undermining the stability of the nation.

Chapter 7 traces the history of the colonial enterprises of European nations, contrasts the British colonial experience with those of other nations, and explores the consequences of the British colonial policy for its colonies and for Britain itself.

The chapter is divided into three parts.

Part I: "Of the Motives for establishing new Colonies"

Smith begins with a brief review of the differences between the Roman and Greek colonial systems. The former was motivated by a desire to diffuse the frustrations of a subservient class, the latter by a search for more space among equals. This difference is reflected in "the words, which in the original languages denote those different establishments.... The Latin word (*Colonia*) signifies simply a plantation. The Greek word (αποιχια), on the contrary, signifies a separation of dwelling, a departure from home" (*WN*, 558). In both cases, however, the motive was "irresistible necessity, or ... evident utility" (*WN*, 558). Not so the European colonies in America or the East Indies. There was no necessity and utility was not, at least initially, the issue. The initial motive was to share the benefits of the spice trade monopolized by the Venetians.

The Portuguese sought a route around Africa. Ultimately de Gama succeeded in 1497.

During this period "a Genoese pilot ... Columbus very justly concluded, [that] the shorter [route] ... would be by the West" (*WN*, 559). But as history records, he found what became known as the Americas, not the East Indies; and absent the spices, it was the gold trinkets taken from the natives that intrigued his benefactors most.

In consequence of the representations of Columbus, the council of Castile determined to take possession of countries of which the inhabitants were plainly incapable of defending themselves. The pious purpose of converting them to Christianity sanctified the injustice of the project. But the hope of finding treasures of gold there, was the sole motive which prompted it. (*WN*, 561)

These lines richly reflect Smith's conception of ethics and its relationship to religion. Justice lies at the heart of Smith's ethical system and he is consistently concerned that, as here, greed can trample on justice when there is an asymmetry of power. Religion is, in Smith's narrative, not unlike institutionalized civil government, instrumental in humankind's evolution. Either can be an instrument for human improvement, or, in the wrong hands as was the case here, an instrument for human oppression.

In the Americas colonization was represented in the pious pose of bringing Christianity to heathens. But this was a pose, not the purpose. Gold was the goal. Initially it was simply stolen, but when there was none left to steal the effort turned to that "most disadvantageous lottery in the world" (*WN*, 562), mining for gold. No "prudent law-giver" would encourage such a risky project, but "[s]uch in reality is the absurd confidence which almost all men have in their own good fortune, that wherever there is the least probability of success" (*WN*, 562) they believe they will be the winner. Driven by these "strange delusions" (*WN*, 563) adventurers explored and colonized the Americas.

Part II: "Causes of the Prosperity of new Colonies"

When colonies are established in a sparsely populated and fertile land where the indigenous people do not represent a formidable obstacle, the prosperity of the colonists can be quite rapid if they bring

- the human and physical capital of advanced agricultural production: this makes the capital that would normally take "many centuries" to evolve immediately available (*WN*, 564) and
- "some notion of regular government ..., the system of laws which support it, and a regular administration of justice" (*WN*, 565). This prerequisite for the encouragement of individual initiative is also the product of many centuries of evolution.

Settling people with these advantages into a world in which there is a superabundance of fertile, uncultivated land unleashes a dynamic that is incredibly productive.

With all the land one could hope to use, and no landlord to whom one must answer and thus no rent to pay, the first colonists work the land to their great benefit. Seeing ever more untilled lands awaiting human hands, these initial settlers bring in workers at high wages to work even more land. These new arrivals see land for themselves in the endless landscape, and become independent producers. They bring in more workers. Thus agricultural expansion is fed by ready land and ready labor, and the abundant agricultural production provides the means to support large, healthy, working families. Population grows and, the indigenous people being fairly easily displaced thanks to the colonists' superior weapons, there is plenty of additional land available for the expanding numbers of productive hands. In this world, the only way to keep workers from leaving to work their own land is to treat them well.

In other countries, rent and profit eat up wages, and the two superior orders of people oppress the inferior one. But in new colonies, the interest of the superior orders obliges them to treat the inferior one with more generosity and humanity; at least, where that inferior one is not in a state of slavery. (*WN*, 565)

This narrative on colonies reflects Smith's image of the best-case scenario. In such a world the seemingly endless "unclaimed"[21] land means anyone can clear and own land, so no one can extract a rent from him. In such a world of very high wages anyone can accumulate his own capital

---

[21] Clearly the indigenous people didn't see it this way. Smith makes note shortly after of "the cruel destruction of the natives" (*WN*, 568).

stock, so no one can extract interest for providing access to capital. In such a world, the least among the working class do well enough to raise healthy children who themselves become independent, productive farmers or workers. In such a world, "[w]hat encourages the progress of population and improvement, encourages that of real wealth and greatness" (*WN*, 566).

Portugal and Spain, owing to their initial dominance of the oceans as the "two great naval powers," controlled the early years of colonization in America. "But the declension of the naval power of this latter nation, in consequence of the defeat or miscarriage of, what they called, their Invincible Armada" (*WN*, 569) ended that dominance and opened the exploration of the Americas to all of Europe.

Smith proceeds to review which countries moved where in this exploration. In the course of this review he notes that the Danes initially allowed St. Thomas and Santa Cruz to be under "the government of an exclusive company of merchants ... [a condition he describes as] perhaps, the worst of all governments for any country whatever" (*WN*, 570). This attack on government by merchants is a theme he will return to with a vengeance when he turns his attention to the East India Company of Britain.

While Britain's approach to governing colonies in the East was despicable, in the West it was enlightened: "[T]here are no colonies of which progress has been more rapid than that of the English in North America.... [This has been so because] the political institutions of the English colonies have been more favorable to the improvement and cultivation of this land, than those of any of the other three nations" (*WN*, 571–2). Most significantly these institutions ensured individual security and they made land accessible. The latter was true because "engrossing of uncultivated land ... [was] more restrained in the English colonies" (*WN*, 572) and because the diffusion of land wealth was promoted by laws that encouraged alienation or by those such as "in Pennsylvania [where] there is no right to primogeniture" (*WN*, 572).

The English colonies also benefit from low taxes because

- they do not bear the burden of their own defense,
- there is not so much extravagance by their colonial rulers to pay for,
- there is no ecclesiastical government that must be supported, and
- they enjoy a somewhat more liberal access to world markets.[22]

---

[22] Again he notes that "[o]f all the expedients that can well be contrived to stunt the natural growth of a new colony, that of an exclusive company is undoubtedly the most effectual" (*WN*, 574).

The limitations that do exist were established by the "act of navigation" (*WN*, 577).

Smith reviews this act and concludes that it exists at least in part "[t]o increase the shipping and naval power of Great Britain" (*WN*, 577). Asserting that this act is not overly illiberal given defense considerations, he continues:

The liberality of England, however, towards the trade of her colonies has been confined chiefly to what concerns the market for their produce, either in its rude state, or in what may be called the very first stage of manufacture. The more advanced or more refined manufacturers even of the colony produce, the merchants and manufacturers of Great Britain chuse to reserve to themselves, and have prevailed upon the legislature to prevent their establishment in the colonies, sometimes by high duties, and sometimes by absolute prohibitions.... [After reviewing examples, he writes:]

To prohibit a great people ... from making all that they can of every part of their own produce, or from employing their stock and industry in the way that they judge most advantageous to themselves, is a manifest violation of the most sacred rights of mankind.... [Given the endless opportunities due to the expanse of open land, these restrictions] have not hitherto been very hurtful to the colonies.... [They] are only impertinent badges of slavery imposed upon them, without any sufficient reason, by the groundless jealously of the merchants and manufacturers of the mother country. In a more advanced state they might be really oppressive and insupportable. (*WN*, 581, 582)

Of all of mercantilism's policies the most distorting has been the colonial policy. The colonists have not always been responsible in their response, but their grievances are legitimate.

In the course of this narrative on the British colonies, Smith references the time frame with comments like: "the present disturbances" (*WN*, 573, 585, 615) or "at present, October 1773" (*WN*, 581). Clearly much of this was composed or recomposed after he arrived in London in the spring of 1773. This is consistent with the assertion that the mercantile colonies policies being pressed upon the parliament were a story he did not fully appreciate before his arrival in London, but a story he could not, for both philosophical and practical reasons, leave out of his narrative in his *Wealth of Nations*.

Of the greater part of the regulations concerning the colony trade, the merchants who carry it on, it must be observed, have been the principal advisers. We must not wonder, therefore, if, in the greater part of them, their interest has been more considered than either that of the colonies or that of the mother country. (*WN*, 584)

Following this quotation Smith reviews how mercantile policies have been finely tuned to serve that faction's interests. Some of these policies (e.g., paying "drawbacks upon the re-exportation of German linens to American colonies" (*WN*, 584)) hurt the nation's interest "even according to the mercantile ideas of that interest" (*WN*, 584). Clearly the claim of serving the national interest is simply meant to dress the wolf in sheep's clothing.

To Smith mercantilism is a self-serving transformation of a Lockian philosophy. At a philosophical level his objective is to strip away the veil of philosophical credibility that helps mercantilists sell their policies to parliament. At a practical level he seeks to expose the destructive consequences of those policies.

The progress that the American colonies have enjoyed is not because of, but rather in spite of the mercantilist policies. As he repeats yet again, the key to that progress is in fact the freedom and security established by the British system of government:

In every thing, except their foreign trade, the liberty of the English colonists to manage their own affairs their own way is complete. It is in every respect equal to that of their fellow-citizens at home, and is secured in the same manner, by an assembly of the representatives of the people, who claim the sole right of imposing taxes for the support of the colony government. The authority of this assembly over-awes the executive power, and neither the meanest nor the most obnoxious colonist, as long as he obeys the law, has any thing to fear from the resentment, either of the governor, or of any other civil or military officer in the province. The colony assemblies, though, like the house of commons in England, they are not always a very equal representation of the people, yet they approach more nearly to that character; and as the executive power ... has not the means [or "inclinations"] to corrupt them, they are perhaps in general more influenced by the inclinations of their constituents.... [Furthermore i]n none of the English colonies is there any hereditary nobility ... [with] privileges by which he can be troublesome to his neighbours.... There is more equality, therefore, among the English colonists than among the inhabitants of the mother country. Their manners are more republican, and their governments ... have hitherto been more republican too. (*WN*, 584–5)

Again we hear: independent citizens enjoying freedom and security are the ultimate source of *The Wealth of Nations*. The foundation for the success of the English colonies is just such freedom and security, and their phenomenal growth is thanks to the abundance of fertile land available. The similarly situated colonies of "[t]he absolute governments of Spain, Portugal, and France, on the contrary" (*WN*, 586) have enjoyed no such dramatic growth because their institutions undermined rather than enhanced individuals' sense of freedom and security.[23]

---

[23] Although he notes that France is not nearly so oppressive as Spain and Portugal.

The exception to this British advantage in the Americas is among the British sugar-producing colonies that use slave labor. The French sugar colonies generate more wealth than their British counterparts. Smith ascribes this in part to the more liberal refining rules the French have, but primarily to the difference in the treatment of the slaves.[24]

In every country where the unfortunate law of slavery is established, the magistrate, when he protects the slave, intermeddles in some measure in the management of the private property of the master; and in a free country, where the master is perhaps either a member of the colony assembly, or an elector of such a member, he dare not do this but with the greatest caution and circumspection. (*WN*, 587)

As a consequence one finds the well-being of slaves more carefully attended to under more authoritarian regimes (the French case) because the magistrate is more accustomed to imposing his will in such a system. "That the condition of a slave is better under arbitrary than under a free government, is, I believe, supported by the history of all ages and nations" (*WN*, 587). Where slaves are treated more humanely they are more productive, and this, according to Smith, accounts for the superiority of the French sugar colonies over the British.

In closing this second Part, Smith notes that policies for colonial development were not based on coherent plans wisely laid out in advance by the mother country. The engines that drove colonization were "the folly of hunting after gold and silver mines" (*WN*, 588), and the "disorder and injustice of European governments" (*WN*, 589) which sent religious groups (he cites English puritans, English Catholics, Portuguese Jews) in search of asylum in a new world. The colonists took "possession of a country whose harmless natives, far from having ever injured the people of Europe, had received the first adventurers with every mark of kindness and hospitality" (*WN*, 588).

In what way, therefore, has the policy of Europe contributed either to the first establishment, or to the present grandeur of the colonies of America? In one way, and in one way only, it has contributed a good deal.... It bred and formed the men who were capable of atchieving such great actions, and of laying the foundation of so great an empire; and there is no other quarter of the world of which the policy is capable of forming, or has ever actually and in fact formed such men. The colonies owe to the policy of Europe the education and great views of their active and enterprizing founders; and some of the greatest and most important of them, so far as concerns their internal government, owe to it scarce any thing else. (*WN*, 590)

---

[24] He compares the "good management" of slaves to the good management of cattle (*WN*, 586–7).

What advantages did the colonies, East and West, born of folly, oppression, and injustice, bring to Europe? Smith addresses this question in the third Part.

Part III: "Of the Advantages which Europe has derived from the Discovery of America, and from that of a Passage to the East Indies by the Cape of Good Hope"

These advantages must be understood at two levels, according to Smith:

- "Europe, considered as one great country" (*WN*, 591), and
- Each country considered individually.

With the opening of trade to more distant places Europe as a whole enjoyed access to commodities that were heretofore unavailable and its industry enjoyed more encouragement from the extended market. Even European countries "such as Hungary and Poland" (*WN*, 591) that were not directly involved in the colonial enterprise benefited from the colonies because the colonial trade expanded the nexus of trade circulation of which they were a part. The circuits of trade analysis Smith laid out in Book II serves as his framework for understanding this case:

The mass of commodities annually thrown into the great circle of European commerce, and by its various revolutions annually distributed among all the different nations comprehended within it, must have been augmented by the whole surplus produce of America. (*WN*, 592)

The benefit of this expanded nexus of trade is diminished by mercantilist policy. It is a "dead weight upon the action ... which puts into motion a great part of the business of mankind ... It is a clog which, for the supposed benefit of some particular countries, embarrasses the pleasures, and encumbers the industry of all other countries" (*WN*, 592–3).

As for the benefits that can accrue to each colonizing country, there are potentially two: military support and tax revenue. Roman colonies provided both. Greek colonies furnished the former but seldom the latter. None of the European colonies in the Americas have provided help in the defense of the mother country, and, except for Spain and Portugal, none have even contributed revenue for this purpose. "In this respect, therefore, all the European colonies have, without exception, been a cause rather of weakness than of strength of their respective mother countries" (*WN*, 593).

If there is any benefit that individual nations derive from having these colonies, it must therefore come from the exclusive trade each nation enjoys with its colonies.

Smith begins his case that there is no such benefit by reviewing the mercantilist argument that the benefit is real: in the British case, "exclusive trade … [in] enumerated commodities" forces the colonies to sell those commodities only in England. This cheapens them and so it "must contribute more to increase the enjoyments of England, than those of any other country. It must likewise contribute to encourage her industry" because that industry gets more in return (colonial products being artificially cheap) for its surpluses than it would from other countries (*WN*, 595). In classic mercantilist logic, the argument is that with these exclusive trade policies we win and those who are excluded lose.

Having laid out the supposed advantage, Smith turns on that logic:

> This advantage, however, will, perhaps, be found to be rather what may be called a relative than an absolute advantage; and to give a superiority to the country which enjoys it, rather by depressing the industry and produce of other countries, than by raising those of that particular country above what they would naturally rise to in the case of a free trade. (*WN*, 594–5)

Consider the tobacco trade: mercantile restrictions bring Maryland and Virginia tobacco directly and exclusively to England, some of which is then re-exported to France. As a result tobacco is cheaper in England than in France. But if there had been free trade, with the encouragement of a more extended market production would have expanded and tobacco "might by this time, have come cheaper than it actually does, not only to all those other countries [of Europe], but likewise to England" (*WN*, 595). The price of the relative advantage that comes with the "invidious and malignant project of excluding" of others (*WN*, 595) is the loss of an absolute advantage: much cheaper tobacco. And this is not the full price of the "project."

The general monopoly on British colonial trade created "by the act of navigation" led to profits "much above the ordinary level of profit in other branches of trade" (*WN*, 596). This in turn attracted capital from other branches of the British market, a flow that continued until "the profits of all came to a new level, different from and somewhat higher than that at which they had been before" (*WN*, 596).

This distortion of capital flows benefited the merchants by artificially increasing profits, but harmed the economy by directing capital into circuits that were "more distant" (*WN*, 596). Such circuits are, as he laid out in Book II, slower and more risky.

Defenders of the act note that the rate of profit has fallen since its establishment. Smith replies:

[I]t certainly has, [but] it must have fallen still lower, had not the monopoly established by the act contributed to keep it up.

But whatever raises in any country the ordinary rate of profit higher than it otherwise would be, necessarily subjects that country both to an absolute and to a relative disadvantage in every branch of trade of which she has not the monopoly. (*WN*, 599)

This is so because an artificially higher rate of profit raises all prices, making the cost of living higher, the cost of production higher, and the competitive position of exports worse.

Our merchants frequently complain of the high wages of British labour as the cause of their manufactures being undersold in foreign markets; but they are silent about the high profits of stock.... The high profits of British stock, however, may contribute towards raising the price of British manufacturers in many cases as much, and in some perhaps more, than the high wages of British labour. (*WN*, 599)

In Smith's analysis it is a falling rate of profit that goes hand in hand with growth. When trade is free a falling domestic profit rate incentivizes a growing capital stock to spill into ever wider circuits as enterprising entrepreneurs seek opportunities in more distant markets. Extending the market increases the nexus of exchange and encourages specialization among nations. This natural flow of capital to the best risk-adjusted rate of profit grows *The Wealth of Nations*.

Thanks to the liberal British constitution the absurd mercantile regulations of the British colonial trade have not caused the stagnation found in China or the decline found in Bengal (*WN*, 90). But they have significantly impeded British progress and may yet do more harm given the political influence of those interests. His argument is straightforward:

The most advantageous employment of any capital to the country to which it belongs, is that which maintains there the greatest quantity of productive labour, and increases the most the annual produce of the land and labour of the country. But the quantity of productive labour which any capital employed in the foreign trade of consumptions can maintain, is exactly in proportion, it has been shewn in the second book, to the frequency of its returns. (*WN*, 600)

In the name of national interest mercantilist policies have artificially drawn capital into the distant, slower, and less secure colonial trade. This destructive effect is exacerbated because the colonies, constantly understocked with capital, are constantly "running as much in arrear ... [as their] correspondents will allow them" (*WN*, 601). This further slows the circulation of capital, resulting in even less productivity.

The colonial trade monopoly also reduces productivity by diverting capital into "a round-about trade of foreign consumption" (*WN*, 602). He again cites as an example the trade in tobacco between the colonies and the rest of Europe. Tobacco must pass through Britain to get to the rest of Europe. This roundaboutness ties up capital in the tobacco trade. Absent the monopoly, less tobacco would be imported into Britain by a smaller quantity of capital and:

[a]ll the purposes of this trade being ... answered by a much smaller capital, there would have been a large spare capital to apply to other purposes; to improve lands, to increase manufacturers, and to extend the commerce of Great Britain; to come into competition at least with the other British capitals employed in all those different ways, to reduce the rate of profit in them all [thus lowering domestic prices and improving Britain's international competitive position]. (*WN*, 604)

Smith summarizes his case against the mercantilist colonial venture as follows:

The monopoly of the colony trade ... by forcing towards it a much greater proportion of the capital of Great Britain than what would naturally have gone to it, seems to have broken altogether that natural balance which would otherwise have taken place among all the different branches of British industry.... Her commerce, instead of running in a great number of small channels, has been taught to run principally into one great channel. But the whole system of her industry and commerce has thereby been rendered less secure; the whole state of her body politick less healthful, than it otherwise would have been. (*WN*, 604)

This is the voice of Smith the citizen expressing concern about the state of his nation's health. He has stripped away the veil of mercantilism as a system of philosophy and revealed it for what it is: a self-serving and destructive policy regime.

In her present condition [having followed the dictates of the mercantile system], Great Britain resembles one of those unwholesome bodies in which some of the vital parts are over grown, and which upon that account, are liable to many dangerous disorders scarce incident to those in which all the parts are more properly proportioned. A small stop in a great blood-vessel, which has been artificially swelled beyond its natural dimensions, and through which an unnatural proportion of the industry and commerce of the country has been forced to circulate, is very likely to bring on the most dangerous disorders upon the whole body politick. (*WN*, 604–5)

Indeed, he continues, Britain has become so dependent on the flow in this one artificially enlarged vessel that "the expectation of a rupture with the colonies ... has struck the people of Great Britain with more terror than they ever felt for a Spanish armada, or a French invasion"[25] (*WN*, 605).

The Wealth of Nations was published in 1776, just as "the expectation of a rupture" became a reality.

Smith recognized that these mercantile distortions are built so deeply into the British system of commerce that a quick solution would be very destabilizing. "Such are the unfortunate effects of all the regulations of the mercantile system! [(A rare use by Smith of an exclamation point.)] They not only introduce very dangerous disorders ..., but disorders which it is often difficult to remedy, without occasioning, for a time at least, still greater disorders" (*WN*, 606).

What is clear is the ultimate solution: "[T]he natural system of perfect liberty and justice ought gradually to be restored.... [The adjustment towards this ideal must be incremental so as not to create these 'greater disorders.' How it should be implemented,] we must leave to the wisdom of future statesmen and legislators to determine" (*WN*, 606).

Smith writes to present the principles of a constructive liberal society. He is not a "man of system" (*TMS*, 233) offering a detailed design that must be immediately and scrupulously followed to achieve success. It is for the "statesmen and legislators" to develop the best government "the prejudices of the people ... can bear" (*TMS*, 233). Each new approximation of the ideal is progress and, *ceteris paribus*, natural selection will improve this approximation over time.

He continues that since "the first of December, 1774" (*WN*, 606)[26] the Articles of Association passed by the First Continental Congress[27] have cut off trade to the American colonies. The "great disorders" to be expected from this severance of trade have been ameliorated by factors that are "transitory and accidental" (*WN*, 607). We should expect to feel the very significant consequences of this exclusion in due time.

This reflects what the narrative in Book III demonstrates: the real course of events may not follow a scripted version of the model because there are all kinds of disturbing forces in political and social dimensions of human society that make the course of economic events unpredictable. What is predictable is that the underlying principles will ultimately

[25] "It was this terror, whether well or ill grounded, which rendered the repeal of the stamp act, among the merchants at least, a popular measure" (*WN*, 605).

[26] Clearly, this part of his narrative was added after he arrived in London in 1773.

[27] In response to trade grievances, in 1774 the first Continental Congress passed the Articles of Association prohibiting trade with Great Britain. See Gould (383).

prevail. They did in medieval Europe, and they will 1770s in Britain yet again. Do not, he suggests, let the current lack of severity in the consequences of mercantile policies obscure the clear logic that demonstrates that these distortions will bear bitter fruit.

To be clear, it is not colonial trade per se that is perverse. In a "natural and free state" this trade can be very beneficial[28] (*WN*, 608). The problem lies not in the trade, but in the mercantile distortions of this trade. In the British case if the colonial trade has been beneficial, and it has, "it is not by means of the monopoly, but in spite of the monopoly" (*WN*, 609).

Indicative of the worst case are Spain and Portugal where the colonial policies, "above all, that irregular and partial administration of justice" (*WN*, 610), are so perverse that trade with the colonies has actually led to a decline in production in the mother countries. If England has not suffered this worst case it is due "above all ... [to the] equal and impartial administration of justice" (*WN*, 610).

Spain and Portugal may be worse cases but his concern is England, so he turns again to the perverse effects of the mercantile system there. After reviewing the points he has already made he cites another, and to him the most perverse, effect of mercantilism: "Light come light go, says the proverb" (*WN*, 613).

Under the mercantile system merchants enjoy an artificially high rate of profit. Not only does this lower wages and rents and distort the price system, it distorts the mercantilists' behavior. They become less parsimonious and, as models for lesser men, they encourage that same behavior across the nation. With this "dissolute ... [behavior t]he capital of the country, instead of increasing [with accumulation], gradually dwindles away" (*WN*, 612). Again the dynamic of economic activity intersects with the role of ethical behavior that Smith lays out in *TMS*. In this case, the mercantile system undermines the parsimony of individuals, diminishing the accumulation of capital that fuels economic activity. And all this at what cost?

The initial costs of the colonies – discovery, reconnoitering, and "fictitious possession" (*WN*, 614) – were pretty meager. The subsequent costs during peacetime had also been modest. There are, however, the costs of two wars, both of which he lays squarely "to the account of the colonies" (*WN*, 615). These were very expensive, and to what end has Britain defended these colonies?

---

[28] He uses the refrain "natural and free state" three times in this paragraph.

[The] pretended purpose ... [was] to increase the commerce of Great Britain. But its real effect has been to raise the rate of merchant profit ...

Under the present system of management ... Great Britain derives nothing but loss from the dominion which she assumes over her colonies. (*WN*, 616)

So how can Britain relieve itself of this colonial burden? Smith suggests that granting the colonies their independence should be considered.

Writing in the context of the "present disturbances" (*WN*, 615), he clearly appreciates that this is an implausible outcome. Given national "pride ... [and] the private interest of the governing part of it [(the nation)] ... The most visionary enthusiast would scarce be capable of proposing such a measure, with any serious hopes at least of its ever being adopted" (*WN*, 617). Nevertheless, he believes it is worthy of serious discussion. Granting independence would transform a burden into a benefit: from dependent colonies to vibrant partners in free trade and natural allies.

Because independence is not going to happen, what then, he asks, should we reasonably expect from our colonies? In peacetime the colonies should contribute revenue that pays the full costs of their own administration and a proportionate share of the general administrative costs of the national government. In wartime they should bear that extraordinary expense in the same proportion as their share of the general administration in peacetime. This, he suggests, is the only fair way to share the burden. Is this the current case? No. Is this deficit compensated, as the mercantilists suggest, by the higher tax revenue generated by the colonial trade? No:

That neither the ordinary nor extraordinary revenue which Great Britain derives from her colonies, bears this proportion to the whole revenue of the British empire, will be readily allowed. The monopoly, it has been supposed, indeed, by increasing the private revenue of the people of Great Britain, and thereby enabling them to pay greater taxes, compensates the deficiency of the publick revenue of the colonies. But this monopoly, I have endeavoured to show, though a very grievous tax upon the colonies, and though it may increase the revenue of a particular order of men in Great Britain, diminishes instead of increasing that of the great body of the people; and consequently diminishes instead of increasing the ability of the great body of the people to pay taxes. (*WN*, 618)

In order to generate tax revenue from the colonies for support of the empire they "may be taxed by their own assemblies" (*WN*, 619). But it is very unlikely that the assemblies would impose such a tax.

When parliament was reticent to tax, the king used patronage to encourage cooperation. But this strategy won't work in the colonies.

Colonial leaders are too far away, too many in number, too removed from the institutions of British government, and too ignorant of the military needs of the empire for the patronage system to influence them.

The "proposed" solution has been therefore that the colonies "be taxed by requisition, the parliament in Great Britain determining the sum" (*WN*, 620), each colonial administration being responsible for determining the optimal tax plan to generate that sum. "Though the colonies should in this case have no representatives in the British parliament, yet, if we may judge by experience, there is no probability that the parliamentary requisition would be unreasonable.... [T]he colonies might in this case be considered as virtually represented in parliament" (*WN*, 620). The French do something similar so there is precedent.

This simple system has, however, one very strong drawback. Lacking any incentive to do so, it is highly unlikely that the colonial assemblies will cooperate. Thus for the requisition system to be effective parliament must make the "requisitions immediately effectual" (*WN*, 621). But this, in effect, eviscerates the colonial assemblies, an action that comes at another cost that is now playing out: resistance. Indeed, the colonies' elites are currently resisting just such a move because it deprives them of the source of their power, however "imagine[d]" (*WN*, 622) that power might be.

They have rejected ... the proposal of being taxed by parliamentary requisition, and like other ambitious and high-spirited men, have rather chosen to draw the sword in defence of their own importance. (*WN*, 622)

Drawing on Roman precedent, Smith offers his solution to this apparent impasse. If we will not let the colonies go and the leading men of the colonies will not accept virtual representation, let us co-opt the opposition of that colonial elite by offering them "a new method of acquiring importance, a new and more dazzling object of ambition" (*WN*, 622). Let us offer the citizens of the colonies all the rights and privileges of citizens in Great Britain, including full freedom of trade, and let us bring their leaders into the parliament as their representatives.

Unless this or some other method is fallen upon, and there seems to be none more obvious than this, of preserving the importance and of gratifying the ambition of the leading men of America, it is not very probable that they will ever voluntarily submit to us; and we ought to consider that the blood which must be shed in forcing them to do so, is, every drop of it, the blood either of those who are, or of those whom we wish to have for our fellow-citizens. (*WN*, 623)

And make no mistake about that difficulty of the current undertaking. These are very determined people who are inspired by their cause:

From shopkeepers, tradesmen, and attornies, they are become statesmen and legislators, and are employed in contriving a new form of government for an extensive empire, which, they flatter themselves, will become, and which, indeed, seems very likely to become, one of the greatest and most formidable that ever was in the world.... [Every man involved in this enterprise has a station beyond any he ever imagined in life and] he will die in defence of that station. (*WN*, 623)

Smith clearly believes that this senseless bloodshed should and can be avoided by offering the citizens of the colonies full rights and real representation as British citizens. The "constitution ... would be completed by it, and seems to be imperfect without it" (*WN*, 624). Certainly the transformation would be full of challenges but none seem to him "insurmountable" (*WN*, 625).

The greatest of these challenges is, as Smith recognizes, the "prejudices and opinions" of the people on both sides. Those in Britain fear that the delicate balance between the "monarchical and democratical parts of the constitution" (*WN*, 625) would be disturbed by the sudden influx of a "multitude of American representatives" (*WN*, 625). He responds to this concern by pointing out that with proportional representation the American influence will grow slowly and so too will any constitutional changes.

For citizens on the other side of the Atlantic, their concern would be how much influence they would have on their representatives who serve so far away. To this Smith responds that so long as your representatives are beholden to you for their office, they will be responsive to your needs in office. Then, following this geographic theme, he speculates on the future locus of power: given the growth potential of this vast new land called America, it seems plausible

that in the course of little more than a century, perhaps, the produce of America might exceed that of British taxation. The seat of the empire would then naturally remove itself to that part of the empire which contributed most to the general defence and support of the whole. (*WN*, 625–6)

As Smith writes this in London, the British colonists in America are taking up arms against Britain. The motives of the colonial leaders may be self-serving at some level (personal power and glory) but, as Smith recognizes, they see their cause as noble and they are highly motivated.

Smith's position: a war with these colonists will be very costly and very difficult to win. It will be a war with our own people. If independence is not acceptable and subjugation is not possible, eliminate the shackles of the mercantile system, give them representation in parliament, and let us grow together as one powerful nation.

Having made his case on the immediate and pressing issue, Smith turns again to his larger theme: colonies, mercantile distortions, and the virtues of free trade.

He begins by taking the long view: these discoveries "of America and ... of a passage to the East Indies ... are the two greatest and most important events recorded in the history of mankind" (*WN*, 626). But human history is a very long story, of which this age of colonization is but a very short, new chapter. Much remains to be written: "What benefits, or what misfortunes to mankind may hereafter result from those great events no human wisdom can foresee" (*WN*, 626).

The great discoveries to the east and west have created the potential for a much more extensive market, and with it the possibility of great progress. They have also come at an egregious cost: the brutal treatment of the "natives ... [because by "accident" (*WN*, 626) of history] the superiority of force happened to be so great on the side of the Europeans, that they were enabled to commit with impunity ever sort of injustice" (*WN*, 626).

He envisions a time when the power will be more balanced and "by inspiring mutual fear ... respect for the rights of one another" will emerge (*WN*, 626). This prospect is most likely to be realized if there is

mutual communication of knowledge and of all sorts of improvements which an extensive commerce from all countries to all countries naturally, or rather necessarily, carries along with it. [This point brings him back to the mercantile system. He continues:]
In the mean time one of the principal effects of those discoveries has been the rise of the mercantile system to a degree of splendor and glory which it could have never otherwise have attained to. (*WN*, 627)

What an irony this is. The opening of the East and West have given Europe an opportunity to reach markets that span the globe. Because extending markets is, as he explained in the opening pages of Book I, both a prerequisite for the ever finer division of labor and an opportunity to generate the capital to finance those improvements, this new era of global trade centered in Europe should have been a great benefit, directly and indirectly, to all the nations of Europe. But this golden opportunity has been undermined by mercantilist policies.

Nominally meant to "enrich a great nation" (*WN*, 627), the mercantile constraints have in fact "frequently [been] more hurtful to the countries in favour of which they are established than to those against which they are established" (*WN*, 627).

After all the unjust attempts, therefore, of every country in Europe to engross to itself the whole advantages of the trade of its own colonies, no country has yet been able to engross to itself any thing but the expence of supporting in time of peace and of defending in time of war the oppressive authority which it assumes over them. (*WN*, 628)

It is easy to understand the persuasive power of the mercantile system:

At first sight, no doubt, the monopoly of the great commerce of America, naturally seems to be an acquisition of the highest value. To the undiscerning eye of giddy ambition, it naturally presents itself amidst the confused scramble of politicks and war, as a very dazzling object to fight for. (*WN*, 628)

But the mercantile prospect is an illusion, a "golden dream" (*WN*, 947). Free trade is the path to the progress of opulence. When trade is free:

[t]he mercantile stock of every country, it has been shewn in the second book, naturally seeks, if one may say so, the employment most advantageous to that country. (*WN*, 628–9)

In pursuit of its best advantage capital flows into successively broader circuits of trade: first the home trade, then foreign trade, and ultimately the carrying trade. With each circuit, if men are parsimonious, the capital stock grows. This unfettered flow ensures that capital is most productive, creating the greatest possible growth in the wealth of the nation.

Without any intervention of law ... the private interests and passions of men naturally lead them to divide and distribute the stock of every society, among all the different employments carried on in it, as nearly as possible in the proportion which is most agreeable to the interest of the whole society. (*WN*, 630)

In this natural dynamic wherever there is a "superiority of profit [this advantage] will draw stock ... till the profits of all return to their proper level" (*WN*, 629). That level is inversely related to the aggregate capital stock. Because that stock grows with each circuit of production, the rate of profit in a growing, healthy economy will fall until it just covers the cost of superintendence.

It is clearly in the interest of the mercantile faction to ensure that this dynamic is thwarted so that profits remain high. Controlling markets sustains advantage, thus it is "[m]onopoly of one kind or another ... [that] seems to be the sole engine of the mercantile system" (*WN*, 630).

This distinction of monopoly as "one kind or another" brings Smith to the difference between the monopolies established by mercantilists in the American colonies and those established in the East.

In the American case, with few exceptions, British colonial trade must be carried by British ships but all British companies can participate. In contrast, "the trade to the East Indies has in every European country [except Portugal and France] been subjected to an exclusive company" (WN, 631). In England that company is the East India Company.

If the first kind of monopoly (in America) is foolish, "the absurdity of this second [(in the East)] ... is much more manifest" (WN, 631). The people of England have to pay ...

not only for all the extraordinary profits which the company may have made ... in consequence of their monopoly, but for all the extraordinary waste which the fraud and abuse, inseparable from the management of the affairs of so great a company, must necessarily have occasioned. (WN, 631)

These two kinds of monopolies (West and East) both "derange more or less the natural distribution of the stock of the society: but they do not always derange it in the same way" (WN, 631). The former (the Americas) attracts too much capital to the monopoly. In the latter case (the East Indies), while small countries may establish a company where they might not have otherwise participated thus sending more capital than they otherwise would have, big countries send less because the one company established as the exclusive trader is limited to its own resources.

One argument for exclusive trading privileges is that developing these new, large markets requires too many sorts of expertise for any one company to enter without the incentive of an exclusive monopoly. Smith's response to this is based on a point he made earlier in Book IV: the division of labor applies to the supply chain just as it does to production. If left to natural forces, where there is an opportunity, individual interests will pursue that opportunity and the market process will determine what entities play which roles in the supply chain (WN, 530–1). He cites Cape of Good Hope and Batavia as colonies that play such supply chain roles.[29]

But mercantilist interests have prevailed so the model for trade with the East has been to grant an exclusive monopoly to a company. Under that model "[t]he English and Dutch companies ... have both made considerable conquests in the East Indies" (WN, 635). And in both cases we see the absurdity of the mercantilist model at work.

---

[29] In the course of his description of the African continent he applies his four stages theory to his analysis of the tribes found there and how they relate to the tribes found in the Americas.

By grant of their respective governments these companies are in effect the sovereigns of the lands they have conquered. As sovereigns they stand to benefit most *in the long run* by ensuring conditions that maximize the productivity of the workers: security and independence.

But a company of merchants are, it seems, incapable of considering themselves as sovereigns, even after they have become such.... Their mercantile habits draw them ... to prefer upon all ordinary occasions the little and transitory profit of the monopolist to the great and permanent revenue of the sovereign. (*WN*, 637–8)

Instead of encouraging the indigenous people to produce for the market by offering them independence, security, and just compensation, these companies see such private production as competition and discourage it. Indeed, in the extreme they see the people themselves as a threat and, as the Dutch have done, they use "different arts of oppression ... [to] reduce the population" (*WN*, 636).

In India control is maintained by a "government that is ... military and despotical ... [a] government [that is] subservient to the interest of the monopoly" (*WN*, 638). In such an environment, far from the eyes of owners in London, the whole superstructure of the company becomes corrupted as employees at all levels see opportunities to enjoy a share of the monopoly profits. Not wanting to offend any individual, Smith adds the caveat:

I mean not ... by any thing which I have here said, to throw any odious imputation upon the general character of the servants of the East India company, and much less upon that of any particular person. It is the system of government, the situation in which they are placed, that I mean to censure; not the character of those who have acted in it. They have acted as their situation naturally directed, and those who have clamoured the loudest against them would, probably, not have acted better themselves. (*WN*, 641)

In keeping with the *TMS* representation of humans as formed from "coarse clay" (*TMS*, 162) by socialization, Smith sees these people as "bred" by "their situation" to exhibit these behaviors (*WN*, 641). Our being is not determined by society, but it is certainly shaped by "education, experience, ... [and] example" (*WN*, 641).

This concludes Smith's analysis of the mercantile system in the original edition (1776) of *WN*. In his 1784 edition, having served several years as a Commissioner of Customs, he adds the entirely new chapter 8: "Conclusion of the Mercantile System."

CHAPTER 8: "CONCLUSION OF THE MERCANTILE SYSTEM"

Smith begins this added chapter with a review of trade laws that mercantilists have "extorted from the legislature" (*WN*, 643), always "pretend[ing that these will] ... enrich the country" (*WN*, 642), but always aiming to enrich themselves.

Clearly well-schooled in the history and intricacies of these laws from his years in the customhouse, as an instructive example he details the rules put in place to control the linen yarn market. His point is clear:

> It is not by the sale of their work [("our spinners ... poor people, women commonly, scattered about in all different parts of the country, without support or protection" (*WN*, 644))], but by that of the compleat work of the weavers, that our great manufacturers make their profits. As it is their interest to sell the compleat manufacturers as dear, so is it to buy the materials as cheap as possible. By extorting from the legislature bounties upon the exportation of their own linen, high duties upon the importation of all foreign linen, and a total prohibition of the home consumption of some sorts of French linen, they endeavour to sell their goods as dear as possible. By encouraging the importation of foreign linen yarn, and thereby bringing it into competition with that which is made by our own people, they endeavour to buy the work of the poor spinners as cheap as possible. They are as intent to keep down the wages of their own weavers, as the earnings of the poor spinners, and it is by no means for the benefit of the workman, that they endeavour either to raise the price of the compleat work, or to lower that of the rude materials. It is the industry which is carried on for the benefit of the rich and the powerful, that is principally encouraged by our mercantile system. (*WN*, 644)

The mercantile system has been meticulously constructed to ensure the control of the market for the "benefit of the rich and the powerful." In the name of global competitiveness,[30] laws have been aligned to favor employers over workers who, "without support or protection," cannot resist. For Smith this is a destructive distortion of the law. The foundation of the progress of opulence is not a positive trade balance; it is a healthy, secure, independent working class.

In 1784 Smith's pen is aimed directly at these mercantilist laws that dictate the terms of trade and exploit labor to the detriment of the nation. In this new chapter he lays bare the problem and asserts that something should and can be done to address it. Indeed, two of the bounties on which this

---

[30] Absent the persuasiveness of that argument, these laws reflect the political power of the mercantilists that enables the mercantilists to "intimidate the legislature" (*WN*, 471).

system has been built, having been renewed twice, "expire with the end of the session of parliament which shall immediately follow the 24th of June 1786" (WN, 644). They should not be renewed.

To support his case he cites the American bounties, writing in 1784: "It is unnecessary, I apprehend, at present to say any thing further, in order to expose the folly of a system, which fatal experience has now sufficiently exposed" (WN, 647). The American debacle is now history.

As a classic example of mercantilist influence on the nation's laws Smith cites the "woollen manufacturers [who] have been more successful than any other class ... in persuading the legislature that the prosperity of the nation depended upon the success and extension of their particular business" (WN, 647). To protect this national interest parliament passed a law "[t]o prevent the breed of our sheep from being propagated in foreign countries" (WN, 648). The initial statute prohibiting the exportation of sheep went so far as to include the death penalty for a second violation.

[T]he cruellest of our revenue laws, I will venture to affirm, are mild and gentle, in comparison of some of those which the clamour of our merchants and manufacturers has extorted from the legislature, for the support of their own absurd and oppressive monopolies. Like the laws of Draco, these laws may be said to be all written in blood.[31] (WN, 648)

Mercantilists justified these "burdensome and oppressive restrictions" on the wool market (WN, 649), arguing that English wool is superior to that of the rest of the world. So, by denying foreigners access to the source of our wool we can "monopolize ... almost the whole woolen trade of the world ... This doctrine ... confidently asserted [by many and] ... implicitly believed [by many more] ... is, however, ... perfectly false" (WN, 651). In fact, if there is a superior wool, it is Spanish not English wool.

The effect of these restrictions on wool exports, a lower price and reduced production, is ameliorated by the fact that wool is a joint product with mutton. As a result the distortion is not as great as it might be. Nevertheless ...

To hurt in any degree the interest of any one order of citizens, for no other purpose but to promote that of some other, is evidently contrary to that justice and equality of treatment which the sovereign owes to all the different orders of his subjects. (WN, 654)

As he reviews the history and current state of mercantile restrictions Smith reiterates a point he has made several times before. Mercantile

---

[31] "[W]ritten in blood" is not hyperbole for Smith. Blood has been the real and dearest cost of the wars fought for the sake of these "absurd and oppressive monopolies."

market power is facilitated by the ease of merchants' collusion and by the disorganization of labor. In Book I he cites the location of traders and artificers together in towns as enhancing their ability to collude (*WN*, 141). Earlier in Book IV he cites the case of "our spinners ... poor people, women commonly, scattered about in all different parts of the country, without support or protection" (*WN*, 644). Now we hear that "[g]raziers separated from one another, and dispersed through all the different corners of the country, cannot without great difficulty, combine together ... [either to impose a monopoly or to resist one] imposed upon them by other people" (*WN*, 655).

The goal of the mercantilists is to acquire the "material[s] of manufacture" (*WN*, 658) and unfinished goods as cheaply as possible, and to export finished products with as little competition as possible. "As long as any thing remains to be done, in order to fit any commodity for immediate use and consumption, our manufacturers think that they themselves ought to have the doing of it" (*WN*, 655).

Mercantilist restrictions were imposed on capital as well as goods, and these restrictions on capital flows out of the country were not limited to physical capital. "When such heavy penalties were imposed upon the exportation of the dead instruments of trade, it could not well be expected that the living instrument, the artificer, should be allowed to go free" (*WN*, 659). Anyone convicted of trying to recruit a skilled worker to move abroad "to practice or teach his trade" (*WN*, 659) was subject first to fines, and for continued offenses to imprisonment. Any artificer who, having been warned to return home, did not do so, lost any property in England and was "declared an alien in every respect" (*WN*, 660).

These laws reflect the fact that "[o]ur master manufacturers think it reasonable, that they themselves should have the monopoly of the ingenuity of all their countrymen" (*WN*, 660).

It is unnecessary, I imagine, to observe, how contrary such regulations are to the boasted liberty of the subject, of which we affect to be so very jealous; but which, in this case, is so plainly sacrificed to the futile interests of our merchants and manufacturers. (*WN*, 660)

The mercantilists' constant claim is that their system, by enabling domestic manufacturers to "win" in the arena of global trade competition, increases the wealth of the nation and thus serves the interests of the people. Nonsense, says Smith:[32]

---

[32] Or, as my father-in-law, Ed Kamps, would say: "Baloney!"

Consumption is the sole end and purpose of all production; and the interest of the producer ought to be attended to, only so far as it may be necessary for promoting that of the consumer. The maxim is so perfectly self-evident, that it would be absurd to attempt to prove it. But in the mercantile system, the interest of the consumer is almost constantly sacrificed to that of the producer. (*WN*, 660)

It is the consumer who pays the price of the protections extorted from the parliament by the mercantilists. The consumer pays directly in taxes levied to cover the costs of bounties and of protecting the monopolized market, and in higher prices caused by bounties, prohibitions, or restrictions. The most egregious example of this cost was the price paid for our colonial adventure:

For the sake of that little enhancement of price which this monopoly might afford our producers, the home-consumers have been burdened with the whole expense of maintaining and defending that empire. For this purpose, and for this purpose only, in the last two wars, more than a hundred and seventy millions have been contracted over and above all that had been expended for the same purpose in former wars. The interest of this debt alone is not only greater than the whole extraordinary profit, which, it ever could be pretended, was made by the monopoly of the colony trade, but than the whole value of that trade or than the whole value of the goods, which at an average have been annually exported to the colonies.
    It cannot be difficult to determine who have been the contrivers of this whole mercantile system; not the consumers, we may believe, whose interest has been entirely neglected; but the producers whose interest has been so carefully attended to; and among this latter class our merchants and manufacturers have been by far the principal architects. (*WN*, 661)

With this indictment Smith leaves the mercantile system behind to briefly explore that other current (1776) system of thought on political economy: the agricultural system.

CHAPTER 9: "OF THE AGRICULTURAL SYSTEMS, OR OF THOSE SYSTEMS OF POLITICAL ŒCONOMY, WHICH REPRESENT THE PRODUCE OF LAND AS EITHER THE SOLE OR THE PRINCIPAL SOURCE OF THE REVENUE AND WEALTH OF EVERY COUNTRY"

The agricultural systems of political œconomy ["which represent the produce of land as the sole source of the revenue and wealth of every country" (*WN*, 663)] will not require so long an explanation as that which I have thought it necessary to bestow upon the mercantile or commercial system. (*WN*, 663)

The reason for his brevity is simple and practical: this system "has, so far as I know, never been adopted by any nation ... It would not, surely, be worthwhile to examine at great length the errors of a system which never has done, and probably never will do any harm in any part of the world" (*WN*, 663).

Smith clearly respects the philosophers who have designed and who advocate for the agricultural system (the Physiocrats), referring to them as "a few men of great learning and ingenuity in France" (*WN*, 663). But for all of their zeal, they have no apparent prospect of significantly affecting policy, so all Smith offers is "the great outlines of this very ingenious system" (*WN*, 663).

He begins by describing the mercantile economic order that "Mr. Colbert, the famous minister of Lewis XIV" (*WN*, 662), has imposed on France and to which the Physiocrats are responding.

When Mr. Colbert, a very able and admirable administrator, became the minister responsible for the French economy, he "embraced all the prejudices of the mercantile system" (*WN*, 663). Given his manager's mentality he was predisposed to regulate the economy "instead of allowing every man to pursue his own interest in his own way, upon the liberal plan of equality, liberty and justice" (*WN*, 664). These last words, "the liberal plan of equality, liberty and justice," are, in all of Smith's work, the most transparent window into his vision of the ideal state that he envisions as the limiting case. Smith offers this image in the context of his presentation of the agricultural system because while he does not agree with the Physiocrats' analysis, he shares with them a deep desire to see the "liberal plan" realized.

Central to Colbert's mercantile policy was his support of the manufacturing interests in the towns. They were the source of finished products for export – the key to mercantile success. To keep their cost of production down and their products more internationally competitive, Colbert imposed absolute restrictions on the export of corn, the commodity needed to feed the workers. This, along with more traditional restrictions on the internal movement of corn and oppressive taxes, severely depressed agricultural production.

The agricultural system was a response to this oppression of agricultural interests. But, Smith writes, "[i]f the rod be bent too much one way, says the proverb, in order to make it straight you must bend it as much the other" (*WN*, 664). In this case, just as Colbert "over-valued" manufactures, so too the "French philosophers ... [over valued agriculture and] certainly under-valued" manufacturing (*WN*, 664). Having identified the basic error of that system, he then proceeds to lay out its logic.

The agricultural system divides those who participate in economic activity into three classes:

- "proprietors of land ...
- "cultivators, ... farmers and country labourers, whom they honor with the peculiar appellation of the productive class ...
- "artificers, manufacturers and merchants, whom they endeavour to degrade by the humiliating appellation of the barren or unproductive class" (*WN*, 664).

The proprietors of the land contribute to agricultural production by improving the land (e.g., with "buildings, drains, enclosures" (*WN*, 665)). The cultivators contribute to agricultural production by the original expenses ("instruments ..., stock", startup costs) and annual expenses (seed used, depreciation of instruments) they contribute (*WN*, 665).

The return on these expenses, the agricultural product, more than covers all these "productive expenses"[33] (*WN*, 666) as evidenced by the cultivators' ability to pay a rent on the land. This rent then is a measure of the "neat produce" (*WN*, 665) of their activity.

In the agricultural system, if unimpeded, this "neat produce" reflected in rent expands the capital that circulates with each cycle. It is perverse to tax this activity beyond the level of the rent because in doing so the means to replenish the "productive expenses" in each cycle of production are being siphoned off by the government. This in turn would, over time, progressively reduce the amount of capital available for agriculture production and thus agricultural productivity.

This centrality of circuits of capital and the liberal notion of freedom of flows are very much in harmony with Smith's moral philosophy. It is not surprising, then, that, while he rejects their system as flawed, he respects the Physiocrats and their efforts very much.

In their agricultural system the expenses of agriculture are the only "productive expenses" (*WN*, 666) because they are the only expenses that generate a net product. "Artificers and manufacturers" are "unproductive" because in each cycle of capital their production simply reproduces the capital that was initially thrown into the system.

---

[33] "Their original and annual expences are ... called, in this system, productive expences, because, over and above replacing their own value, they occasion the annual reproduction of this neat produce" (*WN*, 666).

The expence ... laid out in employing and maintaining artificers and manufacturers [and similarly "[m]ercantile stock" (*WN*, 667)], does no more than continue, if one may say so, the existence of its own value, and does not produce any new value. (*WN*, 667)

The unproductive class's role in the division of labor is to allow those in the productive class to enjoy the benefits of merchants and manufacturers' production without being distracted from their own productive efforts: "[T]he plough goes frequently the easier and the better by means of the labour of the man whose business is most remote from the plough" (*WN*, 669). Given this mutually beneficial relationship

[i]t can never be in the interest of ... [any] class to oppress the other[s] ... The establishment of perfect justice, of perfect liberty, and of perfect equality, is the very simple secret which most effectually secures the highest degree of prosperity to all the three classes. (*WN*, 669)

Again we hear Smith's core value: a perfect liberal society is the best of all possible worlds. These French philosophers share this value, and so Smith values them.

There are some states, "like Holland and Hamburgh" (*WN*, 670), that are naturally mercantile states because of their lack of tillable land. "It can never be in the interest of ... landed nations ... to discourage" (*WN*, 670) trade with these mercantile states. The effect of such a protectionist policy by landed states would ultimately be to "discourage ... the improvement and cultivation of their own land. The most effectual expedient, on the contrary, ... for encouraging ... improvement ... would be to allow the most perfect freedom" of trade (*WN*, 670). Doing so generates an ever greater surplus product. This in turn would "create a greater capital than what could be employed with the ordinary rate of profit in the improvement and cultivation of land; and the surplus part of it would naturally turn itself to the employment of artificers and manufacturers at home" (*WN*, 670).

This continual increase both of the rude and the manufactured produce of those landed nations would in due time create a greater capital than could, with the ordinary rate of profit, be employed either in agriculture or in manufactures. The surplus of this capital would naturally turn itself to foreign trade. (*WN*, 671)

And so with the growth of the wealth of the nation capital spills into yet a larger circuit, creating new opportunities for commerce, accumulation, and the division of labor. And always it is the "liberal and generous system ... grant[ing] the most perfect freedom of trade" (*WN*, 671) that makes this most productive flow of capital possible. The agricultural system shares with Smith's model presented in Book II the concept of concentric circuits of capital in which as each successive circuit is filled the capital then spills into the next circuit.

To restrain this freedom in the name of national interest discourages agriculture "in two different ways. First, by raising the price of foreign goods …, it necessarily sinks the real value of the surplus produce of the land.… Secondly, by giving a sort of monopoly [to domestic producers] … it raises the rate of mercantile and manufacturing profit," artificially drawing capital away from agriculture (*WN*, 672). This is especially destructive if agriculture is indeed the only sector that offers a net product.

This agricultural system

is represented by Mr. Quesnai, the very ingenious and profound author of this system, in some arithmetical formularies. The first of these, which by way of eminence he peculiarly distinguishes by the name of the Oeconomical Table, represents the manner in which he supposes this distribution [among classes] takes place, in a state of the most perfect liberty, and therefore of the highest prosperity.… Some subsequent formularies represent the [distorted cases]. (*WN*, 672–3)

These "subsequent formularies" represent every such distortion as reducing the wealth of the nation – the greater the distortion the greater the diminution.

Smith believes this logic overly simplifies the reality of human progress.

"Some speculative physicians seem to have imagined that the health of the human body could be preserved only by a certain precise regimen of diet and exercise … [with the cure for any] disease or disorder proportioned to the degree of the violation" (*WN*, 673). Quesnay, a physician, is arguing in this vein that the body politic can only survive and thrive under an "exact regime of perfect liberty and perfect justice" (*WN*, 674).

Smith's view of the progress of opulence is much more nuanced. In his system it is not: be perfect or decline. In his system perfection can never be achieved, but progress is possible even in the face of imperfections. Responding to Quesnay, Smith writes that

[h]e seems not to have considered that in the political body, the natural effort which every man is continually making to better his own condition, is a principle of preservation capable of preventing and correcting, in many respects, the bad effects of a political œconomy, in some degree, both partial and oppressive.… If a nation could not prosper without the enjoyment of perfect liberty and perfect justice, there is not in the world a nation which could ever have prospered. In the political body, however, the wisdom of nature has fortunately made ample

provision for remedying many of the bad effects of the folly and injustice of man; in the same manner as it has done in the natural body, for remedying those of his sloth and intemperance. (*WN*, 674)

Furthermore in rejecting mercantilism Quesnay's system has bent the rod too much in the other direction. "The capital error of this system … seems to lie in its representing the class of artificers, manufacturers and merchants, as altogether barren and unproductive" (*WN*, 674). To make this case Smith applies his own system: the role of productive versus unproductive labor in the self-expansion of capital flowing in circuits.

In Smith's analysis labor that is producing stock to be used in the circuit of production is productive labor even if the stock it produces is not greater than its own maintenance. At the very least it is replenishing the capital stock it used for the next circuit of production. To make his point he offers the following analogy: if parents have a son and a daughter they are less "productive" than a couple who has three children, but they are still productive for they have replenished the stock of humanity to follow them.

Based on his definitions of productive and unproductive labor, Smith considers it an error to compare artificers, merchants, or manufacturers to menial servants. The former employments can at least replace the capital required to sustain them; the work of a menial servant "is not of a nature to repay that expense" (*WN*, 675) so it invariably diminishes the capital stock. This latter effect is the essence of unproductive labor in Smith's system.

Furthermore, the productive power of labor is determined by the degree of the division of labor, and the labor of the "artificers and manufacturers … is capable of being more subdivided … than that of farmers and country labourers, so it is likewise capable of … improvement in a much higher degree" (*WN*, 676). Not only are they more able to increase their productivity, they are more inclined to the parsimony that allows for this ever finer division of labor. In sum, the artificers and manufacturers are very productive workers.

His final critique is that empirical realities belie the logic of the agricultural system. If all wealth comes from the ground, how can one explain the prosperity of a place such as Holland that has so little tillable ground? It is their trading and manufacturing that produces their wealth, for these activities are indeed productive.

This [agricultural] system, however, with all its imperfections is, perhaps, the nearest approximation to the truth that has yet been published upon the subject

of political œconomy ... the notions which it inculcates are perhaps too narrow and confined; yet in representing the wealth of nations as consisting, not in
unconsumable riches of money [like the mercantilists], but in the consumable
goods annually reproduced by the labour of the society; and in representing perfect liberty as the only effectual expedient for rendering this annual reproduction
the greatest possible, its doctrine seems to be in every respect as just as it is generous and liberal. (*WN*, 678)

Clearly, while Smith does not agree with these "Oeconomists" (*WN*,
678), he admires and respects them. As with his own, the realm of their
work "is not only what is properly called Political Œconomy, or of the
nature and causes of the wealth of nations, but of every other branch of
the system of government" (*WN*, 678–9). As does he, so too they value
the principles of and seek to enhance the realization of liberal society.
Indeed, they have achieved some good for their nation: "[B]y influenc-
ing in some measure the publick administration ... the agriculture of
France has been delivered from several of the oppressions which it before
laboured under" (*WN*, 678).

But this good notwithstanding, theirs is a flawed system. As evidence
that undervaluing manufacturing can be just as perverse as overvaluing
it, he cites China, where "policy ... favours agriculture more than all
other employments" (*WN*, 679). Under this policy "[f]oreign trade ... [is]
confined within a much narrower circle than that to which it would naturally extend itself, if more freedom was allowed to it" (*WN*, 680). This
restriction to a narrow circle in turn artificially diminishes the potential of the manufacturing industry, for "[t]he perfection of manufacturing
industry ... depends altogether on the division of labour; and [this] is
necessarily regulated ... by the extent of the market" (*WN*, 680).

China is nevertheless wealthy because it is in itself a large market with
many dimensions (e.g., a "variety of climate" (*WN*, 681)) and excellent
navigable rivers to facilitate trade within its borders. This domestic market may well be almost as extensive as "all the different countries of
Europe put together" (*WN*, 681). But for all of China's success, it has
by its own restrictions denied itself many opportunities for even greater
improvement.

Participating freely in the international nexus of trade creates a fabric of constructive interdependence through mutual learning. In a free
trade system

the Chinese would naturally learn the art of using and constructing themselves
all the different machines made use of in other countries, as well as the other
improvements of art and industry practiced in all the different parts of the world.

Under their present plan they have little opportunity of improving themselves by the example of any other nation; except that of the Japanese [with whom they do trade]. (*WN*, 681)

Such restrictions on trade are more deadly to manufacturing than to agriculture because the greater productivity of manufacturing[34] requires a more extensive market to sustain it. "Agriculture, therefore, can support itself under the discouragement of a confined market, much better than manufacturers" (*WN*, 682).

In ancient Egypt and Indostan the existence of these restrictions is largely a function of the interest of the rulers, for in both cases the revenue of the sovereign was derived from the "the produce of the land" (*WN*, 683).

"[T]he antient republicks of Greece, and that of Rome" (*WN*, 683) also discouraged manufacturing. There, however, the discouragement of manufacturing was not to the favor of agriculture. Rather it seems to have been a cultural bias against the kind of labor involved in manufacturing. "In several of the antient states of Greece [this activity was] ... considered as hurtful to the strength and agility of the human body [making it less fit for war.] ... Such occupations were considered as fit only for slaves" (*WN*, 683).

In Athens and Rome the employment of slaves to carry on these skilled trades was "for the benefit of their masters, whose wealth, power, and protection, made it almost impossible for a poor freeman to find a market for his work, when it came into competition with that of the slaves of the rich" (*WN*, 684).[35] Thus slavery was a tool of the rich that undermined the position of the poor.

Such production does not capture the full benefits of manufacturing, however, because slaves have very little or no incentive to be "inventive" (*WN*, 684). Indeed, an inventive suggestion from a slave might be seen by his master as a "suggestion of laziness, and a desire to save his own labour at the master's expence" (*WN*, 684). The "reward" for such a suggestion therefore might be "punishment" (*WN*, 684).

Slave labor, being much less efficient, is therefore much more costly than that of freemen. Smith cites as evidence Montesquieu's observations on the relative profitability of Hungarian versus Turkish mines in the same

---

[34] "The nature of agriculture ... does not admit of so many subdivisions of labour, nor of so complete a separation of one business from another, as manufactures" (*WN*, 16).

[35] This pitting of rich man's slave against poor freeman to the poor man's detriment is a point Smith made earlier in describing the superintendent and workers of Roman agriculture (*WN*, 557).

neighborhood. The former use freemen and "a great deal of machinery" (*WN*, 684). The latter use only the arms of slaves and are much less profitable. Similarly, Smith attributes the high price of fineries in Greece and Rome to the inefficient slave labor used to produce those goods.

In closing this last chapter of Book IV, Smith returns to his central theme: Within a system of liberty and justice, free trade is beneficial to all parties and any distortions reduce the well-being of all. As he has explained in Book II, and in words that are almost identical to the opening words of Book III, here at the close of Book IV he reminds us yet again that "[t]he greatest and most important branch of commerce of every nation ... is that which is carried on between the inhabitants of the town and those of the country" (*WN*, 686). Any restraint on this innermost circuit of trade reduces the fruitfulness of this circuit. Similarly any preferences for other circuits distort the flow of capital. Such a restraint or preference therefore reduces the accumulation of capital and

retards, instead of accelerating, the progress of the society towards real wealth and greatness; and diminishes, instead of increasing, the real value of the annual produce of its land and labour.

All systems either of preference or of restraint, therefore, being thus completely taken away, the obvious and simple system of natural liberty establishes itself of its own accord. Every man, *as long as he does not violate the laws of justice*, is left perfectly free to pursue his own interest in his own way, and to bring both his industry and capital into competition with those of any other man, or order of men. The sovereign is completely discharged from a duty, in attempting to perform which he must always be exposed to innumerable delusions, and for the proper performance of which no human wisdom or knowledge could ever be sufficient; the duty of superintending the industry of private people, and of directing it towards the employments most suitable to the interest of society. (*WN*, 687, emphasis added)

This is Smith's liberal vision: independent individuals free to pursue their own ends will always move their resources to their best advantage and will always compete most keenly to better their condition. When the market competition is unfettered, just, and fair, this dynamic will serve the well-being of society. It is the height of arrogance for a sovereign to believe that he can think for all these individuals and arrange so complex and fluid a world in a way that would be remotely as "suitable to the interest of society." But, and this is the essential caveat, for freedom to be constructive there must be justice.

So if it is not the role of the sovereign to manage the world, what is that role and how is that role to be financed without distorting the natural flows of the economy? This is the topic of Book V, the last book in

Smith's *Inquiry into the Nature and Causes of the Wealth of Nations*. In a brief preview at the end of Book IV, Smith asserts that "[a]ccording to the system of natural liberty, the sovereign has only three duties to attend to; three duties of great importance ...

- "first, the duty of protecting the society from the violence and invasion of other independent societies;
- "secondly, the duty of protecting, as far as possible, every member of the society from the injustice and oppression of every other member of it, or the duty of establishing an exact administration of justice; and,
- "thirdly, the duty of erecting and maintaining certain publick works and certain publick institutions, which it can never be for the interest of any individual, or small number of individuals, to erect and maintain; because the profit could never repay the expence to any individual or small group of individuals, though it may frequently do much more than repay it to a great society." (*WN*, 687–8)

Carrying out each of these duties entails an expense. Meeting these expenses requires revenue, or debt.

Book V examines the roles of government, the means of defraying the expenses of government, and finally public debt and its consequences for the wealth of the nation.

5

The Wealth of Nations: Book V

Of the Revenue of the Sovereign or Commonwealth

INTRODUCTION

In his "Introduction and Plan of the Work," Smith describes Book V as covering:

- the "necessary expences of the sovereign, or commonwealth" (*WN*, 12) and who should pay each of these expenses;
- "the different methods in which the whole society may be made to contribute towards defraying the expences incumbent on the whole society, and what are the principal advantages and inconveniencies of each of those methods" (*WN*, 12); and
- why "almost all modern governments ... contract debts, and what have been the effects of those debts" (*WN*, 12) on the wealth of nations.

But this is more than a book about revenue. As Smith examines the optimal methods for financing the roles of government that he laid out at the close of Book IV, he develops the content of those roles and explores how their optimal implementation evolves as society evolves.

CHAPTER 1: "OF THE EXPENCES OF THE SOVEREIGN OR COMMONWEALTH"

Part I: "Of the Expence of Defence"

The first duty of the sovereign, that of protecting the society from the violence and invasion of other independent societies, can be performed only by means of a military force. But the expence both of preparing this military force in time of peace, and of employing it in time of war, is very different in the different states of society, in the different periods of improvement. (*WN*, 689)

Again, Smith's four stages theory of progress frames his analysis.

In the first, rude state of hunting "as we find it among the native tribes on North America" (*WN*, 690), the sovereign incurs no expense for defense because "there is properly neither sovereign nor commonwealth" (*WN*, 690). Every man is a hunter. The skills he masters as a hunter prepare him for the defense of the tribe and provide his maintenance in peace and in war.

"Among a nation of shepherds, a *more advanced* state of society, such as we find it among the Tartars and Arabs, every man is, in the same manner, a warrior" (*WN*, 690, emphasis added). This community, with "no fixed habitation" (*WN*, 690), moves as a unit with its flocks. In peace and in war it functions as a unit. All participate in both endeavors, and the fate of each is the fate of all.

The "common pastimes of those who live in the open air" ("[r]unning, wrestling, cudgel-playing, throwing the javelin, drawing the bow, &c." (*WN*, 691)) prepare every man for the rigors of war. Moving with their flocks, all are constantly provisioned for war so the "chief or sovereign ... [bears] no sort of expence in preparing" for war (*WN*, 691).

Shepherding is a more fruitful and dependable mode of production than hunting, so a shepherd society can sustain a much larger force: an "army of hunters can seldom exceed two or three hundred men. The[ir] precarious subsistence ... could seldom allow a greater number to keep together for any considerable time.... An army of shepherds ... may sometimes amount to two or three hundred thousand.... [Thus, while a] nation of hunters can never be formidable to the civilized nations in their neighborhood, a nation of shepherds may" (*WN*, 691).

In "a *yet more advanced* state of society ... [people] live by agriculture"[1] (*WN*, 692–3, emphasis added). The hard work of agriculture prepares the husbandman for the rigors of war and in his leisure he indulges in the same "pastimes ... of war" as the shepherd (*WN*, 693). But the husbandman does not have as much leisure as the shepherd to hone these skills, so while husbandmen are good soldiers, they are "not quite so much masters of their [(the skills of war)] exercise" as shepherds (*WN*, 693).

---

[1] Note that each stage has "advanced" beyond the last. These are the stages of the "progress of opulence" (*WN*, 376).

An agricultural society also differs from a shepherding society in that it "supposes a settlement ... which cannot be abandoned without great loss" (WN, 693) and crops that demand someone's full attention, especially at planting and harvesting times. So unlike the shepherd society, in an agricultural society only about "a fourth or a fifth part of the whole body of the people" is available to fight (WN, 693).[2] But even these hands are hard to spare in the seeding and the harvesting seasons. Conflict is therefore seasonal. Between seeding and harvesting "nature does herself the greater part of the work" (WN, 694–5), and with this support from nature soldiers require no support from the sovereign.

Given its greater productivity, agriculture can support much larger communities than shepherding. So while the portion of citizens available to fight in an agricultural society is smaller than in a shepherding society, the pool from which these soldiers are drawn is much larger. Thus an agricultural society can field a more formidable military.

In the last stage of development, a commercial society, "two different causes contribute to render it altogether impossible that they, who take the field, should maintain themselves at their own expence. Those two causes are, the progress of manufacturers, and the improvement in the art of war" (WN, 694).

Unlike an agricultural society in which nature, as a partner in production, can relieve the husbandman for military duty during the growing season, in a commercial society:

the moment that an artificer, a smith, a carpenter, or a weaver ... quits his workhouse, the sole source of his revenue is completely dried up. Nature does nothing for him, he does all for himself. When he takes the field, therefore, ... he must necessarily be maintained by the publick.

[This is all the more so w]hen the art of war ... [has] grown up to be a very intricate and complicated science, [and when, instead of being] determined as in the first ages of society, by a single irregular skirmish or battle ... [wars are characterized by] campaigns, each of which lasts during the greater part of the year. (WN, 695)

At this most advanced stage in the progress of opulence, government must establish and finance the military.

The initial model for this was a militia,[3] a military in which "the trade of a soldier was not a separate, distinct trade, which constituted the sole

---

2 "The old men, the women, and children, at least, must remain at home to take care of the habitation" (WN, 693).
3 Smith traces this model from the "republicks of antient Greece ... [to] antient Rome ... [to early] feudal governments" (WN, 696).

or principal occupation of a particular class of citizens" (WN, 696–7). But hand in hand with advancements in the art of production came two dynamics that undermined this militia model for defense:

- a general neglect among the population of the art of war, and
- advancements in the art of war that made war more "complicated" (WN, 697).

A shepherd has a great deal of leisure; a husbandman ... has some; an artificer or manufacturer has none at all. The first may, without any loss, employ a great deal of his time in martial exercises; the second may employ some part of it; but the last cannot employ a single hour in them without some loss, and his attention to his own interest naturally leads him to neglect them altogether ... [so] unless the state takes some new measures for the publick defence, the natural habits of the people render them altogether incapable of defending themselves. (WN, 697–8)

This is an unfortunate fact given that the "wealth ... which always follows the improvements of agriculture and manufacturers ... provokes the invasion of all of their neighbours" (WN, 697). But as advancement brings this challenge, it also brings the solution through the very process that makes advancement possible, the division of labor:

The art of war ... as it is certainly the noblest of all arts, so in the progress of improvement it necessarily becomes one of the most complicated among them.... [I]t is necessary[, therefore,] that it should become the sole or principal occupation of a particular class of citizens, and the division of labour is as necessary of the improvement of this, as of every other art. (WN, 697)

This particular division of labor will not occur naturally, however, because soldiering is

- unproductive labor – it does not produce the means to maintain itself; and
- a public good – so other citizens do not have the incentive to provide the means to support the soldier.

Into other arts the division of labour is naturally introduced by the prudence of individuals, who find that they promote their private interest better by confining themselves to a particular trade, than by exercising a great number. But it is the wisdom of the state only which can render the trade of a soldier a particular trade separate and distinct from all others. A private citizen who, in time of profound peace, and without any particular encouragement from the publick, should spend the greater part of his time in military exercises ... certainly would not promote his own interest. It is the wisdom of the state only which can render it for his interest to give up the greater part of his time to this particular occupation. (WN, 697)

This position embroils Smith in a long-standing British debate over whether a militia or a standing army is the appropriate model for the defense of the nation.[4] The "essential difference between those two different species of military force" (*WN*, 698) turns, according to Smith, on his division of labor logic.

The character of the soldiers in a militia is determined by their primary job, which is not soldiering. In a standing army soldering is soldiers' primary job and thus defines their character. The transformation of the technology of warfare, in particular "the invention of fire-arms" (*WN*, 699), makes strong soldiering characteristics (good order and discipline) essential for a modern army to succeed. Those characteristics "can only be acquired ... by troops which are exercised in great bodies [as in a standing army.][5] ... A militia [doesn't instill these characteristics and so it] ... must always be much inferior to a well disciplined and well exercised standing army" (*WN*, 699).[6]

Here, as always, Smith's analysis is evolutionary. Militias were fine when combat was technologically rudimentary. But with the invention of firearms the nature of warfare was transformed, and so too a nation's military must be if it is to compete on the field of battle.

Firearms make the modern battlefield different. The premium on individual dexterity that defined ancient battles is replaced by a premium on "regularity, order, and prompt obedience to command" (*WN*, 699). On a "modern [battlefield where each individual is surrounded by] ... the noise of fire-arms, the smoke, and the invisible death to which every man feels himself every moment exposed" (*WN*, 699), the cohesive performance of an armed force requires "regularity, order, and prompt obedience."

The societies most capable of fielding a formidable standing army are those advanced commercial societies that have the technological sophistication to produce the most modern weaponry and sufficient productivity

---

4 See *WN* (700, footnote 31) for references to Smith's correspondence related to the militia question. See Pocock (426–36) on the militia question.

5 "The soldiers, who are bound to obey their officer only once a week or once a month, and who are at all other times at liberty to manage their own affairs their own way ... can never be under the same awe in his presence, can never have the same disposition to ready obedience, with those whose whole life and conduct are every day directed by him" (*WN*, 700). Some militias, like those of the Tartar, approach the standing army model more closely than others, like the Highlanders. Those more like the standing army are more formidable.

6 Smith notes that if a militia stays in the field for any length of time it may develop the characteristics of a standing army, and he continues: "Should the way in America drag out through another campaign, the American militia may become in every respect a match for that [valorous] standing army" of Britain (*WN*, 701).

to support the unproductive labor of professional soldiers. Natural selection should therefore favor such advanced states, but such "states have not always had this wisdom [(to support a standing army)], even when their circumstances had become such, that the preservation of their existence required that they should have it" (*WN*, 697).

The militia versus standing army debate had long been and remained very hot in Smith's day. To drive home his position Smith proceeds to demonstrate that "the history of all ages ... bears testimony" (*WN*, 701) to the case he is making. As always, history provides the empirical evidence he cites to persuade the reader of the power of his logic.

Philip of Macedon's defeat of "the Greek republics and of the Persian empire ... [and later t]he fall of Carthage, and the consequent elevation of Rome" (*WN*, 702) are testimony to the superiority of standing armies. In both cases the success of the victors was determined by their armies, even if initially they were militias, developing "the exact discipline of a standing army" (*WN*, 702).

"From the end of the second Carthaginian war till the fall of the Roman republick, the armies of Rome were in every respect standing armies" (*WN*, 703). While they faced stiff opposition on occasion, they vanquished every enemy they encountered. Then, having defeated all the formidable opponents, their "heavy armour was laid aside ... and laborious exercises were neglected" (*WN*, 704). When the troops deployed on "the German and Pannonian frontiers ... became dangerous to their masters, against whom they used frequently to set up their own generals" (*WN*, 704), those troops were

dispersed ... in small bodies through the different provincial towns ... Small bodies of soldiers quartered in trading and manufacturing towns, and seldom removed from those quarters, became themselves tradesmen, artificers, and manufacturers. Their civil came to predominate over the military character; and the standing armies of Rome gradually degenerated into a corrupt, neglected, and undisciplined militia, incapable of resisting the attack of the German and Scythian militias, which soon afterwards invaded the western empire. (*WN*, 704)

Smith traces this story from the fall of Rome into the feudal period when these conquering militias became the force that preserved order under their chieftains.[7]

As arts and industry advanced, however, the authority of the chieftains gradually decayed, and the great body of the people had less time to spare for military exercises. Both the discipline and the exercise of the feudal militia, therefore,

---

[7] This is where Book III picks up the narrative.

went gradually to ruin, and standing armies were gradually introduced to supply the place of it. When the expedient of a standing army, besides, had once been adopted by one civilized nation, it became necessary that all its neighbours should follow that example. (WN, 705)

The record of the standing armies that emerged from this feudal period demonstrates that peace does not invariably lead to the corruption of discipline if an army is constantly trained. Citing several examples, he concludes: "In a long peace the generals, perhaps, may sometimes forget their skill; but, where a well–regulated standing army has been kept up, the soldiers seem never to forget their valour" (WN, 705).

Always, the standard Smith applies to test his analysis is the actual course of humankind's history. Here, to support his analysis of the evolution of the sovereign's role in defense he traces the "history [as it] has [been] preserved [by] any distinct or circumstantial account" (WN, 702, 704, same usage in both places) from ancient times to the feudal world, and then from the decline of that world to the emergence of the nation-state as he describes it in Book III.

His point is clear: a "well-regulated standing army is superior to every militia ... [and] can best be maintained by an opulent and civilized nation ... It is[, furthermore,] only by means of a standing army ... that the civilization of any country can be perpetuated, or even preserved for any considerable time" (WN, 705–6).[8]

As for republican fears:

Men of republican principles have been jealous of a standing army as dangerous to liberty. It certainly is so, whenever the interest of the general and that of the principal officers are not necessarily connected with the support of the constitution of the state. [He cites Caesar and Cromwell as examples.] ... But ... where the military force is placed under the command of those who have the greatest interest in the support of civil society ... a standing army can never be dangerous to liberty.[9] On the contrary, it may in some cases be favorable to liberty.... That degree of liberty which approaches to licentiousness can be tolerated only in countries where the sovereign is secured by a well-regulated standing army.[10] It is in such countries, only, that the publick safety does not require, that the

---

[8] Not only does such an army sustain the gains of progress, the path to progress is accelerated by such an army: "As it is only by means of a well-regulated standing army that a civilized country can be defended; so it is only by means of it, that a barbarous country can be suddenly and tolerably civilized" (WN, 706).

[9] One of the advantages of history that England enjoys is that "a system of liberty has been established in England before the standing army was introduced; which as it was not the case in other countries, so it has never been established in them" (LJA, 269).

[10] Where public authority is fragile "the whole authority of the government must be employed to suppress and punish every murmur and complaint against it" (WN, 707).

sovereign should be trusted with any discretionary power, for suppressing even the impertinent wantonness of this licentious liberty."[11] (*WN*, 706–7)

Concluding Part I of chapter 1, Smith writes that "[t]he first duty of the sovereign [defense] ... grows gradually more and more expensive, as the society advances in civilization.... [This is t]he unavoidable effect of the natural progress of improvement" (*WN*, 707–8). In keeping with his larger moral philosophical theme of natural selection as a driving force in humankind's progress, he writes:

> In modern war the great expence of fire-arms gives an evident advantage to the nation which can best afford that expence; and consequently, to an opulent and civilized, over a poor and barbarous nation.... The invention of fire-arms, an invention which at first sight appears to be so pernicious, is certainly favourable both to the permanency and to the extension of civilization. (*WN*, 708)

Part II: "Of the Expence of Justice"

> The second duty of the sovereign, that of protecting, as far as possible, every member of society from the injustice or oppression of every other member of it, or the duty of establishing an exact administration of justice, requires too very different degrees of expence in the different periods of society. (*WN*, 708–9)

The continuity of Smith's thought from Part I on defense to Part II on justice is striking. Both focus on security,[12] Part I on the security of the entire society from external threats and Part II on the security of "every member of society from the injustice or oppression of every other member of it." In both cases the analysis is framed by the evolution of society through the "different periods."

In the first period, the rude state of hunters, "there is seldom any established magistrate or any regular administration of justice ... [because w] here there is no property, or at least none that exceeds the value of two or three days labour ..., civil government is not necessary" (*WN*, 709–10).

---

[11] Smith's reference to "the impertinent wantonness of this licentious liberty" reflects a valuing of diversity in liberal society that John Stuart Mill expresses also:

> "No society in which eccentricity is a matter of reproach, can be in a wholesome state.... [The] multiform development of human nature, those manifold unlikenesses, that diversity of tastes and talents, and variety of intellectual points of view, which not only form a great part of the interest of human life, but by bringing intellects into stimulating collision, and by presenting to each innumerable notions that he would not have conceived of himself, are the mainspring of mental and moral progression" (Mill, 1895, Vol. I, 271).

[12] This connection is also explicit in *LJA* (5–6).

Absent significant property, while "[e]nvy, malice, or resentment" (WN, 709) can drive one to injure one's neighbor in body or reputation, "[a]s their gratification … is not attended with any real or permanent advantage, it is in the greater part of men commonly restrained by prudential considerations"[13] (WN, 709).

"It is otherwise with the injuries to property. The benefit of the person who does the injury is often equal to the loss of him who suffers it" (WN, 709). A thief enjoys the fruits of his injustice. Such fruits are only possible where there is property, therefore, the injustices driven by passions for property "are much more steady in their operation, and much more universal in their influence…. The acquisition of valuable and extensive property, therefore, necessarily requires the establishment of civil government" (WN, 709–10).

With the evolution from hunting to pasturage, property in animals emerges. With the evolution from pasturage to agriculture, property in land emerges. And finally, with the evolution from agriculture to commercial society, property in capital emerges. Each of these kinds of property creates new and more complex challenges for the legal system if property is to be secure, and property must be secure if each of the steps in the progress of opulence is to be sustained. Thus the progress of opulence requires the emergence and maturation of civil government. The success of civil government requires civil citizens.

> Civil government supposes a certain subordination. But as the necessity of civil government gradually grows up with the acquisition of valuable property, so the principal causes which naturally introduce subordination gradually grow up with the growth of that valuable property. (WN, 710)

Classic Smith. Humankind's evolution is a natural process driven in part by characteristics of human nature that supply the requisite conditions for that evolution to proceed. Smith identifies four natural sources of subordination that make the emergence of civil government possible.

"[S]uperiority of personal qualifications, of strength, beauty, and agility of body; of wisdom, and virtue, or prudence, justice, fortitude, and moderation of mind" can be significant but are not generally the determining factor of subordination. Strength absent a good mind can only

---

[13] "Resentment seems to have been given us by nature for defence, and for defence only. It is the safeguard of justice and the security of innocence…. [Injustice] is, therefore, the proper object of resentment, and of punishment, which is the natural consequence of resentment…. [M]ankind [can] go along with, and approve of the violence employed to avenge the hurt which is done by injustice" (TMS, 78).

subordinate a few. "[Q]ualifications of the mind … are invisible qualities; always disputable, and generally disputed." Thus most societies look to "more plain and palpable" distinctions (*WN*, 711). These include:

- "[S]uperiority of age – [this] is a plain and palpable quality which admits of no dispute" (*WN*, 711).
- "[S]uperiority of fortune" – this is most significant as a regulator of rank in a "society [that] does not afford him [(one with wealth)] any manufactured produce" (*WN*, 711–12). In such a world, as in the feudal world Smith describes in Book III, the only vent for wealth is support of dependents. Wealth is a less powerful determinant of rank in an advanced society because most of those who work to supply the needs of the wealthy serve many masters through the market and are thus not totally dependent on the whim of any one individual. Nevertheless, "[t]he authority of fortune … is very great even in an opulent and civilized society. That it is much greater than that, either of age, or of personal qualities, has been the constant complaint of every period of society which admitted of any considerable inequality of wealth" (*WN*, 712).
- "Superiority of birth supposes an antient superiority of fortune in the family of the person who claims it…. Upstart greatness is every where less respected than antient greatness" (*WN*, 713).

Among these sources of distinction "[b]irth and fortune are evidently the two circumstances which principally set one man above another … and are therefore the principal causes which naturally establish authority and subordination among men" (*WN*, 714). The power that birth and fortune afford a leader is greatest "[a]mong a nation of shepherds" (*WN*, 714) when the necessity of civil government first emerges. With this authority comes the responsibility to protect the society from external threats and to ensure internal justice. The tribal head is the leader in war and the "judicial authority" in peace (*WN*, 714).

[Thus] in the second period of society … [the] civil government which is indispensably necessary for its own preservation [emerges] … and it seems to do this naturally, and even independent of the consideration of that necessity.[14] The

---

[14] In his *Lectures on Jurisprudence* Smith makes his evolutionary view of the emergence of government clear as he rejects contractarian origins of government: "[I]t arose, not as some writers imagine from any consent or agreement of a number of persons to submit themselves to such or such regulations, but from the natural progress which men make in society" (*LJA*, 207).

consideration of that necessity comes no doubt afterwards to contribute very much to maintain and secure that authority and subordination (*WN*, 715).

Civil government emerges "naturally," but intentional human actions can and do reinforce and refine the structures of civil government. Both "the rich ... [and the m]en of moderate wealth" see the virtue of defending this system of security, for both have something to lose and both appreciate that property is vulnerable in the absence of an authority that protects security. At the pastoral stage "[c]ivil government, so far as it is instituted for the security of property, is in reality instituted for the defence ... of those who have some property from those who have none at all" (*WN*, 715).

It is evolution that brings forth civil government, and for progress to be sustained civil society must continue to evolve as a system of civil laws and civic duties. Smith's analysis of the emergence of judicial authority in civil government reflects this dynamic.

When civil government was first formed all authority rested in the hands of a powerful individual leader. Included among his powers was that of serving as the judicial authority. This role generated significant revenue for the leader. When people "applied to him for justice ... a present never failed to accompany a petition ... [and once] the authority of the sovereign ... was thoroughly established ... [those] found guilty [not only had to compensate the injured but were also] forced to pay an amercement to the sovereign" (*WN*, 715) to compensate for the intrusion they caused to his tranquility.

> Originally both the sovereign and the inferior chiefs used to exercise this jurisdiction in their own persons. Afterwards they universally found it convenient to delegate it to some substitute, bailiff, or judge. This substitute, however, was still obliged to account to his principal or constituent for the profits of the jurisdiction....
>
> This scheme of making the administration of justice subservient to the purposes of revenue, could scarce fail to be productive of several very gross abuses. The person, who applied for justice with a large present ... was likely to get something more than justice; while he, who applied for it with a small one, was likely to get something less. (*WN*, 716)

As always, Smith cites history to establish the credibility of his case: "That such abuses were far from uncommon, the antient history of every country in Europe bears witness" (*WN*, 717).

This fee-for-service justice – the better the fee, the better the service – continued until other considerations transformed the fiscal needs of the sovereign.

As nations matured they became more ripe and more vulnerable to "invasion of other nations" (*WN*, 718). This led to a "continually increasing expence of defending the nation" (*WN*, 718). "[T]he private estate of the sovereign [became] ... altogether insufficient" (*WN*, 718) to fund this undertaking. The civil government required more revenue and more regular means of acquiring that revenue.

It became "necessary that the people should, for their own security, contribute towards this expence by taxes" (*WN*, 718).

Given this regular and determinate tax revenue stream, the irregular compensation for justice based on presents was abolished and "[f]ixed salaries were appointed to judges" (*WN*, 718). This did not significantly diminish the cost of justice because much of that cost was to cover the fees of lawyers. It did, however, separate the judges' compensation from their judgments, which can contribute to the "prevent[ion] of the corruption of justice" (*WN*, 719).

The salaries for judges need not, Smith notes, be very high, for the very honor of the office attracts many good candidates. Indeed, the entire cost of the administration of justice "makes, in any civilized country, but a very inconsiderable part of the whole expence of government" (*WN*, 719). With this assertion, Smith turns his attention to how "[t]he whole expence of justice ... might easily be defrayed by the fees of court; and, without exposing the administration of justice to any real hazard of corruption" (*WN*, 719).

An optimal system would have regularized fees paid to a "cashier or receiver" and only distributed to the judge or judges after "the process was determined" (*WN*, 719). Payments would be independent of participants and proportioned to the cases resolved. This model provides a constructive alignment of incentives for both impartial and diligent consideration of cases. Note the Smithian policy model for we will see it again and again: he is all about aligning incentives to achieve the desired outcome.

Just such fees, designed to encourage diligence, have had very constructive unintended consequences among "the different courts of justice in England" (*WN*, 720). Again he turns to historical evidence.

In pursuit of more cases and thus more fees, "the different courts of justice" have embraced various "fictions," leaps of interpretation invented to extend their jurisdictions (*WN*, 720). As a consequence these different courts developed overlapping jurisdictions, putting them into direct competition for cases.

In consequence of such fictions it came, in many cases, to depend altogether upon the parties before what court they would chuse to have their case tried; and each court endeavoured, by superior dispatch and impartiality, to draw to itself as many causes as it could. The present admirable constitution of the courts of justice in England was, perhaps, originally in a great measure, formed by this emulation. (*WN*, 720)[15]

In keeping with his evolutionary narrative, Smith sees the increasing integrity of the British judicial system as an unintended consequence of competition among the various courts for cases.

A fee-based system can also generate perverse incentives. Those fees that increased with the number of pages that go into a submission "contrived to multiply words beyond all necessity, to the corruption of the law language of ... every court of justice in Europe" (*WN*, 721).

Never a "man of system ... enamoured with the supposed beauty of his own ideal plan" (*TMS*, 233), Smith's point is not that he knows the ideal system, but rather that any constructive system must align incentives such that they encourage constructive action.

A principle that has emerged from the evolution of judicial administration, and one that Smith is adamant must be protected, is "[t]he separation of the judicial from the executive power" (*WN*, 721): judicial tenure and compensation must be independent of the executive.

When the judicial is united to the executive power, it is scarce possible that justice should not frequently be sacrificed to, what is vulgarly called, politics. The persons entrusted with the great interests of the state may, even without any corrupt views, sometimes imagine it necessary to sacrifice to those interests the rights of the private man. But upon the impartial administration of justice depends the liberty of every individual, the sense which he has of his own security. In order to make every individual feel himself perfectly secure in the possession of every right which belongs to him, it is not only necessary that the judicial should be separated from the executive power, but that it should be rendered as much as possible independent of that power. The judge should not be liable to be removed from his office according to the caprice of that power. The regular payment of his salary should not depend upon the good-will, or even upon the good economy of that power. (*WN*, 721–2)

The first two duties Smith ascribes to the sovereign or commonwealth, providing for defense and justice, both have to do with security. The ultimate purpose of each is to ensure that "every individual feel himself perfectly secure [(from external threats or internal injustices)] in the possession of every right which belongs to him" (*WN*, 722). Security is not a birthright of humankind. Indeed, in the first age of humankind individuals are very insecure. The institutions that provide security are human

---

15 Smith presents this process in his lecture of Thursday, 10 March 1763 in *LJA* (275–82).

constructs that emerge and evolve across many generations of societal experiments. That evolution is driven by chance, circumstance, and the unintended and intended consequences of human actions.

What he has described in these first two parts of chapter 1 of Book V of *The Wealth of Nations* are two of the essential expenses or, in other words, two essential roles that government must mature into if progress toward the "liberal plan of equality, liberty and justice" (*WN*, 664) is to be realized. In Part III he turns to the third expense, the third role of government.

Part III: "Of the Expence of publick Works and publick Institutions"

The third and last duty of the sovereign or commonwealth is that of erecting and maintaining those publick institutions and those publick works, which, though they may be in the highest degree advantageous to a great society, are, however, of such a nature, that the profit could never repay the expence to any individual or small number of individuals, and which it, therefore, cannot be expected that any individual or small number of individuals should erect or maintain. The performance of this duty requires too very different degrees of expence in different periods of society.

... [The] institutions of this kind are chiefly those for facilitating the commerce of the society, and those for promoting the instruction of the people. (*WN*, 723)

As with security, only the state can ensure the provision of these public goods and, as with security, the maturation of these works and institutions is essential if a society is to progress.

Article I. "Of the publick Works and Institutions for facilitating the Commerce of the Society"

"And, first, of those which are necessary for facilitating Commerce in general"

Smith asserts that it "is evident without any proof" (*WN*, 724) that as society progresses through "different periods" the demands on the "publick works which facilitate the commerce" (*WN*, 724) increase. After all, the weight and scope of commerce can only grow as the carrying capacity of the avenues and ports of commerce, the "roads, bridges, navigable canals, harbours, &c." (*WN*, 724), grows.

In most cases these are public goods so there must be public provision if the progress of opulence is to proceed. But while public provision may be necessary, "[t]he greater part of such publick works may easily be so managed, as to afford a particular revenue sufficient for defraying their own expence, without bringing any burden upon the general revenue of the society" (WN, 724).

Smith envisions various kind of user fees as the optimal way to defray the cost of constructing and maintaining many of these public works.[16] "It seems scarce possible to invent a more equitable way of maintaining such works" (WN, 725). And, where appropriate, such fees do not discourage commerce because for "[t]he person who finally pays this tax," the benefit outweighs the burden because "the cheapness of the carriage" (WN, 725) lowers the price much more than the fee raises it.

In keeping with his concern for the least among the working class, Smith also suggests that such fees can be used to accomplish redistribution from rich to poor. By imposing higher fees on luxuries, the fees on necessities can be held down. Thus "the indolence and vanity of the rich is made to contribute in a very easy manner to the relief of the poor" (WN, 725).

Examining the management of public works that facilitate transport, Smith distinguishes those avenues that require constant maintenance, for example, canals, from those that continue to be passable with minimal maintenance, for example, high roads. Given the alignment of incentives, the best way to ensure proper maintenance for the former is to put the toll revenue into the hands of a private person who is responsible for maintenance. The incentives are then properly aligned for him to do that maintenance scrupulously because his well-being depends on keeping the canal passable. In contrast, a high road does not need such constant care, so placing responsibility for maintenance in the hands of a private person might lead to neglect while the person simply collects the tolls. It is better that such roads be managed by a public commission of trustees under the watchful eye of parliament.

If such fees do go to government, it is essential that they stay in a dedicated fund to service the infrastructure that generates them. Allowing these fees to become a resource for the general fund invites abuse. "The facility with which a great revenue could be drawn from them, would probably encourage administration to recur very frequently to this resource" (WN, 727).

---

[16] He cites "[t]he coinage" and "[t]he post-office" as two examples of public provision of services that pay for themselves and even generate a "revenue to the sovereign" (WN, 724).

This could lead to three perverse consequences: first, if diverting fees led to neglected maintenance and in turn an increase in the cost of transport, the extent of the market would be artificially "narrowed" (*WN*, 728), and commerce would be discouraged. Second, because the necessities of life tend to be more gross and heavy than the fineries, fee increases based on weight would be a regressive tax, the burden falling "on those least able to supply it" (*WN*, 728). And finally, the increased funds to the trustees would make it harder and harder to get them to attend to their primary task, caring for the road.

Smith cites France as an example of such perverse incentives. There "the authority of the executive power ... assumes to itself the management of every branch of revenue which is destined for any public purpose" (*WN*, 729). As a consequence, the funds are spent on show rather than utility. The great roads (those "frequently seen by the principal nobility") are in good order, but the many smaller roads, being out of sight, "are entirely neglected" (*WN*, 729).

It is also the case in China that the sovereign exercises great control over infrastructure maintenance. But there the revenue of that sovereign is based largely on land taxes. These taxes are enhanced by agricultural success and this depends on the extent of the market. Thus the sovereign in China has a strong incentive to maintain these public works so that the internal commerce moves well. The European sovereigns have the same incentive, but as this linkage is obscure to them, the incentive is not so keen and the consequence is neglect.

For Smith it is all about the alignment of perceived incentives. Provision is best when the incentives are clear and constructively aligned.

In keeping with this theme, Smith suggests that for "public works [with localized benefits] which are of such a nature that they cannot afford any revenue for maintaining themselves" (*WN*, 730), the responsibility for maintenance should stay local. He cites the streetlights of London as public works that are best supported by taxes from and best managed at the local level. If the funds for their maintenance depended on an allocation from the national treasury, the incentive for allocating funds for that specific purpose would be very weak and the consequence would be neglected provision.

At this point in the first edition of *WN*, Article I titled "Of the publick Works and Institutions for facilitating the Commerce of the Society" ends. This entire, original Article I covers approximately seven pages.

In the third edition (1784) Smith appends to the original title of Article I a section heading: "And, first, of those which are necessary for facilitating

Commerce in general." At the end of this original section, he adds a new section to Article 1 titled "Of the Publick Works and Institutions which are necessary for facilitating particular Branches of Commerce." This new section is approximately four times as long as the original. As does the 1784 addition to Book IV, chapter 8, "Conclusion of the Mercantile System," this addition reflects Smith's growing anger and concern regarding the mercantile interests, and the deeper understanding of the mechanisms of the mercantile system that he gained during his years of service as a Commissioner of Customs. In a letter to his publisher William Strahan (22 May 1783), Smith describes this new section as "A short History and, I presume, a full exposition of the Absurdity and hurtfulness of almost all our chartered trading companies" (*Correspondence*, 266).

"Of the Publick Works and Institutions which are necessary for facilitating particular Branches of Commerce"

Smith begins this new section with the acknowledgment that trade with foreign lands does require public facilitation.

In trade with "barbarours or uncivilized nations" (*WN*, 731) public facilitation may take the form of garrisons to protect the merchants and goods, while in more civilized places "it may be necessary to maintain some ambassador, minister, or counsel" to facilitate relationships where private individuals do not have the necessary "authority … [or] publick character" to do so (*WN*, 732). Indeed, he suggests that it was commerce that "probably introduced the custom of keeping, in all neighbouring countries, ambassadors or ministries … [a custom that seems to have emerged at] the end of the fifteenth or the beginning of the sixteenth century … when commerce first began to extend itself to the greater part of the nations of Europe" (*WN*, 732).

Two general principles that apply to the facilitation of commerce in general also apply to the facilitation of commerce in particular spheres. First, the cost of works and institutions that facilitate commerce, be it general or particular, should ideally be borne by the beneficiary. And second, whether general or particular, the ultimate duty for protecting trade lies with the "executive power" (*WN*, 733).

But given the alignment of incentives and power of the mercantile interests, these principles have not been honored.

[I]n the greater part of the commercial states of Europe, particular companies of merchants have had the address to perswade the legislature to entrust to them the performance of this part of the duty of the sovereign, together with all the powers which are necessarily connected with it.

These companies, though they may, perhaps, have been useful for the first introduction of some branches of commerce, by making at their own expence, an experiment which the state might not think it prudent to make, have in the long-run proved, universally, either burdensome or useless, and have either mismanaged or confined the trade. (*WN*, 733)

This quotation reflects the core point of what follows: there are in limited cases good reasons to grant companies special powers in a new market for a limited period of time. But invariably these advantages have been protected and maintained by the mercantile interests, and this has inevitably led to perverse consequences.

Smith distinguishes two sorts of companies that venture into these foreign adventures: "regulated," in which "each member trade[s] upon his own stock, and at his own risk"; and "joint stock," in which "each member share[s] in the common profit or loss in proportion to his share of this stock" (*WN*, 733). Based on the observations of Sir Josiah Child, Smith describes how the different structures of the regulated companies and joint stock companies lead to significantly different behavior.

The directors of the regulated companies are independent agents each controlling his own capital, and so their interests are not always aligned and capital cannot generally be pooled. In joint stock companies the "private interest [of each director] is connected with the prosperity of the general trade of the company ..., [and given that resources are pooled, they] have always the management of a large capital" (*WN*, 737). An example of the implications of this difference is that the joint stock companies "frequently supported ... forts and garrisons in the countries to which they traded," while the regulated companies did not (*WN*, 737).[17]

Joint stock companies, having the capital and the incentive to establish and maintain fortifications, came to dominate those British colonies that were not self-governing, in particular India.

Another significant difference between "private copartneries" (*WN*, 740) and joint stock companies is that the structure of the joint stock companies incentivizes accumulation and speculation.

---

[17] In 1750 parliament tried to design a regulated company for trade in Africa with a charter that reduced the opportunity for monopoly and forced the company to establish and maintain fortifications. On paper it seemed like an effective design. In fact, the incentives to monopolize trade and ignore responsibilities prevailed. Garrisons, he notes, are best left to the "executive power" that invests in this extension of power to enhance the "pride and dignity of that power" (*WN*, 740). He cites Gibraltar and Minorca as examples of the foolish consequences of that self-aggrandizing incentive.

In the "private copartneries" an individual can only enter the partnership with the permission of other partners. Partners are generally active participants in running the company. Any partner can demand compensation for his share and leave. Each partner is liable for company obligations "to the whole extent of his fortune" (*WN*, 740).

In the joint stock companies an individual can join by buying or leave by selling stock, and the proprietors (the stockholders) enjoy limited liability.

This total exemption from trouble and risk, beyond a limited sum, encourages many people to become adventurers in joint stock companies, who would, upon no account, hazard their fortunes in any private copartnery. Such companies, therefore, commonly draw to themselves much greater stocks than any private copartnery can boast of. (*WN*, 741)

Furthermore, a joint stock company is "managed by a court of directors" (*WN*, 741) that is answerable to the proprietors. But the proprietors seldom understand the workings of the company, so the directors have a largely free hand in running the company. This leads to an agency problem.

The incentive for care when the money at risk is that of others is less keen, so "[n]egligence and profusion" are common in joint stock companies (*WN*, 741). As a consequence, "without an exclusive privilege [they seldom prevail in competition with privately held companies]; and frequently have not succeeded with one" (*WN*, 741).

The Royal African Company is an example of such incompetence (*WN*, 742). The Hudson Bay Company is a rare example of a joint stock company that worked, but it did so largely because of geography that afforded it something of a natural monopoly, and because it was small and thus "approaches very nearly to the nature of a private copartnery" with attendant advantages (*WN*, 744).

The South Sea Company is a classic example of colossal failure. Given that company's "immense capital divided among an immense number of proprietors ... [i]t was naturally to be expected ... that folly, negligence, and profusion should prevail in the whole management of their affairs" (*WN*, 744–5). Lacking an exclusive privilege of any value, the company predictably failed.

British trade with the East Indies offers a particularly instructive joint stock company example. Smith's narrative on East Indian trade begins with the old East India Company.

That Company enjoyed an exclusive charter, but that charter, issued by the king, had not been confirmed by parliament. Over time, as "the principles of liberty were better understood" (*WN*, 747), the validity of the royal charter was challenged in court. This challenge was complicated by the emergence of a new East India Company established by parliament: "[A] negligence in the expression of the act of parliament" (*WN*, 747) allowed shareholders in the new company to freely participate in the trade as individuals. A fierce competition grew up.

The old Company complained of the "miserable effects ... of this competition" (*WN*, 748) citing a lower price in England due to expanded supply. This is for Smith classic, self-serving mercantilist whining about lower prices for their products when in fact the low prices caused by the "more plentiful supply ... [are] to the great advantage and conveniency of the publick" (*WN*, 748). And as for the old Company's additional complaint that increasing demand in India was raising the prices it had to pay there:

The increase of demand ... though in the beginning it may sometimes raise the price of goods, never fails to lower it in the long run. It encourages production, and thereby increases the competition of the producers, who, in order to undersell one another, have recourse to new divisions of labour and new improvements of art, which might never otherwise have been thought of. (*WN*, 748)

Summarizing his dismissive view of the mercantile interests that ran the East India enterprise, Smith writes:

The miserable effects of which the company complained, were the cheapness of consumption and the encouragement given to production, precisely the two effects which it is the great business of political economy to promote. The competition, however, of which they gave this doleful account, had not been allowed to be of long continuance. (*WN*, 748)

In 1708 by act of parliament the erstwhile competitors were merged into "The United Company of Merchants trading to the East Indies ... [which was] fully established in the monopoly of the English commerce to the East Indies" (*WN*, 749).

The ensuing "great increase in their [(the proprietors')] fortune had, it seems, only served to furnish their servants with a pretext for greater profusion, and a cover for greater malversation" (*WN*, 751). He traces this story to 1773 when "[t]he distress which ... accumulated claims brought upon them, obliged them ... to throw themselves upon the mercy of the government" (*WN*, 751).

After an inquiry, parliament made "alterations" (*WN*, 752) to the company's structure that imposed more government regulation to ensure more responsible management. "But [Smith concludes] it seems impossible, by any alterations, to render those courts [of company directors], in any respect, fit to govern, or even share government of a great empire; because the greater part of their members must always have too little interest in the prosperity of that empire, to give any serious attention to what may promote it" (WN, 752).

Given the scale of the returns to corruption by agents of the company, individuals would ante up 1,000 pounds for a share of stock, not for the prospect of the dividend, but for the chance to influence the appointments of those administrators who would be dispatched to plunder India. The real benefit of the stock was not returns to productivity but to plunder.

No other sovereigns ever were, or, from the nature of things, ever could be, so perfectly indifferent about the happiness or misery of their subjects, the improvement or waste of their dominions, the glory or disgrace of their administration; as, from irresistible moral causes, the greater part of the proprietors of such a mercantile company are, and necessarily must be. (WN, 752)

The inevitable outcome of these colonial mercantile policies that resist competition and exploit subjects is failure followed by pleading to the government for help: "The regulations of 1773 ... did not put an end to the disorders of the company's government in India.... [T]he company is now (1784) in greater distress than ever; and, in order to prevent immediate bankruptcy, is once more reduced to supplicate the assistance of government" (WN, 753). As with the colonial policies in America, in this case the mercantilists drain the treasure of the nation for the sake of their profit. But here, unlike in the American colonies where governance was modeled after the British liberal system, the onerous governance by the mercantile courts immiserates the colonies' subjects. The problems became so bad that by 1784 "[e]ven the company itself ... [had become] convinced of its own incapacity" (WN, 753–4) to govern.

Smith summarizes his views on this subject as follows:

When a company of merchants undertake, at their own risk and expence, to establish a new trade with some remote and barbarous nation, it may not be unreasonable to incorporate them into a joint stock company, and to grant them, in case of their success, a monopoly of trade for a certain number of years. It is the easiest and most natural way in which the state can recompense them for hazarding a dangerous and expensive experiment, of which the publick is afterwards to reap the benefit. A temporary monopoly of this kind may be vindicated upon the same principles upon which a like monopoly of a new machine is granted to its inventor, and that of a new book to its author.... [The key word here is clearly "temporary."] By a perpetual monopoly, all the other subjects of the state are taxed very absurdly in two different ways [(by an artificially high price and by an artificial constraint on opportunity)] ... It is for the most worthless of all purposes too that they are taxed in this manner. It is merely to enable the company to support the negligence, profusion, and malversation of their own servants. (*WN*, 754–5)

Joint stock companies suffer agency problems that make them ill suited for free market competition. Free competition is, as Smith describes it, "a species of warfare ... [that, given] occasional variations in the demand ... [and] much greater and more frequent variations in the competition ... [requires] dexterity and judgment ... [and] unremitting exertion of vigilance and attention" (*WN*, 755).

Insulated from this warfare by monopoly, joint stock companies can survive for a while, but monopoly does not allow them to succeed over the long term.[18] The very monopoly that makes their existence possible, by eliminating the discipline of competition, makes inefficiency and decline inevitable.

So is there any condition under which the government should charter a joint stock company? Yes.

"The only trades which it seems possible for a joint stock company to carry on successfully, without exclusive privilege, are those, of which all operations are capable of being reduced to what is called a Routine" (*WN*, 756). He cites four such enterprises: banking,[19] insurance, canal building and maintenance, and water supply to cities. Because the operations of each of these enterprises are "reducible to strict rule and method" (*WN*, 756), they require less vigilance by the stockholders. He cites successful examples of each case.

"[R]educible to strict rule and method" is a necessary but not sufficient condition for the success of a joint stock company. There are two more conditions that are necessary to justify such an arrangement: the undertaking must be "of greater and more general utility than the greater part of common trades; and ... [it must require] a greater capital than can easily be collected into a private copartnery" (*WN*, 757). "Except the four trades above mentioned, I have not been able to recollect any other in which all the three circumstances, requisite for rendering reasonable the establishment of a joint stock company, concur" (*WN*, 758).

---

[18] He cites, with a caveat, Abbe Morellet's data on this (*WN*, 755).

[19] "Though the principles of the banking trade may appear somewhat abstruse, the practice is capable of being reduced to strict rules. To depart upon any occasion from those rules, in consequence of some flattering speculation of extraordinary gain, is almost always extremely dangerous, and frequently fatal to the banking company which attempts it" (*WN*, 756). The genesis of the Great Recession makes Smith seem quite prescient.

The first section of chapter 1, Part III is nominally concerned with expenses of public works and institutions that facilitate commerce. But the theme of this section is really a more fundamental issue: what the government's role in commerce should – and should not – be. As this 1784 addition makes clear, one thing the government should not be doing is granting privileges that serve the few at the expense of the many.

Article II. *"Of the Expence of the Institutions for the Education of Youth"*

Turning to the expense of institutions for the education of youth, Smith returns to a principle he laid out in his examination of the expense of public works and institutions that facilitate commerce. Public provision should to the degree feasible be self-financing:

The institutions for the education of the youth may, in the same manner, furnish a revenue sufficient for defraying their own expence. The fee or honorary which the scholar pays to the master naturally constitutes a revenue of this kind. (WN, 758–9)

If the "reward of the master" is not covered entirely by fees, the difference need not come from the general revenue. It can be and typically is paid by locally established "public endowments" (WN, 759) administered by local trustees. This is the model for most of Europe. But, Smith poses the question: Does it work? This depends on what purpose is assigned to the enterprise.

Again, while the narrative is explicitly about covering the expense of a public provision, the larger story is about the role of government.

Have those publick endowments contributed in general to promote the end of their institution? Have they contributed to encourage diligence, and to improve the abilities of the teachers? Have they directed the course of education towards objects more useful, both to the individual and to the publick, than those to which it would naturally have gone of its own accord? It should not seem very difficult to give at least a probable answer to each of those questions. (WN, 759)

Smith's "probable answer" begins with an analysis of the importance of the alignment of incentives in encouraging diligence. As a general principle:

[i]n every profession, the exertion of the greater part of those who exercise it, is always in proportion to the necessity they are under of making that exertion. This necessity is greatest [where livelihoods depend on performance, and] ... where the competition is free, [because] the rivalship of competitors, who are

all endeavouring to justle one another out of employment, obliges every man to endeavour to execute his work with a certain degree of exactness.[20] (*WN*, 759)

In the case of university professors endowments often diminish their exertion because their salaries are "derived from a fund altogether independent of their success and reputation in their particular profession" (*WN*, 760). He suggests that in universities, where salaries depend on performance as measured by "the affection, gratitude, and favourable report of those who have attended upon his instructions"[21] (*WN*, 760), performance is better than in those universities where salaries are independent of this performance. It is, after all, our nature to respond to incentives.

As he examines the structure of pay for teachers, Smith emphasizes the potential conflict between incentive and "duty" (*WN*, 760). This ties the issue at hand to a much larger concern he has about society. An ideal citizen does his duty – incentives be damned. But real citizens are not ideal and this conflict between the incentives of interest ("vulgarly understood" (*WN*, 760)) and the responsibilities of duty is all too often resolved in favor of incentives. Thus it is important, as we construct institutions, to ensure to the degree possible that the alignment of incentives is consistent with doing one's duty. By encouraging individuals to do their duty institutions align behaviors with the progress of society.

A system of salaries independent of performance is all the more likely to be abused when the trustees of the endowment are themselves those receiving the salaries. Such an arrangement creates a collusion of neglect as incentives trump duty. This is just the case Smith experienced at Oxford: "In the university of Oxford, the greater part of the publick professors have, for these many years, given up altogether even the pretence of teaching" (*WN*, 761).[22]

If on the other hand the authority that exercises discretion in distributing salaries is "extraneous" to the teaching process (i.e., by those who are

---

[20] Smith notes that it is not the tangible returns alone that create the incentive for exertion. The keenness of the competition is itself often a stimulus. "Great objects ... are evidently not necessary in order to occasion the greatest exertions. Rivalship and emulation render excellency, even in mean professions, an object of ambition and frequently occasion the very greatest exertions" (*WN*, 759). John Maynard Keynes makes a very similar point in *The General Theory* (Keynes, 374).

[21] As the editors of *WN* point out in footnote 4 (*WN*, 760), this "was the case in the Scottish universities."

[22] On 24 August 1740, Smith wrote from Oxford where he was in school to his cousin and guardian William Smith that "it will be his own fault if anyone should endanger his health at Oxford by excessive Study" (*Correspondence*, 1).

neither an authority on the subject nor an attendee in the lectures), such jurisdiction, being "arbitrary and discretionary," "is liable to be exercised both ignorantly and capriciously" (*WN*, 761).

> The person subject to such jurisdiction is necessarily degraded by it, and, instead of being one of the most respectable, is rendered one of the meanest and most contemptible persons in society. It is by powerful protection only that he can effectually guard himself against bad usage to which he is at all times exposed; and this protection he is most likely to gain, not by ability or diligence in his profession, but by obsequiousness to the will of his superiors, and being ready, at all times, to sacrifice to that will the rights, the interest, and the honour of the body corporate of which he is a member. (*WN*, 761–2)

Competition for the rewards of reputation among students, and therefore performance, is also diminished when students are forced to attend particular universities to receive credentials in certain fields. Smith compares this to the apprenticeship system, and suggests that it has the same perverse effects.[23] Similarly, "scholarships, exhibitions, bursaries, &c. [that] necessarily attach a certain number of student to certain colleges"[24] (*WN*, 762) limit student choice and therefore the competition for students. Incentives would align more constructively if students were "free to chuse" (*WN*, 763).

But all too often, students have no choice. Students attend their lectures and act respectful, not for the benefit they receive, but because the discipline of the college commands it.

> The discipline of colleges and universities is in general contrived, not for the benefit of the students, but for the interest, or more properly speaking the ease of the masters. Its object is, in all cases, to maintain the authority of the master, and whether he neglects or performs his duty, to oblige the students in all cases to behave to him as if he performed it with the greatest diligence and ability. (*WN*, 764)

"Discipline" extracted by intimidation need not, indeed should not be the model for education.

> Where the masters ... really perform their duty, there are no examples, I believe, that the greater part of the students ever neglect theirs. No discipline is ever requisite to force attendance upon lectures which are really worth attending. (*WN*, 764)

Clearly young children need institutionally enforced discipline for they have not developed mature mechanisms for restraint in the absence of

---

[23] See where he begins his story on apprenticeships in *WN* (137).
[24] Smith was a Snell Exhibitioner at Balliol College, Oxford (Ross, 60).

social sanctions, but modeling is key to instilling this self-discipline as they begin to mature:

Force and restraint may, no doubt, be in some degree requisite in order to oblige children, or very young boys, to attend to those parts of education which it is thought necessary for them to acquire during that early period of life; but after twelve or thirteen years of age, provided the master does his duty, force or restraint can scarce ever be necessary to carry on any part of education. (*WN*, 764)

Mature students are not only willing to work hard for a good teacher, they are willing to forgive the deficiencies of a teacher's less than stellar performance "provided he shows some serious intention of being of use to them" (*WN*, 764).

In England the schools are doing a reasonable job because the incentives are reasonably aligned. Schoolmasters' rewards come primarily at the satisfaction of the students, and students are free to move from school to school. The universities are another matter. There, with all the extant restrictions, "[t]he parts of education taught [there ("the sciences" (*WN*, 474)),] ... are not very well taught" (*WN*, 765).

With this observation Smith proceeds into a lengthy account of how modern universities emerged and evolved into their current form. The account is classic Smith. Through the twists and turns that characterize the course of this history, he draws a thread that represents a story of progress as the university, as an institution, evolves. The thread he follows in this case is the role of language.

His narrative begins with the Catholic Church's need to teach Latin.

"When christianity was first established by law [under the Roman empire] a corrupted Latin had become the common language of all western parts of Europe" (*WN*, 765). After the empire collapsed "Latin gradually ceased to be the language of any part of Europe. But the reverence of the people naturally preserves the established forms and ceremonies of religion long after the circumstances which first introduced and rendered them reasonable are no more" (*WN*, 765).

Latin ceased to be the language of the people but it remained the language of the Church. University education emerged, at least in part, to educate "priests ... [in] that sacred and learned language in which they were to officiate" (*WN*, 765), "the Latin Vulgate" (*WN*, 766).

Because the Church decreed "the Latin translation of the Bible ... to have been equally dictated by divine inspiration, and therefore of equal authority with the Greek and Hebrew originals" (*WN*, 766), those originals were not a part of the university training for priests. Over time, however, differences between the originals and their Latin translations became a battleground. The Church favored its Latin translation of the New Testament, while reformers reached back to "the Greek text of the new testament, and even the Hebrew text of the old, [as] more favourable to their opinions than the vulgate translation, which, as might naturally be supposed, had been gradually accommodated to support the doctrines of the catholick church" (*WN*, 766). The reformers

set themselves … to expose the many errors of that translation, which the Roman catholick clergy were thus put under the necessity of defending or explaining. But this could not well be done without some knowledge of the original languages, of which the study was therefore gradually introduced into the greater part of universities; both of those which embraced, and of those which rejected, the doctrines of reformation. The Greek language was connected with every part of that classical learning, which … happened to come into fashion much about the same time as the doctrines of the reformation were set on foot. (*WN*, 766)

The introduction of classical philosophy into the curriculum of the university was largely the unintended consequence of the debate over doctrine, and in particular translation. Each side needed to return to the Greek originals to establish the bona fides of its interpretation. The texts for the study of Greek were the ancient classics of philosophy.

Over time the structure of that ancient philosophy became the frame for the development of the study of philosophy in the university. Smith describes this structure as follows: "The antient Greek philosophy was divided into three great branches; physicks, or natural philosophy; ethicks, or moral philosophy; and logick. This general division seems to be agreeable to the nature of things" (*WN*, 766). He continues with a very brief digest of the story he tells in his "History of Astronomy":

The great phenomena of nature … are objects which, as they necessarily excite the wonder, so they naturally call forth the curiosity of mankind to enquire into their causes. Superstition first attempted to satisfy this curiosity by referring all those wonderful appearances to the immediate agency of the gods. Philosophy afterwards endeavoured to account for them, from more familiar causes. (*WN*, 767)

Because the first phenomena that inspired wonder in humankind were those observed in the heavens, the first superstitions and subsequently the first endeavors of philosophy were focused on those natural phenomena. This became the realm of Natural Philosophy.

He then turns his attention to the emergence of Moral Philosophy, his own enterprise:

In every age and country of the world men must have attended to the characters, designs, and actions of one another, and many reputable rules and maxims for the conduct of human life, must have been laid down and approved of by common consent. As soon as writing came into fashion, wise men, or those who fancied themselves such, would naturally endeavour to increase the number of those established and represented maxims, and to express their own sense of what was either proper or improper conduct.... [He cites various forms these take in the works of Aesop, Solomon, Theognis and Phocyllides, and Hesiod.] They might continue in this manner for a long time merely to multiply the number of those maxims of prudence and morality, without even attempting to arrange them in a very distinct or methodical order, much less to collect them together by one or more general principles, from which they were all deducible, like effects from their natural causes. The beauty of that systematical arrangement of different observations connected by a few common principles, was first seen in the rude essays of those antient times towards a system of natural philosophy. Something of the same kind was afterwards attempted in morals. The maxims of common life were arranged in some methodical order, and connected together by a few common principles, in the same manner as they had attempted to arrange and connect the phenomena of nature. The science which pretends to investigate and explain those connecting principles is what is properly called moral philosophy. (*WN*, 768–9)

The purpose of Smith's own enterprise is to represent "[t]he maxims of common life ... arranged in some methodical order" and to use that foundation to explain the progress of humankind. By applying this analysis to the history of humankind he offers a "systematical arrangement of different observations connected by a few common principles" (*WN*, 768–9) – a Newtonian effort.

The science "which pretends" (*WN*, 769) to do these things is Moral Philosophy. Smith does not claim to *know* the connecting principles he seeks to represent. He only imagines them. The credibility of his argument lies in his ability to persuade his audience of the power of his principles. Natural philosophers persuade by demonstrating that their principles "arrange and connect the phenomena of nature" in a manner that seems consistent with observations of natural events. As a moral philosopher, Smith lays out the principles that he believes guide humankind's progress, and then seeks to persuade others of the power of his principles by demonstrating that they offer a rich explanation of the observed course of humankind's history. The point of Book III is to demonstrate and thus persuade his audience of the power of his analysis.[25]

---

[25] Where history is unrecorded Smith uses his analysis to represent what "must have" been (*WN*, 768). This is what his biographer, Dugald Stewart (1980), refers to as "conjectural history." Smith would not presume that his conjecture is a description of the actual course of events in the period he describes. Rather his conjecture represents the natural course that must have ultimately unfolded after all effects of human frailty, the twists and

This notion of persuasiveness bring us back to Smith's narrative on the evolution of the university.

Having explained the emergence of Moral Philosophy in early Western universities, Smith turns to the role of Logick.

Different authors gave different systems both of natural and moral philosophy. But arrangements by which they supported those different systems, far from being always demonstrations, were frequently at best but very slender probabilities, and sometimes sophisms.... Gross sophistry has scarce ever had any influence upon the opinions of mankind, except in matters of philosophy and speculation; and in these it has frequently had the greatest. (WN, 769)

With alternative systems competing for the attention and acceptance of the audience,

[t]he patrons of each system of natural and moral philosophy naturally endeavoured to expose the weakness of the arguments adduced to support the systems which were opposite to their own. In examining these arguments, they were necessarily led to consider the difference between a probable and a demonstrative argument, between a fallacious and a conclusive one; and Logick, or the science of the general principles of good and bad reasoning, necessarily arose out of the observations which a scrutiny of this kind gave occasion to. (WN, 769–70)

While Logic emerged after Natural and Moral Philosophy to assess the arguments of each, it was taught "previously to either of those sciences" (WN, 770).

Here again we hear Smith's evolutionary view. The development of philosophy and logic, and more generally of the university as an institution for their study, was not based on the rational design of some committee of wise ones assembled to establish and transmit knowledge. Rather, the institution of the modern university and the subjects of Natural Philosophy, Moral Philosophy, and Logic emerged as the unintended consequence of debates over language, doctrines, and beliefs.

As the modern universities evolved from their original form as "ecclesiastical corporations" (WN, 765), the influence of religion continued to affect their evolution.

In the antient philosophy ... the human mind ... [and] the Deity ... made, as it were, two chapters, though no doubt two very important ones, of the science [physics] which pretended to give an account of the origin and the revolutions of the great system of the universe. But in the universities of Europe, where

turns of history, have been overwhelmed by the power of natural selection to guide the flow of humankind's evolution toward the limiting case.

philosophy was taught only as subservient to theology, it was natural to dwell longer upon these two chapters than upon any other of the science. (*WN*, 770)

Over time this subset of ancient philosophy took on a life of its own and became an independent domain of study:

Metaphysicks or Pneumaticks were set in opposition to Physicks, and were cultivated not only as more sublime, but, for the purposes of a particular profession [the clergy], as the more useful science of the two. The proper subject of experiment and observation, a subject in which a careful attention is capable of making so many useful discoveries, was almost entirely neglected. The subject in which, after a few very simple and almost obvious truths, the most careful attention can discover nothing but obscurity and uncertainty, and consequently produce nothing but subtleties and sophisms, was greatly cultivated. (*WN*, 770–1)

As conflict over translations of the Bible led to evolution of the curriculum in an earlier day, so this "opposition" between metaphysics and physics "naturally gave birth to a third … called Ontology … But if subtleties and sophisms composed the greater part of the Metaphysicks … they composed the whole of this cobweb science of Ontology" (*WN*, 771). Smith has very little use for what he considers this distortion of the philosophical enterprise:

Wherein consisted the happiness and perfection of man, considered not only as an individual, but as the member of a family, of a state, and of the great society of mankind, was the object which the ancient moral philosophy proposed to investigate. In that philosophy the duties of human life were treated of as subservient to the happiness and perfection of human life.... In the antient philosophy the perfection of virtue was represented as necessarily productive, to the person who possessed it, of the most perfect happiness in this life. (*WN*, 771)

This is Smith's own view of what Moral Philosophy should be: an enterprise focused on the path to the happiness of humans individually and collectively in this life. This is not, however, what philosophy became in the modern universities of Europe.

[W]hen moral, as well as natural philosophy, came to be treated of as chiefly subservient to theology, the duties of human life were treated of as subservient to the happiness of a life to come.... [H]eaven was to be earned only by penance and mortification, by the austerities and abasement of a monk; not by the liberal and generous, and spirited conduct of a man. Casuistry and an ascetic morality made up, in most cases, the greater part of the moral philosophy of the schools. By far the most important of all the different branches of philosophy, became in this manner by far the most corrupted. (*WN*, 771)

Smith faults this theologically based philosophy for suggesting that we should manage our lives as if we *know* the intention of the deity, and with an eye toward some next world that the deity offers as a reward for doing his bidding in this one. For Smith this is not only arrogant, but useless and even harmful. It is arrogant because we cannot know the mind of the deity. It is harmful because by focusing on a next world we neglect the duties we have to one another in this one, and thus diminish the human prospect.

This theologically focused philosophy is undermining the university system because, thanks to the dominance of metaphysics, a "short and superficial system of Physicks ... is what still continues to be taught in the greater part of the universities of Europe" (*WN*, 772).

There have been "improvements" in philosophy, but these have not pierced the university "sanctuaries in which exploded systems and obsolete prejudices found shelter and protection, after they had been hunted out of every other corner of the world" (*WN*, 772). Furthermore, there is no incentive for the universities to change when their compensation is independent of "reputation ... [or] attention to the current opinions of the world" (*WN*, 773). This intellectual inertia is, therefore, all the more in evidence in the "richest and best endowed universities" (*WN*, 772).

The consequence of this failure is greater now that the clientele of the universities has expanded. Originally formed to educate the churchmen, over time they have attracted all who seek advanced education. Among these are young "gentlemen and men of fortune" whose fathers send them to the university to fill "the long interval between infancy" and a life in business (*WN*, 773). Given the pathetic state of universities, many fathers have opted instead to send their sons on a tutored international tour for exploration and education.

Smith sees this as perverse.[26] He writes that this "frivolous dissipation [in these] ... most precious years of his life, at a distance from the inspection and controul of his parents and relations" (*WN*, 773), deprives a young man of the personal and intellectual maturity that a good, well-supervised education would afford. "Nothing but the discredit into which the universities are allowing themselves to fall, could ever have brought into repute so very absurd a practice" (*WN*, 774).

It has not always been like this. The "different institutions for education" (*WN*, 774) of the young found in Greece and Rome offer a valuable contrast to the universities of his day.

In Greece "every free citizen was instructed, under the direction of the publick magistrate" (*WN*, 774). The two dimensions of education were

---

[26] Ironic because he guided the Duke of Buccleuch on just such a tour (Ross, 195).

"gymnastic exercises," designed to prepare each citizen for participation in the militia, and music, designed "to humanize the mind, to soften the temper, and to dispose it for performing all the social and moral duties both of publick and private life" (*WN*, 774). Unfortunately the outcomes were only good with respect to developing men for the militia. The system failed to develop good public morals.

Smith identifies a key to developing good public morals by contrasting the Greek and Roman cases. In Greece factions were strong and contentious, and justice was arbitrarily administered: the "courts of justice consisted of numerous and, therefore, disorderly bodies of people, who frequently decided almost at random, or as the clamour, faction, and party spirit happened to determine" (*WN*, 778).

In Rome factions were moderated and justice was more carefully administered. This was so because

the principal courts of justice consisted either of a single judge, or of a small number of judges, whose characters, especially since they deliberated always in publick, could not fail to be very much affected by any rash or unjust decision, ... [These judges] would naturally endeavour to shelter themselves under ... precedent.... This attention, to practice and precedent, necessarily formed the Roman law into that regular and orderly system in which it has been delivered down to us. (*WN*, 779)

Thus in Rome the unintended consequence of individual actions based on private incentive led to a constructive social construction, in this case "regular and orderly" courts of justice.[27]

This maturity of the court system had beneficial effects on the character of the citizenry. "The superiority of character in the Romans over that of the Greeks, so much remarked by Polybius and Dionysius of Halicarnassus, was probably owing to the better constitution of their courts of justice, than to any other circumstances to which those authors ascribe it" (*WN*, 779). This nexus of development, the coevolution of individuals and institutions, is a powerful force driving humankind's progress, for progress comes when, as in this Roman case, this coevolution leads to more ethically mature institutions and individuals.

Smith takes this turn to Greek versus Roman justice as he is describing the way education was provided in those times and places. The one

---

[27] This analysis is very similar to the one Smith tells in his *Lectures on Jurisprudence* of how, to insulate themselves from the wrath of superiors, judges in England shielded themselves by precedent and thereby established the stability and regularity of the English legal system (*LJA*, 275–9).

common virtue he sees in both of these systems of education is that "except in what related to military exercises, the state seems to have been at no pains to" (*WN*, 781) provide for public education. The free market system was the reality of Greek and Roman education. His praise of the incentives it creates contrasts dramatically with his condemnation of the modern university where teaching is dead and what teaching there is focuses on metaphysics at the expense of physics.

Were there no publick institutions for education, no system, no science would be taught for which there was not some demand.[28] ... A private teacher could never find his account in teaching ... an exploded and antiquated system of a science universally believed to be a mere useless and pedantick heap of sophistry and nonsense.... [Such teaching only survives today in] those incorporated societies for education whose prosperity and revenue are in great measure independent of their reputation (*WN*, 780–1).

So, is the free market the way to finance education? Is there any reason for education of the young to be among "the Expences of the Sovereign or Commonwealth"? Or as Smith puts it:

Ought the publick ... to give no attention, it may be asked, to the education of the people? Or if it ought to give any, what are the different parts of education which it ought to attend to in the different orders of the people? and in what manner ought it to attend to them? (*WN*, 781)

His answer to his own question is: it depends on the "state of the society" (*WN*, 781) and that in turn relates to the stage of the society's advancement with respect to the division of labor.

In the progress of the division of labour, the employment of the far greater part of those who live by labour ... comes to be confined to a few very simple operations.... But the understandings of the greater part of men are necessarily formed by their ordinary employments. The man whose whole life is spent in performing a few simple operations ... has no occasion to exert his understanding, or to exercise his invention.... He naturally loses, therefore, the habit of such exertion, and generally becomes as stupid and ignorant as it is possible for a human creature to become.... [I]ncapable of ... bearing a part of any rational conversation ... of conceiving any generous, noble, or tender sentiment, ... of forming any just judgment ... [on the] duties of private life ... [or the] extensive interests of his country, [and] he is ... incapable of defending his country in war.... [I]n every improved and civilized society this is the state into which the labouring poor, that is, the great body of the people, must necessarily fall, unless government takes some pains to prevent it. (*WN*, 781–2)

---

[28] All women's education is private, primarily provided by parents and guardians, and all that they are taught is "useful" (*WN*, 781).

In the first three stages of humankind's evolution, the division of labor is less fine. And precisely because the number of occupations are fewer, the number of skills each person must possess to meet his needs is greater. In learning and exercising these many skills the mind is challenged and developed.[29]

"In a civilized state, on the contrary, though there is little variety in the occupations of the greater part of individuals, there is an almost infinite variety in those of the whole society" (*WN*, 783). As a consequence "all the nobler parts of the human character may be, in a great measure, obliterated and extinguished in the great body of the people" (*WN*, 783–4).

The analysis Smith presents here regarding the education of youth parallels his analysis of the role of the state with respect to defense. In the first three stages of humankind's evolution there is little need for the state to spend much on defense. At these early stages a militia is a natural structure and a sufficient defense. The nature of a commercial society with its much finer division of labor makes a standing army imperative so state financing is necessary.

In the realm of education there is no need for state provision in the first three stages of society. In a commercial society the extreme fine-tuning of skills narrows and diminishes the mind. This effect transforms the role of the state because the benefit of ameliorating this ill effect of "progress" on the great body of the people is a public good:

The state ... derives no inconsiderable advantage from their instruction. The more they are instructed, the less liable they are to the delusions of enthusiasm and superstition, which, among ignorant nations, frequently occasion the most dreadful disorders. An instructed and intelligent people besides are always more decent and orderly than an ignorant and stupid one.... They are more disposed to examine, and more capable of seeing through, the interested complaints of faction and sedition, and they are, upon that account, less apt to be misled into any wanton or unnecessary opposition to the measures of government. In free countries, where the safety of government depends very much upon the favourable judgment which the people may form of its conduct, it must surely be of

---

[29] "The common ploughman, though generally regarded as the pattern of stupidity and ignorance, is seldom defective in his judgment and discretion. He is less accustomed, indeed to social intercourse than the mechanick who lives in a town. His voice and language are more uncouth and more difficult to be understood by those who are not used to them. His understanding, however, being accustomed to consider a greater variety of objects, is generally much superior to that of the other, whose whole attention from morning till night is commonly occupied in performing one or two very simple operations. How much the lower ranks of people in the country are really superior to those of the town, is well known to every man whom either business or curiosity has led to converse much with both" (*WN*, 143–4).

the highest importance that they should not be disposed to judge rashly or capriciously concerning it. (*WN*, 788)

Public provision is necessary because paying to master "[t]he most essential parts of education ... to read, write, and account" (*WN*, 785) is beyond the means of "the common people" (*WN*, 784) who live from hand to mouth and who must send their kids to work early in life to contribute to the family. These essentials of education can be offered to the poor "[f]or a very small expence [to] the publick"[30] (*WN*, 785). The public good warrants this public expense.

To ensure that incentives are aligned constructively, Smith suggests that the public contribution to a child's education should not pay the full salary of the teacher. Some affordable portion should come from the student as a reward for performance.

Basic education is a public good. To ensure that every citizen does indeed master the basics, "[t]he publick can ... oblig[e] every man to undergo an examination or probation in them before he can obtain the freedom in any corporation, or be allowed to set up any trade either in a village or town corporate" (*WN*, 786).[31]

Smith is a man with a system, but no "man of system" (*TMS*, 233–4). Here he proposes a screen on market access, an imposition that elsewhere he decries as absurd. In this case, however, the screen is designed to ensure the successful provision of a public good, an educated citizenry, not a private monopoly.

In keeping with this public good theme, Smith notes that, while not sufficient for defense, citizens' participation in a militia might serve the public by building individuals' courage. Cowardice, like ignorance, is a "mutilation" of being (*WN*, 787), and courage, like education, is a public good.

In the course of Article II we see two themes in Smith woven together. He is a classical liberal, the father of liberal thought in economics emphasizing individualism, free choice, market mechanisms, and the power of incentives. But he also has a civic humanist voice. He believes that good citizens are the *sine qua non* of a constructive liberal state, that citizenship is an "active duty" (*TMS*, 237).[32]

---

[30] There is no need for public provision to the children of the rich. "If they are not always properly educated it is seldom from the want of expence laid out upon their education; but from the improper application of that expence" (*WN*, 784).

[31] He returns to and expands on this scheme later (*WN*, 796).

[32] See Harpham (1984).

Article III. *"Of the Expence of the Institutions for the Instruction of People of all Ages"*

The institutions for the instruction of people of all ages are chiefly those for religious instruction. This is a species of instruction of which the object is not so much to render the people good citizens in this world, as to prepare them for another and a better world in the life to come. (*WN*, 788)

As we have seen, Smith feels that this next-world emphasis is the wrong priority. Education should be about rendering the people "good citizens in this world." Our "active duty" is to the here and now. So clearly, if civic education is the goal there is no public purpose in public financing of religious education.

Is there *any* public purpose served in public financing of religion? David Hume says yes. Smith says no.

Both men agree that established religions are less prone than new religions to enthusiasm, a characteristic both men abhor. The logic Smith employs to explain this phenomenon is a variation on the incentives theme he applies in his analysis of teaching.

The teachers of the doctrine which contains this instruction [(religion)], in the same manner as other teachers, may either depend altogether for their subsistence upon the voluntary contributions of their hearers; or they may derive it from some other fund to which the law of the country may entitle them.... Their exertion, their zeal and industry, are likely to be much greater in the former situation than in the latter. In this respect the teachers of new religions have always a considerable advantage in attacking those antient and established systems of which the clergy, reposing themselves upon their benefices, had neglected to keep up the fervour of faith. (*WN*, 788–9)[33]

As with his analysis of teaching incentives, it is a market argument. The erstwhile monopolist, initially fat and happy, is "indolent" and cannot match the "popular and bold, though perhaps stupid and ignorant [appeal of the] enthusiasts" (*WN*, 789). Following the classic strategy of a monopolist under siege, as did the mercantilists the established "clergy ... call upon the civil magistrate to persecute, destroy, or drive out their adversaries, as disturbers of the peace. It was thus that the Roman catholic clergy called upon the civil magistrate to persecute the protestants; and the church of England, to persecute the dissenters" (*WN*, 789).

---

[33] One of the great strengths of "the church of Rome ... [is that it maintains the] zeal of the inferior clergy" (*WN*, 789) by requiring them to generate their own income. "It is with them, as with the hussars and light infantry of some armies; no plunder, no pay" (*WN*, 790).

Smith and Hume[34] agree that enthusiasm and superstition undermine the maturation of society, that new religions are more prone to such because they are keen to whip up enthusiasm to gain adherents, and that the leaders of established religions tend to be more indolent. For Hume this suggests that the best strategy to avoid the scourge of enthusiasm is for the state to finance an established religion to, in effect, "bribe their indolence" (Hume cited in *WN*, 791).

Smith disagrees. He sees a large, established religion as an independent power base that can "over-awe the chiefs and leaders" of the party in power (*WN*, 792). There is a history here. In periods of political disorder religious leaders aligned themselves with a party in the dispute. The *quid pro quo* for exerting themselves on behalf of that party was power and resources. If their party won

[t]heir first demand was generally, that he ["the civil magistrate"] should silence and subdue all their adversaries; and their second, that he should bestow an independent provision on themselves. (*WN*, 792)

Smith envisions a case that he believes is much more constructive: a free competition among sects in a state that "dealt equally and impartially with all the different sects, and ... allowed every man to chuse his own priest and his own religion as he thought proper" (*WN*, 792). This would lead to a great many small sects, diminishing the influence of any one sect and thus the power of any one enthusiasm or superstition.

The teachers of each little sect, finding themselves almost alone, would be obliged to respect those of almost every other sect, and the concessions which they would mutually find it both convenient and agreeable to make to one another, might in time probably reduce the doctrine of the greater part of them to that pure and rational religion, free from every mixture of absurdity, imposture, or fanaticism, such as wise men have in all ages of the world wished to see established. (*WN*, 793)[35]

Such a competition emerges when the state "allow[s] every man to chuse his own priest and his own religion as he thought proper." Smith uses exactly the same language – "chuse ... as he thought proper" – when he writes of individuals making choices among "the different employments of labour and stock ... in a society where things were left to follow

---

[34] Smith refers to Hume as "the most illustrious philosopher and historian of the present age" (*WN*, 790).

[35] He suggests that the Pennsylvania experiment has demonstrated the credibility of this position (*WN*, 793).

their natural course, where there was perfect liberty" (*WN*, 116). It is a market argument.

Aside from the benefits already cited, more thoughtful religion and a government independent of religious influence, Smith believes that a many sects, market solution to the provision of religion can offer a valuable service in a liberal society.

"In a society where things were left to follow their natural course, where there was perfect liberty, and where every man was perfectly free both to chuse what occupation he thought proper, and to change it as often as he thought proper" (*WN*, 116) people move about the country in search of opportunities. As men move from the community of their "country village" to the anonymity of the "great city" they lose the moral compass of those familiar spectators whom they know and who can, through approbation and disapprobation, constructively influence their behavior. In this anonymous and lonely condition it is easy to sink into "low profligacy and vice" (*WN*, 795). "[B]ecoming a member of a small religious sect" (*WN*, 795) can provide a new community and thus a new moral compass. It is a morality enforced by the powerful threat that "expulsion or excommunication" (*WN*, 796) can throw one back into lonely isolation. "In little religious sects, accordingly, the morals of the common people have been always remarkably regular and orderly" (*WN*, 796).

Smith sees his scheme of many sects competing as superior to Hume's suggestion that the state institutionalize religion. But even under his scheme he fears that the destructive potential of religion, enthusiasm and superstition, could infect the citizenry. So, he offers

two very easy and effectual remedies ... by whose joint application the state might, without violence, correct whatever was unsocial or disagreeably rigorous in the morals of all the little sects into which the country was divided.
The first of those remedies is the study of science and philosophy, which the state might render almost universal among all people of middling or more than middling rank and fortune; not by giving salaries to teachers in order to make them negligent and idle, but by instituting some sort of probation, even in the higher and more difficult sciences, to be under gone by every person before he was permitted to exercise any liberal profession or before he could be received as a candidate for any honourable office of trust or profit.... Science is the great antidote to the poison of enthusiasm and superstition, and where the superior ranks of the people were secure from it, the inferior ranks could not be much exposed to it. (*WN*, 796)

The second remedy is ensuring the "entire liberty" (*WN*, 796) of public diversions.

Where individuals enjoy the opportunity to be entertained by the arts they are in a less "melancholy and gloomy humour which is always the nurse of popular superstition and enthusiasm" (*WN*, 796). Indeed, those who seek to whip up the public frenzy are often the subject of ridicule by these artists, and thus freedom of the arts is a tool in extinguishing the effect of their hot rhetoric.

An ongoing theme in Smith's analysis of the role of the state is that for its own sake a liberal state must structure institutions that enhance the civic maturity of its citizens. If working-class citizens' minds are numbed by the monotony of their work, they can become easy prey to the man of system who offers simplistic, seductive solutions to complex problems. If citizens' lack of martial participation makes them cowardly, they will not have the will to defend the state from internal or external threats. If citizens are caught up in the enthusiasms of a religion, the power of that religion can become formidable to the state.

The remedy to these problems lies in state incentives for/provision of education. State provision of a basic public education for working-class citizens can ameliorate the mind-numbing effect of their work. A militia, while not sufficient to defend the state, is a valuable tool for maintaining the martial spirit in individuals, and it makes possible a smaller standing army, making that army less formidable to the state. Screens on access to higher pursuits, public or private, that require study of science and philosophy ensure that those in the higher ranks of society are equipped to resist the simplistic, yet powerful appeals of enthusiasm.

An "immature" citizenry can be led by a demagogue down a path that would destroy the very liberty that gave that demagogue the freedom to express his views.

The[se demagogues] ... hold out some plausible plan of reformation which, they pretend, will not only remove the inconveniencies and relieve the distresses immediately complained of, but will prevent, in all time coming, any return of the like inconveniencies and distresses. They often propose, upon this account, to new-model the constitution, and to alter, in some of its most essential parts, that system of government under which the subjects of a great empire have enjoyed, perhaps, peace, security, and even glory, during the course of several centuries together. The great body of the ... [people] are commonly intoxicated with the imaginary beauty of this ideal system, of which they have no experience, but which has been represented to them in all the most dazzling colours in which the eloquence of their leaders could paint it. (*TMS*, 232)

Smith appreciates that the ideal liberal solution to this potential liberal dilemma is not to still the voices of demagogues, but rather to empower the citizenry to take thoughtful measure of all ideas and reject demagoguery.

Having laid out his theoretical position regarding the importance of education for the security of the state and in turn the important role of the state in education, and his rejection of a role for religion in the state's institutions, Smith turns to an historical analysis of the role of the Church in Europe. What he describes is an evolutionary process in which the immense power of the Church was eroded away, an essential transformation that made possible the emergence of more liberal forms of government.

He begins by describing the power of an established church:

The clergy of every established church constitute a great corporation. They can act in concert, and pursue their interest upon one plan and with one spirit, as much as if they were under the direction of one man; and they are frequently too under such direction. Their interest as an incorporated body is never the same with that of the sovereign, and is sometimes directly opposite to it.... [Deference is demanded] in order to avoid eternal misery.... Should [a sovereign] ... oppose any of their pretensions or usurpations [or defend a citizen who does so], the danger is equally great. (*WN*, 797)[36]

The clergy of an established church are beyond the power of the sovereign to control, for the people respect and fear the church more than they do the sovereign. Even the army of the sovereign, if locally recruited, may be more beholden to the church than to the sovereign. So the only way for the sovereign to influence the church is by "management and persuasion" and the best tool for that is "the preferment which he has to bestow upon them" (*WN*, 799). But in the Catholic Church, those preferments were internally managed, and the power of that management became concentrated in the Pope. Thus over time "[t]he clergy of all the different countries of Europe were thus formed into a sort of spiritual army ... directed by one head, and conducted upon one uniform plan ... [with] detachments quartered" in every country (*WN*, 800).

As did the medieval barons Smith describes in Book III, the Church sustained its power over tenants who were "entirely dependent ... [on its] hospitality and ... charity" (*WN*, 801) and it became

the most formidable combination that ever was formed against the authority and security of civil government, as well as against the liberty, reason, and happiness

---

[36] This sounds very much like Smith's criticism of Mercantilists as an "overgrown standing army" (*WN*, 471).

of mankind, which can flourish only where civil government is able to protect them. (*WN*, 802–3)

The perverse effect of the large institutional Church was very much like that of the barons, but on a much grander scale. It stretched across Europe and established an illiberal dependency of men. And, as with the barons so too the demise of the Church was not a product of design, but rather of an evolution of events that restructured incentives.[37]

Had this constitution [based on "private interest"] been attacked by no other enemies but the feeble efforts of human reason, it must have endured forever. But that immense well-built fabric, which all the wisdom and virtue of man could never have shaken, much less have overturned, was by *the natural course of things*, first weakened, and afterwards in part destroyed, and is now likely, in the course of a few centuries more, perhaps, to crumble into ruins altogether.

The gradual improvements of arts, manufactures, and commerce, the same causes that destroyed the power of the great barons, destroyed in the same manner, through the greater part of Europe, the whole temporal power of the clergy. (*WN*, 803, emphasis added)

As with the barons, "[t]he clergy could [initially] derive advantage from its immense surplus" (*WN*, 801) only through largess. But as did the barons, with the emergence of an extended market they "discovered the means of spending their whole revenues upon their own persons" (*WN*, 803). And again, as with the barons this encouraged production for the market in order to earn more to spend in the market. This led to a transformation of the relationship with the tenants of their land from custodial, sharing some of the produce, to legal, a lease-based rent. This transformation made tenants "in a great measure independent" (*WN*, 803). They now responded to the market rather than to a benefactor.

This corrosion of the power of the clergy opened up the opportunity for temporal sovereigns to take back power. Across Europe they did so,

---

[37] In the case of the feudal lords "what all the violence of the feudal institutions could never have effected, the silent and insensible operation of foreign commerce and manufactures gradually brought about. These gradually furnished the great proprietors with something for which they could exchange the whole of their surplus produce of their lands, and which they could consume themselves without sharing it wither with tenants or retainers. All for ourselves, and nothing for the other people, seems, in every age of the world, to have been the vile maxim of the masters of mankind.... For a pair of diamond buckles perhaps, or for something as frivolous and useless, they exchanged the maintenance, or what is the same thing, the price of the maintenance of a thousand men for a year, and with it the whole weight and authority which it could give them ... and thus, for the gratification of the most childish, the meanest and the most sordid of all vanities, they gradually bartered their whole power and authority" (*WN*, 418).

largely by taking control of election and distributions of benefices. "The authority of the church of Rome was in this state of declension, when the disputes which gave birth to the reformation, began in Germany" (*WN*, 805).

The Reformation came in a world ripe for change because the existing hierarchy was often resented as old, inert, and self-serving. The enthusiasm of those who offered the new doctrines and their greater command of the history of ideas gave their movement energy and credibility. "The austerity of their manners [in contrast to the 'vanity, luxury, and expence of the richer clergy' (*WN*, 804)] gave them authority with the common people" (*WN*, 805). Some sovereigns seized on this popularity, and, seeking to eliminate a long-standing challenge of the Church, "established the reformation in their own dominions" (*WN*, 806).

Lacking a pope to resolve differences of doctrines, inevitable divisions emerged among the reformers. This "gave birth ... [to] the Lutheran and Calvinistic sects" (*WN*, 807). The Lutherans followed an "episcopal" model of governance and, by control of benefices, "rendered ... [the sovereign] the real head of the church" (*WN*, 807). This model led to a clergy that was, for the sake of self-interest, polished and well connected to the "sovereign, to the court, and to the nobility and gentry of the country" (*WN*, 807). But it was a clergy that was out of touch with the concerns of the common man, and thus less able to persuade that public to reject the "ignorant enthusiast" (*WN*, 808).

In its initial form the Calvinist model was much more individualistic and democratic. Power derived from election by the people of the parish and all clergy were of equal rank. This election process invited fanaticism and conflict and thus led to "disorder and confusion" (*WN*, 808). The government in Scotland, the largest country to follow this sect, saw fit to manage the process so that these perverse effects did not become destabilizing.

The evolution of the Scottish church is for Smith an example of a serendipitous process that led to an unintended but desirable outcome. While the management of the elections and benefices largely diminished the fanaticism, what remained of the presbyterian model was the equality of authority and the near equality of benefice. This meant that a clergyman had no incentive to

pay court to his patron ... In all the presbyterian churches, where the rights of patronage are thoroughly established, it is by nobler and better arts that the established clergy in general endeavour to gain the favour of their superiors; by their learning, by the irreproachable regularity of their life, and by the faithful and diligent discharge of their duty.... Nothing but the most exemplary morals can give dignity to a man of small fortune. (*WN*, 809–10)

The presbyterian clergy live the same manner of life as the people they serve. They enjoy no deference based on wealth. To achieve the respect and affection of the people they must be leaders and caregivers: noble and kind and concerned. This, according to Smith, is precisely the character of the clergy in presbyterian countries, and above all in Scotland.[38] This is why the people of those countries are "converted, without persecution, compleatly, and almost to a man" (*WN*, 810).

The modest benefice these clergy receive has also been beneficial to the universities. There is, after all, a competition between the churches and the universities for the best minds. In places where clergy are liberally rewarded – Smith cites England and France – all the best minds flow to their best advantage, the church, to the detriment of the university. It is not so in Scotland and other places that follow the presbyterian model. There "the mediocrity of the church benefices naturally tend to draw the greater part of men of letters ... to the employment ([teaching)] in which they can be the most useful to the publick, and at the same time, to give them the best education, perhaps, they are capable of receiving" (*WN*, 812).[39]

Part IV: "Of the Expence of supporting the Dignity of the Sovereign"

This Part is only 178 words. Smith's point is yet again contextualized by his evolutionary frame: "This expence [of supporting the dignity of the sovereign] varies with the different periods of improvement, and with the different forms of government" (*WN*, 814). With the progress of opulence the price of dignity goes up.

---

[38] "There is scarce perhaps to be found any where in Europe a more learned, decent, independent, and respectable set of men, than the greater part of the presbyterian clergy of Holland, Geneva, Switzerland, and Scotland" (*WN*, 810).

[39] "To impose upon any man the necessity of teaching, year after year, any particular branch of science, seems, in reality, to be the most effectual method for rendering him completely master of it himself. By being obliged to go every year over the same ground, if he is good for anything, he necessarily becomes, in a few years, well acquainted with every part of it: and if upon any particular point he should form too hasty an opinion one year, when he comes in the course of his lectures to reconsider the same subject the year thereafter, he is very likely to correct it. As to be a teacher of science is certainly the natural employment of a mere man of letters, so is it likewise, perhaps, the education which is most likely to render him a man of solid learning and knowledge" (*WN*, 812).

"Conclusion of the Chapter"

In chapter 1 Smith has examined the roles of government and how these roles are optimally financed.

His general points are clear: wherever possible government should accomplish its ends by laws and regulations that align incentives to meet the desired objective. Where there is a role for government and incentives alone will not suffice, government provision and thus expenditure are warranted.

Where there are such expenditures the costs should be borne, as much as feasible, by the beneficiaries. This seems just and it aligns incentives constructively, for if the beneficiary pays for the provision he will hold the provider accountable for the quality of that provision relative to cost: "The proper performance of every service seems to require that its pay ... should be ... proportioned to the nature of the service" (*WN*, 813).

If the benefits are a public good (e.g., the nation's defense) the financing should come from the public revenue, to which citizens should contribute "in proportion to their respective abilities" (*WN*, 814). In chapter 2 Smith examines the sources of public revenue.

CHAPTER 2: "OF THE SOURCES OF THE GENERAL OR PUBLICK REVENUE OF THE SOCIETY"

The state has two sources of revenue with which to cover its expenses: the revenue of the sovereign or commonwealth and the revenue of the citizens. Smith begins by examining the first of these.

Part I: "Of the Funds or Sources of Revenue which may peculiarly belong to the Sovereign or Commonwealth"

"The funds or sources of revenue which may peculiarly belong to the sovereign or commonwealth must consist, either in stock, or in land" (*WN*, 817). The former yields profit or interest (depending on who superintends it), the latter a rent.

To derive revenue from the profit of stock the government must act as a merchant, superintending the business of making the profit.

Smith traces the role of profits in states' revenues from the "earliest and rudest state of civil government" (*WN*, 817). Only in the shepherding stage of civil government has "profit ... ever made the principal part of the publick revenue of a monarchical state" (*WN*, 817). Managing stock in this stage requires little superintendence because the eye of the sovereign is easily cast over the source of his revenue, his herds.

In more advanced states, when a sovereign undertakes a mercantile project the enterprise is managed by "agents" (*WN*, 818) of that sovereign. This leads to an agency problem. The sovereign lives in profusion and his agents tend to emulate that lifestyle, focusing more on their own well-being than the efficiency of the projects. "It was thus, as we are told by Machiavel, that the agents of Lorenzo of Medicis … carried on his trade" (*WN*, 819).

Mercantile projects and governing are not a good mix:

No two characters seem more inconsistent than those of trader and sovereign. If the trading spirit of the English East India company renders them very bad sovereigns; the spirit of sovereignty seems to have rendered them equally bad traders.[40] (*WN*, 819)

There are governments such as the "republick of Hamburgh" or the "aristocracies … of Venice and Amsterdam" (*WN*, 817, 818) that have succeeded in deriving revenue from a state bank. But Smith does not think this would work for "such a government as that of England; which [suffers the] … slothful and negligent profusion that is perhaps natural to monarchies" (*WN*, 818).

The only mercantile project that seems to have been universally profitable for states is the post office: "The capital to be advanced is not very considerable. There is no mystery in the business. The returns are not only certain, but immediate" (*WN*, 818).

Another possible source of revenue is interest derived from the state lending a portion of accumulated treasure to its citizens or to other governments. The former is the principal source of funding for "[t]he city of Hamburgh" (*WN*, 820). The primary example of the latter is the "canton of Berne" (*WN*, 820), and a variation of the latter has been used in the American colonies. Such lending can be functional, Smith suggests, so long as it is done in moderation, but he is not sanguine about the moderation of states when employing this tool.

Both profit and interest can contribute to the revenues of a state, but these returns are far too fickle to be the foundation of finance for a great state. "Land is a fund of a more stable and permanent nature; and the rent of publick lands, accordingly, has been the principal source of the

---

40 This is a story he tells earlier (*WN*, 747).

publick revenue of many a great nation that was much advanced beyond the shepherd state" (*WN*, 821). In all but the most advanced, commercial stage of humankind's evolution, rents have been more than sufficient to meet the revenue needs of governments. It is the evolution of the nature of war that has made rents insufficient to meet revenue needs in a commercial state.

"War and the preparation for war, are the two circumstances which in modern times occasion the greater part of the necessary expence of all great states" (*WN*, 821). In the "ancient republicks of Greece and Italy ... [as well as] the ancient monarchies of Europe" (*WN*, 821), government expense for both preparation and engagement in war was small because defense was based on a militia. Rents were sufficient to meet this need.

With the emergence of commerce came the transformation of warfare, and this transformation made necessary a standing army (*WN*, 699). Such an army requires a much greater revenue to cover the cost: "In the present state of the greater part of the civilized monarchies of Europe, the rent of all the lands in the country, managed as they probably would be if they all belonged to one proprietor [(i.e., not very efficiently)], would scarce perhaps amount to the ordinary revenue which they levy upon the people even in peaceable times" (*WN*, 822).

Smith advocates selling off most public lands. This would immediately add to the public revenue, and it would serve the public welfare more generally because the enhanced management of land resources in private hands would contribute to the growth of the wealth of the nation. The only lands Smith believes that the government should hold on to are "[l]ands, for the purposes of pleasure and magnificence, parks, gardens, publick walks, &c." (*WN*, 824).

Smith's point is clear:

Public stock and publick lands ... [generate] insufficient funds for defraying the necessary expence of any great and civilized state; [so] it remains that this expence must ... be defrayed by taxes of one kind or another; the people contributing a part of their own private revenue in order to make up a publick revenue to the sovereign or commonwealth. (*WN*, 824)

Part II: "Of Taxes"

Smith's plan for Part II reflects a principle presented in Book I: the revenue of the people comes in three forms: wages, profit, or rent. It follows that taxes must come from one or some combination of these revenues. In this Part he examines taxes levied on each form of revenue, and then he examines a tax that falls on all three "indifferently" (WN, 825). He notes, as he begins, that appearances can be deceptive because many taxes "are not finally paid from the ... source of revenue, upon which it was intended they should fall" (WN, 825).

Smith cites four general "maxims" (WN, 825) that should guide taxation:

- Taxes should fall most heavily on those most able to pay them: "The subjects of every state ought to contribute towards the support of the government, as nearly as possible, in proportion to the revenue which they respectively enjoy under the protection of that state"[41] (WN, 825). Indeed he favors progressive taxes because "[i]t is not very unreasonable that the rich should contribute to the publick expence, not only in proportion to their revenue, but something more than in that proportion" (WN, 842).
- Taxes "ought to be certain, and not arbitrary" (WN, 825). "[U]ncertainty of taxation encourages the insolence and favours the corruption" of tax collectors (WN, 826).
- Taxes should be levied with the convenience "in the time and mode of payment" (WN, 896) of the payer in mind.
- Tax collection should be as monetarily and psychologically efficient as possible. To this end, taxes should not:
  - Entail an unnecessarily expensive collection process.
  - Unnecessarily discourage commerce.
  - Be so high that they encourage perverse behavior, for example, smuggling.
  - Be collected in a manner that entails an onerous experience for the payer.

These maxims, Smith asserts, achieve both "justice and utility" (WN, 827).

The history of taxation is unfortunately largely a story of failure to honor these maxims. To demonstrate this Smith presents a short history of taxes on each revenue source.

Article I. "Taxes upon Rent; Taxes upon the Rent of Land"

The British land rent tax is fixed and "payable in money" (WN, 829). The good news about this system is that it is certain, convenient, and

---

[41] In a footnote Smith cites Lord Kames' "six rules regarding taxation. [including the assertion:] ... 'To remedy the "inequality of riches" as much as possible, by relieving the poor and burdening the rich'" (WN, 827).

efficient in collection. Furthermore, because the tax does not increase with improvements, it does not discourage them. Finally, falling on the residual in the price, the rent, it reduces the share to rent but it does not raise prices.

This fixed tax does, however, have drawbacks. Because of the fact that the overall level of rents is not constant over time, depending on the direction of change, the landlord or the sovereign is a winner vis-à-vis taxes. Furthermore, because rents on various parcels vary over time, those who initially paid the same tax on initially similar rents could in time pay the same tax on very different rents. Finally, a fixed tax payable in money suffers from the effects of inflation or deflation, creating winners and losers between the payee and payer depending on the direction of the price level change.

Smith cites the Physiocrats as believers that "[a]ll taxes ... fall ultimately upon the rent of land" (*WN*, 830), so for efficiency all taxes should be directly and fully on land rent. To ensure that such a land rent tax is "imposed equally" (*WN*, 831), as rents vary the tax must vary with them.

Smith entirely agrees with the principle that taxes should reflect ability of those upon whom they ultimately fall to pay, but he rejects the premise that all taxes ultimately fall on rent. And even if that premise were correct, a scheme that adjusts taxes on rents to changes in the level of rents to maintain the equity of the burden would involve a significant implementation challenge. It would require constant assessments to keep the rent roles up to date. This can lead to violations of his certainty, efficiency, and intrusiveness maxims.

Smith proceeds to imagine what the design of a rent tax that ameliorates these problems might look like. As always, his focus is on the alignment of incentives.

To discourage misreporting of rents, he imagines a system of landlord/tenant rent reporting that sets up a quasi-prisoner's dilemma structure.

To discourage landlords' tax avoidance by charging signing fees in lieu of higher rents – an "expedient of a spendthrift, who for a sum of ready money sells a future revenue of much greater value" (*WN*, 831) and a system that would consume the capital of the tenant and thus discourage improvements – he suggests that signing fees be discouraged by taxing them more heavily.

In the case of landlords who cultivate their own land, rent taxes could be negotiated based on rents on comparable land in the community. It is important not to over tax the landlord's use of his own land because

[t]he landlord can afford to try experiments, and is generally disposed to do so. His unsuccessful experiments occasion only a moderate loss to himself. His successful ones contribute to the improvement and better cultivation of the whole country. (*WN*, 832)

It is equally important not to under tax landlords. Given their capital resources, they are not as dependable a custodian of the day-to-day management of cultivation as the "sober and industrious tenants, who are bound by their own interest to cultivate as well as their capital and skill will allow" (*WN*, 832). Ideally, landlords are using some of the land creatively while yeoman farmers are using most of it dependably and productively.

These seem to Smith like plausible and not inordinately expensive solutions to the challenge of dynamic land tax assessment advocated by the Physiocrats. But there is one more very important complication that is invisible to a Physiocratic eye because they deny its existence: capital is productive so a land "rent" tax actually falls on a joint distribution of rent and profit.

The return to the land itself is the rent. The return to the improvements on the land is a profit. If the latter is confounded as part of the former, all the return being treated as a rent and taxed as a rent, then "the sovereign, who contributed nothing to the expence ... [would] share in the profit of the improvement" (*WN*, 833). This would discourage investment in improvements, to the detriment of society as a whole.

To address this requires an honest, careful assessment of land value prior to improvement.[42] Given such an assessment, a land rent tax system would encourage the improvement without "any other inconveniency to the landlord, except always the unavoidable one of being obliged to pay the tax" (*WN*, 834).

Smith believes that this "variable land-tax" (*WN*, 833), implemented as he describes, would be "just and equitable" (*WN*, 834). If "established as a perpetual and unalterable regulation" (*WN*, 834) incentives would be properly aligned and, in this case as it should be in all dimensions of the market, the role of the sovereign would be to:

encourage, by every means in his power, the attention both of the landlord and of the farmer; by allowing both to pursue their own interest in their own way, and according to their own judgment; by giving both the most perfect security that they shall enjoy the full recompence of their own industry; and by procuring to both the most extensive market for every part of their produce, in consequence of establishing the easiest and safest communications both by land and by water,

---

[42] Smith describes such a process (*WN*, 833).

through every part of his own dominions, as well as the most unbounded freedom of exportation to the dominions of all other princes. (*WN*, 833)

Having imagined how a variable land tax could work, Smith surveys cases in which something akin to this have been implemented. Concluding his remarks on "land-tax assessment according to a general survey and valuation" (*WN*, 836), Smith suggests that, given the difficulty of keeping such surveys up to date, this method is bound to lead to inequality. All the exertions of government to avoid this problem "will probably in the long-run occasion much more trouble and vexation than it can possibly bring relief to the contributors" (*WN*, 836).

"Taxes which are proportioned, not to the Rent, but to the produce of Land"

Taxes proportioned to the produce of the land, while originally paid by the farmer, are "finally paid the landlord" (*WN*, 836–7) because they reduce the amount the farmer can afford to pay as rent.

One such tax is the church tithe. It seems equitable on its face, but it is in fact very inequitable. It is a regressive tax that impacts poorer land and poorer farmers more than richer land and richer farmers. Furthermore, it discourages improvements and distorts choices of farmers (e.g., which crops to grow) because "the church, which lays out no part of the expence, is to share so very largely in the profit" (*WN*, 838).

In Asia, unlike Europe, the assessment on the produce of the land is a government tax rather than a church tithe. That has one salutary effect. The tax gives the government an incentive for making internal improvements (roads and canals) to extend markets, thereby increasing the production and increasing the tax yield. The tithe, on the other hand, is collected by a parish of very limited geography so there is no such incentive. He concludes: "Such taxes, when destined for the maintenance of the state, have some advantages which may serve in some measure to balance their inconveniency. When destined for the maintenance of the church, they are attended with nothing but inconveniency" (*WN*, 838).

Payments of taxes on production can be made in kind or in money.

Payments in kind work fine for "[t]he parson of a parish" (*WN*, 839) who personally collects the product. They do not work well for a head of state because they offer too much opportunity for fraud by underlings.

Payments in money that are fixed are less likely to discourage improvements in cultivation than payments in kind, but they are subject to inflationary or deflationary effects.

"Taxes upon the Rent of Houses"

An analysis of taxes on the rent of houses requires a clear distinction between the two components of that rent: "Building rent ... [and] Ground rent" (*WN*, 840).

"The building rent is the interest or profit of the capital expended in building the house" (*WN*, 840). The capital invested in the house could instead have been used to earn interest as a loan to others, so the return must cover that opportunity cost (that forgone interest). The owner must also superintend the house ("keep the house in constant repair" (*WN*, 840)) so there is a net profit (return for superintendence) that must be covered to make the pursuit worthwhile. In a competitive market, therefore, the building rent is determined by the "ordinary interest of money" (*WN*, 840) plus the normal net rate of profit.

The ground rent is a pure rent determined by the land's "advantage of situation" (*WN*, 840).[43]

A tax on rent of a house will not fall at all on the building rent. This must be covered to compensate the market-determined and required interest and profit. The tax burden therefore falls entirely on the occupant and on the owner's ground rent. The owner pays in lost revenue because, since demand is not perfectly inelastic, he cannot pass on the entire cost of the tax to the occupant. The occupant pays in lost opportunity because increased rents due to the rental tax means he can now only afford a lesser house.

This tax would be progressive because the rich, Smith believes, spend a much larger portion of their incomes on housing. Progressive taxes are to his liking because "[i]t is not very unreasonable that the rich should contribute to the publick expence, not only in proportion to their revenue, but something more than in that proportion" (*WN*, 842).

Applying the productive versus unproductive distinction to land, Smith places housing in the unproductive land category: "Neither the house nor the ground which it stands upon produce any thing" (*WN*, 842), so the rent must ultimately be paid by some other source of revenue. In contrast, the rent on farmland is replenished by the productive activity of nature. "The land which pays it produces it" (*WN*, 842).[44]

---

[43] As they say in the real estate trade: it's all about "location, location, location."

[44] "No equal capital puts into motion a greater quantity of productive labour than that of the farmer.... In agriculture too nature labours along with man.... [Farmers labor at] planting and tillage frequently regulate more than they animate the active fertility of nature; after all their labour, a great part of the work always remains to be done by her" (*WN*, 363).

This distinction leads him to the following policy prescriptions: house rent taxes should be based on the market rent (actual or imputed).[45] This is a desirable source of tax revenue because it is progressive. Ground rents are an even better target for taxes. The entire burden of the tax falls on the landowner "who acts always as a monopolist" (*WN*, 843) and a tax on a monopolistic return has no effect on the alignment of incentives.

Both ground-rents and the ordinary rent of [agricultural] land are a species of revenue [like interest] which the owner, in many cases, enjoys without any care or attention of his own. Though a part of this revenue should be taken from him in order to defray the expences of the state, no discouragement will thereby be given to any sort of industry. The annual produce of the land and labour of the society, the real wealth and revenue of the great body of the people, might be the same after such a tax as before. (*WN*, 844)

While ordinary rents on agricultural land include that profit return to "the attention and good management of the landlord" (*WN*, 844) and thus should be judiciously applied so as not to discourage improvements, a ground rent (a rent on the ground under a house) includes no such return to a private action. Indeed, "[g]round-rents, so far as they exceed the ordinary rent of land, are altogether owing to the good government of the sovereign" (*WN*, 844). It is, after all, good government that, "by giving both the most perfect security ... and by procuring ... the most extensive market" (*WN*, 833), makes the enjoyment of this rent possible.

Nothing can be more reasonable than that a fund which owes its existence to the good government of the state, should be taxed peculiarly, or should contribute something more than the greater part of other funds, towards the support of that government. (*WN*, 844)

In practice, because of the challenge of distinguishing the building and ground rents as shares of total rent, the taxes on rent of houses in Europe have not been focused on ground rents. Instead, the target of the tax has typically been the assessed value of the property as representative of its rent-generating potential. But this value varies over time so assessments are often outdated, resulting in inequitable taxation.

To avoid this problem tax assessment systems have resorted to easily observed proxies to determine the value of houses, for example: a hearth tax, more hearths – more tax. But as this required "that the tax-gatherer should enter every room ... it was abolished as a badge of slavery" (*WN*, 846).

---

[45] A cost of production-based rent would too onerous because in the case of the wealthy estates those costs have been accumulated by many generations.

To avoid such intrusions governments resorted to systems such as window taxes, more windows – more tax – and windows can be counted from outside. "The principal objection to all such taxes is their inequality, an inequality of the worst kind, as they must frequently fall much heavier upon the poor than upon the rich" (*WN*, 846). This regressiveness is due to the fact that country houses of the poor may well have more windows than city houses of the rich.

Article II. *"Taxes upon Profit, or upon the Revenue arising from Stock"*

The revenue of profit arising from stock naturally divides itself into two parts; that which pays the interest, and which belongs to the owner of the stock; and that surplus part which is over and above what is necessary for paying the interest.

This latter part [(the net or pure profit)] … is compensation … for the risk and trouble of employing the stock. The employer must have this compensation, otherwise he cannot, consistently with his own interest, continue the employment.[46] (*WN*, 847)

If a tax is laid upon the "whole profit" (*WN*, 847), to stay in business the employer of the stock must still receive a share of that gross profit sufficient to compensate him for his "risk and trouble." He can do this by either increasing the whole profit (in agriculture by paying less rent, in manufacturing by charging a higher price), or by keeping more of the whole profit, which means he will pay less interest.

So if taxing of the whole profit may cause a price rise to ensure the necessary profit to compensate the undertaker's "risk and trouble," why not avoid that potential problem by taxing the interest component directly, as he proposes with land rent?

The interest on money seems at first sight a subject equally capable of being taxed directly as the rent on land. Like the rent of land, it is a neat produce which remains after compleatly compensating the whole risk and trouble of employing the stock. As a tax upon the rent of land cannot raise rents [it just absorbs a part of this surplus] … so, for the same reason, a tax upon interest of money could not raise the rate of interest; the quantity of stock or money in the country, like

---

[46] This distinction between interest and the profit net of interest is one Smith laid out in Book I: "The revenue … derived from stock, by the person who manages or employs it, is called profit. That derived from it by the person who does not employ it himself, but lends it to another, is called interest or the use of money. … The interest of money is always a derivative revenue … [which is normally, unless the borrower is a 'spendthrift,'] paid from the profit which is made from the use of the money" (*WN*, 69, 70).

the quantity of land, being supposed to remain the same after the tax as before it. (*WN*, 487–8)

Interest, like rent, is a scarcity return.[47] Absent taxes, the level of a rent or interest return is determined by the size of the surplus (the return beyond that required to compensate the undertaker) available to bid for the "fixed" resource (land or money capital).

A tax on rent does not change the size of that surplus nor does it change the amount of land available on which to bid; it simply channels some of that surplus into the government coffers and thus out of the bidding (*WN*, 834). As a result, as the tax rises the rent falls, but the behavior of the farmer, the productive actor in this case, is not affected.

Interest, like rent, is a scarcity return, so a tax on interest does not change the incentives for the productive actor involved, in this case the employer of stock. Why not, therefore, as he proposes with rent, tax the interest component directly?

Because, while interest is the same kind of return as rent, the resources involved, money capital and land respectively, are very different.

His proposed plan for making the assessment of land rent manageable is premised on knowing who owns how much of what land, a reasonable premise. But with money capital stock it is not so easy to ascertain how much a man has or even where it is. The size and location of one's capital holdings is much more fluid than the size and location of one's landholdings. To assess capital holdings would require "[a]n [ongoing] inquisition into every man's private circumstances" (*WN*, 848).

Furthermore, because, unlike land, money capital stock is mobile, if it is treated harshly by the tax collector, it can flee the country.

The proprietor of stock is properly a citizen of the world, and is not necessarily attached to any particular country. He would be apt to abandon the country in which he was exposed to the vexatious inquisition, in order to be assessed to a burdensome tax, and would remove his stock to some other country where he could, either carry on his business, or enjoy his fortune more at ease. By removing his stock he would put an end to all the industry which it had maintained in the country which he left. Stock cultivates land; stock employs labour. A tax which

[47] "The lowest ordinary rate of interest must ... be something more than sufficient to compensate the occasional losses to which lending, even with tolerable prudence, is exposed. Were it not more, charity or friendship could be the only motives for lending[, just as in the absence of rent there would be no incentive to let others use your land] ... [In a prudent environment, interest is a very small compensation for risk. So i]n a country which had acquired its full complement of riches ... the ordinary rate of clear profit would be very small ... so low as to render it impossible for any but the very wealthiest people to live upon the interest of their money" (*WN*, 113).

tended to drive away stock from any particular country, would so far tend to dry up every source of revenue, both to the sovereign and to the society. (*WN*, 848–9)

Clearly Smith believes that taxing interest is just, would be fruitful, and (absent the opportunity to flee) is non-distorting. But capital, being mobile, can flee, and chasing it away is counterproductive.

Nations that have "attempted to tax the revenue arising from stock" (*WN*, 849) have resorted to very loose, nonintrusive methods of assessing the quantity of stock one holds. Given the "extreme inequality and uncertainty" (*WN*, 849) of these methods, to avoid the ire of capital holders governments have been very light handed with capital taxes. He cites examples in England, in Hamburgh, in various parts of Switzerland, and in Holland.

In England the effect is so light as to be of little consequence. In the other places the tax is not trivial, but the culture makes it work. For example, in Hamburgh:

[e]very man assesses himself, and, in the presence of the magistrate, puts annually into the publick coffer a certain sum of money ... without declaring what it amounts to, or being liable to any examination on the subject. This tax is generally supposed to be paid with great fidelity. In a small republick, where the people have entire confidence in their magistrates, are convinced of the necessity of the tax for the support of the state, and believe that it will be faithfully applied to that purpose, such conscientious and voluntary payment may sometimes be expected.[48] (*WN*, 850)

This behavior reflects a theme in Smith's moral philosophy that transcends the subject of taxes.

In a liberal society civil government can be less intrusive to the degree that citizens share a common definition of and commitment to civic ethics and have the self-command to self-govern so they live up to that commitment.

As Book V makes clear civil government is instrumental in nurturing such citizens: by offering education to those who cannot afford it, by creating incentives to acquire education in those who can afford it, and by carrying out the essential functions of government in a way that instills "entire confidence [of citizens] in their magistrates" (*WN*, 850) civil government shows respect for its citizens and wins the respect of those citizens.

Such citizens, in turn, participate constructively in making their government ever more efficient and just.

---

[48] He cites another trust-based system in Switzerland (*WN*, 850–1).

"Taxes upon the Profit of particular Employments"

A tax ... upon the profits of stock employed in any particular branch of trade, can never fall finally upon the dealers (who must in all ordinary cases have their reasonable profit, and, where the competition is free, can seldom have more than that profit), but always upon the consumers, who must be obliged to pay in the price of the goods the tax which the dealer advances. (*WN*, 853)

In a perfectly competitive environment, the dealers' compensation is the profit return necessary and sufficient to make the enterprise worthwhile. To receive less would put them out of business, so they must pass on the tax burden.

There are several ways to levy a tax through the dealer. Each has its issues.

A dealer tax that is "proportioned" (*WN*, 853) to the quantity the dealer sells may require a very intrusive investigation to ensure accounting. A flat rate license does not require such intrusion. But if a tax is a flat rate for doing business, small dealers have a higher tax per unit that they cannot pass along to the consumer. Thus, a high, flat-rate tax drives out the small dealers, creating a "monopoly of trade" for the larger ones (*WN*, 853). For example, flat-rate general business licenses like those issued for alehouses "give some advantage to the great, and occasion some oppression to the small dealers" (*WN*, 853), while per-coach taxes on hackney coaches do not have this effect.

The most significant example of a tax on profits is the taille in France.[49]

The "personal taille" is a terribly arbitrary and inconsistent tax. This is due in part to information problems that would plague even the most upright collector, and it is exacerbated by the lack of probity among the collectors and to the constant need for adjustments in obligations as the sovereign's requirements change.

The personal taille also sets up perverse incentives: because it is assessed on the portion of personal stock that the farmer "appears to employ in cultivation" (*WN*, 856), the farmer has a strong incentive to "cultivate with the meanest and most wretched instruments of husbandry that he can. Such is his distrust in the justice of the assessors, that he counterfeits poverty, and wishes to appear scarce able to pay any thing for fear of being obliged to pay too much.... The publick, the farmer, the landlord, all suffer more or less by this degraded cultivation" (*WN*, 856).

---

[49] In discussing the French case, he refers to it as "at present (1775)" so clearly this is written in London.

Earlier we heard Smith describe a constructive relationship between the citizen and civil government in Hamburg. Here we hear Smith describing a destructive relationship in France. In this latter case the citizens' distrust of civil government undermines the progress of opulence.

Taxes on slaves are another form of a tax "upon the profits of a certain species of stock employed in agriculture" (*WN*, 857). While slaves are an "object" of taxation, paying such a tax "is to the person who pays it, not a badge of slavery, but of liberty. It denotes that he is subject to government, indeed, but that, as he has some property, he cannot himself be the property of a master" (*WN*, 857).

Appendix to Articles I and II. *"Taxes upon the Capital Value of Lands, Houses, and Stock"*

Taxes upon the capital value of lands, houses, and stock are incurred when property is transferred, as in a bequest. Unlike the taxes already examined that take some of the revenue generated by capital, these taxes "take away some part of … [the] capital" itself (*WN*, 858).

Taxing a bequest to children who have lost a father on whom they were dependent would be "cruel and oppressive" (*WN*, 859) because they have also lost the support of his current income. It is otherwise with children who are "emancipated."

[They] are supported by funds separate and independent of those of their father. Whatever part of his succession might come to such children, would be a real addition to their fortune, and might, therefore, perhaps, without more inconveniency than what attends all duties of this kind, be liable to some tax. (*WN*, 859)[50]

Smith briefly reviews the various methods for administering taxes on transfers[51] and then examines the incidence of different transfer taxes.

---

[50] Smith anticipates John Stuart Mill to some degree on inheritance. Mill writes: "Were I framing a code of laws according to what seems to me best in itself, without regard to existing opinions and sentiments, I should prefer to restrict, not what any one might bequeath, but what any one should be permitted to acquire, by bequest or inheritance. Each person should have power to dispose by will of his or her whole property; but not to lavish it in enriching some one individual beyond a certain maximum, which should be fixed sufficiently high to afford the means of comfortable independence. The inequalities of property which arise from unequal industry, frugality, perseverance, talents, and to a certain extent even opportunities, are inseparable from the principle of private property, and if we accept the principle, we must bear with these consequences of it: but I see nothing objectionable in fixing the limit to what any one may acquire by the mere favour of others, without exercise of his faculties, and in requiring that if he desires any further accession of fortune, he shall work for it" (Mill, 227–8).

[51] He notes that by adopting and adapting methods of other governments, each becomes much more effective at implementing such taxes: "There is no art which one government

Keenly interested in the final burden of any tax, he traces eight cases to determine for each on whom the tax will ultimately "fall" (WN, 862).

To the degree that any of these taxes on capital value take accumulation from the productive circuits in the economy and are squandered on "unproductive labourers" (WN, 862) who serve the fancy of the sovereign, these taxes reduce the wealth of the nation.

Article III. *"Taxes upon the Wages of Labour"*

Smith begins his analysis of taxes on wages by reminding us that the determinates of wages are "the demand for labour, and the ordinary or average price of provisions" (WN, 864). Demand relative to the size of the labor force determines the level of subsistence that labor must be paid, be it "liberal, moderate, or scanty subsistence" (WN, 864). The price of provisions determines the money price of this subsistence.

With this frame in mind Smith turns to the incidence of a tax on wages. As is often his style, beginning with "Let us suppose" (WN, 864), he spins out scenarios to examine for different tax regimes where the tax burden would ultimately fall.

For "[a] direct tax upon ... wages ... [t]he final payment would[, assuming constant subsistence and prices,] ... fall upon" someone other than the worker (WN, 684–5). Upon whom it falls will be different in "different cases" (WN, 685). In manufacturing it would be passed along to the employer who, in turn, would raise his prices. In farming it would be passed along to the landlord as a lower rent.

If it were the former case, a tax-induced increase in manufacturing prices, this would raise the price of subsistence, creating a feedback effect on wages. For workers to afford subsistence, wages would have to rise more than proportionally to the tax because the increment would have to compensate for both the tax on the base wage and the tax's effect on the price of subsistence. This is so unless the tax increase "occasioned a considerable fall in the demand for labour" (WN, 865).

These taxes generally lead to "the decrease of employment for the poor, [and] the diminution of the annual produce of the land and labour of the country.... Absurd and destructive as such taxes are, however, they take place in many countries" (WN, 865). He cites examples in France and in Bohemia, noting that when such a tax distorts the relationship

sooner learns of another than that of draining money from the pockets of the people" (WN, 861).

among wages of different employments it distorts the distribution of labor in the market.[52]

Article IV. *"Taxes which, it is intended, should fall indifferently upon every different Species of Revenue"*

"The taxes which, it is intended, should fall indifferently upon every different species of revenue, are capitation taxes and, and taxes upon consumable commodities" (*WN*, 867).

"Capitation Taxes"

Capitation taxes on "fortune or revenue … become altogether arbitrary" (*WN*, 867). A person's fortune "varies day by day, and without an inquisition more intolerable than any tax … can be only guessed at" (*WN*, 867), leaving wide discretion and potential for abuse by the collectors. Rank is a very poor proxy for fortune and revenue. People of the same rank often have very different fortunes. A gross inequality of assessment for such a tax is tolerable if the tax is light, but "in a heavy one it is altogether intolerable" (*WN*, 867).

To illustrate this point Smith traces the history of capitation taxes in England and in France.

In France the government dictates that the tax must be adjusted as necessary to meet the desired revenue yield. In England the government sets the tax and takes the yield that comes. The tax, being heavier in France, falls there most heavily on those least able to resist:

Capitation taxes are levied at little expence; and, where they are rigorously exacted, afford a very sure revenue to the state. It is upon this account that in countries where the ease, comfort, and security of the inferior ranks of the people are little attended to, capitation taxes are very common. (*WN*, 869)

Again we find this thread that weaves its way through Smith's narrative: the metric of the goodness of a society is how it treats the least among its working class. He clearly has little use for a severe regime in which "the ease, comfort, and security of the inferior ranks of the people are little attended to."

"Taxes upon Consumable Commodities"

The difficulty in taxing people based on revenue has led to taxing individuals based on what they consume as a proxy for what they earn. But

---

[52] Smith offers the caveat that taxes on the labor of public officers is less distorting because they are commonly overpaid in the first place (*WN*, 866).

treating all commodities the same with respect to such a tax leads to gross inequalities.

> Consumable commodities are either necessaries or luxuries. By necessaries I understand, not only the commodities which are indispensably necessary for the support of life, but whatever the custom of the country renders it indecent for creditable people, even the lowest order, to be without.... [I]n the present times, through the greater part of Europe ... [this would include] a linen shirt. (*WN*, 869–70)

His standard, then, for social subsistence as opposed to "immediate subsistence" (*WN*, 691) is "the established rules of decency" determined by "custom" (*WN*, 870). He demonstrates the social relativity of this latter standard by contrasting the current standards in England with those in France.

All beyond necessaries "I call luxuries, without meaning by this appellation, to throw the smallest degree of reproach upon the temperate use of them" (*WN*, 870).

Because the compensation of the labor must be sufficient to purchase the necessaries of life "a tax on the necessaries of life, operates exactly in the same manner as a direct tax upon the wages of labour" (*WN*, 871). As with a tax on labor in manufacturing, a tax on necessaries will be passed on in higher prices, and the nominal wage increase has to be more than proportional to the tax to maintain the subsistence real wage. In agriculture a tax increase on necessaries will fall upon the landlord in lower rents.

"It is otherwise with taxes upon what I call luxuries; even upon those of the poor. The rise in the price of the taxed commodities, will not necessarily occasion any rise in the wages of labour" (*WN*, 871). Smith cites the effect of taxes on tobacco, tea, sugar, chocolate, and "spirituous liquors" (*WN*, 872) as examples.

Taxes on these luxuries are reasonable social policy, according to Smith:

> [Such taxes] act as sumptuary laws, and dispose them ["the sober and industrious poor" (*WN*, 872)] either to moderate, or to refrain altogether from the use of superfluities.... Their ability to bring up families, in consequence of this forced frugality, ... [is] increased by the tax. It is the sober and industrious poor who generally bring up the most numerous families, and who principally supply the demand for useful labour. All the poor indeed are not sober and industrious, and the dissolute and disorderly might continue to indulge themselves in the use of such commodities ... without regarding the distress which this indulgence might bring upon their families. Such disorderly persons, however,

seldom rear up numerous families; their children generally perishing from neglect, mismanagement, and the scantiness or unwholesomeness of their food. (*WN*, 872)

The poor are generally good folks and they do the vast majority of the productive labor in society. These good folks produce more and better kids for the next generation than the dissolute because their prudence ensures that they have the resources to nurture their children. Government can encourage such behavior with luxury taxes that discourage consumption of commodities such as "spirituous liquors." As always, for Smith it is about the alignment of incentives.

In contrast, a tax on necessities is literally counterproductive:

Any rise in the average price of necessaries, unless it is compensated by a proportionable rise in the wages of labour, must necessarily diminish more or less the ability of the poor to bring up numerous families, and consequently to supply the demand for useful labour. (*WN*, 872–3)

A tax on the wages or necessaries of labor is generally passed on such that the ultimate burden, "with a considerable over-charge" (*WN*, 873), is borne by the "[t]he middling and superior ranks of the people... [So] if they understood their own interest, [they] ought always to oppose all [such] taxes" (*WN*, 873). But while it is a bad idea for them, is it a bad idea for the nation?

He reviews the current state of British taxes on necessaries such as salt, leather, soap, candles, and coal. After citing some of the perverse effects, he nevertheless concludes: "Such taxes, though they raise the price of subsistence, and consequently the wages of labour, yet they afford a considerable revenue to government, which it might not be easy to find in any other way. There may, therefore, be good reasons for continuing them" (*WN*, 875).[53]

Then there is the question of their collection. Should it be from the dealer or from the consumer? The optimal choice depends on the durability of the commodity.

More durable commodities, like a coach, are best taxed over time in the hands of the consumer. This allows a large tax to be spread out over a number of years (e.g., a "licence" (*WN*, 877) fee paid in increments), making the tax burden more manageable for the purchaser.

---

[53] Not so with "[t]he bounty upon the exportation of corn ... or [t]he high duties upon the importation of corn ... [These] have all the bad effects of taxes upon the necessaries of life, and produce no revenue to government" (*WN*, 875).

It is better to collect the tax on less durable commodities from the dealer before delivery. The burden of such a tax would be passed on to the consumer in small increments as he bought each unit for immediate consumption (e.g., An increment of the tax would be paid as each pint of ale is consumed.). To follow the "proposal of Sir Matthew Decker" (*WN*, 877) and levy a fee for the right to consume these less durable commodities (e.g., ale) would result in very large upfront outlays for poor people, gross inequalities due to differences in levels of consumption, and a reduced incentive to be prudent in the consumption of those commodities that are best consumed in moderation (With respect to spirits ... once you've paid the fee why not have more?).

Excise and customs are the most common way to collect a tax from the dealer. "[D]uties of excise are imposed chiefly upon goods of home production destined for home consumption" (*WN*, 878). "The duties of customs are much more ancient" (*WN*, 878). Beginning with the etymology of the term,[54] Smith explores this most ancient source of state revenue.

Customs originated "[d]uring the barbarous times of feudal anarchy" (*WN*, 878). Just as the nobility allowed the king to impose a tax on the feudal tenants, so too on those "despised [merchants] ... whose gains were envied ... In those ignorant times, it was not understood, that the profits of merchants are a subject not taxable directly; or that the final payment of all such taxes must fall, with a considerable over-charge, upon the consumers" (*WN*, 879).

Because "the gains of the alien merchants were looked upon more unfavorably than those of the English merchants" (*WN*, 879), the taxes on imports were more onerous than those of the domestic producers. "This distinction ... begun from ignorance, has been continued from the spirit of monopoly" (*WN*, 879).

The acts of parliament that established or adjusted the system of customs were enacted "sometimes to relieve the exigencies of the state, and sometimes to regulate the trade of the country, according to the principles of the mercantile system ... [a] system [that] has come gradually more and more into fashion" (*WN*, 880).

Reflecting mercantilist interests and influence, "the ancient duties of customs were imposed equally upon all sorts of goods" (*WN*, 879) but as the system has evolved the duties have become more focused on imports. Those on exports have been reduced or eliminated and in some cases

---

[54] "[M]uch more ancient than those of excise ... [t]hey seem to have been called customs, as denoting customary payments which had been in use from time immemorial" (*WN*, 878).

even replaced by bounties, and drawbacks have been offered to compensate for duties on imports that are re-exported. "This growing favour of exportation, and the discouragement of importation, have suffered only a few exceptions, which chiefly concern the materials of some manufacturers" (WN, 881). Not surprisingly, these exceptions align precisely with the mercantile interests: raw materials needed from overseas are allowed in duty free, and the exportation of those inputs over which Britain enjoys a monopoly are prohibited.

> That the mercantile system has not been very favourable to the revenue of the great body of the people, to the annual produce of the land and labour of the country, I have endeavoured to shew in the fourth book of this inquiry. It seems not to have been more favourable to the revenue of the sovereign; so far at least as that revenue depends upon the duties of customs. (WN, 881)

Ideally, government policies align incentives so as to encourage constructive behaviors. In the case of these mercantile policies the incentives are aligned such that they lead to very perverse outcomes.

> The saying of Dr. Swift, that in the arithmetick of the customs two and two, instead of making four, make sometimes only one, holds perfectly true with regard to such heavy duties, which never could have been imposed, had not the mercantile system taught us, in many cases, to employ taxation as an instrument, not of revenue, but of monopoly. (WN, 882)

Mercantilist policies also undermined the revenue from customs by eliminating or reducing imports that could have been taxed (foreign woolens and foreign silks and velvets, respectively), and they have encouraged smuggling.

In some cases the perverse effects of this smuggling are compounded by fraud as re-exported commodities are given drawbacks and then smuggled back into the country (WN, 882). This and other forms of fraud (e.g., "cooked" books showing more exports and fewer imports than actually occurred) not only drain the treasury, they also lead to a gross overestimate of the nation's positive trade balance.

> Our exports, in consequence of these different frauds, appear upon the custom-house books greatly to overbalance our imports; to the unspeakable comfort of the politicians who measure the national prosperity by what they call the balance of trade. (WN, 883)[55]

---

[55] As Smith traces the history of the customs, it is obvious that he is well schooled on the subject. At least some of this was clearly written after Smith arrived in London in 1773; there are references to laws and data that postdate 1773.

Clearly this is all very galling to Smith.

Most customs taxes have "been imposed for the purpose, not of revenue, but of monopoly, or to give our own merchants an advantage in the home market" (*WN*, 884). Customs duties should "by proper management …, without any loss to the publick revenue, and with great advantage to foreign trade, be confined to a few articles only" (*WN*, 883). By lowering or eliminating most of these duties competition would be encouraged, generating more economic activity. Domestic workers and the public revenue would benefit from such a change.

He goes on to describe what he believes is a well-designed system for the administration of the excise that should and could, if the range of commodities involved was suitably limited, be adopted for the administration of customs as well, concluding that "by such a system of administration smuggling, to any considerable extent, could be prevented" (*WN*, 885).

Under his proposal "duties of customs" (*WN*, 884) would be "an instrument of revenue and never of monopoly … [and they would exhibit] the same degree of simplicity, certainty, and precision, as those of excise" (*WN*, 885). The elimination drawbacks and bounties, both of which are at best abused and at worst encourage fraud, would reduce customhouse costs, making up for much of the revenue lost from proposed cuts in customs rates. Whatever the marginal negative effect on revenue, the gain in economic activity due to increased competition unleashed when the onerous, customs-enforced monopolies are eliminated would mean a big boost to the wealth of the nation.

Those commodities that would become freely traded would include "all the necessaries of life," so the cost of labor would fall "without reducing in any respect its real recompence" (*WN*, 885–6). This, along with the fall in the cost of "materials of manufacture" (*WN*, 885), would mean a fall in the cost of production in the domestic market and an improvement in the nation's global competitive position: "The cheapness of their goods would secure to our own workmen, not only the possession of the home, but a very great command of the foreign market" (*WN*, 886).

So if it makes so much sense, why hasn't this system been adopted already?

It was the object of the famous excise scheme of Sir Robert Walpole to establish … a system not very unlike that which is here proposed…. [Walpole's proposal was limited to just two commodities (wine and tobacco), but in fear that this was just the beginning, f]action, combined with the interest of smuggling merchants, raised so violent, though so unjust, a clamour against the bill, that the minister thought proper to drop it; and from a dread of exciting a clamour of the same kind, none of his successors have dared to resume the project. (*WN*, 886)[56]

It is all about political influence.

If customs reform is not a prospect, where can the nation find revenue? Smith makes the case that if an excise tax is going to generate serious revenue it must tax the "inferior" as well as the middling and upper classes. Although those in the inferior class spend less per capita, "taking them collectively, [their expense] amounts always to by much the largest portion of the whole expence of the society" (*WN*, 887).

He has demonstrated that taxing necessities does not extract revenue from the inferior class, taxing luxuries does.[57] So he identifies adjusting the taxes on malt, beer, and ale as a constructive opportunity: "[B]y the taking off all the different duties upon beer and ale, and by tripling the malt-tax ... a greater revenue, it is said, might be raised by a single tax than what is at present drawn from all those heavier taxes"[58] (*WN*, 889). Smith rejects "[t]he objections of Dr. Davenant" (*WN*, 891) that this would be injurious to the maltster because he would see smaller profits as unfounded. "No tax can ever reduce, for any considerable time, the rate of profit in any particular trade, which must always keep its level with other trades in the neighbourhood" (*WN*, 892).

As for the effect of this tax on land rents, if the land has alternative uses a tax that reduced rental return on one use would cause some land use to be shifted to the best alternative. This shift would continue until all rents adjusted to a new normal neighborhood return. The effect, distributed over all land, would be small.

It would be different for "[a] tax upon the produce of those precious vineyards, of which the wine falls so much short of effectual demand, that its price is always above the natural proportion to that of the produce of other equally fertile well cultivated land ... [In this case t]he whole weight of the tax ... would fall ... *properly* upon the rent [(the monopoly return)] of the vineyard" (*WN*, 893, emphasis added).

Sugar producers complained that they, rather than the consumer, bore the burden of sugar taxes. Smith's reply: if that is the case, this

---

[56] Smith has obviously been thinking about this system for a while, for references to Walpole's failed system can be found in his *Lectures on Jurisprudence* (*LJB*, 532).

[57] It is in this section that Smith cites "the year which ended on the 5th of July 1775" (*WN*, 887–8), indicating that this section was written in London.

[58] Clearly Smith enjoys a good beer with friends: "Spirituous liquors might remain as dear as ever; while at the same time the wholesome and invigorating liquors of beer and ale might be considerably reduced in their price" (*WN*, 891).

tax incidence is clear evidence that the return you are enjoying is, like that of the precious vineyard, a monopoly price. The tax therefore is "a proper one ... [for] the gains of monopolists, whenever they can be come at ... [are] certainly of all subjects [of taxation] the most proper" (*WN*, 893).

As for his proposed tax increase on the barley used to make malt:

> The only people likely to suffer by the change of system here proposed, are those who brew for their own private use. But the exemption, which this superior rank of people at present enjoy, from very heavy taxes which are paid by the poor labourer and artificer [(who cannot afford to produce their own brew)], is surely most unjust and unequal, and ought to be taken away.... It has probably been the interest of this superior order of people, however, which has hitherto prevented a change of system that could not well fail both to increase the revenue and to relieve the people. (*WN*, 893)

Again we see his concern that political power derived from superior resources can buy influence to affect and/or effect economic policy in unjust and inefficient ways.

If consumption taxes are the primary source of revenue for a state, then "absentees" (*WN*, 895) who derive their revenue from inside that state but who live outside of that state:

> may derive a great revenue from the protection of a government to the support of which they do not contribute a single shilling. This inequality is likely to be greatest in a country of which the government is in some respects subordinate and dependent upon that of some other. The people who possess the most extensive property in the dependent, will in this case generally chuse to live in the governing country. Ireland is precisely in this situation. (*WN*, 895)

Excepting "this very peculiar situation" (*WN*, 895), consumption taxes meet the first three of Smith's four maxims for taxation very nicely: any inequality is compensated by the fact that the tax is "altogether voluntary" (*WN*, 895). If properly administered it is perfectly certain. And, because it is "paid piece-meal" (*WN*, 896) as one purchases, it is very convenient. However, "[t]hey offend in every respect the fourth" maxim: they are inefficient (*WN*, 896). He cites four reasons:

- Administration is very labor-intensive, this labor is unproductive, and the labor is expensive because of all the "perquisites" (*WN*, 896) the customs officers have come to enjoy.
- These taxes distort prices and in turn they distort the natural flow of capital.
- They encourage smuggling.

Smith blames the government as much as the smuggler for his perverse behavior. The smuggler:

> though no doubt highly blamable for violating the laws ... would have been, in every respect, an excellent citizen, had not the laws of his country made that a crime which nature never meant to be so. In those corrupted governments where there is at least a general suspicion of much unnecessary expence, and a great misapplication of the publick revenue, the laws which guard it are little respected. (*WN*, 898)

Here again we hear Smith emphasizing that the relationship between the citizen and the state is a reciprocal obligation. If the state is to reasonably expect a commitment of the citizen to its laws, then the citizen has a right to expect that those laws are just and are justly administered. Absent this, the citizenry views the laws scornfully, and as in the case of smuggling, the criminal enjoys "the indulgence of the publick" (*WN*, 898). Not surprisingly, in "corrupted governments ... the laws ... are little respected" (*WN*, 898).

- And finally, consumption taxes are inefficient because they can be intrusive.

In some cases, customs and excises officers visit and examine the inventory of merchants to the point of being oppressive. This intrusion is carried to absurd levels in Spain. There the tax is imposed at every stage in the supply chain, employing an army of officers to impose it. This gross intrusion is, in effect, a state-imposed barrier to trade. As a consequence the extent of the market is limited to a very narrow neighborhood. This severely limits the growth of the wealth of the nation because, as he demonstrates in Book II, growth comes from the free flow in the inland trade, deepening capital, and capital spilling into successively wider circuits. Apropos of this he writes:

> The uniform system of taxation, which, with a few exceptions of no great consequence, takes place in all the different parts of the united kingdom of Great Britain, leaves the interior commerce of the country, the inland and coasting trade, almost entirely free.... This freedom of interior commerce ... is perhaps one of the principal causes of the prosperity of Great Britain; every great country being necessarily the best and most extensive market for the greater part of the production of its own industry. (*WN*, 900)

He continues: "If the same freedom ... could be extended to Ireland and the plantations, both the grandeur of the state and the prosperity of every part of the empire, would probably be still greater than at present"

(*WN*, 900). This point picks up a theme Smith developed in Book IV: the best way to deal with the colonies is to fully integrate their inhabitants into the larger political/market nexus as citizens with all the rights and responsibilities of those in Britain (*WN*, 581–2).

France is not as sad a case as Spain, but it is not as free as Britain. France deploys a "multitude of revenue officers" (*WN*, 900) to collect revenue not only at the international border but also at provincial borders. Making matters more complicated, and thus more inefficient, tax schemes are not uniform across provinces. These many tax schemes enforced by this multitude of officers are "restraints upon the interior commerce of the country" (*WN*, 901). The only exception to this is the wine from "[t]he provinces most famous for" that commodity (*WN*, 901). The wine from those provinces is subject to fewer restraints. This allows for a more extensive market and in turn "encourages good management" (*WN*, 901).

If taxes on consumables are employed, how should they be collected? Should they be levied by government in which case revenue will vary from year to year, or farmed out to collectors at a rent certain? Smith's opinion is clear: "The best and most frugal way of levying a tax can never be by farm" (*WN*, 902).

Farming taxes has several drawbacks: There is a barrier to entry: Implementation by private collectors ("farmers") requires that these individuals have large capital resources and some knowledge of the tax system. Very few individuals have such resources and fewer still have any expertise at this. This leads to collusion. "The very few, who are in condition to become competitors, find it more for their interest to combine together" (*WN*, 902) to drive down the farm bid. Indicative of this power, "[i]n countries where the publick revenue are in farm, the farmers are generally the most opulent people" (*WN*, 902).

Furthermore, the farmers have no compassion for the people. They lobby for very strict laws regarding collection and they enforce these laws severely.

Even a bad sovereign feels more compassion for his people than can ever be expected from the farmers of his revenue. He knows that the permanent grandeur of his family depends upon the prosperity of his people, and he will never knowingly ruin that prosperity for the sake of a momentary interest of his own. It is otherwise with the farmers. (*WN*, 903)

The exploitive potential of the farmer is all the greater if he also has a monopoly over the exchange of the commodity being taxed. Salt in France is such a case. The consequence is an exorbitant price and an "irresistible" "temptation to smuggle" (*WN*, 903). While the French government's revenue from this tax is very high, it is collected with "the blood of the people" (*WN*, 904) on it. Only "[t]hose who consider the blood of the people as nothing in comparison with the revenue of the prince, may perhaps approve of this method of levying taxes" (*WN*, 904).

Smith suggests three "reformations" of the French system (*WN*, 904) that would streamline it and make it more equitable, but, he observes, "opposition ... [from] favoured subjects ... [and] from the private interest of individuals" (*WN*, 904, 905) makes such changes very unlikely. Again, he abhors a case in which the currency that pays for the benefits of those with power is the blood of the people.

As evidence that France's tax system is much worse than Britain's, he observes that while France has every advantage over Britain when it comes to tax base (three times the population, better soil and climate, "longer ... state of improvement, better stocked with ... great towns and convenient and well-built houses" (*WN*, 905)), its tax yield does not reflect these advantages. This is the perverse consequence of a tax system in France that is more oppressive than that in Britain.

Holland's citizens are even more heavily taxed than France's. This burden is necessary for this small nation is in a constant struggle to "preserve [its] ... existence" (*WN*, 906) against an unrelenting sea and strong enemies. So, given these high taxes how does Holland maintain its grandeur?

> The republican form of government seems to be the principal support of the present grandeur of Holland. The owners of great capitals, the great mercantile families, have generally either some direct share, or some indirect influence in the administration of that government. For the sake of the respect and authority which they derive from this situation, they are willing to live in a country where their capital, if they employ it themselves, will bring them less profit, and if they lend it to another, less interest.... The residence of such wealthy people keeps alive, in spite of all disadvantages, a certain degree of industry in the country. (*WN*, 906)

In Holland the capital holders have developed a civic humanist culture, a common commitment as citizens to the commonwealth. If, Smith continues, the republic was dissolved and the merchants felt that their influence was gone, they would leave, taking their capital with them. As Smith makes clear on several occasions, capital is not a citizen of any nation (*WN*, 364, 848–9, 927).

CHAPTER 3: "OF PUBLICK DEBTS"

Prior to "the extension of commerce and the improvement of manufactures" any surplus production was in the form of "a large quantity of the necessaries of life, in the materials of plain food and coarse clothing" (*WN*, 907). Given the limited capacity of one's stomach and the limited desire for such coarse clothing there is little opportunity for ostentation. The only vent for the surplus production acquired by a lord was the support of retainers. This kind of hospitality, "[a] hospitality in which there is no luxury, and a liberality in which there is no ostentation" (*WN*, 907), cannot be the ruin of any man.[59]

To drive home his point that this "rustick hospitality" (*WN*, 907) cannot ruin a person, Smith cites the "long time during which estates used to continue in the same family, [as] sufficiently demonstrat[ing] the general disposition of people to live within their income" (*WN*, 907).

Accumulation was the norm because the lack of opportunities to squander what money (gold and silver) they did accumulate was complemented by a strong incentive for lords to hoard that money given the "violence and disorder" (*WN*, 908) of the times. The possibility of being driven from their homes made it "convenient to have a hoard of money at hand … [so] they might have something of known value to carry with them to some place of safety" (*WN*, 908). As with the lords, so too the sovereigns of those times supported retainers, and they horded treasure for the contingencies that might arise.

It is a very different story "[i]n a commercial country abounding with every sort of expensive luxury" (*WN*, 908). As Book III makes clear, the opportunity for conspicuous consumption led the lords and the sovereign to redirect their surplus from retainers to the market to purchase "all the costly trinkets which compose the splendid, but insignificant pageantry of a court" (*WN*, 908).

In such a commercial world a sovereign may "spend upon those pleasures so great a part of his revenue as to debilitate very much the defensive power of the state" (*WN*, 909). But even for one who is not so foolish, whatever resources are left once defense is cared for will be spent on those frivolous pleasures. "The amassing of treasure can no longer be expected, and when extraordinary exigencies require extraordinary expences, he must necessarily call upon his subjects for an extraordinary aid" (*WN*, 909).

---

[59] "[T]hough the hospitality of luxury and a liberality of ostentation" certainly can (*WN*, 907).

"The want of parsimony in time of peace, imposes the necessity of contracting debt in time of war" (*WN*, 909). War is immensely expensive. The mere threat of war requires that money be spent immediately, for delay can be deadly. Even if there are available revenue sources, these can seldom be tapped as quickly as the need dictates. Therefore, absent an accumulated fund, government must turn to borrowing. Not a problem:

> The same commercial state of society which ... brings government in this manner into the necessity of borrowing, produces in the subjects both an ability and an inclination to lend. ...
> A country abounding with merchants and manufacturers, necessarily abounds with a set of people through whose hands not only their own capitals, but the capitals of all those who either lend them money, or trust them with goods, pass as frequently, or more frequently, than the revenue of a private man. (*WN*, 910)

Drawing on his circuits of production analysis, Smith explains that while the capital of the private man circulates "only once a year ... the capital ... of a merchant, who deals in trade of which the returns are very quick" (the domestic circuit) circulates much more often. Merchants can therefore put their hands on a large quantity of capital very quickly. This access to capital means the commercial society has subjects with "the ability ... to lend" as the need of the state arises. (*WN*, 910) And they are willing:

> Commerce and manufacturers can seldom flourish long in any state which does not enjoy a regular administration of justice, in which the people do not feel themselves secure in the possession of their property, in which the faith of contracts is not supported by law, and in which the authority of the state is not supposed to be regularly employed in enforcing the payment of debts from all those who are able to pay. Commerce and manufacturers, in short, can seldom flourish in any state in which there is not a certain degree of confidence in the justice of government. The same confidence which disposes great merchants and manufacturers, upon ordinary occasions, to trust their property to the protection of a particular government; disposes them, upon extraordinary occasions, to trust that government with the use of their property. (*WN*, 910)

Yet again Smith emphasizes the central prerequisite for a successful commercial society: a commercial system is based on capital flowing in circuits of trade. If individuals are to accumulate wealth and pour that accumulation into these circuits, they must feel that their capital will be secure. The ultimate guarantor of this security is the civil government. So for commercial societies to succeed, government must mature into an institution that instills confidence in the justice of its administration. If government evolves in that way, the fruits of commerce will grow. With those fruits come the means for citizens to provide for the financial needs of their government when the exigencies of war dictate such a need. This symbiotic relationship between the citizens and the government is a source of the strength of commercial society that allows it, *ceteris paribus*, to emerge, to survive, and to progress in the course of the evolution of humankind.

This transformation of the relationship between the citizen and the state is not the product of some grand human plan. It is, as Smith explains in detail in Book III, the interplay of a complex weave of incentives (greed, ostentation, desire for security, competition for power ...) that leads to this relationship between more independent citizens and a more powerful state. Mutual trust is the *sine qua non* of this relationship.

Lending to the government does not impair the commercial activity of the merchants. Quite to the contrary, the government generally borrows on very generous terms. This and the confidence that a just government enjoys makes the debt paper very marketable. "The merchant or monied man makes money by lending money to the government, and instead of diminishing, increases his trading capital" (WN, 910–11).

The unfortunate element in all of this is that, secure in the knowledge that it can borrow as needed, the state "therefore dispenses itself from the duty of saving" (WN, 911).[60] This has led to a perverse dependence on debt among the governments of commercial societies: "The progress of the enormous debts which at present oppress, and will in the long-run probably ruin, all the great nations of Europe, has been pretty uniform" (WN, 911).

To understand the origins and consequences of this debt dilemma Smith examines the structure of Great Britain's debt and its history. His theme is straightforward. Loans were initially tied to a revenue stream committed to their repayment. But borrowing invariably exceeded the revenue streams available for repayment. This meant that while some loans were repaid, the term for other debt repayments had to be extended. As the debt grew over time it became impossible to repay any of the principal; only the interest was paid. This "necessarily gave birth to the more ruinous practice of perpetual borrowing" (WN, 915). This practice was exacerbated by the imprudent inclination of governments

---

[60] It is not so in an immature state where the people "distrust of the justice of government" (WN, 911). In such a state the people fear the government and hide whatever wealth they may accumulate for fear that the government will take it. This requires that the sovereign save, for he will not be able to borrow.

to grasp at short-term solutions, leaving the long-term consequences for their successors:

> To relieve the present exigency is always the object which principally interests those immediately concerned in the administration of publick affairs. The future liberation of the publick revenue, they leave to the care of posterity. (*WN*, 915)

By lowering, over time, the interest paid on this public debt Britain was able to save some of its revenue. This saving was committed to a "Sinking Fund" (*WN*, 915). While "instituted for the payment of old [debts], [it represents a resource that] facilitates very much the contracting of new debts" (*WN*, 916).

A significant portion of state borrowing is done by issuing annuities in return for the loan. These annuities can be either perpetual or for a term based on the lives of the lenders. Smith's information suggests that "[i]n France a much greater proportion of the publick debt consists in annuities for lives than in England" (*WN*, 918).[61]

This difference is due to the different character of the lenders. "In England, the seat of government being in the greatest mercantile city in the world, the merchants are generally the people who advance money to government" (*WN*, 918). These merchants want the debt paper they receive to be an asset that will enhance their capital stock. "[I]f by advancing their money they were to purchase, instead of perpetual annuities, annuities for lives only ... they would not always be so likely to sell them with a profit" (*WN*, 919) because the value of the latter falls with time for the passing of time brings the end of the life and of the annuity nearer. In France those who lend to the government are more often than not wealthy bachelors who for various reasons "have little or no care for posterity" (*WN*, 919). A life annuity is perfect for them.

The great driver of government borrowing is war.

In peacetime budgets tend to exhaust available revenue. With war there comes a sudden surge in expenditure well beyond the current revenue. Government is loath to raise taxes to cover this shortfall because the level of need is often unclear and the public's commitment to the war may be eroded by such a tax. Borrowing allows the government to get the funds it needs without a sudden large increase in taxes. If the war is

---

[61] It is "information that suggests" because, as Smith appreciates, data is often an approximation of truth. In this case he writes that "[t]hese estimations [(on which he is basing his assertion)], I know very well, are not exact, but having been presented by so very respectable a body as approximations to the truth, they may, I apprehend, be considered as such" (*WN*, 918). Again we see Smith's keen sense that one has to "consider the source" when using any information from that source.

remote, then for the citizens who feel no real sacrifice the war becomes an exciting "amusement ... [as they read] in the newspapers the exploits of their own fleets and armies" (*WN*, 920).

Even in peacetime the government avoids raising taxes because "[e]very new tax ... occasions always some murmur, and meets with some opposition" (*WN*, 920–1). The more the tax the more the opposition. "To borrow from the sinking fund is always an obvious and easy expedient for getting out of the present difficulty" (*WN*, 921). Ironically and unfortunately, this is all the more likely as an expedient when a nation is heavily burdened with debt because citizens already feel over taxed. "In Great Britain, from the time that we had first recourse to the ruinous expedient of perpetual funding, the reduction of the publick debt in time of peace, has never borne any proportion to its accumulation in time of war" (*WN*, 921).

It was the Nine Years' War, begun in 1688 and concluded with the treaty of Ryswick in 1697, that laid the foundation for the present enormous debt of Great Britain. From there Smith traces, citing a great deal of data,[62] the pattern of growth in the public debt: it surges with war and is only partially reduced from that new, higher level during periods of "profound peace" (*WN*, 922). Even "the prudent and truly patriotic administration of Mr. Pelham, was not able to" significantly affect this pattern (*WN*, 923).

The last data he cites are from "the 5th of January 1775 ... [Certainly our debt problems will get worse, he continues, because] we are now involved in a new war which, in its progress, may prove as expensive as any of our former wars" (*WN*, 924).[63]

To demonstrate the strength of his case that unrestrained growth in public debt is destructive, Smith directly addresses the counterargument made by an author who claims that the borrowing of the government represents an augmentation of the capital stock of the nation. No, says Smith, quite to the contrary. To transfer funds from the hands of merchants to the government is to take those funds out of the productive circuits of capital and turn them to a dead end.[64] They go from "serving

---

[62] He shows care in reporting when in the first revision to the *WN* he corrects a transposed number. See Editors note *h-h* (*WN*, 922).

[63] In a note Smith added for the third edition he confirms his prediction and adds that the pattern he had cited has continued. See editor's note *k-k* (*WN*, 924).

[64] Smith notes that these merchants may indeed have received a marketable annuity that they in turn could sell at a profit to replace their capital. That does not, however, mean that their lending created a net national increase in capital. It simply means that the source from which the government ultimately obtained its capital was not the immediate

the function of capital, to serve in that of revenue; from maintaining productive labourers to maintain unproductive ones, and to be spent and wasted ... without any hope of any future reproduction" (*WN*, 924).

Not only does borrowing redirect capital from productive channels, it has a greater negative effect on capital base than taxing. To the degree that a tax falls on money that would have gone to consumption, the tax is simply replacing one kind of unproductive labor, that which satisfies consumer demand, with another kind of unproductive labor, that which the government employs. Only that share of the money that would have gone into accumulation is lost from the circuit of production. In the case of borrowing 100 percent of the money is taken from the circuit of production.

Borrowing does have one advantage. By leaving more in individuals' pockets ...

the frugality and industry of private people can more easily repair the breaches which the waste and extravagance of government may occasionally make in the general capital of the society.
It is only during the continuance of war, however, that the system of funding has this advantage over the other system. (*WN*, 925)

In peacetime and at the outset of war government should finance itself on a pay as you go basis, that is, by taxes. Doing so protects existing capital. It also diminishes the impact on future capital accumulation because the tax burden, unlike the burden of a debt, can end with the war.

Furthermore, if financed by taxes "[w]ars would in general be more speedily concluded, and less wantonly undertaken" (*WN*, 926). Again we see his focus on the alignment of incentives: bearing the full and immediate financial burden, the tolerance of the people for such an undertaking would be very closely associated with their perception of its necessity.

Some argue that the interest paid financing a public debt is not a national problem because we owe it to ourselves; "it is the right hand which pays the left.... [Smith replies that t]his apology is founded altogether in the sophistry of the mercantile system" (*WN*, 926, 927).

There are two problems with this logic: we do in fact owe some of this debt to foreigners (e.g., "the Dutch" (*WN*, 927)). But this is of no major consequence. The real problem is that to repay the debt we must tax ourselves, and these taxes shrink the amount of capital in the circuit of production.

merchant who made the loan. "Though it replaced to them what they had advanced to the government, it did not replace it to the country" (*WN*, 925).

Some of these taxes fall on our landlords, who cannot escape for their land is fixed in location. This additional levy makes it more difficult for them to make or maintain improvements on their land. As a consequence the "agriculture in the country must necessarily decline" (*WN*, 927).

When the burden of the taxes falls on "the owners and employers of capital stock" (*WN*, 927), if these taxes become sufficiently onerous they will move their capital out of the country. "The industry of the country will necessarily fall with the removal of the capital which supported it, and the ruin of trade and manufacturers will follow the declension of agriculture" (*WN*, 927–8).

The interest paid on the public debt is a transfer of resources from those who use and superintend it as productive capital to those "creditors of the publick, who have no such particular interest" in supporting the system of production (*WN*, 928). These creditors may have a general interest in the well-being of the nation, but their well-being is not tied to any particular productive enterprise. They live off of the scarcity value of capital, the interest they receive. They need not concern themselves with the long-term distress the public debt can cause the nation. There are, after all, other places they can take their capital.

This is not simply a theoretical argument. The Italian republics seem to have invented this debt financing and it has enfeebled them. Spain, and later the United Provinces, followed suit and they too are now enfeebled. "The practice of funding has gradually enfeebled every state which has adopted it" (*WN*, 928). "France, notwithstanding all its natural resources, languishes under an oppressive load" of debt (*WN*, 928). Is there any reason, Smith asks rhetorically, to believe the experience of Britain will be different?

The good news is that Britain has a more "just and equitable" (*WN*, 834) tax system than any other nation.

To the honor of our present system of taxation, indeed, it has hitherto given so little embarrassment to industry, that, during the course even of the most expensive wars, the frugality and good conduct of individuals seem to have been able, by saving and accumulation, to repair all the breaches which the waste and extravagance of government had made in the general capital of the society. (*WN*, 929)[65]

---

[65] This echoes the point Smith made about why the English colonies are successful in spite of the constraints of the mercantile system. It is because they are free and treated justly as individuals under English law. This encourages accumulation and unleashes capital, so in spite of the onerous mercantile constraints progress prevails. See *WN* (585).

But as our debt pushes us to find ever more revenue will the wisdom of our system be sufficient? Can the success we have enjoyed in the face of our own fiscal foolishness continue? Smith clearly has grave doubts. At some point, he suggests, debt can become so large that it simply cannot be repaid. Nations then resort to bankruptcy, or they degrade the currency to cover the nominal obligations by either "direct[ly] raising of the denomination of the coin … [or by t]he adulteration of the standard" (WN, 932).

Degrading the currency is for Smith a "real publick bankruptcy … disguised under the appearance of pretended payment … and the creditors of the publick would really be defrauded" (WN, 929, 930). The cascading effect of such a fraud would be a disaster for the economy. The consequent general inflation would cause an implicit transfer from creditor to debtor, from frugal to frivolous individuals, and as a consequence the movement of money from capital to consumption. Better the state should openly declare its bankruptcy than disguise it with this "juggling trick" (WN, 930). Unfortunately, however, history records more tricks than truth.

In the current British case, the debt is so significant that it can only be addressed by "either some very considerable augmentation of the publick revenue, or some equally considerable reduction of the publick expence" (WN, 933). He suggests that "a more equal land-tax, a more equal tax upon rent of houses, and such alterations in the present system of customs and excise" (WN, 933) as he laid out earlier,[66] would "distribute the weight of … [the tax burden] more equally upon the whole, [and] produce a considerable augmentation in revenue" (WN, 933). But even this, he continues, would not be enough to solve the problem.

So where do we turn?

A significant augmentation of the national tax revenue could be had by "extending the British system of taxation to all the different provinces of the empire inhabited by people of either British or European extraction" (WN, 933). But if this is to be consistent "with the principles of the British constitution" then these provinces must enjoy representation in parliament in "proportion to the produce of its taxes" (WN, 933).

This is a very unlikely prospect given "[t]he private interests of many powerful individuals, [and] the confirmed prejudices of great bodies of people" (WN, 933–4). Nevertheless, "in a speculative work of this kind" (WN, 934) it seems reasonable to imagine how such a system would play

---

[66] For example, eliminating drawbacks and bounties.

out. "Such a speculation can at worst be regarded but as a new Utopia" (*WN*, 934). Because there was no harm in imagining the old one why not imagine again, and so he does...

The land-tax, the stamp duties, and the different duties of customs and excise, constitute the four principal branches of the British taxes. (*WN*, 934)

The land tax and the stamp duties could be justly imposed across the empire with little adaptation.

The extension of the custom-house laws of Great Britain to Ireland and the plantations, provided it was accompanied, as in justice it ought to be, with an extension of the freedom of trade, would be in the highest degree advantageous to both. All the invidious restraints which at present oppress the trade of Ireland ... [and] America, would be entirely at an end.... The trade between all the different parts of the British empire would ... be as free as the coasting trade of Great Britain is at present. The British empire would thus afford within itself an immense internal market for every part of the produce of all its different provinces. (*WN*, 935)

The only tax that might, justifiably, be inconsistent among the dominions of the empire would be the excise. This is so because "the produce and consumption are so very different" (*WN*, 935–6) across the dominions. He cites, for example, the fact that the kind of liquor consumed in America does not have the same shelf life as British beer. To tax it like British beer would require intrusions "inconsistent with liberty" (*WN*, 936). But this is a problem that should and can be addressed, "for the sake of equity" (*WN*, 936), without major consequence.

The biggest change in the present system of taxation would no doubt apply to "[s]ugar, rum, and tobacco, ... commodities which are no where necessaries of life, which are become objects of almost universal consumption, and which are therefore extremely proper subjects of taxation" (*WN*, 936). Adjusting the system of taxing these items would be a challenge, but it can be effectively addressed.

So how much revenue would this imagined union generate? Smith proceeds to estimate, admittedly grossly, the additional revenue as well as the additional costs associated with the union.[67] Given his caveat that this is speculation,[68] Smith extrapolates that if 10 million pounds

---

[67] In the process he refers to data from "March 1775" and he notes "the present disturbances" (*WN*, 937), so clearly some of this section was written in London.

[68] He suggests that he is purposely being conservative to give his case more credibility. For example, he takes the low end of the estimate of the population of the American colonies because "[t]hose accounts [he cites] ... may have been exaggerated, in order, perhaps, either encourage their own people, or to intimidate those of this country" (*WN*, 937).

can be collected from the 8 million inhabitants of Great Britain, then over 16 million would be generated by the 13 million inhabitants of the entire empire he envisions. Given his estimates of government costs, this revenue would be enough to retire the public debt and reinvigorate the empire. Furthermore, given this enhanced revenue

> people might be relieved from some of the most burdensome taxes; from those which are imposed wither upon the necessaries of life, or upon the materials of manufacture. The labouring poor would thus be enabled to live better, to work cheaper, and to send their goods cheaper to market. The cheapness of their goods would increase the demand for them, and consequently for the labour of those who produce them. This increase in the demand for labour, would both increase the numbers and improve the circumstances of the labouring poor. (*WN*, 938)

A very desirable outcome, for the goodness of a society is measured by the "the circumstances of the labouring poor."

Smith told us, as he began to describe the new empire he imagines, that it was his "Utopia." And what lies at the heart of that Utopian vision: "labouring poor ... enabled to live better" (*WN*, 938). This reflects the heart of Smith's values. Here in the last section of the last chapter of the last book of *The Wealth of Nations*, he reiterates a point he made in Book I:

> Is this improvement in the circumstances of the lower ranks of the people to be regarded as an advantage or as an inconveniency to the society? ... [W]hat improves the circumstances of the greater part can never be regarded as an inconveniency to the whole. No society can surely be flourishing and happy, of which the far greater part of the members are poor and miserable. It is but equity, besides, that they who feed, cloath and lodge the whole body of the people, should have such a share of the produce of their own labour as to be themselves tolerably well fed, cloathed, and lodged. (*WN*, 96)

Smith believes in the possibilities of union, but he recognizes that the benefits would not be immediate because given the porous boundaries of Scotland and the American colonies, smuggling would have to be addressed. He believes that the policy he has proposed does this. Confining duties to a few select imports would make administering these duties much easier while at the same time reducing the incentive for smuggling the many currently heavily tax-burdened imports. As always, it is about getting the alignment of incentives right.

Some might object that the Americans will not have sufficient specie available to pay their taxes because they use paper currency for their domestic transactions. These sceptics assert that "[w]e already get all the gold and silver which they have. How is it possible to draw from them what they have not?" (*WN*, 940).

A red herring, says Smith. The absence of gold and silver in the American colonies is "the effect of choice, and not of necessity" (WN, 940). As he described in Book II, the inner, domestic circuit uses paper currency to free gold and silver for use in wider circuits of trade. In both America and in Scotland "it is not the poverty, but the enterprizing and projecting spirit of the people, their desire of employing all the stock which they can get as active and productive stock, which has occasioned this" absence of metals (WN, 941). The Americans have the wealth to command those metals when they need them, as reflected in the ability of "the northern colonies" to pay the trade deficit they normally run with specie (WN, 942).

If Britain has had occasional trouble getting full payment from the colonies, it is not for lack of ability but rather due to bad management. This has been a particular problem in those colonies with much "uncultivated land" because unwise speculation has led to "irregular and uncertain" returns (WN, 943). "It is not because they are poor that their payments are irregular and uncertain; but because they are too eager to become excessively rich" (WN, 943).

The system he proposes is, Smith believes, fair to Ireland and America:

It is not contrary to justice that both Ireland and America should contribute towards the discharge of the publick debt of Great Britain. That debt has been contracted in support of the government established by the Revolution, a government to which the protestants of Ireland owe, not only the whole authority which they at present enjoy in their own country, but every security which they possess for their liberty, their property, and their religion; a government to which several of the colonies of America owe their present charters, and consequently their present constitution, and to which all the colonies of America owe the liberty, security, and property which they have ever since enjoyed. That publick debt has been contracted in the defence, not of Great Britain alone, but of all the different provinces of the empire... (WN, 944)

As Smith makes his case for the union he imagines, it is a case laid out on a foundation of his values: Ireland and America should share the burden of financing the government because they[69] have shared the blessings of "liberty, security, and property" that we in Britain have established and defended for them.

Ireland would gain more with union than free trade. As it was in Scotland so too in Ireland, with union "the middling and inferior ranks of the people ... [would gain] compleat deliverance from the power of

---

[69] "They" being white males and Protestant males in America and Ireland, respectively.

an aristocracy.... [An aristocracy] much more oppressive [than that of
Scotland, because unlike the aristocracy of Scotland which was based
on] natural and respectable distinctions of birth and fortune; ... [that
in Ireland is based on] the most odious of all distinctions, those of religious and political prejudices" (*WN*, 944). This religious divide, "more
than any other, animate[s] both the insolence of the oppressors, and the
hatred and indignation of the oppressed" (*WN*, 944), thereby nurturing
immense hostility. "Without a union with Great Britain, the inhabitants
of Ireland are not likely for many ages to consider themselves as one
people" (*WN*, 944).[70]

As for the full benefits of his plan of union for the American colonies
(given his reference herein to the "present disturbances," this is clearly
written after he arrived in London in 1773):

No oppressive aristocracy has ever prevailed in the colonies. Even they, however,
would, in point of happiness and tranquility, gain considerably by a union with
Great Britain. It would, at least, deliver them from those rancorous and virulent
factions which are inseperable from small democracies, and which have so frequently divided the affections of their people, and disturbed the tranquility of
their governments, in their form so democratical. In the case of total separation
from Great Britain, which, unless prevented by a union of this kind, seems very
likely to take place, those factions would be ten times more virulent than ever.
Before the commencement of the present disturbances, the coercive power of the
mother-country had always been able to restrain those factions.... In all great
countries which are united under one uniform government, the spirit of party
commonly prevails less in the remote provinces than in the centre of the empire.[71]
The distance of those provinces from the capital, from the principal seat of the
great scramble of faction and ambition, makes them enter less into the views of
the contending parties, and renders them more indifferent and impartial spectators of the conduct of all.[72] (*WN*, 944–5)

Thus as part of a union the British in America, being at a distance from
London, would be less plagued by faction and more likely to "enjoy a
degree of concord and unanimity at present unknown" (*WN*, 945). Taxes
would be higher, but those taxes would only be in place until the union's
debt was addressed. There is the even prospect that the tax burden could

---

[70] Smith does not make many specific predictions. In this case he does and it certainly seems
prescient.

[71] Smith himself became keenly aware of this when he moved from Kirkcaldy to London
in 1773.

[72] Smith's analysis of the virulence of faction in small democracies is very similar to the
concern James Madison expressed in Federalist No. 10 (Madison, 53). Smith predicts
for the colonies without union very much what Madison predicts without union, albeit
a different union, tumult, and breakdown.

be reduced by the higher tax revenues generated from reducing the oppression and corruption in the British East Indies.

Absent an increase in government revenue, the only way to reduce the debt is to reduce expenditures.

Where to cut?

"In the mode of collecting, and in that of expending the publick revenue; though in both there may be still room for improvement; Great Britain seems to be at least as oeconomical as any of her neighbours" (*WN*, 946). Indeed, her peacetime spending on the military establishment for "her own defence" (*WN*, 946) is not so great as her neighbors'.

The cost of maintaining the colonies in peacetime is "very considerable, and is an expence which may, and if no revenue can be drawn from them, ought certainly to be saved altogether. This constant expence in time of peace though very great, is insignificant in comparison with what the defence of the colonies has cost us in time of war" (*WN*, 946).

He recounts the huge expense of the wars with Spain and France, noting that "[h]ad it not been for those wars ... [the] debt might, and probably would by this time, have been compleatly paid" (*WN*, 946).

It was because the colonies were supposed to be provinces of the British empire, that this expence was laid out upon them. But countries which contribute neither revenue nor military force towards the support of the empire, cannot be considered as provinces. They may perhaps be considered as appendages, as a sort of splendid and showy equipage of the empire. (*WN*, 946)

Our "empire" and its mercantile benefits have been an illusion. "It has hitherto been, not an empire, but the project of an empire; not a gold mine, but the project of a gold mine" (*WN*, 947). It is a project undertaken at immense public expense that has returned no public benefit. Nor was it intended to. It is a project of a monopolist faction designed to serve, as he has demonstrated at length, not public good but private greed.

Smith concludes his *Inquiry into the Nature and Causes of the Wealth of Nations* with the following sober assessment of this dream of empire:

It is surely now time that our rulers should either realize this golden dream,[73] in which they have been indulging themselves, perhaps, as well as the people; or, that they should awake from it themselves, and endeavour to awaken the people. If the project cannot be compleatd, it ought to be given up. If any of the provinces of the British empire cannot be made to contribute towards the support of the whole

---

[73] He uses the same term, "golden dreams," to describe the irresponsible expectations of projectors who use expensive funding schemes to finance projects for which they envision "great profit" (*WN*, 310).

empire, it is surely time that Great Britain should free herself from the expence of defending those provinces in time of war, and of supporting any part of their civil or military establishments in time of peace, and endeavour to accommodate her future views and designs to the real mediocrity of her circumstances. (*WN*, 947)

As he wrote in Book IV when he first proposed his vision of a union:[74] it is not the challenges of implementation that are "insurmountable ... [it is the] prejudices and opinions of the people both on this and on the other side of the Atlantic" (*WN*, 625).

For any nation, and so too for humankind, the promise of our shared prospect is as real or illusory as our shared commitment to inclusive common values and the commonweal.

---

[74] Union is a vision he suggested earlier in Book IV: the "constitution ... would be compleatd by it, and seems to be imperfect without it" (*WN*, 624).

Epilogue

Adam Smith and Laissez-Faire

The *Wealth of Nations* is a stupendous palace erected upon the granite of self-interest.... The immensely powerful force of self-interest guides resources to their most efficient uses, stimulates labourers to diligence and investors to splendid new divisions of labour, in short, it orders and enriches the nation which gives it free rein.

George Stigler

(Stigler, 1975, 236)

If, as Stigler asserts, Smith believes that "self-interest ... orders and enriches the nation which gives it free rein," then clearly Smith must believe that the optimal government policy is laissez-faire.

Among the very best, full-length arguments for interpreting Smith as an advocate for laissez-faire is James Otteson's *Adam Smith*, published as Volume 16 in the series "Major Conservative and Libertarian Thinkers." Therein Otteson writes:

The baseline for a Smithian state is quite limited: protections of person, property, and voluntary contract, punishments for attacks on person or property or breach of contract, and – little else.... Because Smith believes history shows that people do better under conditions of limited government, the strong presumption will be against third party interposition into human affairs and in favor of allowing individuals to find their own ways.... [H]e thus recommends a largely – though not completely – laissez-faire state.... [But Smith's] liberalism ... is pragmatic: he is willing to allow for exceptions to the default presumptions if there are specific cases in which local circumstances warrant it. (Otteson, 2011, 81)

Otteson's case for Smith as an advocate for laissez-faire is based in part on three complementary arguments that he finds in Smith's work:

The "Local Knowledge Argument" maintains that "everyone has unique knowledge of his own 'local' situation" so a distant other (e.g., the proverbial "Government bureaucrat") is by definition less informed to make "local" decisions (Otteson, 2011, 98).

The "Economizer Argument" maintains that "local knowledge provides ... a better chance of knowing how best to use ... resources" (Otteson, 2011, 98).

The "Invisible Hand Argument" asserts that given the first two arguments, our self-interest has the unintended consequence of serving the public good, for as we seek to benefit ourselves by serving the market more efficiently and effectively, we serve others (Otteson, 2011, 99).

The fourth element of Smith's work that, according to Otteson, seals the deal for Smith's laissez-faire position is what Otteson refers to as the "Great Mind Fallacy." Not only can individuals manage their own affairs quite well, thank you, but we need to manage our own affairs. There is no one "out there [no 'Great Mind'] smart enough and benevolent enough to make ... decisions for us ... [There is no big brother looking after us,] leaving us peacefully secure in the knowledge that somebody somewhere is protecting and taking care of us. It would be nice. Alas, here on earth there is no such Great Mind. And no fallible human beings – not even 'government experts' [(those grey-suited bureaucrats)] – ever will be" (Otteson, 2011, 101–2).

This all seems to be very consistent with Smith, who writes:

All systems either of preference or of restraint ... being thus completely taken away, the obvious and simple system of natural liberty establishes itself of its own accord. Every man, *as long as he does not violate the laws of justice*, is left perfectly free to pursue his own interest his own way, and to bring both his industry and capital into competition with those of any other man, or order of men. The sovereign is completely discharged from a duty, in the attempting to perform which he must always be exposed to innumerable delusions, and for the proper performance of which no human wisdom or knowledge could ever be sufficient; the duty of superintending the industry of private people, and of directing it towards the employments most suitable to the interest of the society. (*WN*, 687, emphasis added)

Clearly, when the conditions consistent with natural liberty are realized it is the height of arrogance for the sovereign to micro manage the citizenry.

But those conditions are not trivial and their realization does involve government action, not as a micro manager of human action but as an institution that constitutes and enforces fair and just principles of participation by all in the "race for wealth" (*TMS*, 83). Smith continues:

According to the system of natural liberty, the sovereign has only three duties to attend to; *three duties of great importance*, indeed, but plain and intelligible to common understandings: first, the duty of protecting the society from the violence and invasion of other independent societies; secondly, the duty of protecting, as far as possible, every member of the society from the injustice or oppression of every other member of it, or the duty of establishing an exact administration of justice; and, thirdly, the duty of erecting and maintaining certain publick works and certain publick institutions, which it can never be for the interest of any individual, or small number of individuals, to erect and maintain; because the profit could never repay the expence to any individual or small number of individuals, though it may frequently do much more than repay it to a great society. (*WN*, 687–8, emphasis added)

In Smith's vision government's role is limited, but it is a role of "great importance."

If the "simple system of natural liberty [is to] establish … itself," government must secure society from foreign threats, ensure fairness in the race for wealth by establishing justice among citizens, and take responsibility when the market fails.

This list requires minimal government intrusion in the life of the citizenry "as long as … ['every man'] does not violate the laws of justice" (*WN*, 687). It would be nice if every man was so noble, but alas, every man isn't.

Individuals may well be uniquely situated to accrue local knowledge that makes them more efficient at allocating their resources to maximize their utility, but such allocations based on self-interest are not invariably socially optimal. Given that we are all engaged with one another in a "race for wealth," optimal individual choices may well involve trying to "justle, or throw down" (*TMS*, 83)[1] our competitors, or in the modern vernacular: "rent-seeking" – using our resources to achieve market power. Or, they may involve undertaking activities that generate negative externalities – personally optimizing, but doing so based on a truncated assessment of costs, considering only the costs we personally bear and not taking into account the full social cost of our activity.

In Smith's analysis such market-distorting behaviors are not "quite limited," including only "attacks on person or property or breach of contract, and – little else." Smith sees the scope of potential market power and market failure distortions as much broader with significant microeconomic and macroeconomic implications. Recall, for example, his description of the bold projectors manipulation of bank credit that

---

[1] "In the race for wealth, and honours, and preferments he may run as hard as he can, and strain every nerve and every muscle, in order to outstrip all his competitors. But if he should justle, or throw down any of them, the indulgence of the spectators is entirely at an end. It is a violation of fair play, which they cannot admit of" (*TMS*, 83).

caused a systemic failure of the nation's banking system (Sounds very familiar in light of the Great Recession, doesn't it?). Recall as well his passionate concern that the self-serving policies of the mercantilist faction, implemented by a "captured" and/or intimidated parliament, were undermining all the progress that had been achieved by the nation (Ever been to K Street in DC?).

In Smith's analysis market power and market failure are not "exceptions to the default presumptions" (Otteson, 2011, 81). They *are* the default presumptions.

Given the alignment of incentives, in an ungoverned system where self-interest is unbridled market power and market failure are the norm because power pays and taking account of perverse external consequences of one's actions is costly.[2] In the absence of some form of government (personal ethics and/or civil institutions) society does not move toward an ideal natural and harmonious order; it descends into chaos.

I agree with Otteson that Smith rejects the Great Mind Fallacy. He writes passionately to this effect in revisions to *TMS* published the year he died:

> The man of system ... is apt to be very wise in his own conceit; and is often so enamoured with the supposed beauty of his own ideal plan of government, that he cannot suffer the smallest deviation from any part of it....
>
> Some general, and even systematical, idea of the perfection of policy and law, may no doubt be necessary for directing the views of the statesman. But to insist upon establishing, and upon establishing all at once, and in spite of all opposition, every thing which that idea may seem to require, must often be the highest degree of arrogance. It is to erect his own judgment into the supreme standard of right and wrong. It is to fancy himself the only wise and worthy man in the commonwealth, and that his fellow-citizens should accommodate themselves to him and not he to them. (*TMS*, 233–4)

But it does not follow from the "arrogance" of the "man of system" that civil government is invariably oppressive and destructive – or unnecessary.

Laissez-faire is fine for a community of angels, but there are devils among us and there is a bit of the devil in each of us. Given this "human frailty" (*Correspondence*, 221), government is necessary if human society is to be more than a chaos of power grabbing and vigilantism. Self and

---

[2] Otteson writes that "policy-makers routinely bias their cost/benefit calculations in favor of their proposals by leaving out 'unseen,' but no less real, costs" (Otteson, 2011, 109). So too do private individuals. The problem, challenge, is symmetric. The only advantage on the public side is that there is the potential for accountability to the public.

civil government are sources of order. Clearly, however, the establishment of government does not invariably give rise to a just or fair order. North Korea's government achieves great order at the price of human dignity. Government is simply an instrument for establishing order – it can be used for evil, or for good.

It is the "improvement" of self-government and civil government, the development of an ever more just and an inclusive order, that enhances the well-being of an ever widening scope of those who live within that order. As his *Inquiry into the Nature and Causes of the Wealth of Nations* makes clear, for Smith the progress of governance and the inclusive progress of opulence go hand in hand.

Creating a government that functions constructively (ensuring security, justice and fairness, and addressing market failures) is a complex challenge, and clearly the perfection of civil government is impossible, but "like Solon, when … [we] cannot establish the best system of laws, … [we should] endeavour to establish the best that the people can bear" (*TMS*, 233).

Every system of positive law may be regarded as a more or less imperfect attempt towards a system of natural jurisprudence, or towards an enumeration of the particular rules of justice. As the violation of justice is what men will never submit to from one another, the public magistrate is under a necessity of employing the power of the commonwealth to enforce the practice of this virtue. Without this precaution, civil society would become a scene of bloodshed and disorder, every man revenging himself at his own hand whenever he fancied he was injured. To prevent the confusion which would attend upon every man's doing justice to himself, the magistrate, in all governments that have acquired any considerable authority, undertakes to do justice to all, and promises to hear and to redress every complaint of injury. (*TMS*, 340)

The question of government in Smith's analysis is not:

Is government necessary? … It is.[3]
Nor is it …
Is government's role significant for the success of society? … It is.

The question of government in Smith's analysis is: How do we as citizens constitute a government that with the least possible intrusion

---

[3] Smith "had little trust in the competence or good faith of government. He knew who controlled it, and whose purposes they tried to serve…. He saw, nevertheless, that it was necessary, in the absence of a better instrument, to rely upon government for the performance of many tasks which individuals as such would not do, or could not do, or could do only badly. He did not believe that laissez faire was always good, or always bad. It depended on circumstances" (Viner, 231–2).

into our lives realizes, or at least ever more closely approximates, the necessary and sufficient conditions for liberty and justice for all? If we as a community are to "improve the constitution," how do we go about it? How do we, a community of less than angels, discern and agree on principles that can make liberal society function constructively?[4]

James Buchanan understood this necessity of civil government and imagined that in a second best world of less than angels we can approximate the best government by establishing its constitution behind what Buchanan described as a "veil of uncertainty" (Buchanan, 1991, 48).[5] Behind that veil we are each unsure about where we will be "standing" when the veil is lifted, so as we constitute our shared order we each have a strong incentive to ensure that the constitution we establish is just, efficient, and effective no matter the position in which we may find our self when the veil is lifted. An order constituted in such a manner is stable because under such a constitution every citizen will have a stake in its preservation.

But such a veiled condition is clearly an abstraction. Any real constitutional negotiation begins from a known status quo and that status quo is the product of a long evolutionary process. Recognizing this, Buchanan assumes that the negotiations start from an "existential acceptance of the status quo" (Buchanan, 1991, 205). But that concept is inherently problematic. Who would, for example, want to existentially accept a status quo in which he or she is a slave?[6]

---

[4] Those who drafted the U.S. Constitution, contemporaries of Smith's, understood that this is what they were doing. The preamble reads: "We the people of the United States, in order to form a more perfect union, establish justice, insure domestic tranquility, provide for the common defense, promote the general welfare, and secure the blessings of liberty to ourselves and our posterity, do ordain and establish this Constitution for the United States of America."

[5] "[A]greement on rules is much more likely to emerge than agreement on policy alternatives within rules because of the difficulties in precisely identifying the individual's economic interest in the first setting. The rule to be chosen is expected to remain in being over a whole sequence of time periods and possibly over a wide set of separate in-period choices during each period. How can the individual, at the stage of trying to select among rules, identify his or her own narrowly defined self-interest? ... He or she is necessarily forced to choose from behind a dark '*veil of uncertainty*.' In such a situation, utility maximization dictates that generalized criteria, such as fairness, equity, or justice enter the calculus rather than more specific arguments like net income or wealth" (Buchanan, 1991, 47–8, emphasis added). For more detail on Buchanan's analysis see Evensky (2005, chapter 11).

[6] Buchanan tries to address this very question, but it remains problematic to say the least (Buchanan, 1991, 204).

Smith appreciated these challenges of social contracts. Otteson, following Hayek, is correct that Smith envisioned humankind's evolution not as a series of social contracts but as an evolving spontaneous order. As Otteson aptly and eloquently notes, Smith's analysis of the evolution of language reflects this dynamic. "[F]or Smith language is ... [t]he result ... [of] a system of 'spontaneous order': a self-enforcing, orderly institution created unintentionally by the free exchanges of individuals who desire only to satisfy their own individual wants" (Otteson, 121–2).[7] This development of language through spontaneous order is, for Otteson, analogous to the spontaneous order of the market guided by the invisible hand.

The analogy is indeed apt, but it is not so benign as Otteson suggests. As is the market, language is a contested space subject to power, a space in which individuals and/or government can exert constructive or destructive influence.

In the 1950s in the United States the black community was kept "in its place" in part by the language created by the white community. "Colored" was a dismissive term for a black person. "Negro" was a term for a "good" black person, one who knew his or her "place."[8] Language became a contested space: the black community responded by acting on language – self-identifying with terms that reflected pride not oppression: African-American and black.

Similarly, in those days while Mr. and Master distinguished the age of a male person, Mrs. and Miss distinguished a female person by her relationship to a male: Mrs. in the custodial care of her husband. Miss in the custodial care of her father or brother or the community as a whole. Language became a contested space: the women's movement responded by acting on language – coining a term to clearly identify oneself as an independent adult woman: Ms.

---

[7] Otteson's analysis of Smith's work on language is by far the best I have seen.
[8] The "old" South Africa had quite a formal "taxonomy of being." Consider the following blurb that appeared in the news in July 1983:

> JOHANNESBURG, South Africa: Lize Venter is 4 weeks old and nobody knows who her parents are. In a society where the races are separated by law, that means the government will decide if she's black, white, or of mixed race and set the course of her life.
>
> The decision on her race will determine who can adopt her, where she goes to school, what neighborhood she may live in, who she can marry, whether she can vote, where she can eat, what she can hope for in life.
>
> This is decreed by the Population Registration Act of 1950, adopted by the governing National Party two years after it took control of the white minority government.

Language, markets, government, these are just various dimensions of an evolving, spontaneous, contested order. At any given stage in this evolution, the extant order is only as stable as the power structure that supports it. The less inclusive that power structure, the greater the "internal contradiction" (Marx, 245) built into that order for the fewer are the participants who have a stake in its survival. In such an environment, the government that serves the few must be diligent in policing the many (e.g., North Korea or apartheid South Africa or the segregated South).

A power system that is baked into language, norms, government, and markets and that ignores the interests of a segment of the community is inefficient. By marginalizing citizens and engendering their resentment it loses many of the potential contributions of that marginalized community, even as it has to pay the price of enabling its power: police, paddy wagons, jails, and so forth[9] ... all enforced, as Smith would say, by unproductive labor.

The broader the foundation of the collective voice that shapes civic ethics and civil government, the less policing necessary – for the broader the participation of citizens in shaping those standards, the broader the share of the participants who have an investment in those standards, and the fewer "deviant" behaviors with which government must deal. A civil discourse that leads to an inclusive system of shared ethics and civil governance generates an evolutionary approximation of the results achieved behind Buchanan's "veil."[10]

"Deviant" captures an important point in Smith's vision. Smith appreciated that deviance can be a constructive evolutionary force. "[T]he unfortunate Galileo" (*HA*, 84), whose work advanced our understanding of

---

[9]   "Religious orders, legal codes, and numerous cultural practices manifest and propound a community's moral standards, and these standards will last as long as those institutions and practices enjoy the reverence of the community's members – which, of course, is not forever" (Otteson, 2011, 123). These standards do indeed evolve but at any given time they do not "enjoy the [universal] reverence of the community's members" and so they require enforcement mechanisms – respectively: hell, jail, or loneliness. These institutions that govern our behavior are necessary for social order, including government. But to the degree they are unjust, they are inherently unstable.

[10]   Amartya Sen is effusive in his praise of Buchanan for recognizing the importance of this public discourse: "As he [(Buchanan)] puts it: "The market economy, basically as described by Adam Smith, is a necessary part of the social order – indeed perhaps its most important part. But the economy cannot function in vacuo; it must be incorporated in, and must be understood to be incorporated in, a structure of 'law and institutions' (Buchanan, 1977). The choice and functioning of these other institutions remain, again, as part social decisions to be taken through public discussion and social interchange" (Sen, 2013).

our universe, was punished for his deviance from church doctrine. Smith's dearest friend, David Hume, was a religious deviant, and one whose attack on "some of the prevailing systems of superstition" (*Correspondence*, 219) Smith admired very much.

In Smith's narrative humankind's history reflects the evolutionary path of human progress: a path full of twists and turns caused by distortions of power (governmental and/or nongovernmental), but progressive nevertheless because that is the prospect nature has afforded us. Individuals like Galileo and Hume can contribute to that progress by challenging the extant, inert power structure. Government can contribute when it ensures justice and constructively aligns incentives – and sometimes that involves "incursions into the market" (Otteson, 2011, 143).

As Otteson writes, "it is of course true that ... Smithian markets require quite a bit of artificial regulative assistance to operate smoothly. Thus Smith was not so naïve that he thought that markets would be perfect" (Otteson, 2011, 127). As a consequence, he writes, Smith "perhaps fell prey to his own Great Mind Fallacy (GMF). In several places in *WN*, Smith endorses incursions into the market by third parties, often members of government" (Otteson, 2011, 143).

Given this apparent slippage by Smith into the GMF, Otteson writes: "There are some uncharitable conclusions about Smith's argument one might draw.... One of the uncharitable conclusions is that Smith is really a progressive, not a classical, liberal" (Otteson, 2011, 144). Otteson suggests that a more charitable interpretation is that Smith believes "that human life is messier than many theorists would have it, and so sometimes exceptions to the principles are warranted for the benefit of the individuals or the local society involved" (Otteson, 2011, 144–5).

Adam Smith did indeed believe that human life is messy.[11] But he did not believe that this messiness is an aberration to be addressed in an ad hoc fashion as theory is translated into practice. For Smith messiness is the essence of the human condition[12] – indeed, its pervasiveness is what distinguishes

---

[11] As Joseph Spengler expressed in his Southern Economic Association Presidential Address: "Man, as represented by the social theorist, inhabits two realms of being, a realm that is *real* and a realm that is *analytical* or *hypothetical*. <u>The realm that is real comprehends the earthy, dissonant, bumbled, and seemingly confused (albeit not wholly disorderly) world of affairs</u>.... The realm of the hypothetical consists of the mental constructs more or less wittingly built by the social theorist ... out of his precepts and concepts of the real realm and attaining an understanding of and (possibly) control over this realm" (Spengler, 1948, 1, italics in original, underline added).

[12] "Contemporary researchers have discovered that the knowledge that others would disapprove of us free riding, breaching contracts, reneging on promises, or making

the challenges of Social Science (Smith's Moral Philosophy) from those of the Physical Sciences (Newton's Natural Philosophy). As a Moral Philosopher Smith sought to imagine the invisible connecting principles of the ideal human order so that we could by their approximation bring a more constructive order to this messy world. And he sought to persuade policy makers to use these principles as a guide.

He expresses this view of his role and his purpose in writing the *Wealth of Nations* quite clearly in the following quotation. Note his clear enthusiasm for "public virtue," "public spirit," and a "great system of public police" in realizing the "superior advantages the subjects of a well-governed state enjoy," which enhance "the happiness of the society."[13]

[I]f you would implant *public virtue* in the breast of him who seems heedless of the interest of his country, it will often be to no purpose to tell him, what *superior advantages the subjects of a well-governed state enjoy*; that they are better lodged, that they are better clothed, that they are better fed. These considerations will commonly make no great impression. You will be more likely to persuade, if you describe the *great system of public police which procures these advantages*, if you explain the connexions and dependencies of its several parts, their mutual subordination to one another, and their general subserviency to the happiness of the society; if you show how this system might be introduced into his own country, what it is that hinders it from taking place there at present, how those obstructions might be removed, and all the several wheels of the machine of government be made to move with more harmony and smoothness, without grating upon one another,[14] or mutually retarding one another's motions. It is scarce possible that a man should listen to a discourse of this kind, and not feel himself animated to some degree of *public spirit*. He will, at least for the moment, feel some desire to remove those obstructions, and to put into motion so beautiful and so orderly a machine. Nothing tends so much to promote public spirit as the study of politics, of the several systems of civil government, their advantages and disadvantages,

exceptions for ourselves from the rules of behavior by which we expect others to live acts as a surprisingly effective disincentive to engage in such practices.... [T]hese are *natural* incentives – present, that is, without the aid of third-party intervention. Hence even if it is true that self-interest by itself is not enough to generate stable and beneficial social orders, it would not follow that the systems of unintended-order generated by Smithian invisible-hand mechanisms cannot allow people to spontaneously adopt behavioral norms that enable stable and beneficial social interaction" (Otteson, 157–8). Smith would see this as a very Pollyannaish view.

13 "In [Edwin] Cannan's view, Smith's linkage between pursuit of self-interest and the social good is successful when, *but only when*, appropriate institutions direct people towards the collective interests" (Levy and Pert, 372, emphasis added).

14 In *TMS* Smith writes: "[V]irtue, which is, as it were, the fine polish to the wheels of society, necessarily pleases; while vice, like the vile rust, which makes them jar and grate upon one another, is as necessarily offensive" (*TMS*, 316).

of the constitution of our own country, its situation, and interest with regard to foreign nations, its commerce, its defence, the disadvantages it labours under, the dangers to which it may be exposed, how to remove the one, and how to guard against the other. Upon this account political disquisitions, if just, and reasonable, and practicable, are of all the works of speculation the most useful.[15] Even the weakest and the worst of them are not altogether without their utility. They serve at least to animate the public passions of men, and rouse them to *seek out the means of promoting the happiness of the society.* (TMS, 186–7, emphasis added)

Smith is quite clear about government: the absence of a civil government does not result in a society that spontaneously gravitates to a harmonious natural order.[16] Quite to the contrary, the absence of civil government is an invitation to the chaos of factional conflict, which will ultimately lead to the dominance of one faction that will deem itself the government (as the lords did after the fall of Rome) in order to restore order based on its vision of the ideal order.

There will be civil government. The contested question is: What will be its character?

In his last published work (*TMS* revisions, 1790) Smith implores those with the power to lead to take on the role of the statesman (a la Solon), one who acts not for the well-being of self or faction, but for the well-being of the entire community.

The leader of the successful party ... if he has authority enough to prevail upon his own friends to act with proper temper and moderation (which he frequently has not), may sometimes render to his country a service much more essential and important than the greatest victories and the most extensive conquests. He may re-establish and improve the constitution, and from the very doubtful and ambiguous character of the leader of a party, he may assume the greatest and noblest

---

[15] Recall: Smith writes that inquiries into what is "properly called Political Economy ... [are inquiries into] the nature and causes of the wealth of nations" (*WN*, 678–9).

[16] "Given these human characteristics ['that man is naturally deceitful and unscrupulous and will quite willingly employ predatory practices so long as such practices are available to him'] it is plain that the mere absence of external restraints and the freedom to pursue self-interest do not suffice, in Smith's view, to establish social harmony or to protect society from 'the passionate confidence of interested falsehood.' What are required, above all, are institutional mechanisms which compel man, in his 'natural insolence,' 'to use the good instrument' " (Rosenberg, 1960, 558).

"Adam Smith's employment of self-interest in the *Wealth of Nations* ... does not mean either that he regarded self-love as the only actuating principle in human nature, or that he recommended unrestrained selfishness as the best means of promoting public wealth. It merely means that Smith was preaching, in the economic world, the same gospel of individual rights and individual liberty which in one form or another was the burden of eighteenth-century social thought. It expresses his faith in the value of the individual and in the importance of freeing the individual man from the fetters of outworn economic institutions" (Morrow, 331).

of all characters, that of the reformer and legislator of a great state; and, by the wisdom of his institutions, secure the internal tranquillity and happiness of his fellow-citizens for many succeeding generations. (*TMS*, 232)

In Smith's *Inquiry into the Nature and Causes of the Wealth of Nations* the evolution of society is driven by chance, circumstance, and the unintended and *intended* consequences of individuals' actions. Every generation leaves as its legacy the foundation on which successive generations build. To the degree a given generation's legacy is constructive, it contributes to that society's approximation of the ideal. Given human frailty the ideal is not achievable, but given humankind's capacity for progress, it is approachable.

In Smith's analysis progress emerges from a constructive co-evolution of civic ethics and civil government. As these mature together, freedom and security follow and the constructive potential of the market system is unleashed.

How do we know if our community is successfully nurturing good citizens and calibrating the role of government correctly? What are the signs of progress? For Smith the best observable metric is distribution.

As society progresses ...

Those unproductive individuals who live off of their returns from the scarcity value of capital (interest) or land (rent) would be few in number ...

In a country which had acquired its full complement of riches, where in every particular branch of business there was the greatest quantity of stock that could be employed in it, as the ordinary rate of clear profit would be very small, so that usual market rate of interest which could be afforded out of it, would be so low as to render it impossible for any but the very wealthiest people to live upon the interest of their money. (*WN*, 113)

... [and few would live off of rents because] very old families, such as have possessed some considerable estate from father to son for many successive generations, are very rare in commercial countries. (*WN*, 422)

What we would find is that with progress those who comprise the majority of the productive hands in society would be doing "tolerably well":

No society can surely be flourishing and happy, of which the far greater part of the members are poor and miserable. It is but equity, besides, that they who feed, cloath and lodge the whole body of the people, should have such a share of the produce of their own labour as to be themselves tolerably well fed, cloathed, and lodged. (*WN*, 96)[17]

---

[17] Smith's "prejudices, such as they were, were against the powerful and the grasping, and it was the interests of the general masses that he wished above all to promote, in an age when even philosophers rarely condescended to deal sympathetically with their needs" (Viner, 231-2).

Given this standard for progress, a growing gap in income distribution between those who derive their revenue from capital or land and those whose well-being is derived from their productive labor represents a *prima facie* case that there are power distortions somewhere in the system.

Are such power distortions an inevitable part of capitalism? Is capitalism fatally flawed?

This is a recurring question in the history of economic thought. In 1848 in the midst of revolutions in Europe that were inspired by dramatic distributive disparities, in the year Karl Marx published *The Communist Manifesto*, John Stuart Mill wrote in his *Principles of Political Economy*:

The principle of private property has never yet had a fair trial in any country; and less so, perhaps, in this country [(Britain)] than in some others. The arrangements of modern Europe commenced from a distribution of property which was the result, not of just partition, or acquisition by industry, but of conquest and violence.... [Subsequently, t]he laws of property ... have not held the balance fairly between human beings, but have heaped impediments upon some, to give advantages to others; they have purposely fostered inequalities, and prevented all from starting the race fair. That all should indeed start on perfectly equal terms, is inconsistent with any law of private property: but if as much pains as has been taken to aggravate the inequality of chances arising from the natural working of the principle, had been taken to temper that inequality by every means not subversive of the principle itself; if the tendency of legislation had been to favour the diffusion, instead of the concentration of wealth ... the principle of individual property would have been found to have no necessary connection with the physical and social evils which almost all Socialist writers assume to be inseparable from it. (Mill, 208–9)

Mill dearly wants the liberal experiment to succeed because no other proposed system of human society is as "consistent with that multiform development of human nature, those manifold unlikenesses, that diversity of tastes and talents, and variety of intellectual points of view, which not only form a great part of the interest of human life, but by bringing intellects into stimulating collision, and by presenting to each innumerable notions that he would not have conceived of himself, are the mainspring of mental and moral progression" (Mill, 210–1).[18]

Adam Smith would heartily agree.

The opportunity humankind has been afforded to make progress toward the liberal ideal is, he believed, a gift of nature.[19] If that opportunity is to be realized, the liberal experiment must be continuously and

[18] For a more detailed discussion of Mill on this topic, see Evensky (2005, chapter 12).
[19] The deity? See Evensky (2005, chapter 1).

actively nurtured. Smith wrote his *Inquiry into the Nature and Causes of the Wealth of Nations* as one piece of a moral philosophical vision that he hoped would be a contribution to the progress of that liberal experiment.

Smith dedicated his life to this work because he believed that "[h]e is not a citizen who is not disposed to respect the laws and to obey the civil magistrate; and he is certainly not a good citizen who does not wish to promote, by every means in his power, the welfare of the whole society of his fellow-citizens" (*TMS*, 231).

For Adam Smith citizenship must be an active virtue because the fate of our collective future lies

> not in our stars,
> But in ourselves....
> William Shakespeare
> (*Julius Caesar*)

References

Anderson, Gary M., William F. Shughart, and Robert D. Tollison. 1985. "Adam Smith in the Customhouse." *Journal of Political Economy.* 93(4): 740–59.

Baumol, William J. 1999. "Retrospectives: Say's Law." *The Journal of Economic Perspectives.* 13(1): 195–204.

Berry, Christopher, Maria Pia Paganelli, and Craig Smith (eds.). 2013. *The Oxford Handbook of Adam Smith.* Oxford: Oxford University Press.

Bittermann, Henry J. 1940. "Adam Smith's Empiricism and the Law of Nature, II." *Journal of Political Economy.* 48(5): 703–34.

Blaug, Mark. 1978. *Economic Theory in Retrospect,* 3rd. ed. Cambridge: Cambridge University Press.

Bryce, J. C. 1983. "Introduction," in *Lectures on Rhetoric and Belles Lettres.* Edited by J. C. Bryce. Vol. 4 of *The Glasgow Edition of the Works and Correspondence of Adam Smith.* General editing by D. D. Raphael and Andrew Skinner. Oxford: Clarendon Press, pp. 1–37.

Buchan, James. 2003. *Crowded with Genius – The Scottish Enlightenment: Edinburgh's Moment of the Mind.* New York: HarperCollins.

2006. *The Authentic Adam Smith: His Life and Ideas.* New York: Atlas Books – W. W. Norton & Company.

Buchanan, James. 1991. *The Economics and the Ethics of Constitutional Order.* Ann Arbor: University of Michigan Press.

1994. *Ethics and Economic Progress.* Norman: University of Oklahoma Press.

2008. "Let Us Understand Adam Smith." *Journal of the History of Economic Thought.* 30(1): 21–8.

Buchanan, James, R. D. Tollison, and Gordon Tullock (eds.). 1980. *Toward a Theory of a Rent-Seeking Society.* College Station: Texas A&M University Press.

Campbell, R. H., and Andrew Skinner. 1976. "General Introduction," in *An Inquiry into the Nature and Causes of the Wealth of Nations.* Edited in two vols. by W. B. Todd. Vol. 2 of *The Glasgow Edition of the Works and*

Correspondence of Adam Smith. General editing by D. D. Raphael and Andrew Skinner. Oxford: Clarendon Press, pp. 1–60.

Campbell, Tom. "Adam Smith: Methods, Morals, and Markets," in *The Oxford Handbook of Adam Smith*. Edited by Christopher Berry, Maria Paganelli, and Craig Smith. Oxford: Oxford University Press, pp. 559–80.

Cannan, Edwin. 1926. "Adam Smith as an Economist." *Economica*. 17: 123–34.

Coats, A. W. 1975. "Adam Smith and the Mercantile System," in *Essays on Adam Smith*. Edited by Andrew Skinner and Thomas Wilson. Oxford: Clarendon Press, pp. 218–36.

Cohen, Avi J., and G. C. Harcourt. 2003. "Retrospectives: Whatever Happened to the Cambridge Capital Theory Controversies?" *The Journal of Economic Perspectives*. 17(1): 199–214.

Dobb, Maurice. 1973. *Theories of Value and Distribution since Adam Smith*. London: Cambridge University Press.

Ekelund, Robert, and Gordon Tullock. 1981. *Mercantilism as a Rent-Seeking Society: Economic Regulation in Historical Perspective*. College Station: Texas A&M University Press.

Evensky, Jerry. 2005. *Adam Smith's Moral Philosophy: A Historical and Contemporary Perspective on Markets, Law, Ethics, and Culture*. Cambridge: Cambridge University Press.

2011. "Adam Smith's Essentials: On Trust, Faith, and Free Markets." *Journal of the History of Economic Thought*. 33(2): 249–68.

Friedman, Milton. 1977. "Adam Smith's Relevance for Today." *Challenge*. 20(1): 6–12.

Gaillot, B. J. 1960. "God Gave the Law of Segregation (as well as the 10 Commandments) to Moses on Mount Sinai." Hattiesburg: University of Southern Mississippi. http://digilib.usm.edu/cdm/compoundobject/collection/manu/id/2139/rec/6.

Gay, Peter. 1954. "The Enlightenment in the History of Political Theory." *Political Science Quarterly*. 69(3): 374–89.

Gould, Philip. 2008. "Wit and Politics in Revolutionary British America: The Case of Samuel Seabury and Alexander Hamilton." *Eighteenth-Century Studies*. 41(3): 383–403.

Griswold, Charles. 1999. *Adam Smith and the Virtues of Enlightenment*. Cambridge: Cambridge University Press.

Haakonssen, Knud. ed. 2006. *The Cambridge Companion to Adam Smith*. Cambridge and New York: Cambridge University Press.

Hanley, Ryan Patrick. *Adam Smith and the Character of Virtue*. New York: Cambridge University Press.

Harpham, Edward J. 1984. "Liberalism, Civic Humanism, and the Case of Adam Smith." *The American Political Science Review*. 78(3): 764–74.

Hollander, Jacob H. 1927. "Adam Smith 1776–1926." *Journal of Political Economy*. 35(2): 153–97.

Hollander, Samuel. 1973. *The Economics of Adam Smith*. Buffalo: University of Toronto Press.

Howell, Wilbur Samuel. 1975. "Adam Smith's Lectures on Rhetoric: An Historical Assessment," in *Essays on Adam Smith*. Edited by Andrew Skinner and Thomas Wilson. Oxford: Clarendon Press, pp. 11–43.

Hueckel, Glenn. 2000. "On the 'Insurmountable Difficulties, Obscurity, and Embarrassment' of Smith's Fifth Chapter." *History of Political Economy*. 32(2): 317–45.

Hutchison, Terence, W. 1976. "Adam Smith and the *Wealth of Nations*." *Journal of Law and Economics*. 19(3): 507–28.

Kammen, Michael. 1970. *Empire and Interest: The American Colonies and the Politics of Mercantilism*. Philadelphia, PA: J. B. Lippincott Company.

Keynes, John Maynard. 1964. *The General Theory of Employment, Interest, and Money*. First Harbinger Edition. New York: Harcourt Brace Jovanovich.

Levy, David, and Sandra Pert. 2013. "Adam Smith and the State: Language and Reform." in *The Oxford Handbook of Adam Smith*. Edited by Christopher Berry, Maria Paganelli, and Craig Smith. Oxford: Oxford University Press.

Madison, James. 1959. "The Federalist No. 10." In Alexander Hamilton, John Jay, and James Madison. *The Federalist*. New York: The Modern Library by Random House.

Marshall, Alfred. 1936. *Principles of Economics*, 8th Ed. London: MacMillan.

Marx, Karl. 1959. *Capital: A Critique of Political Economy*, Vol. III. Moscow: Progress Publishers.

Meek, Ronald. 1976. *Social Science and the Ignoble Savage*. Cambridge: Cambridge University Press.

  1977. *Smith, Marx, & After: Ten Essays in the Development of Economic Thought*. London: Chapman & Hall.

Meek, Ronald L., D. D. Raphael, and P. G. Stein. 1978. "Introduction" to *Lectures on Jurisprudence*. Edited by R. L. Meek, D. D. Raphael, and P. G. Stein. Vol. 5 of *The Glasgow Edition of the Works and Correspondence of Adam Smith*. General editing by D. D. Raphael and Andrew Skinner. Oxford: Clarendon Press.

Meek, Ronald L., and Andrew S. Skinner. 1973. "The Development of Adam Smith's Ideas on the Division of Labour." *The Economic Journal*. 83 (332): 1094–1116.

Mill, John Stuart. 1929. *Principles of Political Economy: With Some of Their Applications to Social Philosophy*. Edited by W. J. Ashley. Based on the 7th edition, the last revised by Mill. London: Longmans, Green, and Co.

Morrow, Glenn R. 1927. "Adam Smith: Moralist and Philosopher." *Journal of Political Economy*. 35: 321–42.

Naldi, Nerio. 2013. "Adam Smith on Value and Prices," in *The Oxford Handbook of Adam Smith*. Edited by Christopher Berry, Maria Paganelli, and Craig Smith. Oxford: Oxford University Press.

Otteson, James R. 2002. *Adam Smith's Marketplace of Life*. Cambridge: Cambridge University Press.

  2011. *Adam Smith*. New York: Continuum International Publishing Group.

Pocock, J. G. A. 1975. *The Machiavellian Moment: Florentine Political Thought and the Atlantic Republican Tradition*. Cambridge: Cambridge University Press.

Raphael, D. D. 1975. "The Impartial Spectator," in *Essays on Adam Smith*. Edited by Andrew Skinner and Thomas Wilson. Oxford: Clarendon Press, pp. 83–99.

Raphael, D. D., and Andrew Skinner. 1980. "General Introduction" to *Essays on Philosophical Subjects*. Edited by W. P. D. Wightman and J. C. Bryce. Vol. 3 of *The Glasgow Edition of the Works and Correspondence of Adam Smith*. General editing by D. D. Raphael and Andrew Skinner. Oxford: Clarendon Press.

Reisman, David A. 1998. "Adam Smith on Market and State." *Journal of Institutional and Theoretical Economics (JITE) / Zeitschrift für die gesamte Staatswissenschaft*. 154(2): 357–83.

Robinson, Joan. 1953. "The Production Function and the Theory of Capital." *The Review of Economic Studies*. 21(2): 81–106.

Rockoff, Hugh. 2013. "Adam Smith on Money, Banking, and the Price Level," in *The Oxford Handbook of Adam Smith*. Edited by Christopher Berry, Maria Paganelli, and Craig Smith. Oxford: Oxford University Press.

Rosenberg, Nathan. 1960. "Some Institutional Aspects of the Wealth of Nations." *Journal of Political Economy*. 68(6): 557–70.

1965. "Adam Smith on the Division of Labour: Two Views or One?" *Economica* (New Series). 32(126): 127–39.

1976. "Another Advantage of the Division of Labor." *Journal of Political Economy*. 84(4): 861–8.

1979. "Adam Smith and Laissez-Faire Revisited," in *Adam Smith and Modern Political Economy: Bicentennial Essays on The Wealth of Nations*. Edited by Gerald R. O'Driscoll Jr. Ames: Iowa State University Press, pp. 19–34.

Ross, Ian. 1995. *The Life of Adam Smith*. Oxford: Clarendon Press.

Rothschild, Emma, and Amartya Sen. 2006. "Adam Smith's Economics," in *The Cambridge Companion to Adam Smith*. Edited by Knud Haakonsen. Cambridge: Cambridge University Press, pp. 319–65.

Samuels, Warren J. 1962. "The Physiocratic Theory of Economic Policy." *The Quarterly Journal of Economics*. 76(1): 145–62.

1984A (1973). "Adam Smith and the Economy as a System of Power." Reprinted in *Adam Smith: Critical Assessments*. Edited by John Cunningham Wood. London: Croom Helm.

1984B (1976). "The Political Economy of Adam Smith." Reprinted in *Adam Smith: Critical Assessments*. Edited by John Cunningham Wood. London: Croom Helm.

Samuelson, Paul. 1971. "Understanding the Marxian Notion of Exploitation: A Summary of the So-Called Transformation Problem between Marxian Values and Competitive Prices." *Journal of Economic Literature*. 9(2): 399–431.

1977. "A Modern Theorist's Vindication of Adam Smith." *The American Economic Review: Papers and Proceedings of the Eighty-Ninth Annual Meeting of the American Economic Association*. 67(1): 42–9.

Scott, William Robert. 1937. *Adam Smith as Student and Professor*. Glasgow: Jackson, Son & Company – Publishers to the University.

Sen. Amartya. 2011. "The Uses and Abuses of Adam Smith." *History of Political Economy*. 43(2): 257–71.

2013. "On James Buchanan." http://lijian267.blog.sohu.com/252974528.html. Accessed 3/10/2015.

Shakespeare, William. 2006. *Julius Caesar*. New Haven, CT: Yale University Press.

Skinner, Andrew. 1972. "Adam Smith: Philosophy and Science." *Scottish Journal of Political Economy*. 19(3): 307–19.

1975A. "Introduction," in *Essays on Adam Smith*. Edited by Andrew Skinner and Thomas Wilson. Oxford: Clarendon Press, pp. 1–10.

1975B. "Adam Smith: An Economic Interpretation of History," in *Essays on Adam Smith*. Edited by Andrew Skinner and Thomas Wilson. Oxford: Clarendon Press, pp. 154–78.

1979. *A System of Social Science: Papers Relating to Adam Smith*. Oxford: Clarendon Press.

Skinner, Andrew, and Thomas Wilson. 1975. *Essays on Adam Smith*. Oxford: Clarendon Press.

Smith, Adam. 1937. "An Early Draft of Part of The Wealth of Nations (c. 1763)," in *Adam Smith as Student and Professor*. Edited by William Robert Scott. Glasgow: Jackson, Son & Company – Publishers to the University.

1976a. *The Theory of Moral Sentiments*. Edited by D. D. Raphael and A. L. Macfie. Vol. 1 of *The Glasgow Edition of the Works and Correspondence of Adam Smith*. General editing by D. D. Raphael and Andrew Skinner. Oxford: Clarendon Press.

1976b. *An Inquiry into the Nature and Causes of the Wealth of Nations*. Vol. 2 of *The Glasgow Edition of the Works and Correspondence of Adam Smith*. General editing by D. D. Raphael and Andrew Skinner. Textual editing by W. B. Todd. Oxford: Clarendon Press.

1977. *The Correspondence of Adam Smith*. Edited by Earnest Campbell Mossner and Ian Simpson Ross. Vol. 5 of *The Glasgow Edition of the Works and Correspondence of Adam Smith*. General editing by D. D. Raphael and Andrew Skinner. Oxford: Clarendon Press.

1978. *Lectures on Jurisprudence*. Edited by R. L. Meek, D. D. Raphael, and P. G. Stein. Vol. 5 of *The Glasgow Edition of the Works and Correspondence of Adam Smith*. General editing by D. D. Raphael and Andrew Skinner. Oxford: Clarendon Press.

1980. *Essays on Philosophical Subjects*. Edited by W. P. D. Wightman and J. C. Bryce. Vol. 3 of *The Glasgow Edition of the Works and Correspondence of Adam Smith*. General editing by D. D. Raphael and Andrew Skinner. Oxford: Clarendon Press.

1980. "Of the External Senses," in *Essays on Philosophical Subjects*. Edited by W. P. D. Wightman and J. C. Bryce. *The Glasgow Edition of the Works and Correspondence of Adam Smith*. Oxford: Clarendon Press.

1980. "The Principles Which Lead and Direct Philosophical Enquiries; Illustrated by the History of Ancient Physics," in *Essays on Philosophical Subjects*. Edited by W. P. D. Wightman and J. C. Bryce. *The Glasgow Edition of the Works and Correspondence of Adam Smith*. Oxford: Clarendon Press.

1980. "The Principles Which Lead and Direct Philosophical Enquiries; Illustrated by the History of Astronomy," in *Essays on Philosophical Subjects*. Edited by W. P. D. Wightman and J. C. Bryce. *The Glasgow Edition of the Works and Correspondence of Adam Smith*. Oxford: Clarendon Press.

1983. Lectures on Rhetoric and Belles Lettres. Edited by J. C. Bryce. Vol. 4 of *The Glasgow Edition of the Works and Correspondence of Adam Smith*. General editing by D. D. Raphael and Andrew Skinner. Oxford: Clarendon Press.

Smith, Craig. 2013. "Adam Smith and the New Right," in *The Oxford Handbook of Adam Smith*. Edited by Christopher Berry, Maria Paganelli, and Craig Smith. Oxford: Oxford University Press.

Sparkes, Ivan. 1975. *Stagecoaches & Carriages: An Illustrated History of Coaches and Coaching*. Buckinghamshire: Spurbooks Limited.

Spengler, Joseph J. 1948. "The Problem of Order in Economic Affairs." *Southern Economic Journal*. 15(1): 1–29.

1959A. "Adam Smith's Theory of Economic Growth: Part I." *Southern Economic Journal*. 25(4): 397–415.

1959B. "Adam Smith's Theory of Economic Growth: Part II." *Southern Economic Journal*. 26(1): 1–12.

Stewart, Dugald. (1793) 1980. "Account of the Life and Writings of Adam Smith, LL.D," in *Essays on Philosophical Subjects*. Edited by W. P. D. Wightman and J. C. Bryce. Vol. 3 of *The Glasgow Edition of the Works and Correspondence of Adam Smith*. General editing by D. D. Raphael and Andrew Skinner. Oxford: Clarendon Press, pp. 269–351.

Stigler, George J. 1951. "The Division of Labor Is Limited by the Extent of the Market." *Journal of Political Economy*. 59(3): 185–93.

1958. "Ricardo and the 93% Labor Theory of Value." *The American Economic Review*. 48(3): 357–67.

1975. "Smith's Travels on the Ship of State," in *Essays on Adam Smith*. Edited by Andrew Skinner and Thomas Wilson. Oxford: Clarendon Press, pp. 237–46.

1976. "The Successes and Failures of Professor Smith." *Journal of Political Economy*. 84(6): 1199–1213.

Teichgraeber, Richard F., III. 1986. *"Free Trade" and Moral Philosophy: Rethinking the Sources of Adam Smith's Wealth of Nations*. Durham, NC: Duke University Press.

Viner, Jacob. 1927. "Adam Smith and Laissez Faire." *Journal of Political Economy*. 35(2): 198–232.

Weinstein, Jack. 2013. *Adam Smith's Pluralism: Rationality, Education, and the Moral Sentiments*. New London, CT: Yale University Press.

Williamson, Oliver E. 1979. "Transaction-Cost Economics: The Governance of Contractual Relations." *Journal of Law and Economics*. 22(2): 233–61.

2000. "The New Institutional Economics: Taking Stock, Looking Ahead." *Journal of Economic Literature*. 38(3): 595–613.

Young, Jeffrey. 1997. *Economics as a Moral Science: The Political Economy of Adam Smith*. Cheltenham: Edward Elgar.

Index

Page numbers with an "n" refer to footnotes.

"Account of the Life and Writings of Adam Smith" (Stewart), 12n24
Adam Smith (Otteson), 253–54
advancement, measures of, 34–36
Africa, 155n29, 187n17, 188
African Americans, power of language and, 259
agency problem, 188, 191, 214
agriculture
  capital and, 85–87, 105, 131–32, 160–68, 220n44
  colonial policy and, 86n12, 139–40
  early stages of, 49–50, 57–58, 91–95, 171–72
  monopolies and, 115, 131, 132, 164
  "neat produce," 162–63
  as source of revenue and wealth, 160–68
  surpluses in, 51, 91–93, 134, 163–64
  taxation and, 162, 237–38, 245
alignment of incentives, 181, 185, 192, 193, 217, 221, 230, 244, 248, 256
  teachers, 193–195
ambition, 9n13
American colonies, 137–56, 247–51
  agriculture, investment in, 86n12, 139–40
  diffusion of land in, 103n30
  financing, 149–51, 214, 249–52
  government of, 148, 258n4
  growth of, 103n30
  material conditions in, 34–35

  monopolies in, 154–56, 190
  motives for establishing, 137–38, 190
  paper money in, 74, 248–49
  prosperity in, 139–44
  rights of citizenship, 151–53
  taxation and, 144, 150–51, 248–52
  tobacco trade, 145, 147
  trade with, 87–89, 112, 145, 147, 148, 247–49
annuities, 242, 243n64
apprenticeship law, 42–45, 46
armies. *See* defense
Articles of Association, U.S., 148
autonomy, interdependence vs., 20–21
Ayr Bank (Scotland), 71–72

Bank of England, 70, 72
bankruptcy, 38, 190, 246
banks and banking
  competition among, 74–75
  corruption and fraud in, 70–72, 74–75, 85, 255–56
  joint stock companies and, 191
  principles of, 74–75
  role of, 72–73
  See also credit; interest; money
beer taxes, 234, 247
Bengal, 22–23, 34, 37n36, 55, 146
Bohemia, 227–28
borrowing. *See* credit, public debt
bounties, 127–36, 233

Brazil, 136
Britain. *See* England; Scotland
Buccleuch, Duke of, 123, 125
Buchanan, James, 5, 258–59, 260
bullion
   bounties and, 128–29
   coinage of, 137
   controlling flow of, 109–11, 129
   hoarding of, 107, 108, 111
   role in extended markets, 86
   "treaties of commerce" and, 136–37
   See also gold and silver
burghers, 95–99

Calvinism, 211–12
Campbell, R. H., 125n15
Cannan, Edwin, 262n13
capital, 64–93
   agriculture and, 85–87, 105, 131–32,
      160–68, 220n44
   circuits of flow, 64–66, 85–90
   deepening of, 36, 236
   defined, 64, 65–70, 75
   distortions to flow of, 109, 113–15, 126,
      136–37, 145–48, 159, 235
   efficiency of, 72
   forms of, 65–70
   four employments of, 40–41, 85–89
   joint stock companies and, 187
   manufacturing and, 85–89, 91–93
   micro vs. macro conceptions of, 66
   mobility of, 45–46, 104n32, 223–24
   redirection of, 127–28
   risk of loss, 87n13, 92
   scarcity value of, 245, 264–65
   success of, 67
   taxation and, 223–28, 235
capitalism, 265
capitation taxes, 228
carrying trade, 69, 87–90, 113–14, 154
cattle, 49–50, 57–59
Child, Josiah, 187
children, 46n47, 93–94, 104,
   140, 226–27
China
   extent of market in, 23, 166–67
   infrastructure costs, 185
   interest rates in, 29–30
   laws and institutions in, 34, 37–38, 55
   market maturation in, 83–84, 112
   market stagnation in, 146
   success of trade in, 166–67
church and state, 205–212

church tithe, 219
circulating capital
   defined, 65–70
   mercantile system and, 113–14, 136–37
   overflow of, 86–89, 236
cities and towns, rise and growth of, 91,
   95–105, 115, 159, 168
citizenship
   as "active duty," 204
   classical liberalism and civic
      humanism, 204
   effects of constructive laws on, 82
   reciprocal nature of relationship with
      government, 236, 240–41, 260
   role of education in, 208–9, 224
class
   condition of as metric, 19, 33–34, 46,
      60–61, 117, 208–9, 248
   taxation and, 234
Coats, A. W., 15n31
Colbert, Jean-Baptiste, 116, 124, 161–62
collusion
   "conspiracy against the public", 44
   corn trade and, 131, 132
   self-interest and, 40
   taxation and, 237
   town vs. country, 115, 159
   See also factional interests; monopolies
colonial policy, 137–56
   advantages of, 144–56
   agriculture and, 86n12, 139–40
   establishment of, 137–38
   financing, 80n8, 149–51, 214, 249–52
   full citizenship, 151–53
   "golden dream", 251
   mercantile distortions of, 149, 187–92
   prosperity of, 139–44
   taxation and, 144, 150–51, 248–52
   union proposal, 248–252
commerce, facilitation of. *See* regulation
commercial system. *See* mercantile system
commodities
   as component of price, 27–31
   market and natural prices of, 31–32
   measure of value and, 25–27
   micro vs. macro perspectives, 67–68
   taxation and, 228–38
Communist Manifesto, The (Marx),
   265
competition
   among banks, 74–75
   dynamics of, 38–39, 83
   educational, 193–94, 212

religious, 206–7, 212
role of, 29
conjectural history, 23, 197n25
conspicuous consumption, 101, 239
consumption
  characteristics of, 51, 58n62
  desire for food vs. desire for
    "conveniencies", 51
  feudalism and, 101, 239
  immediate, 65
  progress and, 77
  as sole purpose of production, 160
  taxation and, 228–38, 247–48
  as use of stock, 75, 101
  wholesale trade and, 87–88
corn
  bounties on, 128–30, 134
  as measure of value, 26, 53–55
  trade in, 130–36, 161
  wheat vs., 53n58
corn laws, 130–36
corporations, effects of structure on
    behavior of, 187–92
corruption and fraud
  apprenticeship law and, 43
  corporate, 187–92
  credit and, 71–72, 110n5, 255–56
  individual and institutional, 14,
    24, 255–57
  monetary, 24, 55, 70–72, 74–75, 85,
    128–30, 246, 255–56
  public debt and, 246
  smuggling, 232–34, 248
  taxation, 237
  See also collusion; factional interests;
    monopolies
country/town dichotomy, 91, 99–105, 115,
    159, 168
courts,
  costs of, 180–83
  evolution of, 180–183
credit, 82–85
  bankruptcy, 38, 190, 246
  corruption and, 71–72, 110n5,
    255–56
  irresponsible use of, 110n5
  multilateral nature of, 120
  public debt, 239–52
customs duties. *See* duties and tariffs

dealer taxes, 225, 231
debt, public, war and growth of, 239–52

defense
  colonial policy and, 144
  division of labor and, 14n28, 173–74
  evolution of, 171
  expense of, 80n8, 149–51, 170–77,
    182–83, 203, 215, 240, 251
  four stages theory and, 171–72, 203
  militia vs. standing army, 172
  and public debt, 239–52
  taxation and, 180–81, 242–44
demand
  effective, 31–32
  manufacturing and, 58n62, 99
  productivity and, 21–23
  rent and, 47–48
  role of, 21–23
Denmark, 55, 140
diamond-water paradox, 24
distribution
  distortions of, 33n26, 42–45
  as metric of progress, 264–65
diversity, value of, 177n11
division of labor, 17–23
  caveats to, 35, 46
  education and, 202–3
  extent of market and, 19, 21–23, 64–65,
    100, 166
  marketing process and, 132
  military defense and, 14n28, 173–74
  propensity to truck, barter, and
    exchange, 19
  as source of productivity, 14n28, 17–19,
    60–61, 64–65, 163, 165
  "well-governed society" and, 18–19
drawbacks, as tool to limit imports,
    126–27, 142, 233
durable goods, taxation and, 230–31
duties and tariffs, 116–17, 126, 130–36,
    148n25, 231–33, 247

East India Company, 112, 123n13, 140,
    155, 156, 188–92, 214
East Indies
  colonial policy in, 138, 153, 155–56
  demand for silver in, 55
  extent of market in, 22–23
  interest rates in, 37n36
  laws and institutions in, 34
  mercantile system and, 112
education, 192–212
  competition and, 193–94, 212
  necessity of, 46

education (*cont.*)
  religious, 205–12
  role of state in, 35, 204, 224
  subsidies for, 45
effective demand, 31–32
Egypt, 22, 167
Elliot, Gilbert, 11n17
empirical analyses, 50n53, 53–55, 59,
    93, 96n25, 106, 175
  See also history and historians
England
  banking in, 70, 72
  education and religion in, 212
  extent of privilege of
      incorporation, 42–43
  long historical view of growth in, 80–82
  rise of wealth and revenue in,
      83–84, 104–5
  Scotland and, 49–50, 58, 248
England's Treasure in Foreign Trade
    (Mun), 109
ethics, 12–15, 20–21, 138, 256, 260–66
  See also moral philosophy
Europe
  after fall of Rome, 92–99
  carrying trades in, 90
  early trade in, 99
  feudalism in, 67, 76–77
exchange
  labor as measure of value, 25–27
  propensity of, 19–21
  value in, 24
excise taxes, 126, 231, 233–34,
    236, 246–47
exports/imports. *See* duties and
    tariffs; trade
extent of market
  in China, 23, 166–67
  constraints on, 14, 42
  division of labor and, 19, 21–23, 64–65,
    100, 166
  in East Indies, 22–23
  effects of fees on, 185
  effects of free trade on, 111–12
  effects of taxation on, 95–96, 236
  four stages theory and, 22
  prices and, 31
  rents and, 48–49
  See also trade
externalities, 255

factional interests
  contested space and, 259–61

democracy and, 250–51, 263
effects on distribution, 33n26, 42–45
effects on laws and institutions, 37–38,
    94, 104
free trade and, 111–12, 123
in Greece and Rome, 201
market advantage and, 39, 118–19,
    154, 256
use of government, 74, 80–82, 157n30
farming taxes, 237–38
Federalist No. 10, 250n72
fees
  durable commodity, 230–31
  educational, 192
  extent of market and, 185
  fee-for-service justice, 180–85
  rent as fee, 28, 29, 217
  signing, 217
  town, 96
feudalism, 67, 76–77, 95–105, 175–76,
    210n37, 239
fixed capital, 66, 68–70
fixed taxes, 216–17
flat-rate taxes, 225
food, rising rents and, 48–52, 58n62
four stages theory
  Africa and, 155n29
  concept of, 10–16
  defense and, 171–72, 203
  evolution of, 64–66, 91–99, 138,
    259–67
  extent of market as tipping point, 22
  laws and institutions in, 104
  material improvement
      through, 26–28
  religion and, 138
  security and, 93–99, 177–83
frailty. *See* human frailty
France
  cost of war with, 80n8
  education and religion in, 212
  government in, 97n26, 185
  growth in, 55, 142
  mercantile system in, 123–24, 161–62
  Physiocracy and, 160–68
  protectionism in, 116–17
  public debt and, 242, 245, 251
  Smith in, 33n25, 123–24
  taxation and, 225–26, 227–28, 229,
    237–38, 251
  trade in, 104, 116–17, 121–22, 134,
    136–37, 143, 145, 155
fraud. *See* corruption and fraud

free market system
   adaptivity and, 118
   in context of Smith's lifetime, 20–21
   education and, 202
   effects of a bounty on, 127
   joint stock companies in, 191
   natural course of events in, 83
   religion in, 207–8
   See also invisible hand; laissez-faire
free trade
   arguments for, 121–22, 130–36, 145,
      154–55, 168–69
   effects of rapid adjustment to, 117–18
   factional interests and, 111–12, 123
   interdependence and, 166–67
   use of drawbacks and, 126–27, 142, 233
free will, 12–13
frugality, 77–79, 81, 131, 229, 245–46
full employment, 30

Germany, 55, 142, 175, 211
   See also Hamburgh
*Glasgow Edition of the Works and
      Correspondence of Adam
      Smith,* 125n15
gold and silver
   American colonies and, 249
   degradation of, 128–29
   exploitation of, 138
   as measure of value, 26, 52–56,
      59–60, 70
   as source of wealth, 52, 54, 59–60, 78
   See also bullion
government
   absence of, 262
   administration of, 168–69, 170, 177–83
   character of, 263–64
   city and town, 91, 95–106, 115,
      159, 168
   distrust of, 226
   feudalism, 67, 76–77, 95–105, 175–76,
      210n37, 239
   institutional vs. personal, 15, 21, 136, 264
   origins of, 179–83
   Physiocracy and, 21
   prodigality and, 79
   role and duties of, 43, 82, 106–7,
      135–36, 168–71, 177, 182–84,
      224, 254–57
   as tool of destructive policy, 74, 80–82
   "well-governed society" and, 15–16,
      18–19, 29–30
   See also laws and institutions; security

government debt, 80n8, 239–52
government revenue, 170, 180–83, 192–93,
      213–15
   See also fees; taxation
Great Britain. *See* England; Scotland;
      specific colony
Great Mind Fallacy (GMF), 254, 256,
      261
Greece
   colonial system in, 137–38, 144
   defense of, 175, 215
   education and, 195–96, 200–202
   rise and decline of, 92n16
   slavery in, 167–68
growth
   destructive policies regarding, 74, 80–82
   goal of, 66
   keys to, 30–31, 64, 121
   productivity as engine of, 16
   theory of, 58, 115, 122

Hamburgh, 163, 214, 224
Hayek, Friedrich, 259
Heuckel, Glenn, 26n17
history and historians
   aim of, 10n14
   conjectural, 22–23, 197n25
   long view of, 80–82, 90, 93, 98, 117–18,
      176
   See also empirical analyses
History of Astronomy (Smith), 7, 8–9, 12,
      54n59, 196
Holland
   growth and prosperity in, 55, 165–66
   interest rates in, 84n9
   as a mercantile state, 163
   taxation and, 224, 238
   trade in, 50, 165–66
   as a "well-governed society," 29–30
home trade
   capital flows into, 109, 113, 154
   foreign trade vs., 87, 99, 109
   monopoly and, 129
   as subdivision of wholesale trade, 87–89
houses, taxation and, 220–22, 226–27
Hudson Bay Company, 188
human frailty
   defined, 15n30
   as distortion, 79, 80, 92–93, 100
   necessity of government due to, 256–57
   progress and, 92–93, 197n25, 264
   rent-seeking behavior and, 100
   "well-governed society" and, 15

humankind
  characteristics of, 7–12, 149, 156
  evolution of values, 133
  impact of religion on, 37n34
  invisible hand in evolution of, 80
  limiting case of, 12, 15, 34, 36–38,
    161, 197n25
  messiness as essence of, 10–11, 12, 14,
    21, 32, 74, 156, 261–62
  metrics of, 19, 33–34, 46, 60–61,
    208–9, 264–65
  "natural course" of, 92–93, 98–99
  self-love and, 20–21, 77, 263n16
  sources of distinction, 178–79
  spontaneous order and, 259–61
  success of, 34–36, 67
  See also four stages theory
Hume, David, 9n10, 84, 100, 205, 206,
    207, 261
Hungary, 167–68

imagination, importance of, 9–10, 17n1
immediate consumption, 65
imports/exports. *See* duties and
    tariffs; trade
incentives, 185, 186–92
  citizenship and, 241
  educational, 192–93, 200, 202, 204,
    205
  lending and, 223n47
  natural, 261n11
  self-interest and, 256, 261n12, 263n16
  taxation and, 217–18, 219, 221, 225
income, growing gap in, 265
  See also profit(s); revenue; wages
independence, as a condition, 35, 82,
    95–99, 103, 104, 156
India. *See* East India Company
Indostan, 167
inflation, 74, 128–30, 246
infrastructure, 183–92, 219, 255
inheritance, 93–94, 104, 140, 226–27
institutions. *See* laws and institutions
interdependence, autonomy vs., 20–21
interest, 82–85
  as component of price, 29–30
  defined, 29, 222n46
  distinction from profit, 29
  public debt and, 245
  public revenue and, 213–15
  regulation of, 85n10

taxation and, 222–24
usury, 37–38, 84–85
inventory, as part of circulating capital, 66
invisible hand
  evolution of humankind and, 80
  "flow" process and, 45–46, 113, 131,
    154, 168
  Otteson on, 254
  of self-interest, 70–71, 89–90, 253–54,
    256, 261n12
  self-love and interdependence, 20–21
  See also free market system; laissez-faire
Ireland, 236, 249–50
Italy, 97n26, 215, 245

joint stock companies, 186–92
justice, 73, 138, 177–83, 255, 258
  See also laws and institutions

Kammen, Michael, 124
Keynes, John Maynard, 29n23,
    121n11

labor
  as component of price, 27–31
  as measure of value, 25–27
  command, 25
  embodied, 25
  mobility of, 45–46
  productive vs. unproductive, 31, 75–82,
    89, 101–2, 165, 227
  scarcity of, 33–34
  surplus, 118
  See also division of labor; slavery;
    wages; value
laissez-faire, 253–58
  See also free market system;
    invisible hand
land and property
  allocation of capital, 92
  appropriation of, 27–28
  colonial policy and, 139–40
  long-term interests, 61–62
  principle of private property, 265
  security and, 93
  taxation and, 214–15, 216–22, 223,
    226–27, 245, 246–47
  See also agriculture; rent
land assessments, 221–22, 223
land tax, 246–47
language, as contested space, 259–60

Law, John, 84
laws and institutions
  apprenticeship law, 42–45, 46
  citizenry and, 236
  constructive systems of, 82, 257–67
  corn laws, 130–36
  cost of administering, 177–83
  distorting effects of, 37–39, 59, 92–93,
    94, 98, 104
  effects of on resource allocation,
    42–47, 59
  evolution of, 93–99, 104, 133, 177–83
  four stages theory and, 104
  as metric of success, 34–36
  poor laws, 45–46
  role and evolution of, 13–16, 55, 82, 95,
    135–36, 201n27
  as security, 18–19, 53, 67, 84,
    135–36, 254–55
  as tools of destructive policy, 74,
    80–82, 95
  trade, 126–27, 130–36, 157–60,
    166–68, 185–92
  union of Scotland and England, 49–50
  usury, 84–85
  "well-governed society" and, 15–16,
    18–19, 29–30
Lectures on Jurisprudence (Smith)
  comparisons to *WN* and *TMS*, 16, 21
  evolution of laws and institutions, 14,
    15–16, 82, 201n27
  Greek and Roman empires, 92n16
  mercantile system, 122–23
  origins of government, 179n14
  "well-governed society," 16
liberty. *See* perfect liberty
limiting case, 12, 15, 34, 36–38,
    161, 197n25
loans. *See* credit
local knowledge, 253–55
Locke, John, 84, 107–8, 123
logic, development and teaching of, 198–99
luxuries, taxation and, 228–38

Madison, James, 250n72
manufacturing
  capital and, 85–89, 91–93
  demand and, 58n62, 99
  factors affecting origin of, 91–92
  Physiocracy and, 160–68
market maturation, 83–85, 112

markets
  access to, 21–23
  distorting behaviors and, 255–56
  role of, 66–67
  security of, 43, 67, 74, 78, 81–82, 84, 156
  See also extent of market
Marx, Karl, 65n2, 265
mercantile system, 107–59
  arguments against, 109–12,
    119–21, 147–48
  capital in, 85–89, 113–14
  Colbert and, 161–62
  commercial system vs., 119n10, 125
  as destructive policy regime, 147–48
  evolving context of Smith's view,
    122–26, 156, 185–86
  goal of, 107, 159
  monopolies as engine of, 154
  Physiocracy's rejection of, 165
  precious metals as wealth of
    nation, 60, 78
  price(s) in, 127–36, 149
  principles of, 107–12, 119, 159
  profit(s) under, 108–9, 145–47, 149, 214
  taxation and, 214–15, 231–32
  trade and, 111–22, 130–36, 157–60,
    163, 186–92
  "treaties of commerce," 136–37
  wages in, 149
  war debt and, 80n8
  See also colonial policy
military. *See* defense
Mill, John Stuart, 16n34, 177n11,
    226n50, 265
mining industry, 51–52, 56
  See also gold and silver
money, 67–75
  as component of circulating capital, 66
  debasement of, 24, 55
  degrading of, 128–29, 246
  denominations of, 73
  fixed capital and, 66, 68–70
  forms and functions of, 64
  inflation, 74, 128–30, 246
  manipulation of, 24, 55, 70–72, 74–75,
    85, 128–30, 246, 255–56
  origin and use of, 23–27
  paper money, 69–75, 86, 110, 248–49
  revenue vs., 68–69
  See also banks and banking; bullion;
    credit; gold and silver; interest

monopolies, 114–19
  agriculture and, 115, 131, 132, 164
  American vs. British, 154–56, 190
  capital and, 114
  carrying trade and, 88–89
  colonial policy and, 147, 187–92
  as engine of mercantile system, 154
  natural prices vs., 47
Montesquieu, 84, 167–68
moral philosophy, 7–17
  central principles of, 9–10, 106–7, 199
  defined, 8, 196–98
  free will, 12–13
  history and, 117–18, 136
  laws and institutions as security, 53,
    67, 135–36
  natural selection as driving force, 14, 177
  origins of, 196–204, 224, 261–62
  parsimony and, 77–79, 149
  Physiocracy and, 162
  progress and, 136, 177
  self-love and, 20–21, 77, 263n16
  Smith's role as moral philosopher, 7–10,
    96n25, 117–18, 196–98, 262
  Smith's "as if" analysis and, 8–9
  social systems and, 13–15, 73–74
  taxation and, 224
  See also four stages theory; humankind
Mun, Thomas, 109, 123

Naldi, Nerio, 27n19
natives, brutal treatment of, 153
natural philosophy, 8–9, 12, 196, 198, 262
natural prices, 31–32, 47–48
natural selection, 14, 177
"neat produce," 162–63
necessities, taxation and, 228–38
Netherlands, 107, 112, 117, 120, 155
  See also Holland
Newton, Isaac, 8–9, 12
nobility, 67, 76–77, 95–106, 175–76,
    210n37, 239

observation, importance of, 9–10, 46
  See also empirical analyses
ontology, 199
opulence, progress of
  defined, 33n25, 65
  elements contributing to, 77–82, 86–90
  origins of, 91–93
  See also progress
Otteson, James, 253–54, 256, 259, 261

paper money, 69–75, 86, 110, 248–49
parsimony, 77–79, 149
perfect liberty
  colonial policy and, 148
  concept of, 31, 36–38, 39, 254–55
  limiting case of, 12, 34, 36–38, 161
  movement of resources under, 45
  Physiocracy and, 164–65
  religious choice and, 207–8
  rents and, 47
  and variations in wages and
    profits, 40–42
philosophy, 7–17, 196–204
  See also moral philosophy; natural
    philosophy; Physiocracy
Physiocracy, 21, 160–68, 217
political economy, definition of, 106–7
  See also mercantile system
poll-taxes, 96
poor laws, 45–46
population growth, 34
Portugal
  flow of bullion in, 129
  growth in, 142
  naval power of, 140
  taxation in, 144
  trade in, 104, 135, 136–37, 149, 155
positive trade balance, 108–9
power
  contested order and, 259–61
  distorting aspects of, 42–45, 261, 265
  public and private sources of, 39–40
  See also factional interests
price(s), 25–32
  component parts of, 27–31, 227
  corn trade, 131–36
  distortion of, 58–59, 132
  inflation, 74, 128–30, 246
  mercantile system and, 127–36, 149
  micro vs. macro perspectives, 67–68
  natural and market, 31–32
  natural vs. monopoly, 47–48
  production and, 128–30
  in a progressing society, 60–61
  See also interest; labor; profit(s); rent;
    value; wages
primogeniture, 93–94, 103n30, 104, 140
Principles of Political Economy (Mill),
    16n34, 265
*Principles of Political Economy and
    Taxation* (Ricardo), 27n20
private property, principle of, 265

prodigality, 77–79
production
  capital and circuits of, 36, 64–66, 85–90,
    154, 240–41
  fixed capital and, 66, 68–70
  inflation and, 128–30
  as key to progress and wealth, 16,
    30–31, 64, 65, 75–77, 89
  Physiocracy and, 165
  role of independence and security
    in, 103–4
  surpluses in, 91–93, 239
  taxation and, 162, 243–44
  "productive expenses," 162–63
productivity
  in agriculture, 51, 162
  conditions ensuring, 156
  division of labor and, 14n28, 17–19,
    60–61, 64–65, 163, 165
  effects of colonial policy on, 147
  as engine of growth, 16
  moral and legal conditions necessary
    for, 14
  role of demand and access to
    markets, 21–23
profit(s), 36–47
  as component of price, 28–31
  defined, 29
  government, 213–15
  mercantile system and, 108–9, 145–47,
    149, 214
  natural causes of variations in, 40–42
  progress and the fall of, 36–38
  taxation and, 222–26
  See also interest; rent; wages
progress, 12–15, 32–38, 91–105
  agriculture as origin of, 91–93
  defined, 12, 33n25, 65
  effects of on expenses, 212–13
  geography of, 91–93, 95–105, 168
  of governance, 257
  human frailty and, 92–93, 197n25, 264
  keys to, 32–36, 46, 55, 64, 77–80,
    121, 264–65
  limiting case of, 12, 15, 34, 36–38,
    161, 197n25
  long-term, 104–5
  material vs. human, 60
  "natural course" of, 12n21, 12n24,
    91–95, 98–99, 100, 104
  of opulence, 33n25, 65, 77–82,
    86–90, 91–93

perfection and, 164
  standard for, 264–65
  as virtuous circle, 15n32
  See also four stages theory
progressive taxes, 220
property. *See* land and property
protectionism, 116–17, 157–60
public debt, 239–52
public goods, 173, 183, 204
public revenue, 170, 180–83, 192–93,
    213–15
  See also fees; taxation
public works, 183–92, 219, 255
Pulteny, William, 124

Quesnay, François, 164–65
  See also Physiocracy

Reformation, 211
regressive taxes, 222
regulation
  of commerce, 185–92
  competition and, 206–7
  corporate structure and, 187–92
  of interest rates, 85n10
  of trade, 126–27, 130–36, 157–60,
    166–68, 185–92
religion
  education and, 195–99, 205–12
  four stages theory and, 138
  impact of, 37n34
  taxation and, 219
  tithing, 219
rent, 47–62
  agricultural, 162
  as component of price, 28–29
  conditions determining, 48–50
  of cultivated land for food, 48–52
  defined, 28, 68
  as measure of "neat produce," 162
  mercantile system and, 62, 149
  mined materials and, 51–56
  taxation and, 214–15, 216–22,
    223, 226–27
resentment, 178n13
resource allocation, 38–47
  effects of laws and institutions on,
    42–47
  natural, 40–42
revenue
  components of, 68–69, 215–16, 222n46
  mercantile system and, 115

revenue (*cont.*)
  in the political economy, 106–7
  self-financing, 192
  See also profit(s); public revenue;
    taxation
Ricardo, David, 16n34, 27n20
risk
  of capital loss, 87n13, 92
  risk-adjusted rate of return, 41–42, 44
  transaction costs and, 45
Roman Empire, 92–101
  colonial system in, 137–38, 144
  defense of, 175–76
  education in, 200–202
  slavery in, 167–68
Royal African Company, 188
Russia, 55

Say's Law, 77n6
scarcity
  corn trade and, 131
  gold and silver, 51, 59
  interest and, 223, 245
  of labor, 33–34
scarcity value of capital, 245, 264–65
Scotland
  banking in, 70, 71–72, 74
  England and, 49–50, 58, 248
  religion in, 211–12
  Smith in, 122–23, 124
  taxation, 248–50
Scott, William Robert, 33nn25–26
security, 91–106
  four stages theory and, 93–99, 177–83
  laws and institutions as, 18–19, 53, 67,
    84, 135–36, 254–55
  of markets, 43, 67, 74, 78, 81–82, 84, 156
  as source of wealth, 142
  See also defense
self-governance, 20–21, 95–99, 257
self-interest
  benefits of, 20–21, 253–54
  collusion and, 40
  incentives and, 256, 261n12, 263n16
  invisible hand of, 70–71, 89–90, 253–54,
    256, 261n12
  social good and, 262n13
  "veil of uncertainty" and, 258n5
self-knowledge, 253–54
self-love, 20–21, 77, 263n16
  "butcher, the brewer, or the baker", 20
Sen, Amartya, 260n10

silver. *See* bullion; gold and silver
Skinner, A. S., 125n15
slavery, 94–95, 143, 167–68, 226
Smith, Adam
  on aim of historians, 10n14
  as Commissioner of Customs,
    125–26, 186
  education of, 45n43, 45n44, 193n22
  in France, 33n25, 123–24
  in London, 124–26, 141
  as moral philosopher, 7–10, 96n25,
    117–18, 196–98, 262
  on nature of children, 46n47
  progressivism of, 10n15
  in Scotland, 122–23, 124
  Utopian vision of, 248
smuggling, 232–36, 248
social systems
  morality and, 13–15
  success of, 34–35, 67
South Sea Company, 188
Spain
  bullion in, 129
  growth in, 142
  naval power of, 140
  public debt and, 245, 251
  taxation and, 144, 236, 237, 251
  trade in, 104, 135, 149
Spengler, Joseph, 261n11
spillover effects, education and, 45
stamp duties, 148n25, 247
status quo, 258–59
Stewart, Dugald, 12n24, 23, 197n25
Stigler, George, 253
stock, 36–47
  accumulation of, 27–34, 36–37,
    44–45, 64–65
  division of, 65–67
  early stages of, 65–66
  mobility of, 45–46, 223–24
  reinvestment of, 64–65
  taxation and, 223–24, 226–27
  uses of, 75–76
  See also banks and banking; capital;
    money; profit(s)
Strahan, William, 186
subordination, 178–79
subsidies
  bounties as, 127–36, 233
  drawbacks as, 126–27, 142, 233
  for education and training, 45
  success, metric of, 34–36, 67

sugar trade, 143, 234–35
supply chain, 85, 135, 155
surpluses
  agricultural, 51, 91–93, 134, 163–64
  emergence of, 91–93, 239
  production, 91–93, 239
Sweden, 55
Switzerland, 97n26, 224
sympathy, 17n1

taille tax, 225–26
takeoff theory, 57–58, 60, 87
tariffs. *See* duties and tariffs
tax assessments, 221–22, 223
taxation, 215–38
  agriculture and, 162, 237–38, 245
  beer taxes, 234, 247
  bounties, 127–36, 223
  of capital, 223–28, 235
  church tithing, 219
  class and, 234
  collusion and, 237
  colonial policy and, 144,
    150–51, 248–52
  on consumption, 228–38, 247–48
  dealers and, 225, 231
  for defense, 180–81, 242–44
  distorting aspects of, 219,
    227–28, 235–36
  duties and tariffs, 116–17, 126, 130–36,
    148n25, 231–33, 247
  excise taxes, 126, 231, 233–34,
    236, 246–47
  farming, 237–38
  fixed, 216–17
  flat-rate, 225
  incentives and, 217–18, 219, 221, 225
  incidence, 226
  inheritance, 226–27
  interest and, 222–24
  land and property, 214–15, 216–22, 223,
    226–27, 245, 246–47
  maxims guiding, 216, 235–36
  mercantile system and, 214–15, 231–32
  moral philosophy and, 224
  non-distorting taxes, 223–24
  Physiocracy and, 217
  poll-taxes, 96
  production, 162, 243–44
  profit(s) and, 222–26
  progressive, 220
  public works, 183–92, 219, 255

regressive, 222
  rents and, 214–15, 216–22, 223, 226–27
  of slavery, 226
  sugar trade, 234–35
  taille, 225–26
  variable, 218–19
  wages and, 227–28
  window taxes, 222
technology, defense and, 174–75
Theory of Moral Sentiments, The
  (Smith), 10–16
  "arrogance" of man, 256–57
  characteristics of humankind, 10–12, 21,
    149, 156
  comparisons to *TMS* and *WN*, 16, 21
  frugality, 77–79
  mature citizenship, 82
  "natural," 12
  nature of children, 46n47
  "progress," 12–15
  revisions of, 256
  virtue vs. vice, 262n14
tithing, 219
tobacco trade, 145, 147
Todd, W. B., 125n15
towns and cities, rise of, 91, 95–105, 115,
  159, 168
Townshend, Charles, 33n25, 123
trade, 87–93, 108–59
  access to markets and, 23
  balance of, 108–9, 120, 122
  capital and, 91–93, 154
  carrying, 69, 87–90, 113–14, 154
  corn, 127–36, 161
  distortions in, 113–14, 123, 127–37,
    149, 153, 168–69
  emergence of, 92, 99
  as foundation of wealth, 104–5
  home trade, 87–89, 99, 109, 113, 154
  mercantile system and, 111–22, 130–36,
    157–60, 163, 186–92
  money and the expansion of, 64, 249
  origins of money and, 23–25
  positive trade balance, 108–9
  regulation and facilitation of, 126–27,
    130–36, 157–60, 166–67, 185–92
  sequential widening of, 64
  smuggling, 232–36, 248
  as subdivision of wholesale trade, 87–89
  sugar, 143, 234
  taxation on, 116–17, 126, 130–36,
    148n25, 231–33, 247

trade (*cont.*)
  tobacco, 145, 147
  velocity of, 87–89
  wholesale, 87–89
  as zero-sum game, 23, 111–12, 120–21
  See also duties and tariffs; free trade
training, subsidies for, 45
transaction costs, 22, 45, 48–49
transportation, 22–23
transfer taxes, 226–27
transportation, 22, 85
"treaties of commerce," 136–37
Turkey, 167–68

unintended consequences, 98–99, 116,
    201, 254
United States, 148, 258n4
  See also American colonies
university, evolution of, 195–200
use, value in, 24
usury, 37–38, 84–85

value
  corn as consistent measure of, 26, 53–55
  diamond/water paradox, 24
  of gold and silver, 26, 52–56, 59–60, 70
  labor embodied vs. commanded
      as, 25–27
  metaphysical perspective of, 27
  real vs. nominal, 24
  Ricardo on, 27n20
  in use vs. exchange, 24
values (ethical), evolution of, 133
variable taxes, 218–19
"veil of uncertainty," 258–59, 260
velocity of trade, 87–88

wages
  as component of price, 28–29,
      32–36, 227
  effects of bounties on, 128
  mercantile system and, 149
  natural causes of variations in, 40–42
  taxation and, 227–28
Walpole, Robert, 233–34
wars and warfare. *See* defense
wealth
  agriculture as source of, 160–68
  diffusion of, 103n30
  mercantilist view of, 107–12, 115,
      137, 159–60

precious metals as source of, 52, 54,
    59–60, 78
production as key to, 16, 30–31, 64, 65,
    76, 77, 89
race for, 254–55
security as source of, 142
trade as foundation of, 104–5
undermining factors of, 38
Wealth of Nations (Smith)
  additions, corrections, and revisions to,
      27, 243n62
  advertisements of, 126
  Book I themes and conceptual frames,
      19, 30, 31, 32, 37, 41, 47, 63
  Book II themes and conceptual frames,
      32, 37, 38, 42, 47, 63, 67, 89
  Book III themes and conceptual frames,
      32, 38, 47, 52, 67, 87, 90, 92–93
  Book IV themes and conceptual frames,
      32, 38, 52, 63, 87–88, 89, 105,
      122–26, 168–69
  Book V themes and conceptual frames,
      46, 168–69, 170, 204, 248
  comparisons to *LJ* and *TMS*, 16, 21
  difficult aspects of, 27n18
  Early Draft of, 33nn25–26
  editorial notes regarding, 92n16
  first edition, 185–86
  John Stuart Mill on, 16n34
  occurrences of the term
      "progress," 12n20
  organization of, 15–16, 170
  overall themes and conceptual frames,
      14, 17n1, 53, 78, 84, 95, 100, 118,
      135–36, 142, 168
  publishing history, 122–26, 156,
      185–86, 243n63
  third edition, 185–86, 243n63
  use of commercial system vs. mercantile
      system as term, 119n10, 125
"well-governed society," 15–16, 18–19,
    29–30
wholesale trade, 87–88
window taxes, 222
witchcraft laws, 133
women
  exploitation of, 157
  power of language and, 259
wool manufacturing, 59, 158
working class, 19, 33–34, 46, 60–61, 117,
    208–9, 248

Printed in the United States
By Bookmasters